ADVANCED G
PROGRAMMI C++

Roger T. Stevens and Christopher D. Watkins

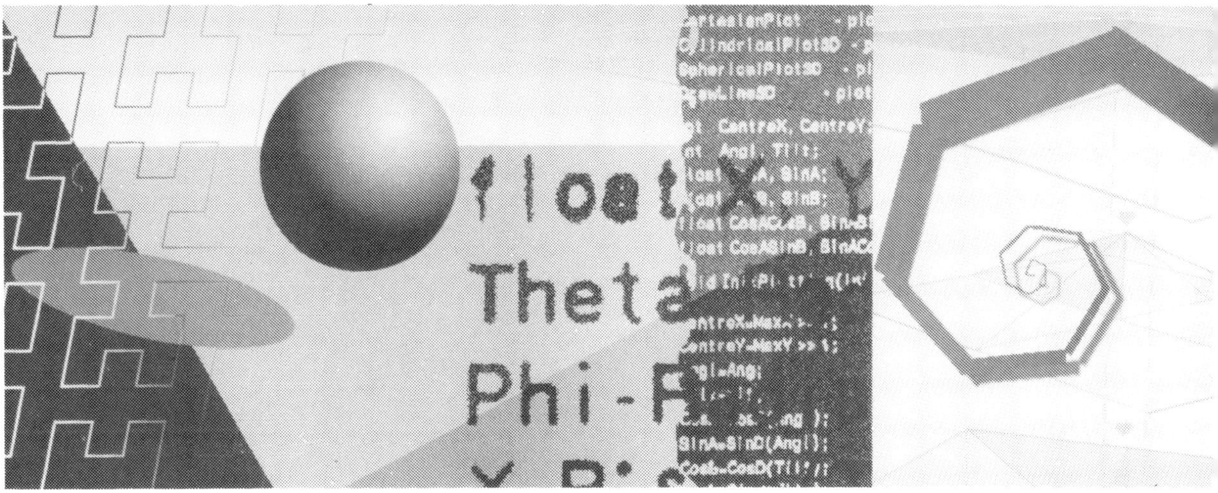

Featuring 16 pages of

full-color graphics you can

create on your computer.

M&T BOOKS

First published in 1991 in North America by M&T Publishing, Inc., 411 Borel Ave, San Mateo, CA 94402-3522, U.S.A., and co-published for sale outside North America by Prentice Hall International (UK) Limited, 66 Wood Lane End, Hemel Hempstead, Hertfordshire, HP2 4RG, England, a division of Simon & Schuster International Group.

British Library Cataloging-in-Publication Data is available from Prentice Hall International (UK) Ltd.

Library of Congress Cataloging-in-Publication Data is available from the Publisher.

Advanced Graphics Programming in C & C++
by Roger T. Stevens and Christopher D. Watkins.

ISBN 0-13-005497-6 (book only)
ISBN 0-13-010463-9 (book/disk)

Cover Design:
Lauren Smith Design

94 93 92 4 3 2

£32-95

ADVANCED GRAPHICS PROGRAMMING IN C AND C++

M&T BOOKS

Dedication

To our families and friends.

Much thanks must go to you all for your consideration and support while we were writing this book. Without your help and understanding, this collection of programs and explanations would never have become a book.

Contents

PART III: Z BUFFERING AND HORIZON RENDERING

Acknowledgments

All of the software in this book was written in Borland C++ and checked with Turbo C++. The compilers were furnished by Borland International, 1800 Green Hills Rd., Scotts Valley, CA 95066.

Computer graphics, including high resolution 1024 x 768 pixel, 256-color displays were produced on Powergraph ERGO-VGA boards with 1 megabyte of memory furnished by STB Systems, Inc., 1651 N. Glenville, Suite 210, Richardson, Texas 75081.

Thanks goes to Martin Jaspan for the ideas and initial BASIC code for the 3 particle orbit simulation program at the beginning of the book.

Thanks goes to Larry Sharp for converting the Turbo Pascal programs to C.

Why this Book is for You

If you have a Borland C++, Turbo C++, or Turbo C compiler, an IBM PC or equivalent with a VGA card, and a color monitor, you may have tried your hand at producing some simple color displays. If you have, perhaps you were disappointed to find that not all of the graphics tools that you wanted were available and that you couldn't find enough information to produce really advanced displays. This book will provide you with the tools and information that you need to perform advanced color graphics work. Although the programs have not been tested with Microsoft C, they should be capable of being compiled and run with it, with only minimal modifications.

This book supplies the tools needed to use advanced color graphics modes not covered by C graphics packages, including extended high-resolution VGA modes and 256-color graphics for highly realistic shading. What follows is a brief outline of some of the material covered in the book.

- Mathematical functions and procedures needed to operate upon vectors, including translation, rotation, and transformation from three-dimensional space to the two-dimensional screen are provided.
- Theory and techniques required for the solid modeling of three-dimensional objects.
- Z-buffering, in which an array is used to store the height of each point in a grid, which is then transformed to two dimensions and plotted on the screen.
- Ray-tracing, in which every ray of light from a three-dimensional scene which intersects the viewing screen and then the eye of the observer is traced back to the object that it came from and thence back to the original light sources. The result is a highly realistic scene filled with the pertinent shadows and reflections. The programs needed to do this are all included, including the code necessary to create interesting object surface textures such as wood and marble.

Introduction

All modern C compilers include a library of graphic routines that permit the user to generate simple types of graphic displays. If you are interested in graphics you have probably already generated a number of pictures and are familiar with how the system works. You may have discovered something else too, as you begin to develop more complex and realistic images, you find yourself running into programming obstacles.

There are two main reasons for this. First, the graphics functions included with a compiler often don't include some of the functions that you really need for producing interesting images. Second, no information is supplied on the mathematics and techniques that are required by more advanced displays, such as solid modeling, z-buffering, and ray tracing. That is where this book comes in.

In the pages that follow, we're going to show you how to create the mathematical and graphics functions that go beyond the standard C compiler libraries and then use them to create several interesting kinds of displays. You'll not only be able to generate all of the displays that are shown and described in this book, but the detailed descriptions of techniques and source code will give you ideas for creating new displays that have never been done before.

It is understood that the accepted usage of solid modeling in the computer graphics community is to refer to B-reps and CSG (boundary representations and Constructive Solid Geometry). We use the terms here to refer to any 3D rendered object that is to have a solid appearance.

The outline and all of the initial software in the book were written by Christopher D. Watkins. Larry Sharp converted the original source code, which was written in Turbo Pascal, to the C language. The text was written by Roger T. Stevens. The programs are written in Borland C++ using the C compiler in Borland's C++ product. If you have another C compiler, you may need to make some modifications for the programs to run properly, since there may be differences in how some standard C functions are implemented.

The book is divided into four parts. Part I describes universal routines for mathematics and graphics. Part II explains how to do wire frame modeling and solid modeling. Wire frame modeling depicts three-dimensional objects as if they consisted of a frame of wires rather than a solid. It is a very fast way of drawing a three-dimensional scene on a two-dimensional display so that you can see the relative positions of objects and determine whether you need to reposition or resize them. Solid modeling renders a three-dimensional scene onto the two-dimensional screen, properly shading each facet of an object so that the scene looks like an artist's rendition. It requires a lot more computer time than wire frame modeling, so you will want to use it only when you're fairly sure that the elements of the picture are positioned and specified in the way you intend. Part III describes how to use the z-buffering and horizon rendering technique to create realistically lighted renditions of three-dimensional scenes. Part IV describes the use of ray tracing and ray casting techniques for creating images with more realistic lighting.

The Mathematics Module

Chapter 1 describes a number of mathematical functions and procedures that are useful in generating graphics scenes. These routines will be used by subsequent programs in the book. They include a number of functions that go beyond the standard C libraries and greatly simplify graphics programming. Also included are a full set of routines for creating and operating upon three-dimensional vectors. Such vectors are used to define and change the position of three-dimensional objects in space and to transform them into a two-dimensional screen. Finally, the module describes functions and procedures that create and operate upon four-dimensional matrices. If you want to take a three-dimensional vector or object and rotate it to a new orientation in space and possibly scale it to a new size at the same time, you will find that the transformation equations can be described by a 3 x 3 matrix. However, if you want a more general transformation that not only includes a rotation and scaling but also a linear translation in space, you need another operation on the vector or object. If this operation is included in a single matrix with the previously described operations, you will need a 4 x 4 matrix. The procedures described in this chapter include creating and initializing such matrices and performing various mathematical operations upon them.

The Graphics Interface Module

Chapter 2 describes a number of useful graphics routines used by other programs in this book. These include a procedure for plotting a pixel to the screen; for clearing the palette register; for setting the palette register; two functions for initializing the 256 colors of the 256 color display; procedures for drawing a circle or a line; a procedure to initialize the proper graphics mode; a procedure that causes the computer to wait for a key stroke; a procedure for exiting from the graphics mode; and a procedure for setting up text screen colors. The chapter also includes a description of three-dimensional and two-dimensional theory, orthogonal and perspective projection, and coordinate conversion. And it lists and describes the functions and procedures that are needed to perform these actions. Procedures that are used to write a pixel to the screen and read a pixel from the screen are described as well as a procedure for drawing a wire outline for a facet of an object. Chapter 2 also provides a procedure for displaying the axes of the coordinate system and the current color palette on the screen and a procedure that permits toggling between having these on the screen or not displaying them.

Using the Mathematics and Graphics Modules

Once you have assimilated the tools provided in the first two chapters, you're going to want to use them to create some interesting displays. Chapter 3 gives examples of a number of images that are typical of those that you can create. The program for each display is listed and described so that you can use it in its current form or modify it to meet your own requirements.

The first program that is described begins by drawing a Mandelbrot set on the left side of the screen. This is the most famous of all fractals. It is well known that the Mandelbrot set is a sort of map of all Julia sets. The program is set up so that after the Mandelbrot set is drawn, a cursor appears. You can move the cursor around on the Mandelbrot set, and as you do, the corresponding Julia set for that particular set of coordinates is immediately drawn on the right-hand side of the screen.

The next two programs simulate two orbiting particles and three orbiting particles, respectively. These particles actually appear to be rotating in orbit in space. The next display is a recursive triangle generator that creates representations of the well-known Sierpinski triangle. Next is a display of the bifurcation diagram. This shows how repeated iteration of the population growth equation for different parameter values can result in cases of settling to one stable solution, two stable solutions, and so on, until chaos is encountered. This illustrates one of the first mathematical discoveries that helped establish the science of chaos. Another program creates a strange attractor, which is representative of a class of iterated equations in which there is a particular set of curves to which the solutions are confined. The next program produces the Lorenz attractor, which is the first strange attractor that was discovered at the beginning of the development of chaos theory.

Solid Modeling Theory and Database Structure

Chapter 4 begins by describing the *Model.Inc* file. This is a file that contains modeling routines to be included within other program files presented later in this book. *Model.Inc* includes variable declarations for defining vertices and facets and *scale data* and *scale image* parameters for integer manipulation. It also provides routines to clear, load, and save vertex and facet data. Procedures are provided for drawing a wire facet and a solid facet. The chapter concludes by showing an example of how to create a file of data for a scene.

Adding Objects to the Scene

Chapter 5 describes and lists the procedures and functions that are needed to add objects to the object list data base. This includes initializing the object buffer, creating an object, specifying transformations (rotation, scaling, and translation), defining its reflective characteristics, assigning it a color, and identifying whether it will reflect in another reflective object. A procedure is provided for setting a flag to indicate that the objects will be sorted for order of placement. Also, procedures are given for adding edge reflectors to a scene. Finally, provisions are made for adding objects to the scene either from a *.SCN* disk file or from a procedure.

Sorting and Displaying Objects in a Scene

Assuming that we have some way of projecting objects on to a two-dimensional screen, it is important that we draw each object and its reflections in the proper order.

If we construct the farthest objects first and the nearest objects last, parts of the nearer object may overlap parts of the farther objects, which is the way that the scene should appear if it is to achieve realism. If a far away object was drawn last, it might overlap nearer objects, which is not the way that the scene would appear when actually viewed. Consequently, Chapter 6 begins with functions and procedures that sort objects and their reflections to place them in the proper order for drawing to the screen. This chapter also includes a procedure that displays an object on the screen, in either vertex format, wire frame format, or solid model format. Another procedure displays objects and any reflections in the scene.

The Description File Maker

Chapter 8 describes the description file maker. This program creates a *.DES* description file from which the solid-state modeling program generates a scene. One purpose of this file is to select the option that causes a complete color palette to be displayed at the side of the screen. The option also enables the three axes of the Cartesian coordinate system to be displayed on the picture. Another option that is selected determines how the model will be displayed.

Since generating a complete solid-state model is somewhat lengthy, two other options are available for faster drawing of the scene. These are displaying vertices only and displaying a wire frame mode. Either of these options quickly creates a scene with sufficient detail for you to determine whether you haves placed objects properly in the scene. Once you are satisfied with the placement, you can switch to the solid modeling option to create the final scene.

The Solid Modeling Program

Chapter 7 puts it all together by describing the complete solid modeling program, *Model.c.* This program begins by setting toggle switches that determine whether the scene should be displayed in the form of a vertex model, a wire frame model, or a solid model. It then performs sorting of the objects. It can also use affine transformations to change the size, position, and/or orientation of any object. The program establishes the position of the viewer and the light source. It includes a procedure for obtaining the vector normal to the surface of an object facet. The program then runs an illumination model which determines the intensity of light on the facet. A test is made as to whether the facet is visible, and the facets for objects and reflections, if visible, are finally projected to the screen to create the final picture. The program also includes the capability to load a *.DES* file—a file that selects various options determining the type of picture created.

Creating Data for a Solid Model

The next two chapters describe how to create the data file from which a solid model scene is generated. Chapter 9 provides programs for generating such shapes as cones, cylinders, spheres, toroids, and solids of revolution. Chapter 10 describes a program for generating scenes and discusses how to use it to create a data file with the description and placement of the objects that you want in the final scene. It is this data file that the *Model* program uses to generate the final picture.

Z-Buffering

Part III of this book is concerned with the rendering of realistic scenes by use of the z-buffering technique. Chapter 11 discusses the theory of z-buffering and horizon rendering. Chapter 12 describes the description file making program which sets the options for the z-buffering rendering program. Chapter 13 provides a z-buffering rendering program and describes how it works and how to use it. Chapter 14 details the programs that are used to generate, examine, and modify a z-buffering database. Such a database contains the data that is used by the z-buffering rendering program to generate the final picture. Finally, Chapter 15 describes fractal programs that are used to create lunar mountains, quaternion dragons, and Mandelbrot and Julia sets using the continuous potential method. Also included is a filtering program for smoothing fractal databases.

Ray Casting and Ray Tracing

The last part of the book is devoted to ray casting and ray tracing. Ray tracing is a technique for drawing a realistic picture of a three-dimensional scene on a two-dimensional display. In this technique computer calculations trace a path from the observer's eye to every pixel on the display screen, to whatever objects are intersected, and then back to the original light sources. All of this information is combined to determine the color of each pixel at the display screen surface and this color is painted on the screen.

Ray casting is somewhat simpler. It doesn't follow the ray to recreate all shadows and mirrored reflections, but instead simply traces far enough to determine object colors.

Chapter 16 outlines ray tracing theory and fundamentals. Chapter 17 covers the procedure used in driving the graphic devices in high resolution 1024 x 768 x 250 mode for the ray tracer. In Chapter 18 we discuss how to create an .RT file for the ray tracer to process. The ray tracing program itself is covered in Chapter 19 along with a detailed description of how it works. Finally, Chapter 20 discusses a color reduction algorithm to allow display of your ray traced images on a VGA graphics card.

Hardware and Software Required

All of the software in this book was written using the compiler present in Borland C++. The programs have also been checked out with Turbo C++ to assure that they are compatible. They may also run on earlier versions of Turbo C or with Microsoft C, but minor changes may be necessary. There are now so many different versions of C available that it is difficult to test the programs with every product.

If you are using a different version of C from that used for the book, we recommend that you upgrade to Borland C++. Borland International has a liberal upgrade policy that will enable you to get the latest version of Borland C++ at a reasonable cost. It has a lot of new features that you'll find very useful. If you really want to stick with your current version of C, a little more effort is required. When you first attempt to compile one of the programs, error messages will quickly show you where incompatibilities lie. You may then need to write some functions of your own to correct these incompatibilities. If you're a neophyte programmer, don't try this until you have a little more experience with the working code.

These programs should run on any IBM PC compatible computer which has a VGA card and VGA monitor. Most of the software uses display mode 19, which is

320 by 200 pixels by 256 colors. With 256 colors, we can produce scenes that adequately represent reality. We prefer superVGA cards which can produce 256 colors at higher resolutions. Unfortunately, the techniques for using these cards are not yet standardized and there are many more superVGA cards on the market than we have testing resources. We used a Powergraph VGA card from STB and a Vega 1024i card from Video Seven in checking the software. We also include a 1024 by 768 pixel by 256 color mode using the PowerGraph card as an alternate in the ray tracing programs. If you have another type of superVGA card, you should be able to use what you have learned from this book to modify the programs to work with it. You'll find that using a 286 or 386 based computer with a math coprocessor will make your life a lot more pleasant by speeding up the computing process, but with adequate patience, any of the programs will run on a slower machine.

Summing it Up

The programs in this book were originally written in Pascal by Christopher Watkins for the book "Advanced Graphics Programming in Turbo Pascal" by Roger Stevens and Christopher Watkins. The software was then ported to C by Larry Sharp.

In translating the programs to the C language, efforts were made to preserve the compatibility between the C programs and the original Pascal code. This meant that, instead of using multiple source files and linking these together, as is the usual case for larger C programs, each program consists of one principal file (a .C file), plus one or more auxiliary files (.INC files). These auxiliary files are incorporated into the principal source code file by use of the preprocessor's *include* directive.

In addition, experienced C programmers will note that some constructs were used in a fashion that resembles Pascal. For example, sequences of *if-else* statements nest rather than using the *else-if* construct in C. These stylistic variations are minor and do not detract from the efficiency or correctness of the programs.

If you're like most C programmers, you have not yet attempted to use the capabilities of your computer to produce any advanced graphics. Even if you have a superVGA, you've seen its power mainly in the good-quality character display during word processing or the fine Solitaire game found in Microsoft Windows 3.0. After trying the programs in this book, you'll be amazed at the graphics capabilities that lie hidden in your computer.

These new graphics applications may inspire you to generate some new ones of your own and to investigate fields that have never been looked at before. After all, self-similar fractal curves lay dormant for nearly a hundred years because they required the power of modern computers for their investigation. It wasn't until Mandelbrot applied computer power to them that they came into their own. There are probably other areas of mathematics that are not new, but can be brought into new light with computer graphics power. Why don't you try to find some?

The following table presents a summary of the programs discussed in this book. For each program in the book, the following information is given:

- which chapter the program is shown in
- the name of the program or module (a module is code that does not stand alone, but is meant to be included in another program).
- a synopsis or brief description of what the program does
- a list of the modules which the program uses or includes within it

Ch.	Program/Module	Synopsis	Uses/Includes	Input Files	Output Files
1	*Math.inc*	Basic mathematical functions, used by subsequent programs.	none	none	none
2	*Graph.inc*	Basic graphics functions, used by subsequent programs	none	none	none
3	*MSetJSet.c*	Browse Mandelbrot set, display Julia set	*Math.inc* *Graph.inc*	none	none
3	*Orbit2P.c*	Simulator for 2 Particle Orbit	*Math.inc* *Graph.inc*	none	none
3	*Orbit3P.c*	Simulator for 3 Particle Orbit	*Math.inc* *Graph.inc*	none	none
3	*Triangle.c*	Generate a Sierpinski Triangle	*Math.inc* *Graph.inc*	none	none
3	*Bifurcat.c*	Generate a Bifurcation Diagram	*Math.inc* *Graph.inc*	none	none

Ch.	Program/Module	Synopsis	Uses/Includes	Input Files	Output Files
3	*StrAtr3d.c*	Generate a 3-D Strange Attractor	*Math.inc* *Graph.inc*	none	none
3	*Lorenz3D.c*	Generate a 3-D Lorenz Attractor	*Math.inc* *Graph.inc*	none	none
4	*Model.inc*	Vertex and facet routines, used by subsequent programs	none	none	none
5	*AddObjs.inc*	Routines to add objects from a file	none	*grid.DAT* *sphere.DAT* **.SCN*	none
6	*DispObjs.inc*	sort and display objects on screen, used by subsequent routines	none	none	none
7	*DesMake.c*	creates a description (*.DES*) file	none	user input	*Model.DES*
8	*Model.c*	solid modeling program	*Math.inc* *Graph.inc* *Model.inc* *AddObjs.inc* *DispObjs.inc*	**.DES file* **.SCN file*	outputs to screen display
9	*ShpMk.inc*	routines used to assist in creating object data files (*.DAT* files), included by subsequent program	none	none	none
9	*MakeObjs.c*	creates an object data file (*.DAT* file)	*Math.inc* *Graph.inc* *Model.inc* *ShpMk.inc*	user input	**.DAT*
9	*ConePyrm.c*	generates object data files for a cone and a pyramid	*Math.inc* *Graph.inc* *Model.inc* *ShpMk.inc*	user input	*Pyramid.DAT* *Cone.DAT*
9	*Cylinder.c*	generates the object data file for a cylinder	*Math.inc* *Graph.inc* *Model.inc* *ShpMk.inc*	user input	*Cylinder.DAT*
9	*HmSphere.c*	generates the object data file for a hemisphere	*Math.inc* *Graph.inc* *Model.inc* *ShpMk.inc*	user input	*HmSphere.DAT*
9	*Sphere.c*	generates the object data file for a sphere	*Math.inc* *Graph.inc* *Model.inc* *ShpMk.inc*	user input	*Sphere.DAT*

Ch.	Program/Module	Synopsis	Uses/Includes	Input Files	Ouput Files
9	*PlotEqns.c*	generates the object data file for a grid and for 4 different equations	*Math.inc* *Graph.inc* *Model.inc* *ShpMk.inc*	user input	*Grid.dat* *PlotEqn1.DAT* *PlotEqn2.DAT* *PlotEqn3.DAT* *PlotEqn4.DAT*
9	*Toroid.c*	generates the object data file for a toroid	*Math.inc* *Graph.inc* *Model.inc* *ShpMk.inc*	user input	*Toroid.DAT*
9	*SolOfRev.c*	generates the object data file for a number of solids of revolution	*Math.inc* *Graph.inc* *Model.inc* *ShpMk.inc*	user input	*Beads.DAT* *LgBeads.DAT* *Funnels.DAT* *MechPart.DAT* *Rocket.DAT* *ChesPawn.DAT*
10	*ScnMaker.c*	generates scene (*.SCN*) files		user input	**.scn*
11	*Render.inc*	routines for file and structure of z-buffering program, included by subsequent programs	none	none	none
12	*DesMake.c*	creates a description (*.DES*) file to be used by *Render.c* program	*Render.inc*	user input	**.des*
13	*Render.c*	z-buffer rendering program	*Math.inc* *Graph.inc* *Render.inc* *AddOns.inc*	**.dat* **.des* *CPM1* *CPM2* *CPMJ1* *CPMJ2*	
13	*AddOns.inc*	included by z-buffer rendering program (*Render.c*)	none	none	none
14	*HmSphere.c*	generates a z-buffer database for painting a hemisphere on the screen	*Render.inc* *Math.inc*		*HmSphere.DAT*
14	*HmToroid.c*	generates a z-buffer database for painting a hemitoroid on the screen	*Render.inc* *Math.inc*		*HmToroid.DAT* *Bowl.DAT*
14	*PlotEqn.c*	generates a z-buffer database for drawing 4 different equations	*Render.inc* *Math.inc*		*PlotEqn1.DAT* *PlotEqn2.DAT* *PlotEqn3.DAT* *PlotEqn4.DAT*
14	*MagnFlds.c*	generates a z-buffer database for drawing the image of magnetic fields	*Render.inc* *Math.inc*	**.dat*	*MagnFlds.DAT*

Ch.	Program/Module	Synopsis	Uses/Includes	Input Files	Output Files
14	*FndLimits.c*	program to find highest and lowest z-values	*Render.inc*		outputs to screen
14	*ViewSlic.c*	program to view a cross-section of displayed data	*Math.inc* *Graph.inc* *Render.inc*	**.dat*	draws to screen
14	*Smooth.c*	program to correct erroneous or discontinuous points	*Crt* *Render.inc*	**.dat*	corrected file
15	*Mountain.c*	generates fractal mountain databases	*Math.inc* *Graph.inc* *Render.inc*		*mountain.DAT*
15	*CPM.c*	creates data file for 3-D Mandelbrot set	*Math.inc* *Graph.inc* *Render.inc*		*CPM1.DAT*
15	*CPMJ.c*	creates data file for 3-D Julia set	*Math.inc* *Graph.inc* *Render.inc*		*CPMJ1.DAT* *CPMJ2.DAT*
15	*Quater.inc*	math routines used by quaternion file generator	none	none	none
15	*Quater.c*	generates data file for quaternion fractals	*Math.inc* *Render.inc* *Quater.inc*		*dragon.DAT* *revsolid.DAT*
17	*Math2.inc*	file from chapter 1 modified for super VGA	none	none	none
17	*Graph2.inc*	file from chapter 2 modified for super VGA	none	none	none
18	*marbles.RT* *molecule.RT* *office.RT* *park.RT* *planets.RT* *pyramid.RT* *stack.RT*	example text data files used by ray tracing program in Chapter 19 (*RayTrace.c*). Note: these are data files, not programs.	none	none	none
19	*RayTrace.c*	recursive ray tracing program	*Math2.inc* *Graph2.inc*	**.RT files*	**.CPR files*
20	*Display.c*	using a color histogram, display the *.CPR* file created by ray tracing program	*Math2.inc* *Graph2.inc*	**.CPR*	screen display

Part I

UNIVERSAL ROUTINES

CHAPTER 1

The Mathematics Module

Before we get into the actual creation of graphics images with C, we need to develop some mathematical functions which will be used throughout the graphics programs. All of these procedures are included in a file called *Math.Inc* which will be included in each graphics program. The file *Math.Inc* is not a stand-alone source code file, but is meant to be included within the principal source code file of every program in the this book. (Some later programs will use a modified version of this file, which I'll present later.)

There are three types of mathematical functions that are included in the *Math.Inc* file. They are: numerical functions, which have to do with manipulating of numbers; vector and matrix functions, which create and manipulate vectors; and affine transformations, which transform the position of points using a four by four matrix. All three types of functions are listed in Figure 1-1. They are described in detail in the sections that follow.

Numerical Functions

The first thing that we need to do in preparation for designing unique images, is to create a number of numerical functions that are not included in the standard C library but are either necessary or highly useful in creating graphics displays. The functions are described in the sections below and they are all listed in Figure 1-1.

In the listing presented before the functions, four constants are defined. The first is *Ln10.* This is the natural logarithm of 10 (2.3025851). It is used in converting between natural logarithms and logarithms to the base 10. The latter are what are more normally used in the algebra and trig classes that we all have taken, but the only logarithmic function in the standard C libraries is that for finding the natural logarithm (to the base e). Thus we have to roll our own function for the other type of logarithm, which is where this constant is useful. The second constant is *Pi* (3.1415927). The third function is *PiOver180* (0.0174533), as shown in Figure 1-1, and the fourth is *PiUnder180* (57.2957795).

We are used to specifying angles in degrees, but standard C trigonometric functions expect to see angles specified in radians. If we want to use angles in degrees, we need some new functions to handle them, and these two constants are useful in performing the required conversions.

```
/* Math. Inc

                    Mathematical Functions

          Original Material by Christopher D. Watkins

                    'C' conversions by
                        Larry Sharp

   Radians   - converts degrees to radians
   Degrees   - converts radians to degrees
   CosD      - cosine in degrees
   SinD      - sine in degrees
   Power     - power a^n
   Log       - log base 10
   Exp10     - exp base 10
   Sign      - negative=-1  positive=1  null=0
   IntSign   - negative=-1  positive=1  null=0
   IntSqrt   - integer square root
   IntPower  - integer power a^n
*/

#define Ln10 2.30258509299405E+000
#define Pi 3.1415927
#define PiOver180 1.74532925199433E-002
#define PiUnder180 5.72957795130823E+001

typedef enum {false, true} Boolean;
typedef unsigned char      Byte;
typedef unsigned int       Word;
```

```
int Round(float x)
{
  return((int)(x+0.5));
}

int Trunc(float x)
{
  return((int)(x));
}

float SqrFP(float x)
{
  return(x*x);
}

int Sqr(int x)
{
  return(x*x);
}

float Radians(float Angle)
{
  return(Angle*PiOver180);
}

float Degrees(float Angle)
{
  return(Angle*PiUnder180);
}

float CosD(float Angle)
{
  return(cos(Radians(Angle)));
}

float SinD(float Angle)
{
```

```
    return(sin(Radians(Angle)));
  }

  float Power(float Base, int Exponent)
  {
    float BPower;
    int   t;

    if(Exponent==0)
      return(1);
    else
    {
      BPower=1.0;
      for(t=1; t<=Exponent; t++)
      {
       BPower*=Base;
      }
      return(BPower);
    }
  }

  float Log(float x)
  {
    return(log(x)/Ln10);
  }

  float Exp10(float x)
  {
    return(exp(x*Ln10));
  }

  float Sign(float x)
  {
    if(x<0)
      return(-1);
    else
    {
      if(x>0)
        return(1);
      else
      {
```

```
      return(0);
    }
  }
}

int IntSign(int x)
{
  if(x<0)
    return(-1);
  else
  {
    if(x>0)
      return(1);
    else
    {
      return(0);
    }
  }
}

int IntSqrt(int x)
{
  int OddInt, OldArg, FirstSqrt;

  OddInt=1;
  OldArg=x;
  while(x>=0)
  {
    x-=OddInt;
    OddInt+=2;
  }
  FirstSqrt=OddInt >> 1;
  if(Sqr(FirstSqrt)-FirstSqrt+1 > OldArg)
    return(FirstSqrt-1);
  else
    return(FirstSqrt);
}

int IntPower(int Base, int Exponent)
{
  if(Exponent==0)
```

```
    return(1);
  else
    return(Base*IntPower(Base, Exponent-1));
}
/*
```

Vector and Matrix Routines

```
    Vec             - Make Vector
    VecInt          - Make Integer Vector
    UnVec           - Get Components of vector
    UnVecInt        - Get Components of Integer Vector
    VecDot          - Vector Dot Product
    VecCross        - Vector Cross Product
    VecLen          - Vector Length
    VecNormalize    - Vector Normalize
    VecMatxMult     - Vector Matrix Multiply
    VecSub          - Vector Subtraction
    VecSubInt       - Vector Subtraction Integer
    VecAdd          - Vector Addition
    VecAdd3         - Vector Addition
    VecCopy         - Vector Copy
    VecLinComb      - Vector Linear Combination
    VecScalMult     - Vector Scalar Multiple
    VecScalMultI    - Vector Scalar Multiple
    VecScalMultInt  - Vector Scalar Multiple and Rounding
    VecAddScalMult  - Vector Add Scalar Multiple
    VecNull         - Vector Null
    VecNullInt      - Vector Null Integer
    VecElemMult     - Vector Element Multiply
*/

typedef float TDA[3];
typedef int   TDIA[3];
typedef float FDA[4];
typedef float Matx4x4[4][4];

void Vec(float r, float s, float t, TDA A)
{
```

```
  A[0]=r;
  A[1]=s;
  A[2]=t;
}

void VecInt(int r, int s, int t, TDIA A)
{
  A[0]=r;
  A[1]=s;
  A[2]=t;
}

void UnVec(TDA A, float *r, float *s, float *t)
{
  *r=A[0];
  *s=A[1];
  *t=A[2];
}

void UnVecInt(TDIA A, int *r, int *s, int *t)
{
  *r=A[0];
  *s=A[1];
  *t=A[2];
}

float VecDot(TDA A, TDA B)
{
  return(A[0]*B[0] + A[1]*B[1] + A[2]*B[2]);
}

void VecCross(TDA A, TDA B, TDA C)
{
  C[0]=A[1]*B[2] - A[2]*B[1];
  C[1]=A[2]*B[0] - A[0]*B[2];
  C[2]=A[0]*B[1] - A[1]*B[0];
}

float VecLen(TDA A)
{
```

```
  return(sqrt(SqrFP(A[0])+SqrFP(A[1])+SqrFP(A[2])));
}

void VecNormalize(TDA A)
{
  float dist, invdist;

  dist=VecLen(A);
  if(!(dist==0.0))
  {
    invdist=1/dist;
    A[0]*=invdist;
    A[1]*=invdist;
    A[2]*=invdist;
  }
  else
  {
    puts("Zero-Length Vectors cannot be Normalized");
    exit(1);
  }
}

void VecMatxMult(FDA A, Matx4x4 Matrix, FDA B)
{
  int mRow, mCol;

  for(mCol=0; mCol<4; mCol++)
  {
    B[mCol]=0;
    for(mRow=0; mRow<4; mRow++)
      B[mCol]+=A[mRow]*Matrix[mRow][mCol];
  }
}

void VecSub(TDA A, TDA B, TDA C)
{
  C[0]=A[0]-B[0];
  C[1]=A[1]-B[1];
  C[2]=A[2]-B[2];
}
```

```
void VecSubInt(TDIA A, TDIA B, TDA C)
{
  C[0]=A[0]-B[0];
  C[1]=A[1]-B[1];
  C[2]=A[2]-B[2];
}

void VecAdd(TDA A, TDA B, TDA C)
{
  C[0]=A[0]+B[0];
  C[1]=A[1]+B[1];
  C[2]=A[2]+B[2];
}

void VecAdd3(TDA A, TDA B, TDA C, TDA D)
{
  D[0]=A[0]+B[0]+C[0];
  D[1]=A[1]+B[1]+C[1];
  D[2]=A[2]+B[2]+C[2];
}

void VecCopy(TDA A, TDA B)
{
  int i;
  for(i=0; i<3; i++)
  {
    B[i]=A[i];
  }
}

void VecLinComb(float r, TDA A, float s, TDA B, TDA C)
{
  C[0]=r*A[0]+s*B[0];
  C[1]=r*A[1]+s*B[1];
  C[2]=r*A[2]+s*B[2];
}

void VecScalMult(float r, TDA A, TDA B)
{
  B[0]=r*A[0];
  B[1]=r*A[1];
```

```
  B[2]=r*A[2];
}

void VecScalMultI(float r, TDIA A, TDA B)
{
  B[0]=r*A[0];
  B[1]=r*A[1];
  B[2]=r*A[2];
}

void VecScalMultInt(float r, TDA A, TDIA B)
{
  B[0]=Round(r*A[0]);
  B[1]=Round(r*A[1]);
  B[2]=Round(r*A[2]);
}

void VecAddScalMult(float r, TDA A, TDA B, TDA C)
{
  C[0]=r*A[0]+B[0];
  C[1]=r*A[1]+B[1];
  C[2]=r*A[2]+B[2];
}

void VecNull(TDA A)
{
  A[0]=0.0;
  A[1]=0.0;
  A[2]=0.0;
}

void VecNullInt(TDIA A)
{
  A[0]=0;
  A[1]=0;
  A[2]=0;
}

void VecElemMult(float r, TDA A, TDA B, TDA C)
{
  C[0]=r*A[0]*B[0];
```

```
  C[1]=r*A[1]*B[1];
  C[2]=r*A[2]*B[2];
}

/*
```

```
  ┌────────────────────────────────────────────────────────────┐
  │              Affine Transformation Routines                │
  └────────────────────────────────────────────────────────────┘
   ZeroMatrix           - zeros the elements of a 4x4 matrix
   Translate3D          - make translation matrix
   Scale3D              - make scaling matrix
   Rotate3D             - make rotation matrix
   ZeroAllMatricies     - zeros all matricies used in
                                                  transformation
   Multiply3DMatricies- multiply 2 4x4 matricies
   PrepareMatrix        - prepare the transformation matrix
                                                       (Tm=S*R*T)
   PrepareInvMatrix     - prepare the inverse transformation matrix
   Transform            - multiply a vertex by the transformation
                                                           matrix
*/

void ZeroMatrix(Matx4x4 A)
{
  int i,j;

  for(i=0; i<4; i++)
  {
    for(j=0; j<4; j++)
      A[i][j]=0.0;
  }
}

void Translate3D(float tx, float ty, float tz, Matx4x4 A)
{
  int i;

  ZeroMatrix(A);
  for(i=0; i<4; i++)
```

```
    A[i][i]=1.0;
    A[0][3]=-tx;
    A[1][3]=-ty;
    A[2][3]=-tz;
}

void Scale3D(float sx, float sy, float sz, Matx4x4 A)
{
    ZeroMatrix(A);
    A[0][0]=sx;
    A[1][1]=sy;
    A[2][2]=sz;
    A[3][3]=1.0;
}

void Rotate3D(int m, float Theta, Matx4x4 A)
{
    int   m1,m2;
    float c,s;

    ZeroMatrix(A);
    A[m-1][m-1]=1.0;
    A[3][3]=1.0;
    m1=(m % 3)+1;
    m2=(m1 % 3);
    m1-=1;
    c=CosD(Theta);
    s=SinD(Theta);
    A[m1][m1]=c;
    A[m1][m2]=s;
    A[m2][m2]=c;
    A[m2][m1]=-s;
}

void Multiply3DMatricies(Matx4x4 A, Matx4x4 B, Matx4x4 C)
{
    int   i,j,k;
    float ab;

    for(i=0; i<4; i++)
```

```
  {
    for(j=0; j<4; j++)
    {
      ab=0;
      for(k=0; k<4; k++)
      ab+=A[i][k]*B[k][j];
      C[i][j]=ab;
    }
  }
}

void MatCopy(Matx4x4 a, Matx4x4 b)
{
  Byte i, j;

  for(i=0; i<4; i++)
  {
    for(j=0; j<4; j++)
      b[i][j]=a[i][j];
  }
}

void PrepareMatrix(float Tx, float Ty, float Tz,
         float Sx, float Sy, float Sz,
         float Rx, float Ry, float Rz,
         Matx4x4 XForm)
{
  Matx4x4 M1, M2, M3, M4, M5, M6, M7, M8, M9;

  Scale3D(Sx, Sy, Sz, M1);
  Rotate3D(1, Rx, M2);
  Rotate3D(2, Ry, M3);
  Rotate3D(3, Rz, M4);
  Translate3D(Tx, Ty, Tz, M5);
  Multiply3DMatricies(M2, M1, M6);
  Multiply3DMatricies(M3, M6, M7);
  Multiply3DMatricies(M4, M7, M8);
  Multiply3DMatricies(M5, M8, M9);
  MatCopy(M9, XForm);
}
```

```
void PrepareInvMatrix(float Tx, float Ty, float Tz,
       float Sx, float Sy, float Sz,
       float Rx, float Ry, float Rz,
       Matx4x4 XForm)
{
  Matx4x4 M1, M2, M3, M4, M5, M6, M7, M8, M9;

  Scale3D(Sx, Sy, Sz, M1);
  Rotate3D(1, Rx, M2);
  Rotate3D(2, Ry, M3);
  Rotate3D(3, Rz, M4);
  Translate3D(Tx, Ty, Tz, M5);
  Multiply3DMatricies(M4, M5, M6);
  Multiply3DMatricies(M3, M6, M7);
  Multiply3DMatricies(M2, M7, M8);
  Multiply3DMatricies(M1, M8, M9);
  MatCopy(M9, XForm);
}

void Transform(TDA A, Matx4x4 M, TDA B)
{
  B[0]=M[0][0]*A[0]+M[0][1]*A[1]+M[0][2]*A[2]+M[0][3];
  B[1]=M[1][0]*A[0]+M[1][1]*A[1]+M[1][2]*A[2]+M[1][3];
  B[2]=M[2][0]*A[0]+M[2][1]*A[1]+M[2][2]*A[2]+M[2][3];
}
```

Figure 1-1. Listing of *Math. Inc* File

Simple Math Functions

We begin with some very simple conversion functions. The first is *Round*. This function is passed a floating point number, adds 0.5 to it, and then returns an integer, which is the rounded-off value of the original number. The next function is *Trunc*, which is passed a floating point number and then returns it in integer form, which is the truncated value of the original number. Next is the function *SqrFP*, which is passed a floating point number and returns another floating point number which is the square of the original number. Finally comes *Sqr*, which is passed an integer and returns the square of the original integer.

The *Radians* and *Degrees* Functions

The next two functions are equally simple. They make use of the constants *PiOver180* and *PiUnder180* and a multiplication to perform conversions between degrees and radians. The *Radians* function converts degrees to radians. The *Degrees* function works in a reverse manner, converting radians to degrees.

The *CosD* and *SinD* Functions

The *CosD* function finds the cosine of an angle specified in degrees, by converting the angle to radians and then using the C *cos* function to find the angle's cosine. Similarly, the *SinD* function finds the sine of an angle specified in degrees by converting the angle to radians and then using the C sin function to find the angle's sine.

The *Power* Function

The *Power* function finds the value of a real (such as a floating point) number raised to an integer power. It begins by returning a one if the power is zero (since any number raised to the zero power is one). Otherwise, the function begins by initializing the variable *BPower* to one. Then a *for* loop is begun which multiplies *BPower* by the floating point number passed to the function as many times as the integer exponent, placing the new value in *BPower* at each iteration. When the loop ends, the desired result is in *BPower*, which is returned by the function. This function is not really necessary, because C has a standard library function for raising a number to a power, but it is useful in preserving the functioning of programs being converted from Turbo Pascal.

The *Log* Function

The *Log* function finds the logarithm of a number to the base 10. It does this by first taking the natural logarithm of the number (using the C function), and then dividing this by the previously defined constant *Ln10* (the natural logarithm of 10), which gives the desired result, which is then returned by the function.

The *Exp10* Function

The *Exp10* function finds the value of ten raised to a real number power. This is done by first multiplying the desired power by the natural logarithm of 10 and then raising the result to the *e* power by using the *exp* function of C. The function then returns this result.

The *Sign* and *IntSign* Functions

These functions are used to find the sign of a real number and of an integer, respectively. Either function returns an integer. This integer is set to –1 if the number is less than zero, +1 if the number is greater than zero, and 0 if the number is equal to zero.

The *IntSqrt* Function

The *IntSqrt* finds the square root of an integer and returns the square root in the form of an integer number.

The function for doing this is a little obscure and you may have to work out a few examples for yourself to convince yourself that it really works. It begins with a *for* loop that starts with *OddInt* equal to one and *x* equal to the number whose square root is being calculated. At each iteration it reduces *x* by *OddInt* and then increases *OddInt* by 2. When *x* is less than zero, the loop terminates. At this point half of the value of *OddInt* is either the integer square root or one more than the integer square root. The function uses a shift to get half the *OddInt* value, and then uses an if statement to determine whether the conditions are met for which the result should be decremented. Finally, the result is returned by the function.

The *IntPower* Function

IntPower is an elegant little function which makes use of recursion to raise an integer to an integer power. Recursion is the calling of a function by that same function. Not all computer languages have the capability to do this without becoming confused, but C language has been defined so that recursion is permissible. Note that except for the case of zero exponent, the function keeps calling itself at the next decrement of the power. Finally, it is decremented to zero, where one is returned to the previous call. One is then multiplied by the base and returned to the next previous call, and so forth until the highest level is reached.

Vector and Matrix Routines

In order to be able to move objects around in space and convert them to a two-dimensional display, we need to be able manipulate vectors. C doesn't have a vector data type, nor any of the associated vector operations, so we have to create our own. You can do this very easily and elegantly using C++, but for the benefit of those without a C++ compiler, we have implemented these operations in C. The vector portion of the mathematics module begins by defining the vector type TDA, which is an array of three real numbers representing the *x, y,* and *z* components of a three-dimensional vector. Similarly, the type *TDIA* is defined, which is an integer three-dimensional vector. An array *FDA* is defined, which is a four-dimensional vector of real numbers. Finally, the type *Matx4x4* is defined, which is a four-by-four element matrix.

The *Vec* and *VecInt* Functions

The *Vec* and *VecInt* functions are actually used to create vectors. For the *Vec* function, three real numbers and a vector of the real number type are passed to the function. The function then sets the three members of the array to the three real values that were passed. The *VecInt* function works in a similar manner except that three integers and a vector of the integer type are passed.

The *UnVec* and *UnVecInt* Functions

These are the reverse of the functions just described. The same three variables and a vector are passed, but the procedure transfers the three vector components to the three variables instead of the other way around.

The *VecDot* Function

The *VecDot* function computes the dot product of two real number three-dimensional vectors. You will remember from your math courses that the dot product of two vectors is a number which is the sum of the products of corresponding elements of the two vectors. The value of the dot product is:

$$a \cdot b = AB \cos x \qquad \text{(Equation 1-1)}$$

where *a* and *b* are the vectors, *A* and *B* are their magnitudes, and *x* is the angle between them. The parameters passed to the function are two real number three-dimensional vectors. The function returns a real number that is the vector dot product.

The *VecCross* Function

The *VecCross* function finds the cross-product of two real number three-dimensional vectors. The vector cross-product has a length of:

$$|a \times b| = |AB| \sin x \qquad \text{(Equation 1-2)}$$

where *A* and *B* are the lengths of the vectors *a* and *b* respectively and *x* is the angle between the two vectors. The direction of the vector cross-product is perpendicular to the plane defined by the vectors *a* and *b*. The vector cross-product is:

$$a \times b = (a_y b_z - a_z b_y,\ a_z b_x - a_x b_z,\ a_x b_y - a_y b_x) \qquad \text{(Equation 1-3)}$$

The *VecLen* Function

The *VecLen* function finds the length of a vector.

The *VecNormalize* Function

A normalized vector is one that has the same direction as a given vector, but has a unit length of one. Since a zero length vector really has no direction, it is a degenerate case that cannot be normalized. Hence, the first thing that the *VecNormalize* function does is call *VecLen* to find the length of the vector and, if this distance is zero, return after displaying an error message that says that the vector could not be normalized. Otherwise, the inverse of the vector length is found and each component of the vector is multiplied by it. This gives the components of a new vector that has the same direction, but whose length is one. This is therefore the normalization of the given vector. The procedure is designed in such a way that the normalized vector replaces the original vector which was passed to the procedure.

The VecMatxMult Function

The *VecMatxMult* function performs the multiplication of a vector by a four by four matrix. The operation is:

```
b = Matx x a                                    (Equation 1-4)
```

where *a* and *b* are real three-dimensional vectors and *Matx* is a four-by-four matrix. As indicated, the result of the multiplication is a vector. The function uses two nested *For* loops to multiply the appropriate elements together and sum them into the new vector components. The vector *a* and the matrix are passed to the function and the result of the multiplication is returned in *b*.

The VecSub and VecSubInt Functions

The *VecSub* function subtracts one real three-dimensional vector from another and returns the result. Similarly, the *VecSubInt* function subtracts one integer three-dimensional vector from another and returns the result.

The VecAdd and VecAdd3 Functions

The *VecAdd* function adds one real three-dimensional vector to another and returns the result. Similarly, the *VecAdd3* procedure adds three real three-dimensional vectors and returns the result.

The VecCopy Function

The *VecCopy* function simply copies the contents of one vector to another.

The VecLinComb Function

The *VecLinComb* accepts as inputs two real numbers and two vectors. The first real number multiplies all elements of the first vector and the second real number multiplies all elements of the second vector. The resulting vectors are then added. Thus the operation is:

```
c = Ra + Sb                                        (Equation 1-5)
```

where *a*, *b*, and *c* are real three-dimensional vectors and *R* and *S* are real numbers.

The *VecScalMult* and *VecScalMultInt* Functions

The *VecScalMult* function multiplies a real three-dimensional vector by a real number. Each element of the vector is multiplied by the real number to give a new vector. Similarly, the *VecScalMultInt* function multiplies an integer three-dimensional vector by an integer. Each element of the vector is multiplied by the integer to give a new vector.

The *VecAddScalMult* Function

The *VecAddScalMult* Function multiplies a real three-dimensional vector by a real number and then adds the result to another real three-dimensional vector. The operation is:

```
c = R*a + b                                        (Equation 1-6)
```

where *a*, *b*, and *c* are real three-dimensional vectors and *R* is a real number.

The *VecNull* and *VecNullInt* Functions

The *VecNull* function creates a zero or null real three-dimensional vector, i. e. one in which each element is zero. Similarly, the *VecNullInt* function creates a null integer three-dimensional vector.

The *VecElemMult* Function

The *VecElemMult* function multiplies a real three-dimensional vector by a real number and then multiplies the result by another real three-dimensional vector. The operation is:

```
c = R*a * b                                        (Equation 1-7)
```

where *a*, *b*, and *c* are real three-dimensional vectors and *R* is a real number.

Affine Transformation Routines

The affine transformation routines are used to create and manipulate four-by-four matrices. They create matrices for translation, scaling, and rotation, combine these into a single transformation matrix, and perform various matrix mathematical operations.

The ZeroMatrix Function

The *ZeroMatrix* function simply zeroes all the elements of a four-by-four matrix.

The Translate3D Function

The *Translate3D* function creates the matrix for performing a linear translation of a vector to a new location in space. This matrix consists of all zeros, except for the diagonal ones and the first three elements of the last row, which are set to the negative of the three translation parameters passed to the function. This creates the following matrix:

$$T = \begin{bmatrix} 1 & 0 & 0 & 0 \\ 0 & 1 & 0 & 0 \\ 0 & 0 & 1 & 0 \\ -t_x & -t_y & -t_z & 1 \end{bmatrix} \qquad \text{(Equation 1-8)}$$

The Scale3D Function

The *Scale3D* function leaves the origin of a real three-dimensional vector at the same point, but changes the size of the vector. Scale factors for each of the three vector components are passed to the procedure. These components become the first three diagonal elements of the matrix; the last diagonal element is a one. All other elements of the matrix are set to zero. The result is the following matrix:

$$S = \begin{bmatrix} s_x & 0 & 0 & 0 \\ 0 & s_y & 0 & 0 \\ 0 & 0 & s_z & 0 \\ 0 & 0 & 0 & 1 \end{bmatrix} \qquad \text{(Equation 1-9)}$$

The *Rotate3D* Function

The *Rotate3D* function creates a matrix to perform the rotation of a vector. The parameters passed to this procedure are an integer representing the axis about which the rotation is to take place (1 for the *x* axis, 2 for the *y* axis, or 3 for the *z* axis), and a real number, which is the rotation angle in degrees. The procedure begins by zeroing the matrix. It then sets the diagonal elements of the matrix that are not involved in the rotation to one. Next, it determines the indices for the matrix elements which perform the rotation. Following that, the cosine and sine of the rotation angle are calculated. These two variables are then placed in the proper matrix elements (with the proper sign) to perform the rotation. The function returns the completed rotation matrix. The rotation matrix around the *x* axis is:

$$R=\begin{bmatrix} 1 & 0 & 0 & 0 \\ 0 & \cos\theta & \sin\theta & 0 \\ 0 & -\sin\theta & \cos\theta & 0 \\ 0 & 0 & 0 & 1 \end{bmatrix}$$

(Equation 1-10)

The rotation matrix around the *y* axis is:

$$R=\begin{bmatrix} \cos\theta & 0 & -\sin\theta & 0 \\ 0 & 1 & 0 & 0 \\ -\sin\theta & 0 & \cos\theta & 0 \\ 0 & 0 & 0 & 1 \end{bmatrix}$$

(Equation 1-11)

The rotation matrix around the *z* axis is:

$$R=\begin{bmatrix} \cos\theta & \sin\theta & 0 & 0 \\ -\sin\theta & \cos\theta & 0 & 0 \\ 0 & 0 & 1 & 0 \\ 0 & 0 & 0 & 1 \end{bmatrix}$$

(Equation 1-12)

The *Multiply3DMatrices* Function

The *Multiply3DMatrices* function performs the multiplication of two four-by-four real number matrices. The function uses three nested *for* loops to perform the element multiplications and additions that are needed to obtain each element of the new matrix.

The *PrepareMatrix* Function

The *PrepareMatrix* function creates a complete affine transformation matrix. The parameters passed to this function are the translation distances in the *x*, *y*, and *z* directions, the scale factors in the *x*, *y*, and *z* directions, and the rotation angles around the *x, y*, and *z* axes. The function first uses the *Scale3D* function to create the matrix for the rescaling in size operation. It then uses the *Rotate3D* function three times to generate the rotation matrices around each of the three axes. It then uses the *Translate3D* function to create the translation matrix. *PrepareMatrix* multiplies all of these matrices together to create the final affine transformation matrix, which is returned by the function.

The *PrepareInvMatrix* Function

The *PrepareInvMatrix* function begins in the same way as the *PrepareMatrix* function, using the various functions previously defined to create all of the parts of the transformation process. However, it then multiplies these matrices together in the reverse order so that the transformation is the inverse of that done by the previous function.

The *Transform* Function

The *Transform* function performs the multiplication of a real three-dimensional vector by a real four-by-four matrix. The result that is returned is a new real three-dimensional vector.

CHAPTER 2

The Graphics Interface Module

This chapter will describe a number of graphics functions that we will be using to paint our graphics to the display screen. These routines are all included in a module called *Graph.Inc*. This module is listed in Figure 2-1, and the various routines are described in this chapter. As you read each description, refer to the listing for the source code.

The *SetMode* Function

This function makes use of the ROM BIOS video services, which form part of the firmware of the IBM PC architecture, to set the computer display to the desired mode. The mode number is passed to this function, which then sets up the computer registers properly and initiates an interrupt which causes BIOS to execute the mode change.

The *PreCalc* Function

This function initializes an array called *PreCalcY*. Each entry of this array consists of the display *x* resolution multiplied by the row number. This is the offset needed by the *Plot* function to properly locate the memory address where it is to transfer information. Using this pre-initialized array reduces computations during plotting and thereby speeds up the plotting function.

The *Plot* Function

This function plots a point to the screen in a designated color. The variables passed to the function are *x*, which is the horizontal position on the screen, *y*, which is the vertical position on the screen, and *color*, which is the palette number for the selected color. The function begins by checking whether *x* and *y* are within the limits set for the display. If they both are within limits, the memory offset for the display data is calculated.

```
/* Graph. Inc

                    Video Graphics Array Driver

            Original Material by Christopher D. Watkins

                    'C' Conversion by Larry Sharp

   SetMode      - selects the display mode
   Plot         - place pixel to screen
   ClearPalette - clear palette register
   SetPalette   - set palette register
   InitPalette1 - 64 levels of grey, red, green and blue
   InitPalette2 - 7 colors with 35 intensities each
   CyclePalette - cycle through palette
   Circle       - circle draw routine
   Draw         - line draw routine
   InitGraphics - initialize graphics
   WaitForKey   - wait for key press
   ExitGraphics - sound and wait for keypress before exiting
                                                         graphics
   Title          - set up text screen colors
*/

union  REGS reg;
struct SREGS inreg;

void SetMode(int Mode)

{
  reg.h.ah=0;
  reg.h.al=Mode;
  int86(0x10,&reg,&reg);
}
```

```
#define MaxXres 320
#define MaxYres 200
#define MaxX (MaxXres-1)
#define MaxY (MaxYres-1)

int  XRes, YRes;
Word PreCalcY[MaxY+1];

void PreCalc()
{
  Word j;

  for(j=0; j<=MaxY; j++)
    PreCalcY[j]=0;
  for(j=0; j<=MaxY; j++)
    PreCalcY[j]=XRes*j;
}

void Plot(int x, int y, Byte color)
{
  Word Offset;
  char far *address;

  if(!((x<0) || (y<0) || (x>MaxX) || (y>MaxY)))
  {
    Offset = PreCalcY[y] + x;
    address = (char far *)  (0xA0000000L + Offset);
    *address = color;
  }
}

typedef struct
{
  Byte Red;
  Byte Grn;
  Byte Blu;
}
RGB;

typedef RGB PaletteRegister[255];
```

```
PaletteRegister Color;

void ClearPalette(PaletteRegister Color)
{ Word i;

  for(i=0; i<=255; i++)
  {
    Color[i].Red=0;
    Color[i].Grn=0;
    Color[i].Blu=0;
  }
}

void SetPalette(PaletteRegister Hue)
{
  reg.x.ax=0x1012;
  segread(&inreg);
  inreg.es=inreg.ds;
  reg.x.bx=0;
  reg.x.cx=256;
  reg.x.dx=(int)&Hue[0];
  int86x(0x10,&reg,&reg,&inreg);
}

void InitPalette(PaletteRegister Color)
{
  Word i;

  for(i=0; i<64; i++)
  {
    Color[i].Red=i;
    Color[i].Grn=i;
    Color[i].Blu=i;
  }

  for(i=64; i<128; i++)
  {
    Color[i].Red=i-64;
    Color[i].Grn=0;
    Color[i].Blu=0;
```

```
  }

  for(i=128; i<192; i++)
  {
    Color[i].Red=0;
    Color[i].Grn=i-128;
    Color[i].Blu=0;
  }

  for(i=192; i<=255; i++)
  {
    Color[i].Red=0;
    Color[i].Grn=0;
    Color[i].Blu=i-192;
  }
}

void InitPalette2(PaletteRegister Color)
{
  Word i;

  for(i=0; i<36; i++)
  {
    Color[i].Red=0;
    Color[i].Grn=0;
    Color[i].Blu=Round(1.8*i);
  }

  for(i=36; i<72; i++)
  {
    Color[i].Red=0;
    Color[i].Grn=Round(1.8*(i-36));
    Color[i].Blu=0;
  }

  for(i=72; i<108; i++)
  {
    Color[i].Red=0;
    Color[i].Grn=Round(1.8*(i-72));
    Color[i].Blu=Round(1.8*(i-72));
```

```
  }

  for(i=108; i<144; i++)
  {
    Color[i].Red=Round(1.8*(i-108));
    Color[i].Grn=0;
    Color[i].Blu=0;
  }

  for(i=144; i<180; i++)
  {
    Color[i].Red=Round(1.8*(i-144));
    Color[i].Grn=0;
    Color[i].Blu=Round(1.8*(i-144));
  }

  for(i=180; i<216; i++)
  {
    Color[i].Red=Round(1.8*(i-180));
    Color[i].Grn=Round(1.8*(i-180));
    Color[i].Blu=0;
  }

  for(i=216; i<252; i++)
  {
    Color[i].Red=Round(1.8*(i-216));
    Color[i].Grn=Round(1.8*(i-216));
    Color[i].Blu=Round(1.8*(i-216));
  }
}

void CyclePalette(PaletteRegister Hue)
{
  Word i;
  RGB tmp;

  tmp=Hue[0];
  for(i=1; i<=255; i++)
    Hue[i-1]=Hue[i];
  Hue[255]=tmp;
```

```
  SetPalette(Hue);
}

void Swap(int *first, int *second)
{
  int temp;

  temp=*first;
  *first=*second;
  *second=temp;
}

void Circle(Word x, Word y, Word radius, Byte color)
{
  int a, af, b, bf, target, r2;

  target=0;
  a=radius;
  b=0;
  r2=Sqr(radius);
  while(a>=b)
  {
    b=Round(sqrt(r2-Sqr(a)));
    Swap(&target,&b);
    while(b<target)
    {
      af=(120*a) / 100;
      bf=(120*b) / 100;
      Plot(x+af, y+b, color);
      Plot(x+bf, y+a, color);
      Plot(x-af, y+b, color);
      Plot(x-bf, y+a, color);
      Plot(x-af, y-b, color);
      Plot(x-bf, y-a, color);
      Plot(x+af, y-b, color);
      Plot(x+bf, y-a, color);
      ++b;
    }
    --a;
  }
```

```
}

void Draw(int xx1, int yy1, int xx2, int yy2, Byte color)
{
  int LgDelta, ShDelta, Cycle, LgStep, ShStep, dtotal;

  LgDelta=xx2-xx1;
  ShDelta=yy2-yy1;
  if(LgDelta<0)
  {
    LgDelta=-LgDelta;
    LgStep=-1;
  }
  else
    LgStep=1;
  if(ShDelta<0)
  {
    ShDelta=-ShDelta;
    ShStep=-1;
  }
  else
    ShStep=1;
  if(ShDelta<LgDelta)
  {
    Cycle=LgDelta >> 1;
    while(xx1 != xx2)
    {
      Plot(xx1, yy1, color);
      Cycle+=ShDelta;
      if(Cycle>LgDelta)
      {
         Cycle-=LgDelta;
         yy1+=ShStep;
      }
      xx1+=LgStep;
    }
    Plot(xx1, yy1, color);
  }
  else
  {
```

```
      Cycle=ShDelta >> 1;
      Swap(&LgDelta, &ShDelta);
      Swap(&LgStep, &ShStep);
      while(yy1 != yy2)
      {
        Plot(xx1, yy1, color);
        Cycle+=ShDelta;
        if(Cycle>LgDelta)
        {
          Cycle-=LgDelta;
          xx1+=ShStep;
        }
        yy1+=LgStep;
      }
      Plot(xx1, yy1, color);
    }
}

void InitGraphics()
{
  XRes=MaxXres;
  YRes=MaxYres;
  PreCalc();
  SetMode(19);
  ClearPalette(Color);
  InitPalette2(Color);
  SetPalette(Color);
}

void WaitForKey()
{
  char k;

  while(!(k=getch()));
}

void ExitGraphics()
{
  sound(1000);
  delay(500);
```

```
  nosound();
  WaitForKey();
  SetMode(3);
}

void Title()
{
  textcolor(YELLOW);
  textbackground(BLUE);
  clrscr();
}


/*
╔══════════════════════════════════════════════════════════════╗
║            Three Dimensional Plotting Routines               ║
╚══════════════════════════════════════════════════════════════╝

   InitPlotting        - rotation and tilt angles
   InitPerspective     - observer location and distances
   MapCoordinates      - maps 3D space onto the 2D screen
   CartesianPlot       - plot a cartesian system point
   CylindricalPlot3D   - plot a cylindrical system point
   SphericalPlot3D     - plot a spherical system point
   DrawLine3D          - plots a line from 3D coordinates
*/

int   CentreX, CentreY;
int   Angl, Tilt;
float CosA, SinA;
float CosB, SinB;
float CosACosB, SinASinB;
float CosASinB, SinACosB;

void InitPlotting(int Ang, int Tlt)
{
  CentreX=MaxX >> 1;
  CentreY=MaxY >> 1;
  Angl=Ang;
  Tilt=Tlt;
```

```
  CosA=CosD(Angl);
  SinA=SinD(Angl);
  CosB=CosD(Tilt);
  SinB=SinD(Tilt);
  CosACosB=CosA*CosB;
  SinASinB=SinA*SinB;
  CosASinB=CosA*SinB;
  SinACosB=SinA*CosB;
}

Boolean PerspectivePlot;
float   Mx, My, Mz, ds;

void InitPerspective(Boolean Perspective, float x, float y, float
   z, float m)
{
  PerspectivePlot=Perspective;
  Mx=x;
  My=y;
  Mz=z;
  ds=m;
}

void MapCoordinates(float X, float Y, float Z, int *Xp, int *Yp)
{
  float Xt, Yt, Zt;

  Xt=(Mx+X*CosA-Y*SinA);
  Yt=(My+X*SinASinB+Y*CosASinB+Z*CosB);
  if(PerspectivePlot)
  {
    Zt=Mz+X*SinACosB+Y*CosACosB-Z*SinB;
    *Xp=CentreX+Round(ds*Xt/Zt);
    *Yp=CentreY-Round(ds*Yt/Zt);
  }
  else
  {
    *Xp=CentreX+Round(Xt);
    *Yp=CentreY-Round(Yt);
  }
```

```
}

void CartesianPlot3D(float X, float Y, float Z, Byte Color)
{
  int Xp, Yp;

  MapCoordinates(X, Y, Z, &Xp, &Yp);
  Plot(Xp, Yp, Color);
}

void CylindricalPlot3D(float Rho, float Theta, float Z, Byte
   Color)
{
  float X, Y;

  Theta=Radians(Theta);
  X=Rho*cos(Theta);
  Y=Rho*sin(Theta);
  CartesianPlot3D(X, Y, Z, Color);
}

void SphericalPlot3D(float R, float Theta, float Phi, Byte Color)
{
  float X, Y, Z;

  Theta=Radians(Theta);
  Phi=Radians(Phi);
  X=R*sin(Theta)*cos(Phi);
  Y=R*sin(Theta)*sin(Phi);
  Z=R*cos(Theta);
  CartesianPlot3D(X, Y, Z, Color);
}

void DrawLine3D(TDA Pnt1, TDA Pnt2, Byte Color)
{
  int   Xp1, Yp1;
  int   Xp2, Yp2;
  float x1, y1, z1;
  float x2, y2, z2;
```

```
  UnVec(Pnt1, &x1, &y1, &z1);
  UnVec(Pnt2, &x2, &y2, &z2);
  MapCoordinates(x1, y1, z1, &Xp1, &Yp1);
  MapCoordinates(x2, y2, z2, &Xp2, &Yp2);
  Draw(Xp1, Yp1, Xp2, Yp2, Color);
}

/*
                         Pixel

   PutPixel - plots pixel
   GetPixel - gets pixel

   Color 1 - Blue
    2 - Green
    3 - Cyan
    4 - Red
    5 - Magenta
    6 - Brown/Yellow
    7 - Gray Scale

   Intensity levels (0..35) for each color
*/

#define MaxCol   7
#define MaxInten 35

void PutPixel(int x, int y, Byte Color, Byte Intensity)
{
  Byte Col;

  if(Intensity>MaxInten)
  {
    printf("Inten > MaxInten!!\n\nHit any hey to exit.\n");
    getch();
    exit(1);
  }
  Col=((MaxInten+1)*(Color-1)+Intensity) & 255;
```

```
  Plot(x, y, Col);
}

int GetPixel(int x, int y)
{
  reg.x.ax=3328;
  reg.x.dx=y;
  reg.x.cx=x;
  int86(0x10,&reg,&reg);
  return(reg.x.ax&255);
}

/*
```

Set up of Coordinate Axes and Color Palette

```
   PutAxisAndPalette - toggle for Axis and Palette
   AxisAndPalette    - places Axis and Color Palette on screen
*/

Boolean DrawAxisAndPalette;

void PutAxisAndPalette(Boolean PlaceOnScreen)
{
  if(PlaceOnScreen)
    DrawAxisAndPalette=true;
  else
    DrawAxisAndPalette=false;
}

void DisplayAxis()
{
  int x, y, z;

  for(x=-100; x<101; x++)
  {
    CartesianPlot3D(x, 0, 0, 35);
    CartesianPlot3D(100, 0, 0, 251);
  }
```

```
  for(y=-100; y<101; y++)
  {
    CartesianPlot3D(0, y, 0, 71);
    CartesianPlot3D(0, 100, 0,251);
  }
  for(z=-100; z<101; z++)
  {
    CartesianPlot3D(0, 0, z, 107);
    CartesianPlot3D(0, 0, 100, 251);
  }
}

void DisplayPalette()
{
  int  X, Y;
  Byte Color;
  Byte Intensity;

  for(Color=1; Color<=MaxCol; Color++)
  {
    for(Intensity=0; Intensity<=MaxInten; Intensity++)
    {
      for(X=0; X<4; X++)
      {
   for(Y=0; Y<4; Y++)
     PutPixel(X+5*Color, 190-Y-5*Intensity, Color, Intensity);
      }
    }
  }
}

void AxisAndPalette()
{
  if(DrawAxisAndPalette)
  {
    DisplayAxis();
    DisplayPalette();
  }
}
```

Figure 2-1. Listing of *Graph.Inc* File.

The display memory begins at the base address *0xA0000000L*. All that is necessary to find the correct pixel address for the 256-color display mode is to add the proper value of *x* and the proper value from the *PreCalcY* array to the base address. The color value then is sent to this memory address.

The *ClearPalette* Function

The array *PaletteRegister* contains the red, green, and blue components that define the color for each of the 256 color registers that define the display colors in the 256-color mode. This function sets all of these values to zero to clear the array.

The *SetPalette* Function

This function uses the ROM BIOS video services to set the 256 color registers to the 256 colors defined by the array *PaletteRegister*. The function begins by setting the proper contents of the microprocessor registers to cause the proper ROM BIOS function to be called and to indicate that it is to transfer information to the VGA card from the address which marks the beginning of the *PaletteRegister* array. Then, the video services interrupt is called to perform this operation.

The *InitPalette1* Function

This function sets up the color designations in the *PaletteRegister* array. In the 256-color mode, the initial color selections chosen by IBM have the virtue of compatibility with the EGA, but otherwise are rather useless. They begin by assigning the first 64 colors to the 64 colors which can be produced by the EGA. Next are 64 shades of gray. The origin of the shades assigned to the remaining color registers are rather obscure. In most cases, we can replace these default colors with a set of colors that are more adapted to the types of displays that we wish to produce. Using this function, we divide the color registers into four basic groups; gray, red, green, and blue. In the gray group, we assign each of the three primary colors (red, green, and blue) to the same intensity value for each shade, with the shades varying from 0 to 63. For the red group, we assign red to intensities from 0 to 63 and leave the other colors at zero. For the green group, we assign green to intensities from 0 to 63 and leave the other colors at zero. For the blue group, we assign blue to intensities from 0 to 63 and leave the other colors at zero.

The *InitPalette2* Function

This function sets up a different set of color designations in the *PaletteRegister* array, which may be more appropriate for particular displays that we wish to generate. Using this function, we divide the color registers into seven basic groups; blue, green, cyan, red, magenta, brown, and gray. In the gray group, we assign equal values to each of the primary colors, varying the values to give intensities of gray from 0 to 63 in 35 steps. In the brown group, we assign equal values to red and green and assign zero to blue, varying the red and green values to give intensities of brown from 0 to 63 in 35 steps. In the magenta group, we assign equal values to red and blue and assign zero to green, varying the red and blue values to give intensities of magenta from 0 to 63 in 35 steps. In the cyan group, we assign equal values to blue and green and zero to red, varying the blue and green values to give intensities of cyan from 0 to 63 in 35 steps. For the red group, we assign red to intensities from 0 to 63 and leave the other colors at zero. For the blue group, we assign blue to intensities from 0 to 63 and leave the other colors at zero. For the green group, we assign green to intensities from 0 to 63 and leave the other colors at zero.

The *Cycle Palette* Function

This function cycles all of the colors in the *PaletteRegister* array. It begins by saving the first set of color values to a temporary storage variable. It then initiates a *for* loop which moves all of the remaining 255 sets of color values to the next lower member of the array. When the loop is complete, the beginning value is transferred from the temporary variable to the highest member of the array. Note that this cycles the color values in the array, but it has no effect upon the actual colors of the display. To change these colors, the *SetPalette* function must be called to transfer the array information to the VGA color registers.

The *Swap* Function

This function simply swaps two integers. In other words, if *first* contains the value 3 and *second* contains the value 4, then after *Swap* is called, *first* will contain 4 and *second* will contain 3. This is an operation that is often needed for our graphics programs, and therefore we have made a separate function for it.

The *Circle* Function

This function is used to draw a circle on the screen (in the 320 by 200 pixel by 256-color mode) when the coordinates of the circle center, its radius, and its color are specified. Note that there is a symmetry in the circle that permits us to specify offsets from the center of the circle in both the *x* and *y* directions and then, by assigning the proper signs to these offsets, draw eight different points on the circle. By performing these eight plots for each offset computation, when we have computed points for one-eighth of the circle, we have drawn the entire circle, thus minimizing the required computations. Were the pixels defined to be square, we would need only two offsets; since they are not, we need to multiply the offsets for the *x* coordinate by a factor (1.2) to correct the aspect of the circle. Now, take a look at how the computations are performed.

First one offset is assigned to be the radius of the circle; the other, and a target value, are set to zero. We then enter a *while* loop which continues until the second offset is less than the first (indicating that one-eighth of the circle is complete). Within this loop, the function first computes the value of the second offset, using the equation of a circle and then swaps it with the target value. Next a second *while* loop is entered, which iterates until the value of the second offset is greater than or equal to the target value. For each iteration, the computation of the *x* offsets (with factor to correct the aspect ratio) is completed and then the eight symmetrical points are plotted. The second offset is then incremented by one. (The reason for this loop is to fill in sections of the circle where the second offset changes so little that there is no change in terms of pixel location for that offset.) When this loop completes, we decrement the first offset by one pixel and then perform another iteration of the first loop. The result is a circle drawn on the screen with the best accuracy that is allowed for the screen resolution being used.

The *Draw* Function

This function draws a line from one specified point to another, using a designated color. The function begins by calculating *LgDelta,* the distance between the beginning and ending points in the *x* direction, and *ShDelta*, the distance between the beginning and end points in the *y* direction. Associated with each of these is a step parameter (*LgStep* and *ShStep*). If either of the distance parameters is negative, it's sign is changed and the corresponding step parameter is made to be –1; otherwise the step parameter is +1. The rest of the function is determined by an *if* statement which directs one course of action if the *y* line distance is shorter than the *x* line distance and another course of action otherwise. Let's start by looking at the first situation. We first compute a parameter *Cycle* which is half of the *x* line distance (the longer distance). Next we enter a *while* loop which iterates as long as the *x* pixel coordinate (*xx1*) is less than the ending *x* line coordinate. (Initially this coordinate is the beginning line *x* coordinate. First a pixel is plotted at the *x* and *y* coordinates in the designated color. Next, *Cycle* is increased by the shorter distance. If this makes it larger than the longer distance, it is reduced by the longer distance and the *y* coordinate is changed by adding the *ShStep* parameter (which is either + or – 1). Then the *x* coordinate is changed by the *LgStep* parameter (which is also + or – 1). The loop is then iterated again, beginning by plotting the new pixel location. When the loop terminates, the coordinates are positioned at the end of the line, but the final point has not yet been plotted, so that the first thing that happens after loop termination is to plot this final point.

Now let's look at what happens when the *y* line distance is longer than the *x* line distance. First, the *Cycle* parameter is computed to be one-half of *ShDelta* instead of one-half of *LgDelta*. Next the values of *LgDelta* and *ShDelta* are swapped and the values of *LgStep* and *ShDelta* are swapped. The rest of the function is just like the loop previously described, except that the termination of the loop depends upon the value of the *y* pixel parameter instead of the *x* parameter and the order of changing the *x* and *y* pixel coordinates is reversed. This function is an implementation of Bresenham's algorithm, which is generally accepted as the best method for drawing lines on a screen.

The *InitGraphics* Function

This function initializes the screen for graphics. It begins by setting the *XRes* and *YRes* parameters to their maximum values. Next, it calls *SetMode* to set the graphics mode to mode 19, which is the 320-pixel-by-200-pixel-by-256-color mode. It then calls *PreCalc* to fill the *PreCalcY* array. Following that, it calls *ClearPalette* to clear the *Color* array, followed by *InitPalette2* to set up the desired colors in the *Color* array. It then calls *SetPalette* to store the colors designated in the *Color* array into the 256 color registers of the VGA board.

The *WaitForKey* Function

This function stops all program action except that of looking for a key to be pressed at the keyboard. The function terminates when a key having an ASCII value of greater than a space (32) is entered. This includes all alphanumeric characters.

The *ExitGraphics* Function

This function is usually called at the end of generating a display picture. It begins by producing a 1000 Hertz note for one-half second, to alert the user that the display is complete. It then calls *WaitForKey* to wait for a key stroke to be entered on the keyboard. When the keystroke is entered, it resets the display to the text mode.

The *Title* Function

This function prepares the screen for writing out information in the text mode. It begins by setting the color of the text to yellow and the color of the background to blue. It then clears the screen, leaving the blue background color.

Three-Dimensional Plotting Routines

The remaining functions that are listed in the graphics module are used for generating three-dimensional pictures. They include functions for initializing the rotation and tilt angles, for setting up the observer location and distances, for mapping the three-dimensional space onto a two-dimensional screen, for plotting in Cartesian, cylindrical, or spherical coordinates, and for drawing a line when given the three-dimensional coordinates. These functions are described in the following sections.

The *InitPlotting* Function

The *InitPlotting* function initializes variables that are used in three-dimensional plotting and that are dependent upon the rotation and tilt angles. These angles, in integer form, are passed to the function. The first variables that are initialized are *CentreX* and *CentreY*, which are the coordinates of a point at the center of the screen. Next, the parameter *Angl* is set to the rotation angle that was passed to the function. The parameter *Tilt* is then set to the tilt angle that was passed to the function. The function then writes to the screen something like this: *View Direction is 45° around the z-Axis and 62° off of the z-Axis*, where the first angle will actually be the viewer rotation angle that was selected and the second angle will actually be the viewer tilt angle that was selected. Next, the parameters *CosA*, *SinA*, *CosB*, and *SinB* are initialized, where *CosA* and *SinA* are the cosine and sine respectively of the rotation angle and *CosB* and *SinB* are the cosine and sine respectively of the tilt angle. Next, the parameters *CosACosB*, *SinASinB*, *CosASinB*, and *SinACosB*, are calculated where each parameter is the product of two trigonometric functions as indicated by its name.

The *InitPerspective* Function

The *InitPerspective* function is passed a Boolean flag indicating that perspective plotting is to take place, together with the *x*, *y*, and *z* coordinates of the observer position in space, and a parameter that represents the distance of the observer from the display screen. The flag is stored in the variable *PerspectivePlot*. The observer position coordinates are stored in *Mx*, *My*, and *Mz* respectively. The distance is stored in the parameter *ds*.

The *MapCoordinates* Function

This function has passed to it the coordinates of a point in three-dimensional space (*X*,Y,*Z*) as real numbers. These are in a coordinate system whose origin is at the center of the display screen. First, the proper mathematical expressions are solved to project this point onto the two-dimensional screen, yielding the two-dimensional coordinates X_t and Y_t. These expressions are:

$$x_t = m_x + x \cos\theta - y \sin\theta \quad \text{(Equation 2-1)}$$

and

$$y_t = m_y + x \sin\theta \sin\phi + y \cos\theta \sin\phi + z \cos\phi \quad \text{(Equation 2-2)}$$

where x_t and y_t are the two-dimensional coordinates, not yet converted to display coordinates. The angles and *x,y,z* coordinates can be seen in Figures 2-2, 2-3, and 2-4. The parameters m_x and m_y represent the viewer's position and are used when perspective is called for. If there is to be no perspective, these parameters are zero. Next, the function checks to see whether a perspective plot is called for. If so, it computes a *z* coordinate as follows:

$$z_t = m_z + x \sin\theta \cos\phi + y \cos\theta \cos\phi - z \sin\phi \qquad \text{(Equation 2-3)}$$

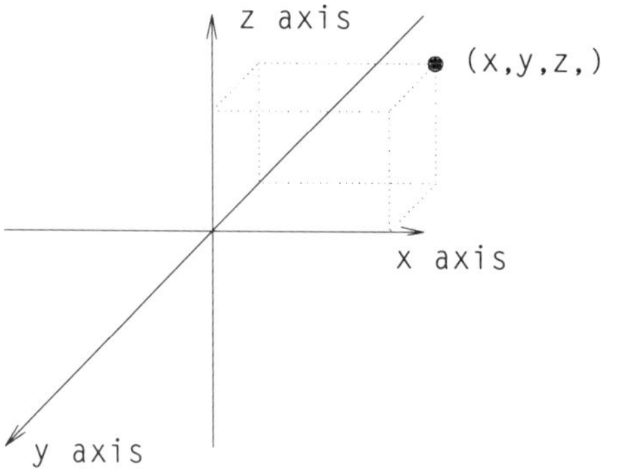

Figure 2-2. Cartesian Coordinates

The function then divides the *x* and *y* coordinates by this *z* coordinate, multiplies them by the viewer distance from the screen, and adds in the center of screen coordinates to convert the pair to integers, *Xp* and *Yp*, which are the column and row representation of the pixel that should be plotted to the screen. If a perspective plot was not called for, the originally-projected coordinate results are modified to the column and row to be displayed (*Xp* and *Yp*) by adding the center of screen coordinates. In either case, the result is returned by the function.

The *CartesianPlot3D* Function

This function is used to plot a point to the screen that is passed to the function as the *x*, *y*, and *z* coordinates of the point in three-dimensional space plus the designated color for the point. Figure 2-2 shows a point plotted in Cartesian coordinates. The function then calls *MapCoordinates* to convert the three-dimensional coordinate information to display screen coordinates and then plots a pixel on the screen at these coordinates in the designated color.

The *CylindricalPlot3D* Function

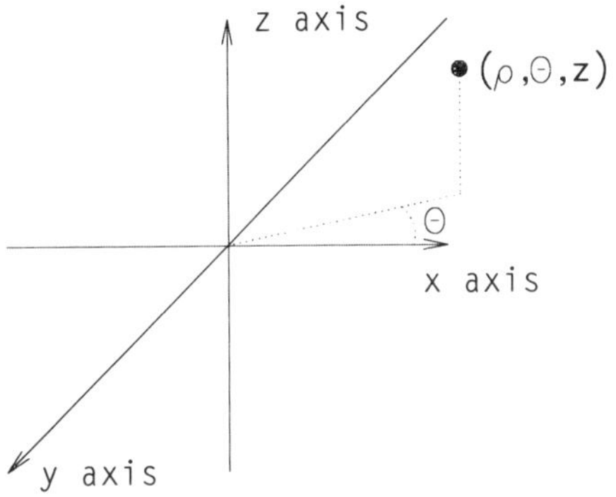

Figure 2-3. Cylindrical Coordinates

This function is used to plot a point to the screen that is passed to the function in the form of cylindrical coordinates *Rho* (radius), *Theta* (angle of radius line in the *xy* plane), and *Z* (height), and a designated color. A point plotted in cylindrical coordinates is shown in Figure 2-3. First, the angle *Theta* is converted from degrees to radians and then the trigonometric relationships are solved to find the three-dimensional coordinates *X* and *Y*. The function *CartesianPlot3d* is then called to plot a pixel on the two dimensional screen using the coordinates *X*, *Y*, and *Z*, and the designated color.

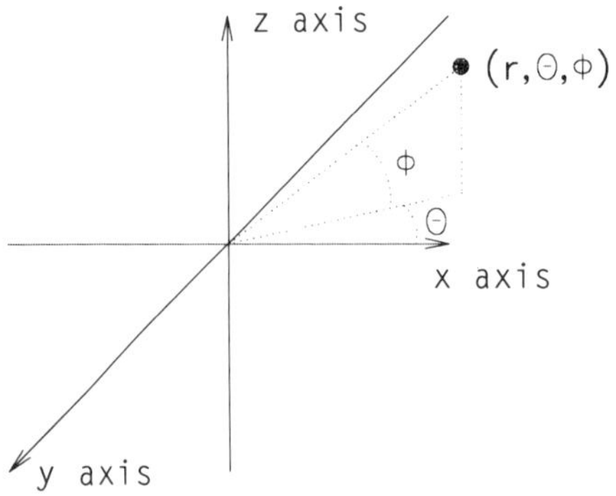

Figure 2-4. Spherical Coordinates

The *SphericalPlot3D* Function

This function is used to plot a point to the screen that is passed to the function in the form of spherical coordinates *r* (radius), *Theta* (angle of radius line in the *xy* plane), and *Phi* (angle of the radius line in the *xz* plane), and a designated color. A point plotted in spherical coordinates is shown in Figure 2-4. First, the angles *Theta* and *Phi* are converted from degrees to radians and then the trigonometric relationships are solved to find the three-dimensional coordinates *X*, *Y*, and *Z*. The function *CartesianPlot3d* is then called to plot a pixel on the two-dimensional screen using the coordinates *X*, *Y*, and *Z*, and the designated color.

The *DrawLine3D* Function

This function is passed two three-dimensional vectors representing the beginning and end of the line respectively and a designated color. The function first uses the function *UnVec* to convert each vector into three separate coordinates. It then calls *MapCoordinates* twice. The first call converts the three-dimensional beginning coordinates of the line to two-dimensional display screen coordinates. The second call converts the three-dimensional ending coordinates of the line to two-dimensional display screen coordinates. Finally, the function calls *Draw* to draw a line on the screen from the beginning display screen coordinates to the ending display screen coordinates in the designated color.

The *PutPixel* Function

The *PutPixel* Function is used to plot a pixel on the screen when the shade of color to be produced is given as a basic color number and an intensity level. First, the function checks to assure that the intensity does not exceed the maximum allowable level. It then computes the color register number (from 1 to 255) of the desired color shade. Next, *Plot* is called to paint the selected color pixel on the screen at the specified coordinates.

The *GetPixel* Function

This function makes use of the ROM BIOS video services to obtain the color of a pixel at a designated set of coordinates on the screen. The microprocessor registers are set to initiate the desired video service interrupt and pass the proper screen coordinates. The interrupt is then initiated to perform the desired video service. Upon completion of the interrupt, the pixel color is contained in register AH. This is extracted by ANDing the AX register with 0xFF. The resulting value is returned by the function.

Displaying the Coordinate Axes and the Color Palette

This group of functions provides the capability to add the display of the coordinate axes and the entire color palette to any display screen. The first function, *PutAxisAndPalette*, simply sets a Boolean variable *DrawAxisAndPalette* to *True* if *True* is passed to the function and to *False* if *False* is passed to the function. The next function, *AxisAndPalette*, checks the above Boolean variable. If it is *True*, the function calls *DisplayAxis* to draw the coordinate axes, and *DisplayPalette* to create the display of palette colors.

The function *DisplayAxis* uses *CartesianPlot3D* to convert points from –100 to +100 along each of the three coordinate axes to their two-dimensional equivalents and display them on the screen as blue, green, and cyan lines for x, y, and z, respectively.

The function *DisplayPalette* uses nested *for* loops to generate 3-by-3 pixel blocks of each color available in the palette. These are located at the left-hand side of the screen.

CHAPTER 3

How to Use the Modules

Now that we understand the use of the Mathematics module and the Graphics Interface module, it is time to try our hand at creating some graphics displays using these new tools. In the paragraphs that follow, we will describe some graphics programs that you can use to create unusual displays, many of them involving fractals. Once you have become familiar with these displays, you should fully understand the techniques and be able to generate some interesting displays of your own.

Walking About on the Mandelbrot Set

The Mandelbrot set is probably the most well known of all fractal curves. Both it and the associated Julia sets are the result of repeated iteration of the equation:

$$z_n = z_{n-1}^2 + c \qquad \text{(Equation 3-1)}$$

where z and c are complex numbers. To generate Mandelbrot sets, we let the display plane represent a range of values for c and at each point on the plane corresponding to some pair of pixel values for x (the real part of c) and y (the imaginary part of c). We let z_0 be equal to zero and then iterate the equation and plot a color to the pixel that represents the behavior of the iterated equation. To generate Julia sets, we select some fixed value for c and let the display plane represent a range of starting values for z_0.

It is often said that the Mandelbrot set is a map or dictionary of the various Julia sets. This is true both because the Mandelbrot set maps the values of c, for each of which there is a unique Julia set, and because interesting features of the Mandelbrot set, such as cusps of the curve, usually correspond to interesting Julia sets. To demonstrate the relationship, the program *MSetJset.c* first generates a Mandelbrot set on the left-hand side of the display and then lets the user move a cursor around this display. At each cursor location, an inverse technique is used to generate the corresponding Julia set on the right-hand side of the display. The Julia display continues to generate points (improving the detail of the rendition) until the user moves the cursor (whereupon the right-hand side of the display is blanked and generation of the new Julia set begins), or until the user hits the *Esc* key, which terminates the program. Figure 3-1 is a listing of the *MSetJSet.c* program.

The main program, which is at the end of the listing, simply calls five procedures. The first of these, *InitGraphics*, was described in the previous chapter. It sets up the computer to use the desired 320-by-200-pixel-by-256-color graphics mode. The next procedure, *InitCursor*, zeroes the members of *ColrArray*, which is later used to store cursor information. The next procedure is *CalcMSet*. This is the procedure that paints the Mandelbrot set on the screen. It begins by using the *Draw* procedure to draw a border for the Mandelbrot set around the left half of the screen and a border for the Julia set around the right half of the screen. It then determines the limit numbers of iterations, *L1* and *L2*, for which displayed colors are to change. Next, it determines the quantities by which *x* and *y* (the parameters of the Mandelbrot equation constant) are to be increased for each increase of a pixel on the display. The procedure then enters a pair of nested *for* loops. The first iterates through values of *y* , which designates the pixel row on the screen, from the edge to the center of the screen. For each one, it determines the value of the iterated equation constant's imaginary part, *cy*. The next loop iterates through the values of *x*, which designates the pixel column on the screen. First, *cx*, the value of the real part of the Mandelbrot constant is determined. Then the function *Iterate* is called to iterate the equation. This function first sets variables *x* (the real part) and *y* (the imaginary part) to the corresponding constant values and then finds their squares. Next, it begins a *while* loop which repeats until either the maximum number of iterations is reached or the value of the sum of the squares is greater than 4. Mathematically, the latter condition shows that the result of the equation is diverging, so it is time to quit. For each repetition of the *while* loop, the Mandelbrot equation is solved to find the next set of values and the number of iterations is incremented. When the loop terminates, the number of iterations that took place is returned by the function. The *CalcMSet* procedure then determines the color, depending upon the number of iterations, and then paints this color on the screen by calling the *Pix* procedure. (This procedure takes advantage of the symmetry of the Mandelbrot set to plot two pixels, one above and one below the center of the screen. It does this using the *Plot* function, which was described in the previous chapter.)

```
/* MsetJset.c

        MSet JSet.c = Walkabout on the Mandelbrot Set -
                     Display the Julia Set

              Program by Christopher D. Watkins

                'C' Conversion by Larry Sharp

*/

#include "stdio.h"
#include "stdlib.h"
#include "dos.h"
#include "conio.h"
#include "math.h"
#include "mem.h"
#include "math.inc"
#include "graph.inc"

#define XMin    -2.20
#define XMax     0.60
#define YMin    -1.20
#define YMax     1.20
#define MaxIter  30.0
#define Res      160.0

char source[160];
int srcoff,srcseg;

int Iterate(float cx, float cy)
{
```

```
  int   Iters;
  float x, y;
  float x2, y2;
  float temp;

  x=cx;
  x2=SqrFP(x);
  y=cy;
  y2=SqrFP(y);
  Iters=0;
  while((Iters<MaxIter) && (x2+y2<4))
  {
    temp=cx+x2-y2;
    y=cy+2*x*y;
    y2=SqrFP(y);
    x=temp;
    x2=SqrFP(x);
    ++Iters;
  }
  return(Iters);
}

void Pix(int x, int y, int col)
{
  int a;

  Plot(x, y, col);
  Plot(x, Res-y-1, col);
}

void CalcMSet()
{
  int   ix, iy;
  int   Iters;
  float cx, cy;
  float dx, dy;
  int   L1, L2;

  Draw(0, 0, Res-1, 0, 35);
```

```
  Draw(Res-1, 0, Res-1, Res-1, 35);
  Draw(Res-1, Res, 0, Res, 35);
  Draw(0, Res, 0, 0, 35);
  Draw(Res, 0, 2*Res-1, 0, 35);
  Draw(2*Res-1, 0, 2*Res-1, Res-1, 35);
  Draw(2*Res-1, Res, Res, Res, 35);
  L1=(MaxIter-(MaxIter*2)/3);
  L2=(MaxIter-(MaxIter*5)/6);
  dx=(XMax-XMin)/(Res-1);
  dy=(YMax-YMin)/(Res-1);
  for(iy=2; iy<=((Res-1)/2); iy++)
  {
    cy=YMin+iy*dy;
    for(ix=2; ix<=Res-3; ix++)
    {
      cx=XMin+ix*dx;
      Iters=Iterate(cx, cy);
      if(Iters==MaxIter)
        Pix(ix, iy, 143);
      else
      {
        if(Iters>L1)
          Pix(ix, iy, 215);
        else
        {
          if(Iters>L2)
            Pix(ix, iy, 35);
        }
      }
    }
  }
}

void CalcJSet(float cx, float cy)
{
  int   xp, yp;
  float dx, dy;
  float r;
  float Theta;
  float x, y;
```

```
  x=0;
  y=0;
  do
  {
    dx=x-cx;
    dy=y-cy;
    if(dx>0)
      Theta=atan(dy/dx)*0.5;
    else
    {
      if(dx<0)
    Theta=(Pi+atan(dy/dx))*0.5;
      else
    Theta=Pi*0.25;
    }
    r=sqrt(sqrt(SqrFP(dx)+SqrFP(dy)));
    if(random(100)<50)
      r=-r;
    x=r*cos(Theta);
    y=r*sin(Theta);
    xp=Res/2+Round(x*36)+Res;
    yp=Res/2+Round(y*36);
    Plot(xp, yp, 143);
  }
  while(!(kbhit()));
}

Byte ColrArray[10];
Byte xx;

void InitCursor()
{
  for(xx=1; xx<=9; xx++)
    ColrArray[xx]=0;
}

void PutCursor(int x, int y, int ox, int oy)
{
  for(xx=1; xx<=5; xx++)
    Plot(ox+xx-3, oy, ColrArray[xx]);
  for(xx=6; xx<=7; xx++)
```

```
    Plot(ox, oy+xx-8, ColrArray[xx]);
  for(xx=8; xx<=9; xx++)
    Plot(ox, oy+xx-7, ColrArray[xx]);
  for(xx=1; xx<=5; xx++)
    ColrArray[xx]=GetPixel(x+xx-3, y);
  for(xx=6; xx<=7; xx++)
    ColrArray[xx]=GetPixel(x, y+xx-8);
  for(xx=8; xx<=9; xx++)
    ColrArray[xx]=GetPixel(x, y+xx-7);
  Draw(x-2, y, x+2, y, 71);
  Draw(x, y-2, x, y+2, 71);
}
void BlockClearHalfScreen()
{
  unsigned int t, i, Offset;
  char far *address;

  for(t=1; t<=Res-1; t++)
  {
      Offset=(t*320)+Res;
      movedata(srcseg,srcoff,0xA000,Offset, Res-3);
  }
}

float cx, cy;

void ViewStats()
{
  ungetch(32);
  ExitGraphics();
  Title();
  printf("Mandlebrot Set :\n\n");
  printf("   XMin = %f\n",XMin);
  printf("   XMax = %f\n",XMax);
  printf("   YMin = %f\n",YMin);
  printf("   YMax = %f\n\n",YMax);
  printf("Julia Set :\n\n");
  printf("   cx = %f\n",cx);
  printf("   cy = %f\n",cy);
  while(!(kbhit()));
  InitGraphics();
```

```
  CalcMSet();
}

void CheckCursor(int *X, int *Y)
{
  if(*X<1)
    *X=1;
  if(*X>158)
    *X=158;
  if(*Y<1)
    *Y=1;
  if(*Y>159)
    *Y=159;
}

void WalkAbout()
{
  int   oCursX, oCursY;
  int   CursX, CursY;
  char  Dir;
  float dx, dy;

  dx=(XMax-XMin)/(Res-1);
  dy=(YMax-YMin)/(Res-1);
  oCursX=3;
  oCursY=3;
  CursX=oCursX;
  CursY=oCursY;
  PutCursor(CursX, CursY, oCursX, oCursY);
  do
  {
    Dir=getch();
    switch(Dir)
    {
      case ' ': ViewStats(); break;
      case 'K': CursX-=1; break;
      case 'M': CursX+=1; break;
      case 'H': CursY-=1; break;
      case 'P': CursY+=1; break;
      case 'G': CursX-=1; CursY-=1; break;
```

```
        case 'I': CursX+=1; CursY-=1; break;
        case 'O': CursX-=1; CursY+=1; break;
        case 'Q': CursX+=1; CursY+=1; break;
      }
      if(Dir!=27)
      {
        CheckCursor(&CursX, &CursY);
        PutCursor(CursX, CursY, oCursX, oCursY);
        oCursX=CursX;
        oCursY=CursY;
        cx=XMin+dx*CursX;
        cy=YMin+dy*CursY;
        BlockClearHalfScreen();
        CalcJSet(cx, cy);
      }
    }
    while(Dir!=27);
}

void main()
{
    int i;
    struct SREGS segregs;

    segread(&segregs);
    srcseg = segregs.ds;
    srcoff = (int) source;

    for (i=0; i<Res; i++)
        source[i] = 0;

    InitGraphics();
    InitCursor();
    CalcMSet();
    WalkAbout();
    ungetch(32);
    ExitGraphics();
}
```

Figure 3-1. Listing of Program to Walk About the Mandelbrot Set

Once the Mandelbrot set has been plotted, the main program calls the function *WalkAbout*, which allows walking about the Mandelbrot set with the cursor and plotting the selected Julia set. The function begins by initializing the parameters that store the cursor location. Next it calls *PutCursor*, which draws the cursor on the screen. *PutCursor* first takes the stored information from the array *ColrArray* and uses it to restore the screen by redrawing the cursor image (a cross 5-by-5 pixels) in the original image colors at its current location. It then fills *ColrArray* with the necessary scene information from the new location of the cursor, and draws the cursor at its new location. It then stores the new cursor location for use for restoring the scene data the next time the function is run. Returning to the *WalkAbout* function, we next enter a *do* loop which continues until the *Esc* key is entered on the keyboard. The loop begins by awaiting a keystroke. When a keystroke is entered, if it is 00, this indicates a special key that outputs two bytes of data, so the second byte is read. Next a *switch* statement is used to take action, depending upon the keystroke that was read. For a left arrow the cursor location is changed one pixel to the left; for the right arrow, the cursor location is changed one pixel to the right; for the up arrow, the cursor location is changed one pixel upward; and for the down arrow, the cursor location is changed one pixel downward. Diagonal cursor position changes are also used. For the *Home* key, the cursor position is changed one pixel to the left and one pixel upward; for the *PgUp* key, the cursor position is changed one pixel to the right and one pixel upward; for the *End* key, the cursor position is changed one pixel to the left and one pixel downward; and for the *PgDn* key, the cursor position is changed one pixel to the right and one pixel downward.

Next, the *PutCursor* function is called to place the cursor at the new position. The values for the real and imaginary parts of the Julia set constant are then calculated. Next the function calls *BlockClearHalfScreen* to clear the half screen of the old Julia set display so as to be ready to draw a new one. We could clear the half screen by using nested *for* loops to send a zero to each pertinent byte of screen memory, but this would be objectionably slow. Borland C++ and Microsoft C have a function called *_fmemset* which permits setting a block of memory at a far location to a desired character. This is ideal for clearing the half screen, but unfortunately the function is not available in the Turbo C family of compilers. Therefore, we have used an alternate technique.

We defined an array *source* to be a half line of characters and in the main program filled the array with zeroes and saved its address. To clear the half screen, a *for* loop is run which at each iteration sets the display address to the next line of the half screen and then transfers the half line of zeroes from the *source* array to the display memory with a call to the standard C function for a block memory move. Next the *CalcJSet* function is called to calculate the Julia set using the inverse technique. This function initializes the *x* and *y* coordinates and then enters a *do* loop which reiterates until a key is pressed. Each iteration begins by computing *dx* and *dy*, the differences between the current values of *x* and *y* and the real and imaginary values of the Julia constant, respectively. Considering these differences as a two-dimensional vector, the vector angle and length are then computed. Next, a random number between 0 and 1 is obtained. If it is less than 0.5, the direction of the vector is reversed. The function then computes new values of *x* and *y* and uses them to generate a new position on the screen. Then, the pixel at this new position is plotted in light red. This process continues until a key is pressed. The function then returns to *WalkAbout*. *WalkAbout* then continues its loop, which permits you to move the cursor and generate a new Julia set. At any time, you can view the values of c_x and c_y for the Julia set being generated by hitting the spacebar. The *WalkAbout* function terminates when the *Esc* key is pressed, whereupon the function returns to the main program. The function *ExitGraphics* is then called, returning to the text mode. This completes the program. A typical Mandelbrot/Julia set display is shown in Plate 1.

Simulating Two Orbiting Particles

In this section, we are going to look at a program that displays two orbiting particles. Normally, a particle that is in motion continues to move in a straight line. If, instead, the particle is moving in a circle at a constant velocity, there is a changing velocity toward the center of the circle. Changing velocity is acceleration, and this acceleration can be shown to be:

$$a = \frac{v^2}{r} \qquad \text{(Equation 3-2)}$$

where a is acceleration, v is the velocity of the particle, and r is the radius of the circular orbit. By Newton's second law of motion, force is equal to mass times acceleration so that:

$$F=ma=\frac{mv^2}{r} \qquad \text{(Equation 3-3)}$$

This is the centripetal force. It is a force acting toward the center of the circle. Thus, when we see a particle moving in an orbit rather than flying off in a straight line, we know that there must be a force acting toward the orbit's center. This is the gravitational force. Suppose each object in the system has a position, represented as (x_n, y_n), and a mass, represented as m_n, where n indicates the number of the object (i.e. n=1 for the first object and n=2 for the second object). Object positions and the distances between the objects are measured in meters and the mass of each object is measured in kilograms. The distance between the two objects is simply the length of a straight line connecting them. Broken down into Cartesian coordinates, it is:

$$d_x=|x_2-x_1| \qquad \text{(Equation 3-4)}$$

$$d_y=|y_2-y_1| \qquad \text{(Equation 3-5)}$$

The length of the distance vector is:

$$D=\sqrt{D_x^2+D_y^2} \qquad \text{(Equation 3-6)}$$

Now that we know the distance between the objects, we can calculate the gravitational force between them using the Law of Universal Gravitation. This law states that the force due to gravity, F_g, is directly proportional to the product of the masses (m_1 and m_2) and inversely proportional to the distance (d) squared. The proportionality term is the Gravitational Constant of Proportionality (g) has the value of $6.67E\text{-}11$ ($N{\cdot}m^2/kg^2$). The resulting equation is thus:

$$F_g=g\frac{m_1 m_2}{D^2} \qquad \text{(Equation 3-7)}$$

This force is an attractive force along the direction of the line connecting the two objects. The force is a vector quantity, namely, it has a direction and a magnitude. It can also be expressed as a horizontal magnitude and a vertical magnitude (F_x and F_y).

For a system of particles to be in equilibrium, the velocity of each particle and its distance from the center of mass must be such that the centripetal force is exactly equal to the gravitational force between the particle and the center of mass. If the gravitational force is too small, the particle will escape from orbit and fly off somewhere; if it is too large, the particle will be pulled in to the center of mass.

Thus combining our equations for gravitational force and acceleration, we obtain:

$$a_{x1}=\frac{gm_2}{D^2}\times\frac{D_x}{D} \qquad \text{(Equation 3-8)}$$

and

$$a_{y1}=\frac{gm_2}{D^2}\times\frac{D_y}{D} \qquad \text{(Equation 3-9)}$$

Because acceleration is change in velocity of an object with respect to change in time, we obtain the following equations:

$$dv_x=a_xt \qquad \text{(Equation 3-10)}$$

and

$$dv_y=a_yt \qquad \text{(Equation 3-11)}$$

If we start with an initial velocity of v_0, then at the end of a time t we have the new velocity components:

$$v_x=v_{x0}+a_xt \qquad \text{(Equation 3-12)}$$

and

$$v_y=v_{y0}+a_yt \qquad \text{(Equation 3-13)}$$

Thus the velocity at the end of the interval is v_0+at. Therefore the average velocity throughout the interval is approximately:

$$v_{avg}=\frac{v_0+v_0+at}{2}=v_0+\frac{at}{2} \qquad \text{(Equation 3-14)}$$

We want our program to show the position of each particle, with continual updating as time passes. Thus we are looking for a formula to express the particle's position. Since velocity is the rate of change of position with respect to time, over any interval of time the change in position is the average velocity multiplied by the time. Therefore, we now have equations that tell us the change in positions of the objects:

$$dx=v_{x0}+\frac{at^2}{2} \qquad \text{(Equation 3-15)}$$

and

$$dy=v_{y0}+\frac{at^2}{2} \qquad \text{(Equation 3-16)}$$

Assuming that we know the initial position (x_0,y_0), then at any time the current position is:

$$x=x_0+v_{x0}t+\frac{a_xt^2}{2} \qquad \text{(Equation 3-17)}$$

and

$$y=y_0+v_{y0}t+\frac{a_y^2t}{2} \qquad \text{(Equation 3-18)}$$

The *Orbit-2P.c* Program

The *Orbit-2P.c* program creates a display that has two parts. Near the center of the screen are the two particles, one a red circle and the other a green circle. They are rotating continually in their orbits, with a blue line connecting them. At the top left-hand corner of the screen is a meter comprised of a blue circle showing the velocity vector of the green particle in dark green and its acceleration vector in light green. The velocity of the red particle is displayed in dark red and its acceleration vector is shown in light red. The program is listed in Figure 3-2. When you run the program, the orbit will be continually changing with time, presenting an interesting display. A static display at any instant of time is not very interesting, however, which is why we haven't shown a color plate of this display.

```
/*

        orbit2P.c = Two Particle Orbit Simulator

          Program by Christopher D. Watkins

            'C' Conversion by Larry Sharp

increase time step size 'dt' to greater than zero to increase speed
*/

#include "stdio.h"
#include "dos.h"
#include "conio.h"
#include "math.h"
#include "math.inc"
#include "graph.inc"

int MSize;
int x, y;
int oVx1, oVy1;
int oAx1, oAy1;
int oVx2, oVy2;
int oAx2, oAy2;

void InitMeters()
{
  MSize=30;
  Circle(MSize, MSize, MSize-4, 35);
  oVx1=MSize;
  oVy1=MSize;
  oAx1=MSize;
  oAy1=MSize;
```

```
    oVx2=MSize;
    oVy2=MSize;
    oAx2=MSize;
    oAy2=MSize;
  }

  void Meter(float dx, float dy, int *xt, int *yt, int Radius,
  int Color)
  {
    float r;

    Draw(MSize, MSize, *xt, *yt, 0);
    r=Radius/sqrt(SqrFP(dx)+SqrFP(dy))-5;
    x=Round(dx*r)+MSize;
    y=-Round(dy*r)+MSize;
    *xt=x;
    *yt=y;
    Draw(MSize, MSize, x, y, Color);
  }

  float X1, Y1, Vx1, Vy1, Ax1, Ay1;
  float X2, Y2, Vx2, Vy2, Ax2, Ay2;
  float OneOverDistSqr, dt;
  float Dx, Dy, Tx, Ty;
  int   M1, M2, Xp1, Yp1, Xp2, Yp2;

  void main()
  {
    M1=6;
    M2=6;

    X1= -40;      Y1= 00.0;
    X2=  40;      Y2= 00.0;

    Vx1= 0.000;  Vy1= 1.000;
    Vx2= 0.000;  Vy2=-1.000;

    dt=0.1;

    InitGraphics();
```

```
  InitMeters();
  do
  {
    Xp1=160+Trunc(X1);
    Yp1=100-Trunc(Y1);
    Xp2=160+Trunc(X2);
    Yp2=100-Trunc(Y2);
    Draw(Xp1, Yp1, Xp2, Yp2, 35);
    Circle(Xp1, Yp1, M1, 71);
    Circle(Xp2, Yp2, M2, 143);
    X1+=Vx1*dt;
    Y1+=Vy1*dt;
    X2+=Vx2*dt;
    Y2+=Vy2*dt;
    Dx=X2-X1;
    Dy=Y2-Y1;
    OneOverDistSqr=1.0/(Sqr(Dx)+Sqr(Dy));
    Tx=Dx*OneOverDistSqr;
    Ty=Dy*OneOverDistSqr;
    Ax1=M2*Tx;
    Ay1=M2*Ty;
    Ax2=-M1*Tx;
    Ay2=-M1*Ty;
    Vx1+=Ax1*dt;
    Vy1+=Ay1*dt;
    Vx2+=Ax2*dt;
    Vy2+=Ay2*dt;
    Meter(Vx1, Vy1, &oVx1, &oVy1, 25, 51);
    Meter(Ax1, Ay1, &oAx1, &oAy1, 12, 71);
    Meter(Vx2, Vy2, &oVx2, &oVy2, 25, 123);
    Meter(Ax2, Ay2, &oAx2, &oAy2, 12, 143);
    Draw(Xp1, Yp1, Xp2, Yp2, 0);
    Circle(Xp1, Yp1, M1, 0);
    Circle(Xp2, Yp2, M2, 0);
  }
  while(!(kbhit()));
  ExitGraphics();
}
```

Figure 3-2. Listing of the *Orbit-2P.c* Program

The program begins by initializing the masses of the particles, their initial positions, and their initial velocities. It then sets the time step to 0.5. This step must always be positive, but can be increased to cause the particles to move faster or decreased to cause them to move slower. Next, *InitGraphics* is called to set up the graphics mode. The function *InitMeters* is then called to initialize the meter part of the display. It draws the initial meter circle and sets up the initial velocity and acceleration coordinates. Next, a *do* loop is begun and reiterated until a key is pressed. At this point, *ExitGraphics* is called to return to the text mode, and the program then terminates. Within the loop, the particle positions are converted to positions on the display screen. A blue line is then drawn between them and then a circle the size of the mass of each is drawn about the coordinate set in the proper color. Next the new position coordinates of each particle after the time step are computed and then the new distances between the particles in the x and y directions. The reciprocal of the distance squared is then computed and used to compute the new accelerations and velocities for each particle. Then *Meter* is called four times to display the two velocities and two accelerations in the meter display. This function has passed to it the beginning and ending x and y coordinates for the vector, the radius of the circle, and the desired color. The function begins by blanking the previous value of the vector by redrawing it in the background color. It then uses the input coordinates and the radius to compute the beginning and end points of the vector in display screen coordinates. It then draws the new vector in the designated color, and then returns to the calling program. Next, the program redraws the two particle circles and their connecting line in the background color to clear them from the screen, and then repeats the loop again to draw them in their new positions.

The *Orbit-3P.c* Program

When three particles are involved, the mathematics is basically similar to that discussed above for two particles, but a bit more complex because the interactions between each pair of particles must be taken into account. We won't go over the equations in detail; after all, this is not a text on mechanics and the equations are all similar to those already discussed for the two particle case. The *Orbit-3P.c* program creates a display that has two parts. Near the center of the screen are three particles, one a red circle, one a white circle, and one a green circle, continually rotating in their orbits, with blue lines connecting each pair of particles. At the top left-hand corner of the screen is a meter comprised of a blue circle showing the velocity vector of the green particle in dark green and its acceleration vector in light green and the velocity of the red particle in dark red and its acceleration vector in light red, and the velocity of the white particle in gray and its acceleration in white. The program is listed in Figure 3-3.

The program begins by initializing the masses of the particles, their initial positions, and their initial velocities. It then sets the time step to 0.4. This step must always be positive, but can be increased to cause the particles to move faster or decreased to cause them to move slower. Next, *InitGraphics* is called to set up the graphics mode. The procedure *InitMeters* is then called to initialize the meter part of the display. It draws the initial meter circle and sets up the initial velocity and acceleration coordinates. Next, a *do* loop is begun and reiterated until a key is pressed. At this point, *ExitGraphics* is called to return to the text mode, and the program then terminates. Within the loop, the particle positions are converted to positions on the display screen. A blue line is then drawn between each pair of particles and then a circle the size of the mass of each is drawn about the coordinate set in the proper color. Next the new position coordinates of each particle after the time step are computed and then the new distances between the particles in the x and y directions. The reciprocal of the distance squared is then computed and used to compute the new accelerations and velocities for each particle. Then *Meter* is called six times to display the three velocities and three accelerations in the meter display. This function has passed to it the beginning and ending x and y coordinates for the vector, the radius of the circle, and the desired color. The function begins by blanking the previous value of the vector by redrawing it in the background color. It then uses the input coordinates and the radius to compute the beginning and end points of the vector in display screen coordinates. It then draws the new vector in the designated color, and returns to the calling program. Next, the program redraws the three particle circles and their connecting lines in the background color to clear them from the screen, and then repeats the loop again to draw them in their new positions.

```
/*
╔══════════════════════════════════════════════════════════════╗
║                                                              ║
║          orbit3P.c = Three Particle Orbit Simulator          ║
║                                                              ║
║             Program by Christopher D. Watkins                ║
║                                                              ║
║               'C' Conversion by Larry Sharp                  ║
║                                                              ║
╚══════════════════════════════════════════════════════════════╝

increase time step size 'dt' to greater than zero to increase speed

/*

#include "stdio.h"
#include "dos.h"
#include "conio.h"
#include "math.h"
#include "math.inc"
#include "graph.inc"

int MSize;
int x,y;
int oVx1, oVy1;
int oAx1, oAy1;
int oVx2, oVy2;
int oAx2, oAy2;
int oVx3, oVy3;
int oAx3, oAy3;

void InitMeters()
{
  MSize=30;
  Circle(MSize, MSize, MSize-4, 35);
  oVx1=MSize;
  oVy1=MSize;
  oAx1=MSize;
  oAy1=MSize;
  oVx2=MSize;
  oVy2=MSize;
```

```
  oAx2=MSize;
  oAy2=MSize;
  oVx3=MSize;
  oVy3=MSize;
  oAx3=MSize;
  oAy3=MSize;
}

void Meter(float dx, float dy, int *xt, int *yt, int Radius,
int Color)
{
  float r;

  Draw(MSize, MSize, *xt, *yt, 0);
  r=Radius/sqrt(SqrFP(dx)+SqrFP(dy))-10;
  x=Round(dx*r)+MSize;
  y=-Round(dy*r)+MSize;
  *xt=x;
  *yt=y;
  Draw(MSize, MSize, x, y, Color);
}

float X1, Y1, Vx1, Vy1, Ax1, Ay1;
float X2, Y2, Vx2, Vy2, Ax2, Ay2;
float X3, Y3, Vx3, Vy3, Ax3, Ay3;
float D12, D23, D31, dt;
float Dx12, Dx23, Dx31;
float Dy12, Dy23, Dy31;
float Tx12, Tx23, Tx31;
float Ty12, Ty23, Ty31;
int   Xp1, Yp1, Xp2, Yp2, Xp3, Yp3;
int   M1, M2, M3;

void main()
{
  M1=1;
  M2=10;
  M3=3;

  X1=-40.0; Y1=0.0;
```

```
X2= 00.0; Y2=0.0;
X3= 90.0; Y3=0.0;

Vx1= 0.1010;  Vy1= 0.2500;
Vx2= 0.0010;  Vy2= 0.0010;
Vx3=-0.0200;  Vy3=-0.1010;

dt=0.4;

InitGraphics();
InitMeters();
do
{
  Xp1=160+Trunc(X1);
  Yp1=100-Trunc(Y1);
  Xp2=160+Trunc(X2);
  Yp2=100-Trunc(Y2);
  Xp3=160+Trunc(X3);
  Yp3=100-Trunc(Y3);
  Draw(Xp1, Yp1, Xp2, Yp2, 35);
  Draw(Xp2, Yp2, Xp3, Yp3, 35);
  Draw(Xp3, Yp3, Xp1, Yp1, 35);
  Circle(Xp1, Yp1, M1, 143);
  Circle(Xp2, Yp2, M2, 71);
  Circle(Xp3, Yp3, M3, 251);
  X1+=Vx1*dt;
  Y1+=Vy1*dt;
  X2+=Vx2*dt;
  Y2+=Vy2*dt;
  X3+=Vx3*dt;
  Y3+=Vy3*dt;
  Dx12=X1-X2;
  Dy12=Y1-Y2;
  Dx23=X2-X3;
  Dy23=Y2-Y3;
  Dx31=X3-X1;
  Dy31=Y3-Y1;
  D12=sqrt(SqrFP(Dx12)+SqrFP(Dy12));
  D12=1.0/(D12*D12*D12);
  D23=sqrt(SqrFP(Dx23)+SqrFP(Dy23));
```

```
    D23=1.0/(D23*D23*D23);
    D31=sqrt(SqrFP(Dx31)+SqrFP(Dy31));
    D31=1.0/(D31*D31*D31);
    Tx31=Dx31*D31;
    Ty31=Dy31*D31;
    Tx12=Dx12*D12;
    Ty12=Dy12*D12;
    Tx23=Dx23*D23;
    Ty23=Dy23*D23;
    Ax1=(M3*Tx31-M2*Tx12);
    Ay1=(M3*Ty31-M2*Ty12);
    Ax2=(M1*Tx12-M3*Tx23);
    Ay2=(M1*Ty12-M3*Ty23);
    Ax3=(M2*Tx23-M1*Tx31);
    Ay3=(M2*Ty23-M1*Ty31);
    Vx1+=Ax1*dt;
    Vy1+=Ay1*dt;
    Vx2+=Ax2*dt;
    Vy2+=Ay2*dt;
    Vx3+=Ax3*dt;
    Vy3+=Ay3*dt;
    Meter(Vx1, Vy1, &oVx1, &oVy1, 25, 123);
    Meter(Ax1, Ay1, &oAx1, &oAy1, 12, 143);
    Meter(Vx2, Vy2, &oVx2, &oVy2, 25, 51);
    Meter(Ax2, Ay2, &oAx2, &oAy2, 12, 71);
    Meter(Vx3, Vy3, &oVx3, &oVy3, 25, 231);
    Meter(Ax3, Ay3, &oAx3, &oAy3, 12, 251);
    Draw(Xp1, Yp1, Xp2, Yp2, 0);
    Draw(Xp2, Yp2, Xp3, Yp3, 0);
    Draw(Xp3, Yp3, Xp1, Yp1, 0);
    Circle(Xp1, Yp1, M1, 0);
    Circle(Xp2, Yp2, M2, 0);
    Circle(Xp3, Yp3, M3, 0);
  }
  while(!(kbhit()));
  ExitGraphics();
}
```

Figure 3-3. Listing of the *Orbit-3P.c* Program

Three Particle Orbits

The parameters that were listed in the program *Orbit3P.c* in Figure 3-3 provide an interesting, though orderly, set of orbits. The orbits are very well-behaved, much like those of the sun and its planets. However, there are other, very interesting, orbital parameters which cause particles to orbit around each other for awhile and then make violent changes to new orbiting paths. If you would like to explore these, parameters for six different orbits are given in Table 3-1.

m1	1	1	1	1	1	1
m2	10	10	10	10	10	10
m3	3	3	3	3	3	3
x1	-60	-40	-40	-40	40	40
y1	0	0	0	0	0	0
x2	0	0	0	0	0	0
y2	0	0	0	0	0	0
x3	90	80	70	90	70	70
y3	0	0	0	0	0	0
vx1	.1000	.1000	.1000	.1010	.1000	.1000
vy1	.1500	.2500	.2500	.2500	.2500	.2500
vx2	.0010	.0010	.0010	.0010	-.0010	-.0010
vy2	.0010	.0010	.0010	.0010	.0010	.0010
vx3	-.0500	-.0500	-.0500	-.0200	-.1010	-.0500
vy3	-.1500	-.1500	-.1500	-.1010	-.1500	-.1500

Table 3-1. Other Orbit Parameters for Three Particles

Generating a Sierpinski Triangle

The Sierpinski triangle is an interesting fractal figure. Aside from the fact that it creates a beautiful and captivating display, the triangle is interesting because there seem to be more ways of generating it than for almost any other fractal. Many of these techniques seem to have very different starting points, yet the resulting figure, when plotted with enough levels of detail, seems to be the same in every case. The book *Fractal Programming in C* shows several ways to generate this triangle. Here is another method, one that makes use of a recursive technique.

At the lowest level, the program simply calls a function called *Triangle*, which just draws a triangle. At higher levels, *Triangle* draws nothing; instead, it calls itself three times at the next lower level for three half-sized triangles along the same sides and having the same apexes as the original triangle. This process repeats until triangles of the lowest level are reached. These are actually drawn. The program that does this is listed in Figure 3-4. The resulting Sierpinski triangle is shown in Plate 2.

The program begins by Displaying the legend "Recursive Triangle Generator", followed by "Level =>". It then reads in the level selected by the user. Next the function *InitGraphics* is run to set up the graphics display mode. The initial color is set and two coordinate parameters *Xo* and *Yo* are initialized. These parameters are then used with a set of trigonometric operations to create the three sets of coordinates for a large equilateral triangle. The program then calls the function *Triangle* for these coordinates and the specified level. This function, if the level is zero, draws a line in the specified color between each pair of coordinates to create a triangle on the screen. If the level is greater than zero, instead of drawing a triangle, the function calls itself three times. Each call has as its coordinate parameters one of the three vertices of the current triangle plus the points half-way along the sides adjoining that vertex. In addition, the level parameter is reduced by one. The color is then changed and the function terminates. Thus a recursive process occurs, with more and more calls to *Triangle* until the zeroth level is reached, at which each call draws a triangle on the screen.

```
/*
    triangle.c = Recursive Triangle Generator

    Program by Christopher D. Watkins

    'C'Conversion by Larry Sharp
*/

#include "stdio.h"
#include "dos.h"
#include "conio.h"
#include "math.h"
#include "math.inc"
#include "graph.inc"

#define Ang1 0
#define Ang2 120
#define Ang3 240

int X1, Y1, X2, Y2, X3, Y3;
int Level, Xc, Yc;
int Col;

void Triangle(int X1, int Y1, int X2, int Y2, int X3, int Y3,
int Level)
{
  int Xp1, Xp2, Xp3;
  int Yp1, Yp2, Yp3;

  if(Level==0)
  {
    Xp1=Xc+X1;
    Yp1=Yc-Y1;
    Xp2=Xc+X2;
    Yp2=Yc-Y2;
    Xp3=Xc+X3;
    Yp3=Yc-Y3;
    Draw(Xp1, Yp1, Xp2, Yp2, Col);
```

```
    Draw(Xp2, Yp2, Xp3, Yp3, Col);
    Draw(Xp3, Yp3, Xp1, Yp1, Col);
  }
  else
  {
    Triangle(X1, Y1, (X1+X2) / 2, (Y1+Y2) / 2, (X1+X3) / 2,
                                    (Y1+Y3) / 2, Level-1);
    Triangle(X2, Y2, (X2+X3) / 2, (Y2+Y3) / 2, (X2+X1) / 2,
                                    (Y2+Y1) / 2, Level-1);
    Triangle(X3, Y3, (X3+X1) / 2, (Y3+Y1) / 2, (X3+X2) / 2,
                                    (Y3+Y2) / 2, Level-1);
    Col=Level*36+35;
  }
}

void main()
{
  Title();
  Level=0;
  puts("Recursive Triangle Generator");
  puts("");
  printf("Level (1-7) => ");
  scanf("%d", &Level);
  InitGraphics();
  Col=35;
  Xc=160;
  Yc=100;
  X1=Round(Xc*CosD(Ang1));
  Y1=Round(Yc*SinD(Ang1));
  X2=Round(Xc*CosD(Ang2));
  Y2=Round(Yc*SinD(Ang2));
  X3=Round(Xc*CosD(Ang3));
  Y3=Round(Yc*SinD(Ang3));
  Triangle(X1, Y1, X2, Y2, X3, Y3, Level);
  ExitGraphics();
}
```

Figure 3-4. Listing of Program to Draw a Sierpinski Triangle

The Bifurcation Diagram

One of the first examples of chaotic behavior in the sciences was a discovered when scientists began looking closely at the population equation, which is supposed to model the behavior of population growth. This is an iterated equation of the form:

$$x_{n+1}=rx_n(1-x_n) \qquad \text{(Equation 3-19)}$$

The bifurcation diagram is a graph created by selecting different values of *r* and performing enough iterations for each one so that the equation settles down to a steady set of values, if it is ever going to. Then the results of a number of iterations are plotted to show whether the equation has settled down to one value, is cycling between two or more values, or has a different value for each iteration. We are going to use a somewhat different equation to obtain our bifurcation diagram, namely:

$$x_n=r\left(\frac{x_{n-1}}{(1+x_{n-1})^b}\right) \qquad \text{(Equation 3-20)}$$

The program to generate a bifurcation diagram from this equation is listed in Figure 3-5. A picture of the final plot is shown in Plate 3. The program begins by listing a number of constants and their variables. It then calls *InitGraphics* to set up the graphics display mode and then initializes several variables. Next, a *do* loop begins, with *lambda* at the minimum value (0). This loop iterates (with *lambda* increasing by *dlambda* at each iteration), until the maximum value (125) is reached, whereupon the loop terminates. The loop begins by setting *x* to the initial value (0.9). It then begins a *for* loop which iterates 300 times. On each pass through the loop the iterated equation is solved. The proper pixel values corresponding to the two coordinates are computed. To give the equation a chance to settle down to its final values, the first 64 iterations are not plotted. After this, the program plots a red pixel at the proper coordinates at each iteration of the equation. When the *for* loop is complete, *lambda* is increased to the next value and the process repeated. When the final value of *lambda* terminates the *do* loop, the program calls *ExitGraphics* to return to the text display mode and then terminates.

```
/*
 ┌──────────────────────────────────────────────────────┐
 │                                                      │
 │       bifurcat.c = Bifurcation Diagram Generator     │
 │                                                      │
 │           Program by Christopher D. Watkins          │
 │                                                      │
 │             'C' Conversion by Larry Sharp            │
 │                                                      │
 └──────────────────────────────────────────────────────┘
*/

#include "stdio.h"
#include "dos.h"
#include "conio.h"
#include "math.h"
#include "math.inc"
#include "graph.inc"

#define min  0.0
#define max  125.0
#define Res  200.0
#define n    300
#define beta 5
#define x0   0.9
#define T    25

float dlambda;
float lambda;
float scale, x;
int   i, Temp;
int   xxx, yyy;

void main()
{
  InitGraphics();
  dlambda=(max-min)/Res;
  scale=Res/max;
  lambda=min;
  do
  {
    x=x0;
```

```
        for(i=1; i<=n; i++)
        {
          x=lambda*x/Power((1+x), (beta));
          xxx=Round(30*x);
          yyy=Round(lambda*scale);
          Temp=GetPixel(xxx, yyy);
          Temp+=1;
          if(Temp<T)
        Plot(xxx, yyy, Temp+128);
          else
          {
        Plot(xxx, yyy, 0);
        Temp-=1;
          }
        }
        lambda+=dlambda;
      }
      while(lambda<=max);
      ExitGraphics();
    }
```

Figure 3-5. Listing of Program to Generate Bifurcation Diagram

Creating a Strange Attractor

This program generates a two-dimensional projection of the three-dimensional strange attractor that illustrates the dynamic system represented by the following set of iterated equations:

$$x_{n+1}=\sin(ay_n)-z_n\cos(bx_n) \qquad \text{(Equation 3-21)}$$

$$y_{n+1}=z_n\sin(cx_n)-\cos(dy_n) \qquad \text{(Equation 3-22)}$$

$$z_{n+1}=esin(x_n) \qquad \text{(Equation 3-23)}$$

The program listed in Figure 3-6 creates this strange attractor and uses the functions that have already been developed to project it onto the two-dimensional screen. The resulting display is shown in Plate 4. There are a number of constants at the beginning of this program, including the coefficients of the equation set and the minimum and maximum values for each of the three coordinates. The program begins with an initialization process that includes calling *InitPerspective* and *InitPlotting* (both described in Chapter 2) and *InitGraphics* to go into the graphics display mode. Next *PutAxisPalette* is called to set up the mode where the axes and palette are displayed on the screen and then *AxisAndPalette* is called to display the palette and the axes of the coordinate system. Next the factors to be used to convert x, y, and z into screen pixel coordinates are set up. The three coordinates are then initialized to zero. The program then begins a *do* loop which continues until a key is pressed. Thus the display continues to add points and become more dense until the user decides to terminate it. At each iteration of the loop, the program generates a new set of x, y, and z values from the previous set. It then converts these to three-dimensional screen pixel coordinates. Following that it generates a color value, using the value of the pixel coordinate in the x dimension.

The program then goes to the coordinate location on the screen and retrieves the color of the pixel there, using the procedure *GetPixel3D*. This procedure first calls *MapCoordinates* to create a pair of two-dimensional screen coordinates from the three-dimensional ones. It then calls *GetPixel* to read the color of the pixel at that screen location. Then, if the color that was generated is a higher number than the color already at the pixel, this color is plotted to the screen. At first, it may not be obvious what is going on here. The color is selected so that its number increases with the increasing of the x coordinate in the three-dimensional system. When three-dimensional coordinates are projected onto the two-dimensional screen, it may turn out that several different three-dimensional locations end up at the same two-dimensional position. If this occurs, then we want the color of that two-dimensional position to be that of the nearest three dimensional-position, since that is the color that we would see. That nearest position is the one with the highest value of the three-dimensional x coordinate, so the program lines just described do indeed assure that the screen is painted with the right color. This completes the loop; it iterates until a key is pressed, continuously adding complexity to the display. When the key is pressed, the function *ExitGraphics* is called to return to the text display mode. The program then terminates.

```
/*
 stratr3d.c = Three-Dimensional Strange Attractor Generator

           Program by Christopher D. Watkins

            'C' Conversion by Larry Sharp
*/

#include "stdio.h"
#include "dos.h"
#include "conio.h"
#include "math.h"
#include "math.inc"
#include "graph.inc"

int GetPixel3D(int x, int y, int z)
{
  int xp, yp;

  MapCoordinates(x, y, z, &xp, &yp);
  return(GetPixel(xp, yp));
}

#define xxmin -2
#define xxmax  2
#define yymin -2
#define yymax  2
#define zzmin -2
#define zzmax  2
#define res    200
#define a      2.24
#define b      0.43
#define c     -0.65
#define d     -2.43
#define e      1.00

float xinc, yinc, zinc;
float x, y, z, xx, yy, zz;
int   xxx, yyy, zzz, col, pix;
```

```
void main()
{
  InitPerspective(false, 0, 0, 500, 500);
  InitPlotting(240, 18);
  InitGraphics();
  PutAxisAndPalette(true);
  AxisAndPalette();
  xinc=res/(xxmax-xxmin);
  yinc=res/(yymax-yymin);
  zinc=res/(zzmax-zzmin);
  x=0;
  y=0;
  z=0;
  while(!(kbhit()))
  {
    xx=sin(a*y)-z*cos(b*x);
    yy=z*sin(c*x)-cos(d*y);
    zz=e*sin(x);
    x=xx;
    y=yy;
    z=zz;
    xxx=Round(xx*xinc);
    yyy=Round(yy*yinc);
    zzz=Round(zz*zinc);
    col=(xxx+XRes/2)%251;
    pix=GetPixel3D(xxx, yyy, zzz);
    if(col>pix)
      CartesianPlot3D(xxx, yyy, zzz, col);
  }
  ExitGraphics();
}
```

Figure 3-6. Listing of Program to Generate a Strange Attractor

Generating the Lorenz Attractor

The Lorenz attractor began as a simplified model for long-range weather predictions. It consists of the dynamic system of the following iterated equations:

$$\frac{dx}{dt}=10(y-x) \quad \text{(Equation 3-24)}$$

$$\frac{dy}{dt}=-xz+28x-y \quad \text{(Equation 3-25)}$$

$$\frac{dz}{dt}=xy-\frac{8}{3}z \quad \text{(Equation 3-26)}$$

The program to generate the Lorenz attractor is listed in Figure 3-7 and the resulting figure shown in Plate 5. The program begins with the familiar initialization process in which we call the functions *InitPerspective*, *InitPlotting*, and *InitGraphics*. The two functions are then called which result in a palette and a set of Cartesian coordinate axes being displayed, as described in the previous section. The initial coordinate value is set to (0.5,0.5,0.5) and the step, time step, and color are set to their initial values. The differential equations are then solved for a time increment which is one twenty-fifth of a step, and the time and coordinate values have the appropriate increments added to them. This is repeated 25 times to complete one step. The program then calls *DrawLine* to draw a line between the beginning and ending points. The function *DrawLine* scales the current coordinate values and converts them to integers. If the time indicates that this is first pass, the coordinates are then converted to a vector, *Tmp*, which is the line beginning, and the procedure returns to the calling program. On all additional passes, the color is computed, based on the elapsed time. The coordinates of the next point are converted to a vector *Pt* that represents the end of the line, and *DrawLine3D*, (which was described in the previous chapter) is called to convert to two-dimensional screen coordinates and draw the line on the screen. The line-ending point is then transferred to be the line-beginning point for the next pass through this function. This entire process is repeated until 500 complete time steps have occurred or until a key is pressed, whereupon the program calls *ExitGraphics* to return to the text display mode and then terminates.

```
/*
┌───────────────────────────────────────────────────────────────┐
│ lorenz3d.c = Three-Dimensional Lorenz Attractor Generator     │
│                                                               │
│              Program by Christopher D. Watkins                │
│                                                               │
│                 'C' Conversion by Larry Sharp                 │
└───────────────────────────────────────────────────────────────┘
*/

#include "stdio.h"
#include "dos.h"
#include "conio.h"
#include "math.h"
#include "math.inc"
#include "graph.inc"

#define Sc      2.2
#define EightThirds 2.6666667

float X, Y, Z;
float T, T9;
float d1, d2, d3;
float Step, Stp;
int   Xo, Yo, Zo;
int   Xn, Yn, Zn;
int   Col=10;
int   oldT9=0;
TDA   Pt, Tmp;

void DrawLine()
{
  Byte i;
  Xn=Round(Sc*X);
  Yn=Round(Sc*Y);
  Zn=Round(Sc*Z);
  if(T9==0)
  {
```

```
      Xo=Xn;
      Yo=Yn;
      Zo=Zn;
      Vec(Xo, Yo, Zo, Tmp);
    }
    if (oldT9 != (int) T9)
    Col++;
    if (Col >= 245)
      Col = 10;
    if ((Col % 35) < 10)
      Col += 10;

    Vec(Xn, Yn, Zn, Pt);
    DrawLine3D(Tmp, Pt, Col);
    Xo=Xn;
    Yo=Yn;
    Zo=Zn;
    for(i=0; i<3; i++)
      Tmp[i]=Pt[i];
  }

  void main()
  {
    InitPerspective(false, 0, 0, 500, 500);
    InitPlotting(-45, 35);
    InitGraphics();
    PutAxisAndPalette(true);
    AxisAndPalette();
    X=5.0;
    Y=5.0;
    Z=5.0;
    Col=0;
    Stp=0.01;
    Step=Stp/25;
    T9=0;
    do
    {
      T=T9;
      do
      {
```

```
        d1=10*(Y-X);
        d2=28*X-Y-X*Z;
        d3=X*Y-EightThirds*Z;
        X+=d1*Step;
        Y+=d2*Step;
        Z+=d3*Step;
        T+=Step;
      }
      while(T<T9+Step);
      DrawLine();
      oldT9 = T9;
      T9+=Stp;
    }
    while(T9<500);
    ExitGraphics();
  }
```

Figure 3-7. Listing of Program to Generate the Lorenz Attractor

Part II

WIRE FRAME AND SOLID MODELING

CHAPTER 4

Solid Modeling Theory and Database Structure

There are many different ways in which a computer can generate a scene that features realistic object shading and reflections. In this section of the book we will examine a method that subdivides each object into a number of small facets. A facet is defined by a number of vertices. We shall usually use four vertices to define a facet. The surface created by connecting sets of vertices together is then assigned a shade of color that varies depending upon the light impinging upon it and its inherent color. This surface is then translated to two-dimensional screen coordinates and painted in the proper shade upon the screen. Additionally, it is possible to define the reflections of objects in the same way and to draw them also upon the screen. By properly selecting which reflections to draw first and by drawing the real objects last, we can produce a scene in which reflections are properly overlaid by the real objects.

Before we jump right in to learning how to break objects into facets and how to handle the resulting data, we need to make some decisions about the kind and amount of data that will be permitted. Mostly, this is a function of the storage space that is easily available to most C compilers. As we get into this, you will see that we can handle quite a few facets, so that we can describe objects of considerable complexity if the need arises. The newest C compilers have techniques for using a lot of extended memory if your computer has it, and if you need gigantic data bases, but we won't consider the subject here. You should investigate it if your interests lie in that direction.

The data structure which contains the facets that make up a scene is part of a file called *Model.Inc* that must be included in all of our solid modeling programs. This file also contains routines to clear, load, and save vertex data, and to draw a wire facet or paint a solid facet on the screen. The file, described in the following paragraphs, is listed in Figure 4-1.

Scale Factors

The first thing that happens in this section of code is that *ScaleData* is initialized to 23000. This is a scale factor that is used in converting real positional data to integers so that processing can take place faster. The number 23000 comes from the fact that the maximum value of a 16-bit signed integer is 32767. If we have a coordinate having the maximum value of 23000, and it is rotated 45 degrees, it may take on a value of approximately 32767. Thus this scaling value assures that we cannot exceed integer bounds with any rotation. Next, *ScaleImage* is set to 100. This is the right factor for converting the integer system we are using to pixel coordinates on the screen.

Vertex and Facet Arrays

Each of the objects that we are going to include in a scene will have its facet and vertex information stored in a separate disk file. When we are ready to paint the object on the screen, this information will be transferred to arrays in the program and operated upon. This places a constraint on the number of facets and vertices that we may have in an object description, since the information must all fit into the available memory. We begin with the constraint that the available memory for data is 65,536 (64K) bytes. Within this memory area, we must include the reflection buffer, which needs one bit for every pixel on the screen. We are using the 320-pixel-by-200-pixel display mode, so we need 64,000 bits, or 8,000 bytes, for this storage task. Next, we must have the object buffer. We'll look at this in more detail later. For the moment, we'll simply say that it can contain a maximum of 40 objects and that each object description requires 70 bytes, so that the total memory requirement is 2,800 bytes. Subtracting these from the total memory available, we find that 54,736 bytes maximum is available for vertex and facet information. We shall call this maximum M_x.

```
/* Model.Inc
 ┌──────────────────────────────────────────────────────────┐
 │                 Variable Declarations                    │
 └──────────────────────────────────────────────────────────┘
*/

#define NumVerticiesInFacet 4
#define MaxVertexNumInFacet 4
#define ScaleData 23000
#define ScaleImage 100

/*
#define MaxFacet 1678          independent : MaxFacet  = n
#define MaxVertex 6712         verticies   MaxVertex = 4 * n
*/

#define MaxFacet 3600
#define MaxVertex 3721

int LastVertex, LastFacet;
int LastVertexNumInFacet;
int VertexNum, FacetNum;
int VertexNumInFacet;
TDIA Vertex[MaxVertex+1];
static int far *Facet;

/*
 ┌──────────────────────────────────────────────────────────┐
 │     Routines to Load and Save Vertex and Facet Data      │
 └──────────────────────────────────────────────────────────┘

   InitVertexBuffer - clear memory for facet and vertex data
   LoadData     - load facet and vertex data
   SaveData     - save facet and vertex data
*/

float InvScaleData, InvScaleImage;

void InitVertexBuffer()
{
```

```
    InvScaleData=1.0/ScaleData;
    InvScaleImage=1.0/ScaleImage;
    for(VertexNum=0; VertexNum<=MaxVertex; VertexNum++)
      VecNullInt(Vertex[VertexNum]);
    for(FacetNum=0; FacetNum<=MaxFacet; FacetNum++)
    {
      for(VertexNumInFacet=0;
      VertexNumInFacet<=MaxVertexNumInFacet;
      VertexNumInFacet++)
        Facet[(FacetNum*5) + VertexNumInFacet]=0;
    }
}

typedef char Name[20];

FILE *DiskFile;
Name FileName;

void LoadData(Name FileName)
{
  TDIA temp;
  int x, y, z;

  DiskFile=fopen(FileName, "r+b");
  LastVertex=getw(DiskFile);
  LastFacet=getw(DiskFile);
  LastVertexNumInFacet=getw(DiskFile);
  for(VertexNum=1; VertexNum<=LastVertex; VertexNum++)
  {
    x=getw(DiskFile);
    y=getw(DiskFile);
    z=getw(DiskFile);
    if((abs(x)>ScaleData) || (abs(y)>ScaleData) ||
      (abs(z)>ScaleData))
    {
      printf("Error : data out of range - Vertex #%d\n",
      VertexNum);
      exit(1);
    }
    else
      VecInt(x, y, z, Vertex[VertexNum]);
  }
```

```
  for(FacetNum=1; FacetNum<=LastFacet; FacetNum++)
   {
     for(VertexNumInFacet=1;
        VertexNumInFacet<=LastVertexNumInFacet;
        VertexNumInFacet++)
        Facet[(FacetNum*5)+VertexNumInFacet]=getw(DiskFile);
   }
  fclose(DiskFile);
}

void SaveData(Name FileName)
{
  int x, y, z;

  DiskFile=fopen(FileName, "w+b");
  putw(LastVertex, DiskFile);
  putw(LastFacet, DiskFile);
  putw(LastVertexNumInFacet, DiskFile);
  for(VertexNum=1; VertexNum<=LastVertex; VertexNum++)
   {
     UnVecInt(Vertex[VertexNum], &x, &y, &z);
     putw(x, DiskFile);
     putw(y, DiskFile);
     putw(z, DiskFile);
   }
  for(FacetNum=1; FacetNum<=LastFacet; FacetNum++)
   {
     for(VertexNumInFacet=1;
     VertexNumInFacet<=LastVertexNumInFacet;
     VertexNumInFacet++)
     putw(Facet[(FacetNum*5)+VertexNumInFacet], DiskFile);
   }
  fclose(DiskFile);
}

typedef struct{
  int x;
  int y;
} PixelVector;
```

```
typedef PixelVector PixelArray[NumVerticiesInFacet+2];
typedef TDA VoxelArray[NumVerticiesInFacet+1];

/*
 ┌──────────────────────────────────────────────────────┐
 │                 Draw a Wire Facet                    │
 └──────────────────────────────────────────────────────┘

   PutWireFacet - draws a wire outline of a facet
*/

void PutWireFacet(PixelArray Pts, Byte Color)
{
  int t;

  for(t=1; t<=4; t++)
    Draw(Pts[t].x, Pts[t].y, Pts[t+1].x, Pts[t+1].y, Color);
}

/*
 ┌──────────────────────────────────────────────────────┐
 │                 Place a Solid Facet                  │
 └──────────────────────────────────────────────────────┘

   PutFacet - Place a Facet
*/

void PutFacet(PixelArray Face2d, Byte Color, Byte Intens)
{
  int xc, yc;
  int i, x;
  int OldVertNum;
  int VertNum;
  int mnx, mxx;
  int mny, mxy;
  float slope;

  mny=Face2d[1].y;
  mxy=Face2d[1].y;
  for(i=2; i<=LastVertexNumInFacet; i++)
  {
```

```
    if(Face2d[i].y>mxy)
      mxy=Face2d[i].y;
    if(Face2d[i].y<mny)
      mny=Face2d[i].y;
  }
  if(mny<0)
    mny=0;
  if(mxy>MaxY)
    mxy=MaxY;
  for(yc=mny; yc<=mxy; yc++)
  {
    mnx=MaxX+1;
    mxx= -1;
   OldVertNum=LastVertexNumInFacet;
   for(VertNum=1; VertNum<=LastVertexNumInFacet; VertNum++)
     {
      if((Face2d[OldVertNum].y>=yc) || (Face2d[VertNum].y>=yc))
       {
         if((Face2d[OldVertNum].y<=yc)
             || (Face2d[VertNum].y<=yc))
          {
            if(Face2d[OldVertNum].y != Face2d[VertNum].y)
             {
                 slope = (float)
                 (Face2d[VertNum].x-Face2d[OldVertNum].x)/
                 (float)(Face2d[VertNum].y-Face2d[OldVertNum].y);
                x=Round(slope*(float)((yc-Face2d[OldVertNum].y))+
                  Face2d[OldVertNum].x);
                 if(x<mnx)
                     mnx=x;
                 if(x>mxx)
                     mxx=x;
             }
          }
       }
      OldVertNum=VertNum;
    }
    if(mnx<0)
      mnx=0;
```

```
        if(mxx>MaxX)
          mxx=MaxX;
        if(mnx<=mxx)
        {
          for(xc=mnx; xc<=mxx; xc++)
          PutPixel(xc, yc, Color, Intens);
        }
      }
    }
```

Figure 4-1. Listing of *Model.Inc* File

We begin our discussion of facets and vertices by deciding to have four-sided facets. Now, for a single facet, we have four vertices, each of which needs to be described by an integer. The facet also has to be described by four integers, one to identify each of the vertices of which it is comprised. So, if we have *n* facets, and each must be described independently, we have a storage requirement of:

$$4n \times 3 + n \times 4 = \frac{M_x}{2} \qquad \text{(Equation 4-1)}$$

The maximum memory available is divided by two because each integer requires two bytes of storage. This tells us that we have space for approximately 1,678 facets and 6,712 vertices, maximum. Fortunately, this is a worst-case situation. Most of the objects we will be dealing with have facets that share vertices. Look at Figure 4-2. Here is a surface composed of 9 facets and 16 shared vertices. If we generalize this, we have n^2 vertices and $(n-1)^2$ facets. The memory storage requirement is then:

$$n^2 \times 3 + (n-1)^2 \times 4 = \frac{M_x}{2} \qquad \text{(Equation 4-2)}$$

This turns out to give us enough storage for approximately 3,721 facets and 3,844 vertices. In the listing, we have commented out the vertex and facet maximums for independent facets and have reduced *n* by one in specifying the maximum number of facets, *MaxFacet* (3,600), and the maximum number of vertices, *MaxVertex* (3,721), to give a little cushion of memory space. The *Vertex* array then consists of 3,721 sets of three-dimensional integer vectors, and the *Facet* array consists of 3,600 sets of four integers per set.

Figure 4-2. Surface Composed of 9 Facets and 16 Vertices

Loading and Saving Vertex and Facet Data

The next routines considered in the listing are those that are involved with loading and saving the facet data. The first of these functions, *InitVertexBuffer*, initializes the various buffers. First, this function computes two inverse scale parameters. It then fills all of the vectors in the *Vertex* array with null vectors. Then all of the members of the *Facet* array are filled with zeroes.

In the next chapter, we are going to show how to add objects to the object list database. Each object will have its own file. In that chapter, we'll go into more detail on the structure of the file. But for now, in the paragraphs that follow, we are going to assume that such an object file already exists and that we are going to load it back into the working program, or alternately that we have all the necessary data already stored in the program and want to save it to a disk file.

The function *LoadData* is passed the name of an object data file. It begins by opening the file and reading the last vertex, last face, last vertex in facet numbers from it. (Note that no error-checking is done on the file; if you provide an incorrect or nonexistent file name, the program will terminate abnormally.) For each vertex, it then reads three integer words that make up the *x*, *y*, and *z* coordinates of the vertex. (Data is stored in the file in binary format.) After reading each set of coordinates for a vertex, the function checks to see if they are within the range of values allowed for such data. If not, the program displays an error message and halts. If the coordinates are within range, they are converted to vector form and stored in the proper member of the *Vertex* array. Next, for each facet, the function reads four word (integers). Each is the number of a vertex that is part of the facet. Each is stored in the proper member of the *Facet* array. After all facets are loaded, the file is closed and the function is complete.

The *SaveData* function works just the opposite of the previous example. It is passed an object data file name and opens it as a text file for writing. Next, the last vertex, last facet, and the last vertex in facet numbers are written to the file. The function then begins a *for* loop which iterates for each vertex. At each iteration, a vertex vector is converted to three integer coordinates and then each coordinate is stored in the output file. When this loop is complete, the four vertex numbers for every facet are written to the output file. The file is then closed and the function is complete.

Drawing a Wire Frame Facet

The *PutWireFacet* function actually draws the outline of the facet to the screen. It is passed an array of x,y pairs of points, which are the two-dimensional screen coordinates of the four vertices of a facet, and a color value. It then runs a *for* loop which draws a line between each adjacent pair of points to frame the facet.

Painting a Solid Facet on the Screen

The function *PutFacet* fills in a facet on the screen with the designated color and intensity. It begins by looping to determine the minimum and maximum values of the y coordinate for the facet. Then a *for* loop begins which iterates once for every value of *y* within the facet. Within the loop, the function computes the slope of the lines connecting critical pairs of vertices and uses the slopes to determine the beginning and ending values of *x* for the current value of *y*. These values are tested to assure that they never come out to be smaller than the minimum *x* for the facet nor larger than the maximum *x* for the facet. Then, if the maximum is greater than or equal to the minimum, the function *DrawHorizLine* is called to draw a line of the proper color for that *y* value. This function simply uses *PutPixel* to plot points at the desired y value for all values of *x* from the beginning value to the end value. The loop continues until all values of *y* within the facet have had their associated lines drawn, resulting in the facet being filled with the desired shade of color. You may have wondered why the Turbo C function *fillpoly* wasn't used to fill the facet, thereby avoiding all of the additional programming. The answer is that the *fillpoly* function can only fill with 16 colors, whereas we need to be able to select from 256 colors for this application. If we had source code available for *fillpoly* it would probably be a fairly simple modification to adapt it for 256 colors; since we do not, we must create our own procedure.

A Sample Manually Generated Data File

In Chapter 9, we'll learn about generating object data files with computer assist. But first, to tie this all together, let's see what a very simple object file might look like. We are going to create a file for an xy plane filling the entire display screen. The first line of this file is

```
4 1 4
```

indicating that there are four vertices, one facet, and that the facet has four vertices. Next come four sets of three coordinates, giving the coordinates of each of the four vertices. Since the plane is in the *xy* system, all values of *z* are zero. The other two coordinates for each vertex are at the maximum limits permitted. Thus we have

```
 23000  23000  0
-23000  23000  0
-23000 -23000  0
 23000 -23000  0
```

Finally, we have a line that lists the vertex numbers for each of the four vertices that make up the facet. They are simply:

```
1  2  3  4
```

CHAPTER 5

Adding Objects to the Scene

In this chapter we will work on techniques for adding objects to a scene. We will assume that, for each type of object (cube, sphere, cone, etc.) that we are interested in displaying, there is an appropriately named disk file containing the necessary vertex and facet information for creating a generic object of the desired type. An array called *ObjList*, which contains a record of information on every object to be displayed, will be needed in order to provide the necessary information to create a scene.

The first item in this array is *ObjectName*, the name of the object file for the desired object type (for example *Sphere.Dat*). Next are *Tx*, *Ty*, and *Tz*, which are the three-dimensional coordinates of the translation vector. This vector moves the object from its nominal position at the center of the screen to the desired location. Next are *Rx*, *Ry*, and *Rz*, which are the three-dimensional coordinates of the rotation vector. This vector rotates the object from its nominal orientation to a new orientation specified by this vector. Following that are *Sx, Sy*, and *Sz*, which are the three-dimensional coordinates of the scaling vector. This vector changes the object from its nominal size by scaling its size in each coordinate as specified by the vector. (Note that the scale factor for an object can be changed separately in each coordinate direction. This makes it possible, for example, to change a sphere to an ellipsoid, or a cube to a rectangular solid.) The next parameter is *Reflection*, which is a Boolean *True* or *False,* that indicates whether this is a reflection or an actual object. Next is *Color*, which is a byte that indicates the color of the object. Next is *Sortable*, another Boolean variable which indicates whether the object is to be a part of the list of objects that are to be sorted before being displayed. The final item is another Boolean variable, *Mirror*, which indicates whether the object is itself a mirror (reflecting object).

The definition of the array for listing objects and the associated functions are included in the file *AddObjs.Inc*, which is listed in Figure 5-1. The functions are described in the sections that follow.

Initializing the Object Buffer

The function *InitObjectBuffer* is used to initialize the list of objects described above. It begins by setting *ObjectName* to be a NULL string. Then the components of the translation, rotation, and scaling vectors are all set to zeroes. Then *Reflection* is set to *False, Color* is set to zero, *Sortable* is set to *False*, and *Mirror* is set *False*. This function is repeated for every one of the 40 objects, the maximum allowable number of objects.

Inserting Object Information into the Object Buffer

Let's briefly examine a number of functions that are used to fill an object record with information. The record number of the record that is being filled is given by *ObjectNum*. The function *AddObject* is passed a string that is the name of the generic object data file for the particular type of object desired. The function writes this string to the proper item in the designated object record. The function *Scale* is passed a set of three scaling coordinates, one for each dimension. It writes these coordinates to the proper items in the designated object record. The function *Rotate* is passed a set of three rotation coordinates, one for each dimension. It writes these coordinates to the proper items in the designated object record. The function *Translate* is passed a set of three translation coordinates, one for each dimension. It writes these coordinates to the proper items in the designated object record. The function *ReflectObject* is passed a Boolean value to establish whether the object is a reflection. It writes this value to the proper item in the designated object record. The function *ObjectColor* is passed a byte which represents the object color. It writes this byte to the proper item in the designated object record. The function *AllowSort* is passed a Boolean value to establish whether the object is to be a part of the list of objects to be sorted. It writes this value to the proper item in the designated object record. The function *Mirrored* is passed a Boolean value to establish whether the object is a mirror. It writes this value to the proper item in the designated object record.

```
/* AddObjs.Inc
 ___________________________________________________________
|                                                           |
|           Add Objects to the Object List Database         |
|___________________________________________________________|

   InitObjectBuffer  - initialize object buffer
   AddObject         - add object of certain name
   Scale             - scale the object
   Rotate            - rotate the object
   Translate         - translate the object
   ReflectObject     - will this object reflect on a reflective
                                                         object
   ObjectColor       - color of object
   AllowSort         - is this object sorted
   Mirrored          - is this object reflective
*/
#define NumObjects 40

int ObjectNum;
int LastObject;

typedef struct{
  Name ObjectName;
  float Tx, Ty, Tz;
  float Rx, Ry, Rz;
  float Sx, Sy, Sz;
  Boolean Reflection;
  Byte Color;
  Boolean Sortable;
  Boolean Mirror;
}ObjL;

ObjL ObjList[NumObjects+1];

void InitObjectBuffer()
{
```

```
  for(ObjectNum=0; ObjectNum<=NumObjects; ObjectNum++)
  {
    strset(ObjList[ObjectNum].ObjectName, 0);
    ObjList[ObjectNum].Tx=0.0;
    ObjList[ObjectNum].Ty=0.0;
    ObjList[ObjectNum].Tz=0.0;
    ObjList[ObjectNum].Rx=0.0;
    ObjList[ObjectNum].Ry=0.0;
    ObjList[ObjectNum].Rz=0.0;
    ObjList[ObjectNum].Sx=0.0;
    ObjList[ObjectNum].Sy=0.0;
    ObjList[ObjectNum].Sz=0.0;
    ObjList[ObjectNum].Reflection=false;
    ObjList[ObjectNum].Color=0;
    ObjList[ObjectNum].Sortable=false;
    ObjList[ObjectNum].Mirror=false;
  }
  ObjectNum=0;
}

void AddObject(Name FileName)
{
  ++ObjectNum;
  strcpy(ObjList[ObjectNum].ObjectName, FileName);
  LastObject=ObjectNum;
}

void Scale(float x, float y, float z)
{
  ObjList[ObjectNum].Sx=x;
  ObjList[ObjectNum].Sy=y;
  ObjList[ObjectNum].Sz=z;
}

void Rotate(float x, float y, float z)
{
  ObjList[ObjectNum].Rx=-x;
  ObjList[ObjectNum].Ry=-y;
  ObjList[ObjectNum].Rz=-z;
}
```

```
void Translate(float x, float y, float z)
{
  ObjList[ObjectNum].Tx=-x;
  ObjList[ObjectNum].Ty=-y;
  ObjList[ObjectNum].Tz=-z;
}

void ReflectObject(Boolean State)
{
  ObjList[ObjectNum].Reflection=State;
}

void ObjectColor(Byte Col)
{
  ObjList[ObjectNum].Color=Col;
}

void AllowSort(Boolean State)
{
  ObjList[ObjectNum].Sortable=State;
}

void Mirrored(Boolean State)
{
  ObjList[ObjectNum].Mirror=State;
}

/*
 ╔══════════════════════════════════════════════════════════════╗
 ║          Routines to Add Edge Reflectors to a Scene          ║
 ╚══════════════════════════════════════════════════════════════╝

   AddReflectorAtZero - adds edge reflectors at x=-100, y=-100
                                                     and z=0
   AddReflectors - adds edge reflectors at x=-100, y=-100 and
                                                        z=-100
*/

Boolean EdgeReflectorAtZero;
Boolean EdgeReflector;
```

```
void AddEdgeReflectorsAtZero()
{
  EdgeReflectorAtZero=true;
  AddObject("GRID.DAT");
  Scale(100.0, 100.0, 100.0);
  Rotate(0.0, 0.0, 0.0);
  Translate(0.0, 0.0, 0.0);
  ReflectObject(false);
  ObjectColor(7);
  AllowSort(false);
  Mirrored(true);
  AddObject("GRID.DAT");
  Scale(50.0, 100.0, 50.0);
  Rotate(0.0, 90.0, 0.0);
  Translate(-100.0, 0.0, 50.0);
  ReflectObject(false);
  ObjectColor(7);
  AllowSort(false);
  Mirrored(true);
  AddObject("GRID.DAT");
  Scale(100.0, 50.0, 50.0);
  Rotate(-90.0, 0.0, 0.0);
  Translate(0.0, -100.0, 50.0);
  ReflectObject(false);
  ObjectColor(7);
  AllowSort(false);
  Mirrored(true);
}

void AddEdgeReflectors()
{
  EdgeReflector=true;
  AddObject("GRID.DAT");
  Scale(100.0, 100.0, 100.0);
  Rotate(0.0, 0.0, 0.0);
  Translate(0.0, 0.0, -100.0);
  ReflectObject(false);
  ObjectColor(7);
  AllowSort(false);
  Mirrored(true);
```

```
  AddObject("GRID.DAT");
  Scale(100.0, 100.0, 100.0);
  Rotate(0.0, 90.0, 0.0);
  Translate(-100.0, 0.0, 0.0);
  ReflectObject(false);
  ObjectColor(7);
  AllowSort(false);
  Mirrored(true);
  AddObject("GRID.DAT");
  Scale(100.0, 100.0, 100.0);
  Rotate(-90.0, 0.0, 0.0);
  Translate(0.0, -100.0, 0.0);
  ReflectObject(false);
  ObjectColor(7);
  AllowSort(false);
  Mirrored(true);
}

/*

        Add Objects to Scene from .SCN Disk File

  AddObjectsToSceneFromDiskFile - add objects to database from
                                              .SCN disk file
*/

typedef char Strg[80];

Boolean Bool(Strg B)
{
  strupr(B);
  if(!(strcmp(B, "FALSE")))
    return(false);
  else
    return(true);
}

void AddObjectsToSceneFromDiskFile(Name FileName)
{
```

```
int I1, I2, I3, I4;
float R1, R2, R3;
Name ObjectFileName;
char blank[256];
FILE *TextDiskFile;
int L1;
Strg B;

strcat(FileName, ".SCN");
TextDiskFile=fopen(FileName, "r+t");
fgets(blank, 255, TextDiskFile);
fgets(blank, 255, TextDiskFile);
fscanf(TextDiskFile, "%s %d %d %d %d", B, &I1, &I2, &I3, &I4);
InitPerspective(Bool(B), I1, I2, I3, I4);
fscanf(TextDiskFile, "%d %d", &I1, &I2);
InitPlotting(I1, I2);
GetViewVector();
fscanf(TextDiskFile, "%d %d", &I1, &I2);
InitLightDirection(I1, I2);
GetLightVector();
fscanf(TextDiskFile, "%s", B);
VertSort(Bool(B));
fscanf(TextDiskFile, "%s", B);
if(Bool(B))
  AddEdgeReflectors();
fscanf(TextDiskFile, "%s", B);
if(Bool(B))
  AddEdgeReflectorsAtZero();
do
{
  strset(ObjectFileName, 0);
  fscanf(TextDiskFile, "%s", ObjectFileName);
  if(ObjectFileName[0]==0)
    goto L1;
  AddObject(ObjectFileName);
  fscanf(TextDiskFile, "%d", &I1);
  ObjectColor(I1);
  fscanf(TextDiskFile, "%f %f %f", &R1, &R2, &R3);
  Scale(R1, R2, R3);
  fscanf(TextDiskFile, "%f %f %f", &R1, &R2, &R3);
```

```
    Rotate(R1, R2, R3);
    fscanf(TextDiskFile, "%f %f %f", &R1, &R2, &R3);
    Translate(R1, R2, R3);
    fscanf(TextDiskFile, "%s", B);
    ReflectObject(Bool(B));
    fscanf(TextDiskFile, "%s", B);
    AllowSort(Bool(B));
    fscanf(TextDiskFile, "%s", B);
    Mirrored(Bool(B));
  }
  while(!(ObjectFileName[0]==0));
L1:  fclose(TextDiskFile);
}

/*
```

Stacked Sphere Scene Generator

```
*/
void StackedSpheres()
{
  float r, s;

  r=16.0;
  s=16.0;
  AddObject("SPHERE.DAT");
  Scale(r, r, r);
  Rotate(0.0, 0.0, 0.0);
  Translate(-2.0*r, -r, s+r);
  ReflectObject(true);
  ObjectColor(1);
  AllowSort(true);
  Mirrored(false);
  AddObject("SPHERE.DAT");
  Scale(r, r, r);
  Rotate(0.0, 0.0, 0.0);
  Translate(0.0, -r, s+r);
  ReflectObject(true);
  ObjectColor(2);
  AllowSort(true);
  Mirrored(false);
```

```
AddObject("SPHERE.DAT");
Scale(r, r, r);
Rotate(0.0, 0.0, 0.0);
Translate(2.0*r, -r, s+r);
ReflectObject(true);
ObjectColor(3);
AllowSort(true);
Mirrored(false);
AddObject("SPHERE.DAT");
Scale(r, r, r);
Rotate(0.0, 0.0, 0.0);
Translate(-r, 0.866*r, s+r);
ReflectObject(true);
ObjectColor(4);
AllowSort(true);
Mirrored(false);
AddObject("SPHERE.DAT");
Scale(r, r, r);
Rotate(0.0, 0.0, 0.0);
Translate(r, 0.866*r, s+r);
ReflectObject(true);
ObjectColor(5);
AllowSort(true);
Mirrored(false);
AddObject("SPHERE.DAT");
Scale(r, r, r);
Rotate(0.0, 0.0, 0.0);
Translate(0.0, 2.732*r, s+r);
ReflectObject(true);
ObjectColor(6);
AllowSort(true);
Mirrored(false);
AddObject("SPHERE.DAT");
Scale(r, r, r);
Rotate(0.0, 0.0, 0.0);
Translate(-r, -0.293*r, s+2.6*r);
ReflectObject(true);
ObjectColor(7);
AllowSort(true);
Mirrored(false);
```

```
  AddObject("SPHERE.DAT");
  Scale(r, r, r);
  Rotate(0.0, 0.0, 0.0);
  Translate(r, -0.293*r, s+2.6*r);
  ReflectObject(true);
  ObjectColor(1);
  AllowSort(true);
  Mirrored(false);
  AddObject("SPHERE.DAT");
  Scale(r, r, r);
  Rotate(0.0, 0.0, 0.0);
  Translate(0.0, 1.5*r, s+2.6*r);
  ReflectObject(true);
  ObjectColor(2);
  AllowSort(true);
  Mirrored(false);
  AddObject("SPHERE.DAT");
  Scale(r, r, r);
  Rotate(0.0, 0.0, 0.0);
  Translate(0.0, 0.5*r, s+4.4*r);
  ReflectObject(true);
  ObjectColor(3);
  AllowSort(true);
  Mirrored(false);
}

/*

              Add Objects to Scene from Procedure

   AddObjectsToSceneFromProcedure - add object to scene from a
      procedure to allow calculation of translation, scaling
      and rotation to be calculated.

*/
void AddObjectsToSceneFromProcedure()
{
  InitPerspective(true, 0, -25, 450, 500);
  InitPlotting(240, 18);
```

```
    GetViewVector();
    InitLightDirection(45, 45);
    GetLightVector();
    VertSort(true);
    AddEdgeReflectorsAtZero();
    StackedSpheres();
}
```

Figure 5-1. Listing of the *AddObjs.Inc* File

Adding Edge Reflectors to a Scene

One feature that we use frequently is to paint three walls on to a scene, each of which consists of a number of small, square mirrored tiles, separated by a black grid. Depending upon the scene, these walls will have their intersection at (–100,–100,0), resulting in a floor at about the center of the screen, and two back walls, or (–100,–100,–100), which results in a floor near the bottom of the screen and two back walls. Since these are used so frequently, we have set up two functions to paint them to the screen. The first case uses function *AddEdgeReflectorsAtZero*. This function makes use of the object data file *Grid.Dat*, which contains the facet and vertex information for a tiled plane. The function calls *Grid.Dat* three times, each time with the proper translation, scaling, and rotation to draw one of the walls. For each wall, it sets *ReflectObject* to *False* to indicate that this is an actual object, not a reflection. It sets *ObjectColor* to 7 , which results in the tiles being a light gray. It sets *AllowSort* to *False*. Since these walls are the boundaries of the scene, the must be drawn first and therefore should not be sorted. It sets *Mirrored* to *True,* since all of the wall tiles are mirrored and are intended to reflect the object that make up the scene.

The second case uses the function *AddEdgeReflectors*. This function is exactly like the previous one except that the translations, rotations and scalings are modified to produce the new wall locations.

Adding Objects to a Scene from a Function

The function *AddObjectsToSceneFromProcedure* may be selected as an option to be run using the *Model* program. It begins by calling the *InitPerspective* and *InitPlotting* functions, which were described in Chapter 2. Next it calls *GetViewVector* to establish a unit vector in the direction of the viewer. Then it calls *InitLightDirection* to establish the direction of the light source. Then it calls *GetLightVector* to set up a unit vector in the direction of the light source. These three functions will be described in Chapter 7. Next, the function *VertSort* is called. This function simply sets the parameter *VerticalSort* to *True*, which will cause objects to be sorted in the proper order later. Next *AddEdgeReflectorsAtZe*ro is called, producing the reflective wall and floor tiles as described above. Finally, the function *StackedSpheres* is called to produce a display of stacked spheres. This function begins by setting a diameter for a sphere and its displacement from the z=0 plane. The *AddObject* function is then called to add this sphere to the data base with the color blue. The function is called again to add a green sphere to the database with a different set of translation coordinates. This process continues until ten different spheres have been added to the data base. Then different colors and differing translation coordinates are adjusted so that the spheres form a pyramid stack.

If you want to use the *AddObjectsToSceneFromProcedure* function to generate your own scene, you may use it with the predetermined mirrored walls, viewer position, and light source position by simply changing the name of the function called in the last statement from *StackedSpheres* to your own function name. Within your new function, you include a number of calls to *AddObject* using the name of one of the generic object data files. You then provide, for each object, calls to scale the size of the object, to rotate it, to translate it to the position where you want it displayed, to specify whether you want its reflections to be displayed, to identify its color, to state whether it is to be sorted, and to determine whether it is to be a mirror or not. If you are not satisfied with the default values for the mirrored walls and for the viewer and light source positions, you will have to modify the default values that are part of the function *AddObjectsToSceneFromProcedure* in addition to creating your own function full of scene data.

Adding Objects to a Scene from a Disk File

In Chapter 10, we are going to show you how to create a *.SCN* file containing the data required for a scene. Here, we are going to assume that you already have such a file and want to transfer it to the variables and arrays from which the scene will be created. The function *AddObjectsToSceneFromDiskFile* performs this task. This function is passed a string which is the file name of the scene data, without the extension. The first thing that happens is that the extension *.SCN* is appended to this file name. The file is then opened and the first two lines are read. The first is a comment line and the second is a blank line. Nothing is done with these lines; they are only for observation when examining the file with a debugger program. Next a line of data is read which contains the parameters for setting up the perspective of the scene. These parameters are passed to the *InitPerspective* function, which then sets up the perspective for the scene. The next line read from the file contains the image and tilt angles. The function *InitPlotting* is then passed these parameters and sets up the viewer position from them. The function *GetViewVector* is then called to establish a unit vector in the position of the viewer. The next line that is read from the file contains light angle information. This is passed to the function *InitLightDirection* to set up the light direction. The function *GetLightVector* is then called to set up a unit vector in the light direction. The next line that is read determines whether *VerticalSort* shall be turned on. The parameter is set to the Boolean value read. The next two lines determine whether the edge reflectors are to be generated. If the first line is *True*, *AddEdgeReflectors* is called. If the second line is *True*, *AddEdgeReflectorsAtZero* is called. We then enter a *Repeat* loop which is continued until the end of the file is reached. At each iteration of this loop, the function begins by reading a blank line. It then reads the file name of the object data file. This is passed to the proper parameter by *AddObject*. Then lines are read from the disk file for the object color, the scaling factors, the rotation parameters, the translation parameters, whether the object can be reflected, whether the object can be sorted, and whether the object is a mirror. Each of these sets of information is loaded into its proper parameters by the associated function. Once the entire file has been read, it is closed and the function is complete.

CHAPTER 6

Sorting and Displaying Objects on the Screen

In this chapter we are going to be concerned with two subjects. The first concerns sorting objects so that we process them in proper order. If we have created an image that contains several objects positioned at different distances from the eye of the viewer, we must make sure that the closer objects overlap the farther ones, just as they would in a photograph or painting. The computer solves this problem by simply drawing the farthest object first and then drawing the others in the order of their distance from the observer. The closest object is then drawn right over the others and the appearance of the picture is realistic. In order to do this, we have to sort the list of objects so that the objects are in proper order with the farthest first and the closest last. Likewise, we have to sort the lists for reflections of objects in the x, y, and z planes.

The second subject to be considered is the actual display of objects on the screen. This involves both the actual objects and their reflections on the three planes. Display of an object requires converting each facet to two-dimensional screen coordinates and then painting the resulting facet on the screen in the appropriate shade of color. The shade is determined by the color of the object, the direction of the light source, the position of the observer, and the surface normal vector of the facet. The program listing for both these subjects is in the file *DispObjs.Inc*. This file is listed in Figure 6-1.

```
/* DispObjs.Inc
   ┌──────────────────────────────────────────────────────────────┐
   │      Routines for Sorting Objects for Order of Placement      │
   └──────────────────────────────────────────────────────────────┘
   PrepareSort                  - setup for sorting routines
   SortObjectsBackToFront       - sort for actual objects
   SortTopToBottom              - sort for reflections in Z
   SortBottomToTop              - sort for actual objects
   SortObjectsFrontToBackInY - sort for reflections in Y
   SortObjectsFrontToBackInX - sort for reflections in X
*/

int First;
int Last;
int FirstObject;
Boolean Sorting;
Boolean ReflSurface;
int NumMirrors;

void PrepareSort()
{
 ReflSurface=false;
 Last=LastObject;
 if(LastObject==1)
 {
  First=Last;
  FirstObject=LastObject;
 }
 else
 {
  First=1;
  while((ObjList[First].Sortable==false) && (First<Last))
   ++First;
  FirstObject=1;
  while((ObjList[FirstObject].Mirror==true) &&
   (FirstObject<LastObject))
  {
   ++FirstObject;
   ReflSurface=true;
  }
 }
```

```
  NumMirrors=FirstObject-1;
  if(First==Last)
   Sorting=false;
  else
   Sorting=true;
}

int Index;

void SwapStrings(Name A, Name B)
{
 Name T;

 strcpy(T, A);
 strcpy(A, B);
 strcpy(B, T);
}

void SwapRealNum(float *A, float *B)
{
 float T;

 T=*A;
 *A=*B;
 *B=T;
}

void SwapByteNum(Byte *A, Byte *B)
{
 Byte T;

 T=*A;
 *A=*B;
 *B=T;
}

void SwapBoolean(Boolean *A, Boolean *B)
{
 Boolean T;
```

```
 T=*A;
 *A=*B;
 *B=T;
}

void SwapData()
{
 SwapStrings(ObjList[Index].ObjectName,
   ObjList[Index+1].ObjectName);
 SwapRealNum(&ObjList[Index].Tx, &ObjList[Index+1].Tx);
 SwapRealNum(&ObjList[Index].Ty, &ObjList[Index+1].Ty);
 SwapRealNum(&ObjList[Index].Tz, &ObjList[Index+1].Tz);
 SwapRealNum(&ObjList[Index].Rx, &ObjList[Index+1].Rx);
 SwapRealNum(&ObjList[Index].Ry, &ObjList[Index+1].Ry);
 SwapRealNum(&ObjList[Index].Rz, &ObjList[Index+1].Rz);
 SwapRealNum(&ObjList[Index].Sx, &ObjList[Index+1].Sx);
 SwapRealNum(&ObjList[Index].Sy, &ObjList[Index+1].Sy);
 SwapRealNum(&ObjList[Index].Sz, &ObjList[Index+1].Sz);
 SwapBoolean(&ObjList[Index].Reflection,
   &ObjList[Index+1].Reflection);
 SwapByteNum(&ObjList[Index].Color, &ObjList[Index+1].Color);
 SwapBoolean(&ObjList[Index].Sortable,
   &ObjList[Index+1].Sortable);
 SwapBoolean(&ObjList[Index].Mirror,  &ObjList[Index+1].Mirror);
}

int i;

void CheckForSwap(float v, float a, float b)
{
 if(v>=0.0)
 {
  if(a<b)
   SwapData();
 }
 else
 {
  if(a>b)
   SwapData();
 }
}
```

```
void OrderX()
{
 for(i=First; i<Last; i++)
 {
  for(Index=First; Index<Last; Index++)
   CheckForSwap(View[0], ObjList[Index].Tx,
   ObjList[Index+1].Tx);
 }
}

void OrderY()
{
 for(i=First; i<Last; i++)
 {
  for(Index=First; Index<Last; Index++)
   CheckForSwap(View[1], ObjList[Index].Ty,
   ObjList[Index+1].Ty);
 }
}

void OrderZ()
{
 for(i=First; i<Last; i++)
 {
  for(Index=First; Index<Last; Index++)
   CheckForSwap(View[2], ObjList[Index].Tz,
   ObjList[Index+1].Tz);
 }
}

void SortObjectsBackToFront()
{
 float x, y, z;

 x=fabs(View[0]);
 y=fabs(View[1]);
 z=fabs(View[2]);
 if((x>y) && (x>z))
  OrderX();
 else
 {
```

```
  if((y>x) && (y>z))
   OrderY();
  else
   OrderZ();
 }
}

void SwapDown(float a, float b)
{
 if(a>b)
  SwapData();
}

void SortTopToBottom()
{
 for(i=First; i<Last; i++)
 {
  for(Index=First; Index<Last; Index++)
   SwapDown(ObjList[Index].Tz, ObjList[Index+1].Tz);
 }
}

void SwapUp(float a, float b)
{
 if(a<b)
  SwapData();
}

void SortBottomToTop()
{
 for(i=First; i<Last; i++)
 {
  for(Index=First; Index<Last; Index++)
   SwapUp(ObjList[Index].Tz, ObjList[Index+1].Tz);
 }
}

void CheckForSwap2(float v, float a, float b)
{
 if(v>=0.0)
 {
```

```
  if(a>b)
   SwapData();
 }
 else
 {
  if(a<b)
   SwapData();
 }
}

void Order_Y()
{
 for(i=First; i<Last; i++)
 {
  for(Index=First; Index<Last; Index++)
   CheckForSwap2(View[1], ObjList[Index].Ty,
   ObjList[Index+1].Ty);
 }
}

void SortObjectsFrontToBackInY()
{
 Order_Y();
}

void Order_X()
{
 for(i=First; i<Last; i++)
 {
  for(Index=First; Index<Last; Index++)
   CheckForSwap2(View[0], ObjList[Index].Tx,
   ObjList[Index+1].Tx);
 }
}

void SortObjectsFrontToBackInX()
{
 Order_X();
}
```

```
/*
 ┌──────────────────────────────────────────────────────────────┐
 │                 Place an Object onto the Screen              │
 └──────────────────────────────────────────────────────────────┘

   PlaceObjectOnScreen - place an object on to the screen in
      Vertex Format, Wire Frame Format or Solid Model Format
*/

Boolean XReflectedObject;
Boolean YReflectedObject;
Boolean ZReflectedObject;

void PreviewVerticies(Byte Color)
{
 float x, y, z;
 TDA Pt;
 for(FacetNum=1; FacetNum<=LastFacet; FacetNum++)
 {
  for(VertexNumInFacet=1;
   VertexNumInFacet<=LastVertexNumInFacet;   VertexNumInFacet++)
  {
   VertexNum=Facet[(FacetNum*5)+VertexNumInFacet];
   VecScalMultI(InvScaleImage, Vertex[VertexNum], Pt);
   UnVec(Pt, &x, &y, &z);
   CartesianPlot3D(x, y, z, ((MaxInten+1)*(Color-1)+MaxInten));
  }
 }
}

void WireFrameDiagram(Byte Color)
{
 VoxelArray Face3d;
 PixelArray Face2d;

 for(FacetNum=1; FacetNum<=LastFacet; FacetNum++)
 {
  for(VertexNumInFacet=1;
   VertexNumInFacet<=LastVertexNumInFacet;   VertexNumInFacet++)
  {
```

```
      VertexNum=Facet[(FacetNum*5)+VertexNumInFacet];
      VecScalMultI(InvScaleImage, Vertex[VertexNum],
      Face3d[VertexNumInFacet]);
     }
     if(Visible(Face3d))
     {
      GetProjectedCoords(Face3d, Face2d);
      PutFacet(Face2d, 1, BLACK);
      PutWireFacet(Face2d, ((MaxInten+1)*(Color-1)+MaxInten));
     }
    }
}

void PlaceFacet(Boolean MirX, Boolean MirY, Boolean MirZ, Byte
   Color)
{
 Byte Intens;
 VoxelArray Face3d;
 PixelArray Face2d;

 MirrorX=MirX;
 MirrorY=MirY;
 MirrorZ=MirZ;
 for(VertexNumInFacet=1;
   VertexNumInFacet<=LastVertexNumInFacet; VertexNumInFacet++)
 {
  VertexNum=Facet[(FacetNum*5)+VertexNumInFacet];
  VecScalMultI(InvScaleImage, Vertex[VertexNum],
   Face3d[VertexNumInFacet]);
 }
 if(Visible(Face3d))
 {
  Intens=Intensity();
  if(Intens>0)
  {
   GetProjectedCoords(Face3d, Face2d);
   PutFacet2(Face2d, Color, Intens);
  }
 }
}
```

```
void SolidModelDiagram(Byte Color)
{
 for(FacetNum=1; FacetNum<=LastFacet; FacetNum++)
 {
  if((!(Reflect)) && (!(ZReflectedObject)) &&
   (!(YReflectedObject)) && (!(XReflectedObject)))
   PlaceFacet(false, false, false, Color);
  else
  {
   if(ZReflectedObject)
    PlaceFacet(false, false, true, Color);
   else
   {
    if(YReflectedObject)
     PlaceFacet(false, true, false, Color);
   else
   {
    if(XReflectedObject)
     PlaceFacet(true, false, false, Color);
   }
   }
  }
 }
}

void PlaceObjectOnScreen(Byte Color)
{
 if(Preview)
  PreviewVerticies(Color);
 if(WireFrame)
  WireFrameDiagram(Color);
 if((SolidModel) && (!(Preview)) && (!( WireFrame)))
  SolidModelDiagram(Color);
}
Name LastObjectName;
Boolean ReflectedObjects;

void DisplayReflectiveSurfaces()
{
 strset(LastObjectName, 0);
```

```
 ReflectedObjects=false;
 Reflect=false;
 for(ObjectNum=1; ObjectNum<FirstObject; ObjectNum++)
  {
  if(strcmp(ObjList[ObjectNum].ObjectName, LastObjectName)!=0)
   {
    InitVertexBuffer();
   LoadData(ObjList[ObjectNum].ObjectName);
   }
  if(ObjList[ObjectNum].Mirror)
   {
    ReflectedObjects=true;
    Mirroring=true;
   AffineTransformation(ObjList[ObjectNum].Tx,
        ObjList[ObjectNum].Ty, ObjList[ObjectNum].Tz,
        ObjList[ObjectNum].Sx, ObjList[ObjectNum].Sy,
        ObjList[ObjectNum].Sz, ObjList[ObjectNum].Rx,
        ObjList[ObjectNum].Ry, ObjList[ObjectNum].Rz);
   PlaceObjectOnScreen(ObjList[ObjectNum].Color);
   InvAffineTransformation(ObjList[ObjectNum].Tx,
        ObjList[ObjectNum].Ty, ObjList[ObjectNum].Tz,
        ObjList[ObjectNum].Sx, ObjList[ObjectNum].Sy,
        ObjList[ObjectNum].Sz, ObjList[ObjectNum].Rx,
        ObjList[ObjectNum].Ry, ObjList[ObjectNum].Rz);
   }
  else
   Mirroring=false;
  strcpy(LastObjectName, ObjList[ObjectNum].ObjectName);
  }
}

void DisplayReflections()
{
 for(ObjectNum=FirstObject; ObjectNum<=LastObject; ObjectNum++)
  {
  if(strcmp(ObjList[ObjectNum].ObjectName, LastObjectName)!=0)
   {
    InitVertexBuffer();
   LoadData(ObjList[ObjectNum].ObjectName);
   }
```

```
    if((ObjList[ObjectNum].Reflection) && (!(Preview)) &&
      (!(WireFrame)))
     {
      Reflect=true;
     Mirroring=ObjList[ObjectNum].Mirror;
     AffineTransformation(ObjList[ObjectNum].Tx,
         ObjList[ObjectNum].Ty, ObjList[ObjectNum].Tz,
         ObjList[ObjectNum].Sx, ObjList[ObjectNum].Sy,
         ObjList[ObjectNum].Sz, ObjList[ObjectNum].Rx,
         ObjList[ObjectNum].Ry, ObjList[ObjectNum].Rz);
     PlaceObjectOnScreen(ObjList[ObjectNum].Color);
     InvAffineTransformation(ObjList[ObjectNum].Tx,
         ObjList[ObjectNum].Ty, ObjList[ObjectNum].Tz,
         ObjList[ObjectNum].Sx, ObjList[ObjectNum].Sy,
         ObjList[ObjectNum].Sz, ObjList[ObjectNum].Rx,
         ObjList[ObjectNum].Ry, ObjList[ObjectNum].Rz);
     }
     else
      Reflect=false;
    strcpy(LastObjectName, ObjList[ObjectNum].ObjectName);
    }
  }

  void DisplayActualImages()
  {
   for(ObjectNum=FirstObject; ObjectNum<=LastObject; ObjectNum++)
    {
    if(strcmp(ObjList[ObjectNum].ObjectName, LastObjectName)!=0)
     {
      InitVertexBuffer();
     LoadData(ObjList[ObjectNum].ObjectName);
     }
    if(!((ObjectNum==1) && ObjList[ObjectNum].Mirror))
     {
      Reflect=false;
     Mirroring=ObjList[ObjectNum].Mirror;
     AffineTransformation(ObjList[ObjectNum].Tx,
         ObjList[ObjectNum].Ty, ObjList[ObjectNum].Tz,
         ObjList[ObjectNum].Sx, ObjList[ObjectNum].Sy,
         ObjList[ObjectNum].Sz, ObjList[ObjectNum].Rx,
```

```
        ObjList[ObjectNum].Ry, ObjList[ObjectNum].Rz);
   PlaceObjectOnScreen(ObjList[ObjectNum].Color);
   InvAffineTransformation(ObjList[ObjectNum].Tx,
        ObjList[ObjectNum].Ty, ObjList[ObjectNum].Tz,
        ObjList[ObjectNum].Sx, ObjList[ObjectNum].Sy,
        ObjList[ObjectNum].Sz, ObjList[ObjectNum].Rx,
        ObjList[ObjectNum].Ry, ObjList[ObjectNum].Rz);
   }
  strcpy(LastObjectName, ObjList[ObjectNum].ObjectName);
  }
}

void DefineReflection(Boolean XRef, Boolean YRef, Boolean   ZRef)
{
 XReflectedObject=XRef;
 YReflectedObject=YRef;
 ZReflectedObject=ZRef;
}

void DisplayObjectsInScene()
{
 PrepareSort();
 DefineReflection(false, false, false);
 if(Sorting)
  SortObjectsBackToFront();
 DisplayReflectiveSurfaces();
 if((!(Preview)) && (!(WireFrame)) && ReflSurface)
  {
  DefineReflection(false, false, true);
  if(Sorting && VerticalSort)
   SortTopToBottom();
  if(ReflectedObjects)
   DisplayReflections();
  if(NumMirrors>1)
   {
   DefineReflection(false, true, false);
    if(Sorting)
    SortObjectsFrontToBackInY();
    if(Sorting && VerticalSort)
    SortBottomToTop();
```

```
    if(ReflectedObjects)
     DisplayReflections();
    DefineReflection(true, false, false);
    if(Sorting)
     SortObjectsFrontToBackInX();
    if(Sorting && VerticalSort)
     SortBottomToTop();
    if(ReflectedObjects)
     DisplayReflections();
   }
  }
  DefineReflection(false, false, false);
  if(Sorting)
   SortObjectsBackToFront();
  if(Sorting && VerticalSort)
   SortBottomToTop();
  DisplayActualImages();
 }
```

Figure 6-1. Listing of *DispObjs.Inc* File

Sorting Objects for Placement on the Screen

First we are going to look at the function *PrepareSort* which does the preparations for the sorting process. This function begins by checking whether there is only one object in our object list. If this is the case, then there are no mirrors and we don't need to worry about either sorting or reflections. If there is more than one object, the function begins a *while* loop which it iterates until it comes upon an object in the object list which is tagged as sortable. If such an object is found, then the parameter *First* is set to the number of this first sortable object. The procedure then begins another *while* loop which checks for the existence of objects having a *Mirror* tag. If there are mirrored objects, we exit from this loop with the parameter *ReflSurface* set to *true* to indicate that mirrored objects exist and with the parameter *FirstObject* set to the number in the list of the first non-mirrored object. The number of mirrors (*NumMirrors* is then set to one less than this number. Next, the function checks whether the first sortable object is the last object. If so, there is no need to sort, so *Sorting* is set to *False*. Otherwise, *Sorting* is set to *true*. This completes this function.

The principal tool used in sorting the list of objects is the procedure *SwapData*. This procedure uses individual procedures to swap the position of two adjacent object descriptions. Note that for each different data item, there is a separate *Swap* procedure. Each one is the same in that it places the first item passed to it into temporary storage, then moves the second item to the first item position and then moves the first item from temporary storage to the second item position. The only difference between these procedures is the data type passed to and from the procedure. Now, looking at the body of the *SwapData* procedure, you can see that the appropriate procedure is called to swap every item that makes up the object description file: the name of the object; the translation, rotation, and scaling vectors; the reflection flag that indicates whether this object will reflect in a reflective object; the object color; and the flags to indicate whether the object is sortable and whether it is reflective.

There are several different sorting procedures, whose names are descriptive of what they do. Which one you use depends upon whether you are sorting actual objects or their reflections in one of the three possible reflective planes. The procedure *SortObjectsBackToFront* procedure sorts actual objects. This procedure begins by checking the values of the coordinates which make up the viewer's position. Which of these is larger determines which coordinate of the viewer and object positions we are to use to order the object list. You will see that a pair of if statements are used call one of the procedures *OrderX*, *OrderY*, or *OrderZ*. The *OrderX* procedure uses a pair of nested for loops to perform all of the pair swaps that are necessary to completely order the list. For each one, it calls the procedure *CheckForSwap*. If the viewer x coordinate is greater than or equal to zero, *CheckSwap* calls *SwapData* to swap the pair if the second is greater than the first. If the view x coordinate is less than zero, the procedure is reversed; the swap occurs if the second is less than the first. The *OrderY* and *OrderZ* procedures are just the same except that they test the y and z coordinates respectively. When the two *for* loops of *SortObjectsBackToFront* are completed, all of the necessary swaps have been made and the object list is in the desired order.

The procedure *SortBottomToTop* is also used for actual objects, but it simply orders the objects by swapping without reference to the viewer position coordinates.

The procedure *SortTopToBottom* is used for sorting reflections in the *z=0* plane. The procedure *SortObjectsFrontToBackInY* is used for sorting reflections in the *y=0* plane. The procedure *SortObjectsFrontToBackInX* is used for sorting reflections in the *x=0* plane. These procedures are all similar in the way that they perform sorting operations, as can be seen from the listing.

Placing an Object on the Screen

This procedure draws an object on the screen. It actually consists of a call to one or more of three other procedures. If the parameter *Preview* has been set to *true* the procedure *PreviewVertices* is called. If the parameter *WireFrame* has been set to *true* the procedure *WireFrameDiagram* is called. If the parameter *SolidModel* has been set to *true* the procedure *SolidModelDiagram* is called.

The *PreviewVertices* procedure uses two nested *for* loops to scan through every facet of the object and every vertex of each facet. Each vertex is then scaled properly for display using the scale factor *InvScaleImage* (defined in Chapter 4). The vertex is then converted from a vector to three separate points, which are used as parameters for the procedure Cartesian*Plot3D*, which, you will remember, converts the position to its two-dimensional counterpart and plots a point to the screen. The point is painted in bright yellow.

The procedure *WireFrameDiagram* begins in just the same way as the previous procedure, except that instead of plotting each converted vertex to the screen, it is saved in an array, *Face3D*. The resulting facet definition is tested to see whether that facet is visible. If it is, the facet is converted to a two-dimensional representation with the procedure Get*ProjectedCoords* and then painted in black on the screen using *PutFacet*. This blanks out any information from facets that are hidden by the one being drawn. The procedure *PutWireFacet* is then used to outline the facet in bright yellow.

The procedure *SolidModelDiagram* is very similar to *WireFrameDiagram*, with a few exceptions. The first difference is that for each facet the procedure sets the parameters *MirrorX*, *MirrorY*, and *MirrorZ*. These parameters indicate whether the facets that are being processed are reflections in the *x=0, y=0,* or *z=0* planes. If they are, the appropriate mirror variable is set to *true*. If the facets are for actual objects, all three variables are set false. From there on, everything proceeds just like *WireFrameDiagram* up to the point where the procedure *PutFacet* is called by the wire frame program. In this case, a different version of the procedure, *PutFacet2* is called. This procedure takes into account mirroring, which the *PutFacet* procedure does not. The procedure is called with the actual facet color and intensity, instead of with black. That ends each loop, instead of having an additional call to draw the wire frame.

At this point, you may be a little confused as to why some of these functions, which are primarily used in the procedure just described, actually appear in other files and are described there. For example, *PutFacet* is included in *Model.Inc* and is described in Chapter 4, whereas *GetProjectedCoords* and *PutFacet2* are included in *Model.c*, which is described in Chapter 8. The reason for this is that some of the variables defined in the first procedure are needed before we come to the *DispObjs.Inc* file, whereas some of the variables needed for *GetProjectedCoords* and *PutFacet2* are not defined until after *DispObjs.Inc* is used. We' re sorry that this makes it harder for you to keep track of where various functions are described, but it is fairly essential to the program design, so we hope you'll bear with us.

Displaying Objects and Reflections

The procedure *DisplayObjectsInScene* performs the task of displaying all of the objects and reflections that make up the scene. This procedure begins by calling the procedure *PrepareSort,* which gets ready for the sorting process. It then calls the procedure *DefineReflectedObject* to indicate that the objects being treated are not reflections. This procedure takes the three parameters that are passed to it and uses them to install the proper Boolean values in *XReflectedObject, YReflectedObject* and *ZReflectedObject.* These indicate which, if any, of the three reflective planes, the reflections of the objects are to be processed for.

Next, if the *Sorting* parameter is set, the *SortObjectsBackToFront* procedure is called to sort properly for the display of actual objects. The *DisplayReflectiveSurfaces* procedure is then called. This procedure properly sets up parameters and then loops through the objects that may represent reflective planes. For each one, the vertex buffer is initialized and then the object information is loaded. If the *Mirror* parameter is *true*, the proper parameters are set, the *AffineTransformation* procedure is called to determine the location of the object's coordinates for the display, and then *PlaceObjectOnScreen* is called to draw the plane to the screen. The *InvAffineTransformation* procedure is then called to restore the original parameters. After this procedure has looped through any or all of the reflective planes that are to be set up in the scene, it terminates.

Next, the *DisplayObjectsinScene* procedure checks to see that we are not in the *WireFrame* or *Preview* modes and that the *ReflSurface* parameter is *true*. If these conditions are met, the procedure begins to display reflections. First, *DefineReflection* is called to define that the reflection is in the *z* plane. The proper sorting for the *z* plane is performed, if indicated. Then, if the *z* plane is identified as a reflective surface, the procedure *DisplayReflections* is called. This procedure uses a *for* loop to cycle through all of the objects that are to be displayed on the screen. For each object, the vertex buffer is initialized and the data for the object are loaded. Then, if we are not in the *WireFrame* or *Preview* modes, and if a reflection is indicated, the proper parameters are set, the affine transformation is performed to determine the location of the object reflection parameters in the *z=0* plane, and the object then painted on the screen. The inverse affine transformation is then performed to restore the original parameters and the loop proceeds through the next iteration.

After performing the *z=0* plane reflection painting tasks, the *DisplayObjectsInScene* checks the parameter *NumMirrors*. This parameter indicates the number of reflecting surfaces. If it is not greater than one, we are through with the reflections. If it is greater than one, the reflection is defined to be in the *y=0* plane, the proper sorting for that plane is performed, and the reflections are painted on the screen. Then the reflections are defined to be in the *x=0* plane and the process is repeated. Next, regardless of mode or of the setting of *ReflSurface*, reflections are defined to be in no planes (actual objects being processed) and the proper sorting is performed, if indicated, for actual objects. The procedure *DisplayActualImages* is then called to paint the actual images on the screen. This procedure is very much like *DisplayReflections* except that it processes the actual objects rather than reflections. When all actual objects have been displayed on the screen, the procedure *DisplayObjectsOnScreen* is complete.

CHAPTER 7

The Model.c Description File Maker

When we run the *Model.c* program to generate solid modeled scenes, there are several options built into the program which are selected by the program reading the *Model.des* file. These options are set up by running the program created by compiling the *Desmaker.c* file before running the *Model.exe* program (which is produced by compiling *Model.c*). The content of this program and the file that it makes are relatively simple. We will describe the program and the options it creates in this chapter.

The program itself and its associated function are in the file *Desmaker.c*, which is listed in Figure 7-1. First let's look at the function *Response*. This function is designed to obtain a response to a question and to make sure that it is either a *Y* or an *N*. It does this by means of two nested *Do* loops. The inner loop keeps trying to read a key from the keyboard until the response is other than a null, indicating that a key has been pressed. Then the character received from the keyboard is converted to a capital letter. If it is a *Y* or an *N*, the outer loop terminates; otherwise the loops continue to iterate until an acceptable response is received. Note that whenever *Response* is called in a program, nothing can happen until you type in either *Y*, *y*, *N*, or n. When a correct response is received, if it is *Y* the function returns *true*; otherwise, it returns false.

Now, let's look at the main program. First it displays the heading "Program to Generate a Description File for Model", followed by a blank line. Then it opens a file called *Model.Des* and prepares it for writing. It next asks, "Display Axis and Palette?", and writes the response to this query to a file line. (You will see in the next chapter how this information is used to decide whether the entire palette and the coordinate axes are displayed on the screen along with the scene.)

Next, the program asks the question, "Display Solid Model?". The response is written to the next line of the file, indicating whether solid facets are to be displayed to comprise the scene. If the response to this query is *true* (solid facets are the display mode), then the program writes *false* to the next two program lines (which indicates that the vertex and wire frame modes of display are not to be used. Otherwise, the program asks the question, "Display Preview of Vertices?" The response to this is written to the next line of the file to indicate whether the vertex mode of display has been selected. Then the program asks the question, "Display Wire Frame Model?". The response to this query is written to the next line of the file to indicate whether the wire frame mode of display has been selected.

Finally, regardless of what display modes have been chosen, the program asks the question, "Load Scene from Disk?" The response to this query is written to the next line of the file. It will be used to determine whether a *.SCN* file will be read to provide the display data or whether the data will come from a procedure. After this, the disk file is closed, completing the operation of the program.

```
/* DesMaker.c

    Program for Generation of Description Files for Model.c

              Program by Christopher D. Watkins

                'C' Conversion by Larry Sharp

*/

#include "stdio.h"
#include "dos.h"
#include "conio.h"
#include "string.h"

/*

                 Keyboard Response Routines

Response  - returns true or false to a Y or N keyboard stroke
*/
```

```
typedef char Name[12];

char Resp[6];

void Response()
{
  char c;

  strcpy(Resp, "\n");
  while((!(c=='Y')) && (!(c=='N')))
  {
    while(!(kbhit()));
    c=toupper(getch());
  }
  putch(c);
  if(c=='Y')
    strcpy(Resp, "true");
  else
    strcpy(Resp, "false");
  puts("");
}

/*
```

Save Description Data

```
SaveDescription - save description of scene
*/

FILE *TextDiskFile;

void SaveDescription(Name FileName)
{
  TextDiskFile=fopen(FileName, "w+t");
  printf("Display Axis and Palette? ");
  Response();
  fprintf(TextDiskFile, "%s\n", Resp);
  printf("Display Solid Model? ");
  Response();
```

```
    fprintf(TextDiskFile, "%s\n", Resp);
    if(strcmp(Resp, "true")==0)
    {
      fprintf(TextDiskFile, "%s\n", "false");
      fprintf(TextDiskFile, "%s\n", "false");
    }
    else
    {
      printf("Display Preview of Verticies? ");
      Response();
      fprintf(TextDiskFile, "%s\n", Resp);
      printf("Display Wire Frame Model? ");
      Response();
      fprintf(TextDiskFile, "%s\n", Resp);
    }
    printf("Load Scene from Disk? ");
    Response();
    fprintf(TextDiskFile, "%s\n", Resp);
    fclose(TextDiskFile);
  }

  void main()
  {
    clrscr();
    printf("Program to Generate a Description File for Model\n\n");
    SaveDescription("MODEL.DES");
  }
```

Figure 7-1. Listing of *Desmaker.c* File

CHAPTER 8

The 3-D Modeling Program

Now that we have examined some of the elements that are needed for three-dimensional modeling, we will consider the 3-D modeling program itself. In this chapter we will assume that we already have a data file ending in the extension *.SCN* which provides all of the data needed to define a scene. In later chapters we'll go into the details of how to create such a data file. To get you started, there are thirteen data files for 3-D modeling included in Appendix A.

The first of these files is *CubePlan.Scn*. The scene produced by this file is a cube on a plane. If you don't specify a file when asked, this is the file that you will get by default. It is illustrated in Plate 5. The third is *SphrWall.Scn*. The scene produced by this file is a sphere in a mirrored room. It is illustrated in Plate 6. The next file is *FourCols.Scn*. The scene produced by this file consists of four columns, each with a sphere at its top. It is illustrated in Plate 7. The next file is *Well.Scn*. The scene produced by this file is a well surrounded by various objects. It is illustrated in Plate 8. (This scene was inspired by the "Old Well" at the University of North Carolina in Chapel Hill, North Carolina.) The next file is *Shapes.Scn*. The scene produced by this file consists of a variety of objects to demonstrate the different shapes that can be produced. It is illustrated in Plate 9. The next file is *SolOfRev.Scn*. The scene produced by this file contains a number of interesting shapes that are produced by solids of revolution. It is illustrated in Plate 10. The next four files demonstrate the use of 3-D modeling to produce plots of equations. These are the files *PlotEqn1.Scn*, *PlotEqn2.Scn*, *PlotEqn3.Scn*, and *PlotEqn4.Scn*. These plots are illustrated in Plates 11, 12, 13, and 14.

Another option, which we will go into later, allows you to generate a scene directly from a function, rather than a stored file. If you select this option, an image of stacked spheres is produced. These are shown in Plate 15. All of the *.SCN* data files are listed in Appendix A, so that you can copy them into your system if you didn't buy the program disk.

The *Model.c* program, when compiled, will take one of these *.SCN* files and use it to create a scene on your display screen. The program and its associated functions are listed in Figure 8-2. Before we look at the main program, though, let's take a look at some of the functions that are used in it.

Viewer and Light Source Vector

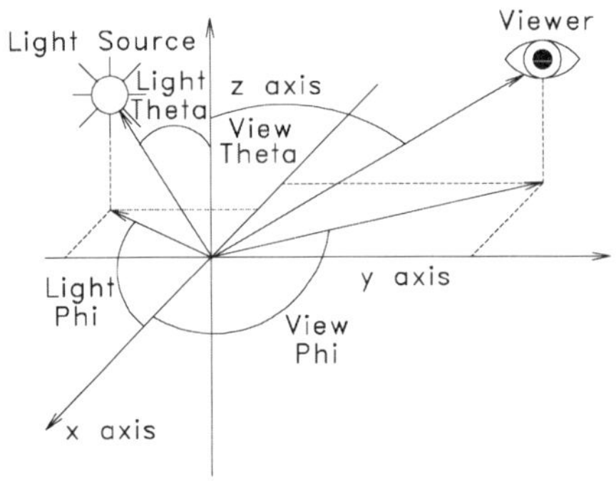

Figure 8-1. Viewer and Light Source Geometry

The position of the viewer determines just what the scene will look like on the display screen. The viewer position is defined by two angles that are obtained from the file of scene information. These are *ViewPhi,* the angle between the viewer position and the *x-z* plane, and *ViewTheta* the angle between the viewer position and the *z* axis. The geometry is shown in Figure 8-1. These angles (in degrees) are passed to the function *GetViewVector*. This function first converts the angles to radians and then uses them to determine the *x*, *y*, and *z* coordinates of a unit vector from the origin pointing in the viewer direction.

There are similar angles *LightPhi* and *LightTheta* which define the position of the light source that illuminates the scene. This determines which part of an object will be brightly colored and which will be dimmer because of the decrease in light intensity. These angles (in degrees) are passed as parameters to the function *InitLightDirection*, which first displays on the screen a description of the two angles and their values and then loads the values into the two parameters described above. Another function, *GetLightVector*, converts these angles to radians and then uses them to determine the *x*, *y*, and *z* coordinates of a unit vector starting at the origin and pointing in the direction of the light source.

```
/* Model.c

        3-D Modeling and Shading Routines for
            Objects Constructed of Facets

          Program by Christopher D. Watkins

            'C' Conversion by Larry Sharp

*/

#include "stdio.h"
#include "dos.h"
#include "conio.h"
#include "math.h"
#include "string.h"
#include "alloc.h"
#include "math.inc"
#include "graph.inc"
#include "model.inc"

/*

                    Toggle Switches

   DoPreview     - display vertices
   DoWireFrame   - display wireframe
   DoSolidModel  - display solid model
   VertSort      - vertically sort objects
*/
```

```
Boolean Preview;
Boolean WireFrame;
Boolean SolidModel;
Boolean VerticalSort;

void DoPreview(Boolean State)
{
  Preview=State;
}

void DoWireFrame(Boolean State)
{
  WireFrame=State;
}

void DoSolidModel(Boolean State)
{
  SolidModel=State;
}

void VertSort(Boolean Sort)
{
  VerticalSort=Sort;
}

 /*
 ╔══════════════════════════════════════════════════════════════╗
 ║                    Affine Transformations                    ║
 ╚══════════════════════════════════════════════════════════════╝

   AffineTransformation - translate, rotate and scale vertices
                                              for viewing
   InvAffineTransformation - return vertices to original value
*/

void DoTransform(Matx4x4 XForm)
{
  TDA temp, temp2;

  for(VertexNum=1; VertexNum<=LastVertex; VertexNum++)
  {
```

```
    VecScalMultI(InvScaleData, Vertex[VertexNum], temp2);
    Transform(temp2, XForm, temp);
    VecScalMultInt(ScaleImage, temp, Vertex[VertexNum]);
  }
}

void DoInvTransform(Matx4x4 XForm)
{
  TDA temp, temp2;

  for(VertexNum=1; VertexNum<=LastVertex; VertexNum++)
  {
    VecScalMultI(InvScaleImage, Vertex[VertexNum], temp2);
    Transform(temp2, XForm, temp);
    VecScalMultInt(ScaleData, temp, Vertex[VertexNum]);
  }
}

void AffineTransformation(float Tx, float Ty, float Tz,
           float Sx, float Sy, float Sz,
           float Rx, float Ry, float Rz)
{
  Matx4x4 XForm;

  PrepareMatrix(Tx, Ty, Tz, Sx, Sy, Sz, Rx, Ry, Rz, XForm);
  DoTransform(XForm);
}

void InvAffineTransformation(float Tx, float Ty, float Tz,
              float Sx, float Sy, float Sz,
              float Rx, float Ry, float Rz)
{
  Matx4x4 XForm;

  PrepareInvMatrix(-Tx, -Ty, -Tz, 1.0/Sx, 1.0/Sy, 1.0/Sz, -Rx, -
      Ry, -Rz, XForm);
  DoInvTransform(XForm);
}

/*
```

```
                    Viewer and Light Source Vectors

   GetViewVector       - unit vector in direction of viewer
   InitLightDirection - get direction for light source
   GetLightVector      - unit vector in direction of light source
*/

#define ViewPhi 270
#define ViewTheta 90

TDA View;

void GetViewVector()
{
  float Phi, Theta;
  float x, y, z;

  Phi=Radians((float)ViewPhi-Angl);
  Theta=Radians((float)ViewTheta-Tilt);
  x=sin(Theta)*cos(Phi);
  y=sin(Theta)*sin(Phi);
  z=cos(Theta);
  Vec(x, y, z, View);
}

float LightPhi;
float LightTheta;

void InitLightDirection(int LgtPhi, int LgtTheta)
{
  printf("Light Direction is %d around the z-Axis and\n",
   LgtPhi);
  printf(" %d off the z-Axis\n", LgtTheta);
  LightPhi=(float)LgtPhi;
  LightTheta=(float)LgtTheta;

}
```

```
TDA Light;

void GetLightVector()
{
  float Phi, Theta;
  float x, y, z;

  Phi=Radians(LightPhi);
  Theta=Radians(LightTheta);
  x=sin(Theta)*cos(Phi);
  y=sin(Theta)*sin(Phi);
  z=cos(Theta);
  Vec(x, y, z, Light);
}

/*
```

Surface Normal Vector

```
   GetSurfaceNormalVector - unit vector normal to surface
*/

TDA SrfNorm;

void GetSurfaceNormalVector(VoxelArray Face3d)
{
  float Length, Length2;
  TDA Dir1;
  TDA Dir2;
  TDA Temp1;
  TDA Temp2;
  TDA Temp3;
  TDA SrfNorm2;

  VecCopy(Face3d[2], Temp1);
  VecCopy(Face3d[1], Temp2);
  VecCopy(Face3d[LastVertexNumInFacet], Temp3);
  VecSub(Temp1, Temp2, Dir1);
  VecSub(Temp3, Temp2, Dir2);
```

```
  VecCross(Dir1, Dir2, SrfNorm);
  Length=VecLen(SrfNorm);
  VecCopy(Face3d[LastVertexNumInFacet], Temp1);
  VecCopy(Face3d[LastVertexNumInFacet-1], Temp2);
  VecCopy(Face3d[LastVertexNumInFacet-2], Temp3);
  VecSub(Temp1, Temp2, Dir1);
  VecSub(Temp3, Temp2, Dir2);
  VecCross(Dir1, Dir2, SrfNorm2);
  Length2=VecLen(SrfNorm2);
  if(Length==0.0)
    VecScalMult(1.0/Length2, SrfNorm2, SrfNorm);
  else
  {
    if(Length2==0.0)
      VecScalMult(1.0/Length, SrfNorm, SrfNorm);
    else
    {
      VecScalMult(1.0/Length, SrfNorm, SrfNorm);
      VecScalMult(1.0/Length2, SrfNorm2, SrfNorm2);
      VecAdd(SrfNorm, SrfNorm2, SrfNorm);
      VecScalMult(0.5, SrfNorm, SrfNorm);
    }
  }
}

/*
                    The Illumination Model

   Intensity - calculated intensity of point on screen
*/

Byte Intensity()
{
  float Ambient=0.30;
  float DifRfl=0.50;
  float SpcRfl=0.20;
  float Gloss=5.0;
  float CosTheta;
```

```
  float CosAlpha;
  TDA Ref;
  float TwoCosTheta;
  TDA temp;

  CosTheta=VecDot(SrfNorm, Light);
  if(CosTheta<=0.0)
    return(Round(MaxInten*Ambient));
  else
  {
    TwoCosTheta=2.0*CosTheta;
    VecScalMult(TwoCosTheta, SrfNorm, temp);
    VecNormalize(temp);
    VecSub(temp, Light, Ref);
    VecNormalize(Ref);
    CosAlpha=VecDot(View, Ref);
    return(Round(MaxInten*(Ambient+DifRfl*CosTheta+SpcRfl *
      pow(CosAlpha, Gloss))));
  }
}

/*
```

Facet Visibility Test

```
   Visible - determine if facet is visible
*/

Boolean Reflect;
Boolean MirrorX;
Boolean MirrorY;
Boolean MirrorZ;

Boolean Visible(VoxelArray Face3d)
{
  float CosBeta;
  float nvx, nvy, nvz;
  TDA temp, v;
  Boolean vt;
```

```
  GetSurfaceNormalVector(Face3d);
  VecCopy(View, v);
  if((!(Preview || WireFrame)) && Reflect && MirrorZ)
    v[2]=-v[2];
  VecElemMult(1.0, SrfNorm, v, temp);
  UnVec(temp, &nvx, &nvy, &nvz);
  vt=true;
  CosBeta=nvx+nvy+nvz;
  if((MirrorZ || (!(MirrorX || MirrorY))) && (CosBeta<0.0))
    vt=false;
  else
  {
    CosBeta=-nvx+nvy+nvz;
    if(MirrorX && (CosBeta<0.0))
      vt=false;
    else
    {
      CosBeta=nvx-nvy+nvz;
      if(MirrorY && (CosBeta<0.0))
        vt=false;
    }
  }
  return(vt);
}

/*
 ╔══════════════════════════════════════════════════════════════════╗
 ║                     Reflection Screen Buffer                     ║
 ╚══════════════════════════════════════════════════════════════════╝

  Stores the reflective states of all screen pixel locations

   InitReflectionBuffer - clear reflective states
   Reflected            - indicates whether or not reflective
   MakeReflected        - makes a screen location reflective
*/

#define XBytes 39

Byte Refl[XBytes+1][MaxY+1];
```

```
void InitReflectionBuffer()
{
  int i, j;

  for(i=0; i<=XBytes; i++)
  {
    for(j=0; j<=MaxY; j++)
      Refl[i][j]=0;
  }
}

Boolean Reflected(int x, int y)
{
  Byte tmp;

  tmp=Refl[x/8][y]&(128>>(x%8));
  if(tmp==0)
    return(false);
  else
    return(true);
}

void MakeReflected(int x, int y)
{
  Refl[x/8][y]=Refl[x/8][y]|(128>>(x%8));
}

#include "addobjs.inc"

/*

              Polygonal Facet Fill Routine

   GetProjectedCoords - 3D point mapped onto 2D screen
   PutFacet2          - fills a facet
*/

void GetProjectedCoords(VoxelArray Face3d, PixelArray Face2d)
{
```

```
   float xt, yt, zt;

   for(VertexNumInFacet=1;
    VertexNumInFacet<=LastVertexNumInFacet;
    VertexNumInFacet++)
   {
     UnVec(Face3d[VertexNumInFacet], &xt, &yt, &zt);
     if(Reflect)
     {
       if(MirrorZ)
       {
    zt=-zt;
    if(EdgeReflector && (!(EdgeReflectorAtZero)))
     zt-=200.0;
     }
     else
     {
     if(MirrorY)
     {
      yt=-yt;
      if(EdgeReflector || EdgeReflectorAtZero)
        yt-=200.0;
    }
    else
    {
      if(MirrorX)
      {
       xt=-xt;
       if(EdgeReflector || EdgeReflectorAtZero)
        xt-=200.0;
      }
     }
      }
     }
     MapCoordinates(xt, yt, zt, &Face2d[VertexNumInFacet].x,
          &Face2d[VertexNumInFacet].y);
   }
  Face2d[LastVertexNumInFacet+1]=Face2d[1];
}
```

```
Boolean Mirroring;

void PutFacet2(PixelArray Face2d, Byte Color, Byte Intens)
{
  int xc, yc;
  int i, x;
  int OldVertNum;
  int VertNum;
  int mnx, mxx;
  int mny, mxy;
  float slope;

  if(Intens<1)
    return;
  if(Reflect && (Intens!=1))
  {
    --Intens;
    if(Intens!=2)
    {
      --Intens;
      if(Intens!=3)
      --Intens;
    }
  }
  mny=Face2d[1].y;
  mxy=Face2d[1].y;
  for(i=2; i<=LastVertexNumInFacet; i++)
  {
    if(Face2d[i].y>mxy)
      mxy=Face2d[i].y;
    if(Face2d[i].y<mny)
      mny=Face2d[i].y;
  }
  if(mny<0)
    mny=0;
  if(mxy>MaxY)
    mxy=MaxY;
  for(yc=mny; yc<=mxy; yc++)
  {
    mnx=MaxX+1;
```

```
mxx=-1;
OldVertNum=LastVertexNumInFacet;
for(VertNum=1; VertNum<=LastVertexNumInFacet; VertNum++)
{
 if((Face2d[OldVertNum].y>=yc) || (Face2d[VertNum].y>=yc))
  {
    if((Face2d[OldVertNum].y<=yc) || (Face2d[VertNum].y<=yc))
     {
       if(Face2d[OldVertNum].y != Face2d[VertNum].y)
        {
           slope=(float)(Face2d[VertNum].x-
                         Face2d[OldVertNum].x)/
                 (float)(Face2d[VertNum].y-
                          Face2d[OldVertNum].y);
           x =  Round(
              slope*(float)((yc-Face2d[OldVertNum].y))+
               Face2d[OldVertNum].x);
           if(x<mnx) mnx=x;
           if(x>mxx) mxx=x;
        }
     }
  }
  OldVertNum=VertNum;
}
if(mnx<0)
  mnx=0;
if(mxx>MaxX)
  mxx=MaxX;
if(mnx<=mxx)
{
  for(xc=mnx; xc<=mxx; xc++)
  {
     if(Mirroring)
        {
          MakeReflected(xc, yc);
          PutPixel(xc, yc, Color, Intens);
        }
     else
     {
       if(!(Reflect))
```

```
        else
        {
          if(Reflected(xc, yc))
            PutPixel(xc, yc, Color, Intens);
        }
      }
      }
    }
  }
}

/*
```

Load Description File and Scene Data

```
   LoadDescAndScene - loads description file ".DES" and scene data
*/

Strg B;


Name SceneFile;

void GetSceneFile()
{
  int i;
  Byte x, y;

  printf("\nEnter File Name -> ");
  x=wherex();
  y=wherey();
  gets(SceneFile);
  if(!(strcmp(SceneFile, "")))
  {
    strcpy(SceneFile, "CUBEPLAN");
    gotoxy(x, y);
    puts(SceneFile);
  }
  puts("");
```

```
    for(i=0; i<strlen(SceneFile); i++)
      SceneFile[i]=toupper(SceneFile[i]);
}

void LoadDescAndScene(Name FileName)
{
  FILE *TextDiskFile;

  TextDiskFile=fopen(FileName, "r+t");
  fscanf(TextDiskFile, "%s", B);
  PutAxisAndPalette(Bool(B));
  if(Bool(B))
    printf("Axis and Palette Display On\n");
  else
    printf("Axis and Palette Display Off\n");
  fscanf(TextDiskFile, "%s", B);
  DoSolidModel(Bool(B));
  if(Bool(B))
    printf("Solid Model Display On\n");
  else
    printf("Solid Model Display Off\n");
  if(SolidModel)
  {
    fscanf(TextDiskFile, "%s", B);
    fscanf(TextDiskFile, "%s", B);
    DoPreview(false);
    DoWireFrame(false);
  }
  else
  {
    fscanf(TextDiskFile, "%s", B);
    DoPreview(Bool(B));
    if(Bool(B))
      printf("Vertex Display On\n");
    else
      printf("Vertex Display Off\n");
    fscanf(TextDiskFile, "%s", B);
    DoWireFrame(Bool(B));
    if(Bool(B))
```

```
      printf("Wire Frame Display On\n");
    else
      printf("Wire Frame Display Off\n");
  }
  fscanf(TextDiskFile, "%s", B);
  fclose(TextDiskFile);
  if(Bool(B))
  {
    printf("Loading Scene from Disk File\n");
    GetSceneFile();
    AddObjectsToSceneFromDiskFile(SceneFile);
  }
  else
  {
    printf("Loading Scene from Procedure\n\n");
    AddObjectsToSceneFromProcedure();
  }
  printf("Hit any key....\n");
  getch();
}

#include "dispobjs.inc"

/*

                    Main Program

*/

void main()
{
  Facet=farcalloc(((MaxFacet+1)*(MaxVertexNumInFacet+1)),
   sizeof(int));
  if(Facet==0)
  {
    printf("Not enough memory!\n");
    getch();
    exit(1);
  }
  Title();
```

```
    printf("3-D Modeling Program\n\n");
    InitReflectionBuffer();
    InitVertexBuffer();
    InitObjectBuffer();
    LoadDescAndScene("MODEL.DES");
    InitGraphics();
    AxisAndPalette();
    if(DrawAxisAndPalette)
      WaitForKey();
    DisplayObjectsInScene();
    ExitGraphics();
    farfree(Facet);
}
```

Figure 8-2. Listing of the Model.c File

Loading the Description File and Scene Data

The function *LoadDescAndScene* loads all of the information that is required to generate the scene with the desired options. The parameter passed to this function is the name of the description file, which is usually *Model.Des*. The function begins by opening this file and reading the first line, which indicates whether the coordinate axes and the palette should be displayed upon the screen. (Note that this function does no error checking on the file open operation.) The file line contains either the string "TRUE" or the string "FALSE". The function *Bool* returns *false* if the string is "FALSE" and *true* otherwise. This Boolean value is passed to the function *PutAxisAndPalette*, which properly sets the parameter for this option. If the Boolean value was *true*, the function next writes to the screen the legend, "Axis and Palette Display On". Otherwise, it writes the line, "Axis and Palette Display Off". The next line determines whether the display is to show 3-D models. The is determined by the parameter *SolidModel*, which is set to the Boolean value obtained from reading the disk file line and passing it through *Bool*. If the value is *true* the line "Solid Model Display On" is written to the display. Otherwise the line "Solid Model Display Off" is written to the display. If the value is *true* the next two lines are read from the file, but disregarded, and the option parameters *Preview* and *WireFrame* are set to *False*. If the value is *false*, the function reads the next line of the disk file and sets *Preview* to the Boolean value specified by the file line. It then displays the line "Vertex Display On", or "Vertex Display Off", as appropriate. The function then reads the next line of the disk file and sets *WireFrame* to the Boolean value specified by the file line. It then displays the line "Wire Frame Display On", or "Wire Frame Display Off", as appropriate.

Once *SolidModel*, *Preview*, and *WireFrame* have all been set to the proper values and the corresponding display output to the screen, the function reads the next line from the disk file, which indicates whether the scene data is to be obtained from a disk file or from a function. It then closes the disk file. If the selected option is to read data from a function, the line "Loading Scene from Procedure" is displayed and *AddObjectsFromProcedure* (described in Chapter 5) is called to load the scene data. If the selected option is to read data from a disk file, the function *GetSceneFile* is called. This function first displays on the screen, "Enter File Name => ". It then saves the current cursor position. Next, the keyboard input is read to the parameter *SceneFile*. If only a carriage return was entered, the file name *CubePlan* is placed in the parameter *SceneFile* by default, the cursor is repositioned at the end of the displayed string, and the default file name is displayed on the screen. This is the end of the *GetSceneFile* function so we return to the *LoadDescAndScene* function, which calls *AddObjectsToSceneFromDiskFile* (described in Chapter 6) to load the scene data from the file named in *SceneFile*. After the scene data is loaded, from whatever source, a 2.5 second delay is introduced, to assure that the user has time to read all of the pertinent information from the screen. The *LoadDescAndScene* function then ends.

Affine Transformations

Given that we have defined a facet by specifying its vertices, we need to transform it from some generic position, size, and orientation, that it assumes in a generic object file, to the position, size, and orientation that we want it to have in the particular scene that we are creating. The function *AffineTransformation* performs these operations. It begins by calling *PrepareMatrix* (described in Chapter 1) to create a transformation matrix from the current translation, scaling, and rotation coordinates. It then executes a *for* loop for every vertex comprising the facet. Each iteration of the loop begins by a scalar multiplication of a vertex vector to convert it to the +23000 to –23000 integer system that is used to speed up calculations. The function *Transform* (described in Chapter 1) is called to multiply the vertex by the transformation matrix. Next an integer vector scalar multiplication is performed to convert to the screen display coordinate system.

The function *InvAffineTransformation* is the opposite of *AffineTransformation*. It takes a set of vertices representing the final position of a facet in display coordinates (the result that is obtained by running *AffineTransformation*) and runs all of the operations in reverse order to obtain the original set of coordinates for each facet vertex.

Finding the Surface Normal Vector

One critical factor in finding the shade of color to be painted on the screen for a particular facet is the surface normal vector to the facet. The function *GetSurfaceNormalVector* generates this vector. It begins by finding two vectors, the first drawn from the first vertex of the facet to the second vertex and the second drawn from the last vertex to the second vertex. It then takes the vector cross-product of these two vectors. If non-zero, this is in the direction of the surface normal. The length of this vector is then found. If it is zero, we need to try again. In that case, we repeat the same function using the last three vertices of the facet. Regardless of which technique is used, the result of the cross-product is divided by its length, resulting in a normalized unit vector which is the surface normal to the facet.

The Illumination Model

The illumination model determines the shade of color that is to be used to paint a particular facet to the screen. This is performed by the function *Intensity*, which returns a byte that represents which of the 256 available colors is to be used to paint the facet to the screen. The function begins by defining the percentage of illumination supplied by ambient, diffuse, and specularly reflected light, as well as the power to be used for shininess in a Phong shading model. This model says that the shininess of a facet is defined by:

$$I = s \cos \alpha^{g} \qquad \text{(Equation 8-1)}$$

where I is the intensity of the light at the surface, s is the spectral reflection coefficient of the facet, *alpha* is the angle between the viewer vector and the facet, and g is the shininess factor. The function then finds the cosine of the angle between the surface normal vector and the light source vector (theta). If this cosine is negative, there is no reflected light, so the ambient light value is returned. If the cosine is positive, the function multiplies the surface normal vector by twice the cosine found above, normalizes the resulting vector, subtracts the light vector from it, and then normalizes the resulting vector. The dot product of this vector and the *View* (viewer direction) vector is then taken to find the cosine of the angle between the two vectors (alpha). The value returned by the function in this case is the maximum intensity value multiplied by the ambient light fraction, plus the diffuse light fraction multiplied by the cosine of theta, plus the specular reflection multiplied by the cosine of alpha raised to the g (glossiness) power.

Testing a Facet for Visibility

The function *Visible* determines whether a facet is visible to the viewer or not. Although this function is listed as part of the *Model.c* file, it is actually used by the function *PlaceObjectOnScreen* (described in Chapter 6). This function is passed the array containing the coordinates of the vertices comprising a facet. It begins by calling *GetSurfaceNormal* to obtain the surface normal vector for the facet. Next, the view vector is copied to a new location. We are going to take the dot product of these two vectors to determine the angle between them. First, however, if we are dealing with a reflection instead of the actual object we have to reverse the direction of one of the coordinates of one of these vectors, in order to make the direction correct. The function therefore uses a series of *if* statements to check which mirror plane is set and adjust the vector coordinates accordingly. It then takes the dot product of the two vectors to form the cosine of beta. If this cosine is negative, the facet is invisible, so the function returns *false*. Otherwise, the facet is visible and the function returns *true*.

The Reflection Screen Buffer

In order to keep track of the reflective state of every pixel on the screen, we need a buffer which contains one bit for every screen pixel. This buffer is *Refl*. It consists of an array whose dimensions are the x resolution 8 (size of byte) by the y resolution. Three functions are associated with this buffer. The function *InitReflectionBuffer* simply uses a pair of nested *For* loops to set every member of the array to zero. The function *Reflected* isolates the bit representing a particular pixel in the array. If it is zero, then the function returns *false*; otherwise it returns *true*. The function *MakeReflected* sets a designated bit in the proper byte in the array to one for *true*.

Obtaining Facet Screen Coordinates

The function *GetProjectedCoords* is passed an array *Facet3d* which comprises the three-dimensional coordinates of each of the vertices which make up the facet definition. For each vertex, the function first decomposes the vertex vector into three separate coordinates. It then looks at the mirror parameters to see if one of the reflections of the actual object is being processed. If this is the case, the coordinates are modified to represent the coordinates of the reflection rather than the actual object. An *if* statement is used to determine the positioning of the edge reflector which is reflecting the object, and then the proper coordinate conversion for whichever edge reflector is being used is performed. Once the coordinate conversions (if any are required) have been completed, the function *MapCoordinates* is called to convert from the three-dimensional coordinates to two-dimensional coordinates representing a position on the display screen surface. These are then placed in a two-dimensional vector *Facet2d[n]*, where *n* is the number of the vector being processed. When all vertices have been processed, the function is complete. The vertex coordinates for the two-dimensional representation of the facet on the screen are then in the array *Facet2d*.

Painting a Solid Facet on the Screen

The function *PutFacet2* fills in a facet on the screen with the designated color and intensity. It is very similar to *PutFacet*, which was described in Chapter 4, except that it takes mirroring into account. It begins by checking whether the parameter *Intens* is large enough for the facet to be visible, and if not, the function terminates right then. Next, the function checks whether an actual object or a reflection is being processed. If a reflection is being processed, the intensity is decreased so that the reflection will be darker than the actual object. Next, the function loops to determine the minimum and maximum values of the *y* coordinate for the facet. Then a *for* loop begins which iterates once for every value of *y* within the facet. Within the loop, the function computes the slope of the lines connecting critical pairs of vertices and uses the slopes to determine the beginning and ending values of *x* for the current value of *y*. These values are tested to assure that they never come out to be smaller than the minimum *x* for the facet nor larger than the maximum *x* for the facet. Then, if the maximum is greater than or equal to the minimum, the function *DrawHorizLine* is called to draw a line of the proper color for that *y* value. This function is different from the *DrawHorizLine* function used in *PutFacet* in that it takes mirroring into account. The function iterates for all values of *x* from the beginning value to the end value at the desired value of *y*. If in the mirroring mode, it makes each pixel in the reflection data matrix *true* and then uses *PutPixel* to paint the pixel on the screen with the proper color. If not in the mirroring mode, the function checks whether we are processing a reflection. If not, it paints the pixel on the screen using *PutPixel*. If we are processing a reflection, it checks whether this particular pixel location is capable of showing a reflection; if it is, it paints the pixel on the screen using *PutPixel*. After all *x* values are processed, the *DrawHorizLine* function is complete. The *PutFacet2* function then loops through another value of y until all values of *y* within the facet have had their associated lines drawn, resulting in the facet being filled with the desired shade of color.

The *Model.c* Program

We are finally done with examining the necessary functions and can proceed with describing the *Model.c* program. It begins by writing the legend "3-D Modeling Program" to the screen. It then initializes the reflection, vertex, and object buffers. Next, the function *LoadDescAndScene* is called. This function reads *Model.Des* to determine which options have been selected. It also sets up for the proper option of solid, vertex, or wire frame modeling. If adding a scene from a function was selected, the function is called to load the scene data in this way. Otherwise, the name of the scene file is requested, and, when given, the scene data is loaded from that file. Next, the program calls *InitGraphics* to initialize for graphics display. It then calls *AxisAndPalette*, which displays the coordinate axes and the color palette on the screen. If that option was selected, the program waits for a keystroke before continuing. Finally, *DisplayObjectsInScene* is called to display all of the objects on the screen. The program now waits for another keystroke, and when one occurs, it exits the graphics mode and terminates.

CHAPTER 9

Creating Object Databases

You have now learned how to model a scene containing objects, assuming that you have a file of object data, or a function that contains the data you need. Whichever technique is used to define scene data, the program makes use of a list of objects, each of which is already defined in a file that is called at the appropriate moment to display the object on the screen. In this chapter, we are going to show you how these object files are created, so that you will understand what's in the file for each primitive object given in this book, and also will know how to create new primitive objects of your own.

We've already described the file format for an object data file in Chapter 4. Let's just go over it quickly here. The file is a binary file and all numbers are written to the file in binary format. The first line of the file consists of the number of vertices in the object, the number of facets in the object, and the number of vertices in each facet. The next section of the file consists of a set of three integers, representing the x, y, and *z* coordinates, for each vertex. The next section of the file consists of a list of the numbers of the vertices that make up each facet, in order. Each of these is also a binary integer taking up two bytes. Keeping this firmly in mind, let's look at some functions that will be needed in creating data files. These functions are included in the file *ShpMk.Inc*, which is listed in Figure 9-1.

Adding Vertices

Perhaps you remember that the vertex information stored in a data file is in the form of an integer having values between –32767 and +32,767. This is a bit misleading, because when you are creating the data file the vertex information you write in is in the form of real numbers between –1 and +1. The transformation to the other scale occurs within the software. The function that is used to add a vertex to the vertex list and ultimately to the object data file is called *AddVertex*. This function is passed three numbers, corresponding to the *x*, *y*, and *z* coordinates of the new vertex. The function first checks that each of these is between –1 and +1. If any one of them is out of limits, an error parameter is set to *true*; otherwise each error parameter is set to *false*. If any coordinate was out of range, a sound is produced, followed by a message on the display telling which coordinate was out of range. The program is then halted, which causes you to return to DOS or C, wherever you were when you ran the program.

Next, the three coordinates are multiplied by the proper scale factor and converted to integers. The function then looks at the parameter *RepeatedVertexCheck*. If this parameter is true, the function *CheckRepeatingVertices* is called. This function first sets the parameter *RepeatedVertex* to false. If this is not the first facet, the function then checks each of the present vertex coordinates against the corresponding coordinate of each of the other vertices in the list. If a set of coordinates matches, *RepeatedVertex* is set to true and the function terminates. If no match is obtained, the function ends with *RepeatedVertex* set to false. Getting back to the *AddVertex* function, if a matching vertex is reported, its number is stored as the present vertex number in the facet description and the function ends. If a match was not reported, either because we weren't supposed to check for matching or because no match was found, then the current vertex is stored in the vertex data array and is scaled and plotted to the screen. Finally, its number is stored as the present vertex number in the facet description, its number is set as the last vertex number, and the index for the next vertex is incremented.

Initializing Before Making Vertices

Before running any of the programs which create facets and vertices, some initialization needs to be done. The function *InitVertexMaker* performs these tasks. First, the functions *InitPerspective*, *InitPlotting*, and *InitGraphics* are called to set up in the graphics mode for plotting a perspective scene. Next, *PutAxisAndPalette* is called, to set up for displaying the axes and the color palette on the screen, and then *AxisAndPalette* is called to actually display this information. The function *InitVertexBuffer* is then called to clear the vertex buffer so that it is ready to receive new data. Finally, *RepeatedVertexCheck* is set to true so that vertices will not be repeated in the list.

```
/* ShpMk.Inc

            Addition of Vertices to Objects

      Original Material by Christopher D. Watkins

            'C' Conversion by Larry Sharp

   ReduceRepeatedVerticies - switch repeated vertex check
   AddVertex          - adds vertex to database
*/

Boolean RepeatedVertexCheck;
Boolean RepeatedVertex;
int OldVertexNum;

void ReduceRepeatedVerticies(Boolean Repeated)
{
  RepeatedVertexCheck=Repeated;
}

void CheckForRepeatingVerticies(int x, int y, int z)
{
  RepeatedVertex=false;
  if(FacetNum>1)
  {
    for(OldVertexNum=VertexNum-1; OldVertexNum>=1;
   OldVertexNum—)
    {
      if((Vertex[OldVertexNum][0]==x) &&
         (Vertex[OldVertexNum][1]==y) &&
         (Vertex[OldVertexNum][2]==z))
      {
         RepeatedVertex=true;
         break;
      }
    }
  }
}
```

```
void AddVertex(float xr, float yr, float zr)
{
  Boolean XError, YError, ZError;
  int x, y, z;
  float sc;

  if((xr<-1.0) || (xr>1.0))
    XError=true;
  else
    XError=false;
  if((yr<-1.0) || (yr>1.0))
    YError=true;
  else
    YError=false;
  if((zr<-1.0) || (zr>1.0))
    ZError=true;
  else
    ZError=false;
  if(XError || YError || ZError)
  {
    sound(1000);
    delay(1000);
    nosound();
    ungetch(32);
    ExitGraphics();
    printf("Out of Range -1 to +1 in ");
    if(XError)
      puts("X !");
    else
    {
      if(YError)
        puts("Y !");
      else
        puts("Z !");
    }
    printf("\n\n\n\nHit any key to exit....\n");
    getch();
    exit(1);
  }
  x=Round((float)ScaleData*xr);
```

```
    y=Round((float)ScaleData*yr);
    z=Round((float)ScaleData*zr);
    if(RepeatedVertexCheck)
      CheckForRepeatingVerticies(x, y, z);
    else
      RepeatedVertex=false;
    if(!(RepeatedVertex))
    {
      VecInt(x, y, z, Vertex[VertexNum]);
      sc=100.0/(float)ScaleData;
      CartesianPlot3D(sc*(float)x, sc*(float)y, sc*(float)z, 215);
      Facet[(FacetNum*5)+VertexNumInFacet]=VertexNum;
      LastVertex=VertexNum;
      ++VertexNum;
    }
    else
      Facet[(FacetNum*5)+VertexNumInFacet]=OldVertexNum;
    ++VertexNumInFacet;
  }

/*
  ┌──────────────────────────────────────────────────────────┐
  │            Initialization of Vertex Database Maker        │
  └──────────────────────────────────────────────────────────┘

   InitVertexMaker - calls routines required to generate an
                                              object database
*/

void InitVertexMaker()
{
  InitPerspective(false, 0, 0, 500, 500);
  InitPlotting(215, 18);
  InitGraphics();
  PutAxisAndPalette(true);
  AxisAndPalette();
  InitVertexBuffer();
  ReduceRepeatedVerticies(true);
}
```

Figure 9-1. Listing of *ShpMk.Inc* File

Creating Objects with the *MakeObj.c* Program

The *MakeObj.c* program, when compiled, gives you the opportunity to create an object data file with a certain amount of computer assistance. This program asks you to name the data file, and then asks for the number of facets. Next, it displays the palette and axes on the screen and allows you to enter all of the necessary vertices (four for each facet). It plots each of these vertices on the screen and then creates an object data file from them.

The program is listed in Figure 9-2. It begins by displaying, "Make Object Databases" followed by a couple of blank lines followed by, "Enter File Name => ". The program then stores the current cursor position. At this point, the user should type in the name that he wants to assign to the new object data file. It may be any acceptable eight-character DOS file name. It should not include an extension.

If, at this point, only the *Ent* key is hit, the program will do the following: First, it will automatically supply the file name N*ewObj*. Then it will return to the stored cursor position and write "NewObj" to the screen. If a file name is entered, it will already be displayed on the screen. The program then adds to the file name the extension *.DAT*. Next, three lines are skipped and the program displays, "Number of Facets=> ". The user then must enter the number of facets of which the object is to be comprised. The function *InitVertexMaker*, which was described earlier in this chapter, is then called to prepare to generate the facet information, including entering the graphics mode and displaying the coordinate axes and color palette on the screen. The program then sets the values of some parameters. *VertexNum* is set to one and *VertexNumInFacet* is set to one. This indicates that we are currently ready to enter data for the first vertex, which is also the first vertex in the facet. The program also initializes La*stFacet*, the number of the last facet with the number of facets that was entered above. The parameter *LastVertexNumInFacet* is set to four, so that all facets used in this program must have four vertices. (If you want a triangular facet, you can get around this very easily by specifying two sequential vertices to be at the same coordinates.) Finally, *LastVertex* is set to the product of the number of facets and the number of vertices per facet. The program is now ready to process vertex data.

For each of the facets that comprise your object, you need to enter a set of three coordinates for each of the four facets. Remember that each coordinate must be between –1 and +1. The coordinates are separated by a space, and after each set, the *Ent* key is hit. When you have entered all of the vertices, the program will give a beep. If you then hit *Ent* again, the program will call the function *SaveData*, which was described in Chapter 4, and which will save your object to the file that you designated. The program then calls *ExitGraphics* to return to the text display mode and then ends.

```
/* MakeObj.c

                           Make Objects

*/

#include "stdio.h"
#include "dos.h"
#include "conio.h"
#include "math.h"
#include "string.h"
#include "alloc.h"
#include "math.inc"
#include "graph.inc"
#include "model.inc"
#include "shpmk.inc"

Name ObjF;

void GetObjF()
{
  int i;
  Byte x, y;

  printf("\nEnter File Name -> ");
  x=wherex();
  y=wherey();
  gets(ObjF);
  if(!(strcmp(ObjF, "")))
  {
    strcpy(ObjF, "NEWOBJ");
```

```
    gotoxy(x, y);
    puts(ObjF);
  }
  puts("");
  strcat(ObjF, ".DAT");
  strupr(ObjF);
}

int NumberOfFacets;

void GetNumberOfFacets()
{
  printf("\nNumber of Facets => ");
  scanf("%d", &NumberOfFacets);
}

void SetupObject(int NumOfFacets)
{
  VertexNum=1;
  VertexNumInFacet=1;
  LastFacet=NumOfFacets;
  LastVertexNumInFacet=4;
  LastVertex=LastFacet*LastVertexNumInFacet;
}

void MakeObjectDataBase()
{
  int T;
  float x, y, z;

  for(FacetNum=1; FacetNum<=LastFacet; FacetNum++)
  {
    for(T=1; T<=LastVertexNumInFacet; T++)
    {
      scanf("%f %f %f", &x, &y, &z);
      AddVertex(x, y, z);
    }
    VertexNumInFacet=1;
  }
}
```

```
/*
┌──────────────────────────────────────────────┐
│                 Main Program                 │
└──────────────────────────────────────────────┘
*/

void main()
{
  Facet=farcalloc(((MaxFacet+1)*(MaxVertexNumInFacet+1)),
   sizeof(int));
  Title();
  printf("Make Object Databases\n\n");
  GetObjF();
  GetNumberOfFacets();
  InitVertexMaker();
  SetupObject(NumberOfFacets);
  MakeObjectDataBase();
  SaveData(ObjF);
  ExitGraphics();
  farfree(Facet);
}
```

Figure 9-2. Listing of *MakeObjs.c* Program

This all sounds pretty simple, but its a little more complicated than it looks. Although each different vertex that you enter is displayed on the screen, unless you have quite a few of them, the display may not tell you very much. Furthermore, you really need to have the coordinates of every vertex well-determined before beginning, and to know precisely which vertices make up each facet and in what order they are to be entered. The problems with not having fully pinned down this data are as follows. First, if any one of your vertex coordinates is out of range (less than –1 or greater than +1) the program will terminate and you will have to fix the problem and begin all over again. Second, if you make a mistake on a line, you can correct it, but once you hit the *Ent* key, its too late for that line. To correct the error, you have to quit and start all over again. Third, if you have an error in the vertex coordinates that causes the vertex to appear in the wrong place on the screen, the same situation occurs, namely its too late to correct so you need to quit and begin again from the beginning. Finally, if all of your vertex information is correct, but you don't assign the correct vertices to a facet, or if you have the right vertices but not in the right order, when you finally use the data file in the *Model.c* program to generate a scene you will find that the does not look like you wanted it to. You will then need to identify your error and regenerate the file from scratch. You can see from this that while manually entering the coordinates for each vertex of each facet is a feasible way of generating the data file for an object, some computer assistance in generating such files would be highly desirable. In the next few sections, we are going to describe some computer programs for generating the data files for various types of objects. Of course, if you bought the program disk that goes with this book, you will have the data files for these objects already, and will therefore not really need the programs themselves. However, the programs provide you with some good techniques for designing your own computer programs to generate data files for new objects that are not included in this book.

Generating a Cone or Pyramid Data File

The program *ConePyrm.c* is used to generate the object data files for both a pyramid and a cone. This program is listed in Figure 9-3.

The program begins by calling *InitVertexMaker* to do the initialization necessary before making an object data file. It then calls the function *SetupCone*. The parameter passed to this function is the number of facets to be used. It must be an even number that divides into 360 without a remainder. At this first pass, we are generating the file *Pyramid.DAT*, which will generate a pyramid. Thus there are only four facets. The function *SetUpCone* first sets starting values into the variables *VertexNum*, *VertexNumInFacet*, *Last Facet*, *LastVertexNumInFacet*, and *LastVertex* in the same way that these parameters were set up in the program described above. It then creates the parameters *DTheta* and *HalfDTheta* which represent angular increments around the base of the cone. The parameter *Theta* is then set to the starting angular position.

Getting back to the main program, the function *MakeConeDataBase* is called next. This function begins with a *for* loop which is iterated for each facet. It adds the four vertices for the facet to the vertex list. These vertices are located at (*cos*(*Theta* – *HalfDTheta*), *sin*(*theta* – *HalfDTheta*), –*1*), (*cos*(*Theta* + *HalfDTheta*), *sin*(*theta*

+ *HalfDTheta*), *–1*), (*0*, *0*, *–1*), and (*0*, *0*, *–1*). Thus each facet is a triangle having a base that is a straight-line segment approximating a short length of the circle that is the base of the cone and having an apex that is the apex of the cone. The function then increments *Theta* by *DTheta*, resets *VertexNumInFacet* to one, and then loops again until all facets have been processed. After the loop is complete, the function E*ndCap* is called to generate the cap at the base of the pyramid or cone. This function first determines the number of facets that will be on the end cap, which is one less than half the number of facets that were used for the rest of the cone surface. It then set up the initial position of the angle *Theta*. Then a *for* loop is run which iterates once for each facet. Each facet is a trapezoid that has as its two sides straight-line segments that approximate a short segment of the circle. When these trapezoids are stacked, they produce an approximation of the circular surface. At the end of each iteration of the loop, Ver*texNumInFacet* is reset to one and *Theta* is increased by *DTheta*. The function ends when the loop has completed its iterations, returning to *MakeConeDataBase*, which also ends, returning to the main program. The main program then calls S*aveData* to create the pyramid object data file and save all of the vertex and facet data to it. The functions S*etupCone*, *MakeConeDatabase*, and *SaveData* are then called again to repeat the entire process with 180 facets to create the object data file for a cone. The program then returns to the text display mode and ends.

```
/* ConePyrm.c

            Cone and Pyramid Database Generator

            Program by Christopher D. Watkins

              'C' Conversion by Larry Sharp

*/

#include "stdio.h"
#include "dos.h"
#include "conio.h"
#include "math.h"
```

```
#include "string.h"
#include "alloc.h"
#include "math.inc"
#include "graph.inc"
#include "model.inc"
#include "shpmk.inc"

int Theta, DTheta, HalfDTheta;

void SetupCone(int NumOfFacets)
{
  VertexNum=1;
  VertexNumInFacet=1;
  LastFacet=NumOfFacets;
  LastVertexNumInFacet=4;
  LastVertex=LastFacet*LastVertexNumInFacet;
  DTheta=360/LastFacet;
  HalfDTheta=DTheta/2;
  Theta=HalfDTheta;
}

int NumFacetsOnEndCap, T;

void EndCap()
{
  int tmp;

  NumFacetsOnEndCap=LastFacet/2-1;
  tmp=NumFacetsOnEndCap&1;
  if(tmp==1)
    Theta=-90+HalfDTheta;
  else
    Theta=-90+DTheta;
  if(LastFacet==4)
    NumFacetsOnEndCap=2;
  for(T=1; T<=NumFacetsOnEndCap; T++)
  {
    AddVertex(CosD(Theta+HalfDTheta), SinD(Theta+HalfDTheta),
                                                          -1.0);
    AddVertex(CosD(Theta-HalfDTheta), SinD(Theta-HalfDTheta),
                                                          -1.0);
```

```
    AddVertex(CosD(180-Theta+HalfDTheta), SinD(180-
         Theta+HalfDTheta), -1.0);
    AddVertex(CosD(180-Theta-HalfDTheta), SinD(180-Theta-
         HalfDTheta), -1.0);
    ++FacetNum;
    ++LastFacet;
    VertexNumInFacet=1;
    Theta+=DTheta;
  }
}

void MakeConeDatabase()
{
  for(FacetNum=1; FacetNum<=LastFacet; FacetNum++)
  {
    AddVertex(CosD(Theta-HalfDTheta), SinD(Theta-HalfDTheta),
      -1.0);
    AddVertex(CosD(Theta+HalfDTheta), SinD(Theta+HalfDTheta),
      -1.0);
    AddVertex(0.0, 0.0, 1.0);
    AddVertex(0.0, 0.0, 1.0);
    Theta+=DTheta;
    VertexNumInFacet=1;
  }
  EndCap();
}

/*
                              Main Program
*/

void main()
{
  Facet=farcalloc(((MaxFacet+1)*(MaxVertexNumInFacet+1)),
   sizeof(int));
  InitVertexMaker();
  SetupCone(4);
  MakeConeDatabase();
```

```
    SaveData("PYRAMID.DAT");
    SetupCone(180);
    MakeConeDatabase();
    SaveData("CONE.DAT");
    ExitGraphics();
    farfree(Facet);
}
```

Figure 9-3 Listing of Program to Generate Cone or Pyramid

Generating the Data File for a Cylinder

The program *Cylinder.c* is used to generate the object data file for a cylinder. This program is listed in Figure 9-4. The program begins by calling *InitVertexMaker* to do the initialization necessary before making an object data file. It then calls the function *SetupCylinder.* The parameter passed to this function is the number of facets to be used. It must be a an even number that divides into 360 without a remainder. This program currently uses 90 facets.

The function *SetUpCylinder* first sets starting values into the variables *VertexNum, VertexNumInFacet, Last Facet, LastVertexNumInFacet*, and *LastVertex* in the same way that these parameters were set up in the program described above. It then creates the parameters *DTheta* and *HalfDTheta* which represent angular increments around the base of the cone. The parameter *Theta* is then set to the starting angular position.

Getting back to the main program, the function *MakeCylinderDatabase* is called next. This function begins with a *for* loop which is iterated for each facet. It adds the four vertices for the facet to the vertex list. These vertices are located at *(cos(Theta – HalfDTheta), sin(Theta – HalfDTheta), –1), (cos(Theta + HalfDTheta), sin(Theta + HalfDTheta), +1).* Thus each facet is a rectangle having a base that is a straight-line segment approximating a short length of the circle that is the base of the cylinder and having a top that is a straight-line segment approximating a short length of the circle that is the top of the cylinder. The function then increments *Theta* by *DTheta*, resets *VertexNumInFacet* to one, and then loops again until all facets have been processed.

After the loop is complete, the function *EndCaps* is called to generate the caps at the top and bottom of the cylinder. This function first determines the number of facets that will be on the end cap, which is one less than half the number of facets that were used for the rest of the cone surface. It then sets up the initial position of the angle *Theta*. Then a *for* loop is run which is iterated once for each facet. Each facet is a trapezoid that has as its two sides straight-line segments that approximate a short segment of the circle. When these trapezoids are stacked, they produce an approximation of the circular surface. At the end of each iteration of the loop, V*ertexNumInFacet* is reset to one and *Theta* is increased by *DTheta*. The function ends when the loop has completed its iterations, returning to *MakeCylinderDatabase*, which also ends, returning to the main program. The main program then calls S*aveData* to create the cylinder object data file and save all of the vertex and facet data to it. The program then returns to the text display mode and ends.

```
/* Cylinder.c

           Cylinder Database Generator

       Program by Christopher D. Watkins

          'C' Conversion by Larry Sharp

*/

#include "stdio.h"
#include "dos.h"
#include "conio.h"
#include "math.h"
#include "string.h"
#include "alloc.h"
#include "math.inc"
#include "graph.inc"
#include "model.inc"
#include "shpmk.inc"

int Theta, DTheta, HalfDTheta;
```

```
void SetupCylinder(int NumOfFacets)
{
  VertexNum=1;
  VertexNumInFacet=1;
  LastFacet=NumOfFacets;
  LastVertexNumInFacet=4;
  LastVertex=LastFacet*LastVertexNumInFacet;
  DTheta=360/LastFacet;
  HalfDTheta=DTheta/2;
  Theta=HalfDTheta;
}

int NumFacetsOnEndCap, T;

void EndCaps()
{
  int tmp;

  NumFacetsOnEndCap=LastFacet/2-1;
  tmp=NumFacetsOnEndCap&1;
  if(tmp==1)
    Theta=-90+HalfDTheta;
  else
    Theta=-90+DTheta;
  for(T=1; T<=NumFacetsOnEndCap; T++)
  {
    AddVertex(CosD(Theta-HalfDTheta), SinD(Theta-HalfDTheta),
                                                          1.0);
    AddVertex(CosD(Theta+HalfDTheta), SinD(Theta+HalfDTheta),
                                                          1.0);
    AddVertex(CosD(180-Theta-HalfDTheta), SinD(180-Theta-
                                              HalfDTheta), 1.0);
    AddVertex(CosD(180-Theta+HalfDTheta), SinD(180-
                                         Theta+HalfDTheta), 1.0);
    ++FacetNum;
    ++LastFacet;
    VertexNumInFacet=1;
    AddVertex(CosD(Theta+HalfDTheta), SinD(Theta+HalfDTheta),
                                                         -1.0);
    AddVertex(CosD(Theta-HalfDTheta), SinD(Theta-HalfDTheta),
                                                         -1.0);
```

```
    AddVertex(CosD(180-Theta+HalfDTheta), SinD(180-
      Theta+HalfDTheta), -1.0);
    AddVertex(CosD(180-Theta-HalfDTheta), SinD(180-Theta-
      HalfDTheta), -1.0);
    ++FacetNum;
    ++LastFacet;
    VertexNumInFacet=1;
    Theta+=DTheta;
  }
}

void MakeCylinderDatabase()
{
  for(FacetNum=1; FacetNum<=LastFacet; FacetNum++)
  {
    AddVertex(CosD(Theta-HalfDTheta), SinD(Theta-HalfDTheta),
      -1.0);
    AddVertex(CosD(Theta+HalfDTheta), SinD(Theta+HalfDTheta),
      -1.0);
    AddVertex(CosD(Theta+HalfDTheta), SinD(Theta+HalfDTheta),
      1.0);
    AddVertex(CosD(Theta-HalfDTheta), SinD(Theta-HalfDTheta),
      1.0);
    Theta+=DTheta;
    VertexNumInFacet=1;
  }
  EndCaps();
}

/*
 ╔════════════════════════════════════════════════════════╗
 ║                    Main Program                        ║
 ╚════════════════════════════════════════════════════════╝
*/

void main()
{
  Facet=farcalloc(((MaxFacet+1)*(MaxVertexNumInFacet+1)),
   sizeof(int));
  InitVertexMaker();
```

```
    SetupCylinder(90);
    MakeCylinderDatabase();
    SaveData("CYLINDER.DAT");
    ExitGraphics();
    farfree(Facet);
}
```

Figure 9-4. Listing of Program to Generate Cylinders

Generating the Data File for a Hemisphere

The program *HmSphere.c* is used to generate the object data file for a hemisphere. This program is listed in Figure 9-5. The program begins by calling *InitVertexMaker* to do the initialization necessary before making an object data file. It then calls the function *SetupHemiSphere*. Two parameters are passed to this function. The first is the number of facets in a horizontal row projected onto the face of the hemisphere and the second is the number of facets in a vertical row. This program sets these values to 60 and 45 respectively, which are the maximum allowable values.

The function *SetupHemiSphere* first sets starting values into the variables *VertexNum*, *VertexNumInFacet*, *LastFacet*, *LastVertexNumInFacet*, and *LastVertex* in the same way that these parameters were set up in the program described above. It then creates the parameters *DTheta* and *HalfDTheta* which represent angular increments horizontally around the base of the hemisphere. The parameter *Theta* is then set to the starting angular position. The function then creates the parameters *DPhi* and *HalfDPhi* which represent angular increments vertically on the hemisphere surface. The parameter *Phi* is then set to the starting angular position.

Getting back to the main program, the function *MakeHemiSphereDatabase* is called next. This function begins by setting *Horz* and *Vert* to one. It then continues with a for loop which is iterated for each facet. At each iteration, the loop begins be computing the sine and cosine of *Phi* and then scaling them appropriately. It then adds the four vertices for the facet to the vertex list. The vertex coordinates are a little too complicated to list here, especially since new values are computed for the sine and cosine of *Phi* before the third and fourth vertices are calculated. However, the vertex coordinate locations should be clear from looking at the program listing. The function then resets *VertexNumInFacet* to one, increments *Horz* by one, and increases *Theta* by *DTheta*. The value of *Horz* is then compared with the maximum allowable value. If the maximum has been reached, *Horz* is reset to one, *Vert* is incremented, *Theta* is reset to its starting value, and *Phi* is increased by *DPhi*. The function then loops again until all facets have been processed. After the loop is complete, the function *EndCap* is called to generate the cap at the base of the hemisphere. This function is very similar to the function of the same name that was used in generating the pyramid and cone, except that the number of facets is determined from the number of horizontal facets rather than the entire number of facets in the sphere, and that the location of the end cap is at zero in the *z* plane rather than at −1. After *EndCap* is complete, we return to the main program, which then calls *SaveData* to create the hemisphere object data file and save all of the vertex and facet data to it. The program then returns to the text display mode and ends.

```
/* HmSphere.c

                 Hemisphere Database Generator

              Program by Christopher D. Watkins

                 'C' Conversion by Larry Sharp

*/

#include "stdio.h"
#include "dos.h"
#include "conio.h"
#include "math.h"
#include "string.h"
#include "alloc.h"
#include "math.inc"
#include "graph.inc"
#include "model.inc"
#include "shpmk.inc"
```

```
int Theta, DTheta, HalfDTheta;
int Phi, DPhi, HalfDPhi, Scale;
int HorzLoop, VertLoop;
int Horz, Vert;
float SinPhi, CosPhi;
int NumFacetsOnEndCap, T;

void EndCap()
{
  NumFacetsOnEndCap=HorzLoop/2-1;
  if((NumFacetsOnEndCap&1)==1)
    Theta=-90+HalfDTheta;
  else
    Theta=-90+DTheta;
  for(T=1; T<=NumFacetsOnEndCap; T++)
  {
    AddVertex(CosD(Theta+HalfDTheta), SinD(Theta+HalfDTheta),
                                                         0.0);
    AddVertex(CosD(Theta-HalfDTheta), SinD(Theta-HalfDTheta),
                                                         0.0);
    AddVertex(CosD(180-Theta+HalfDTheta),    SinD(180-
                                  Theta+HalfDTheta), 0.0);
    AddVertex(CosD(180-Theta-HalfDTheta),    SinD(180-Theta-
                                         HalfDTheta), 0.0);
    ++FacetNum;
    ++LastFacet;
    VertexNumInFacet=1;
    Theta+=DTheta;
  }
}

void SetupHemiSphere(int Horizontal, int Vertical)
{
  VertexNum=1;
  VertexNumInFacet=1;
  HorzLoop=Horizontal;
  VertLoop=Vertical;
  LastFacet=HorzLoop*VertLoop;
  LastVertexNumInFacet=MaxVertexNumInFacet;
  LastVertex=LastFacet*LastVertexNumInFacet;
```

```
  DTheta=360/HorzLoop;
  HalfDTheta=DTheta/2;
  Theta=HalfDTheta;
  DPhi=90/VertLoop;
  HalfDPhi=DPhi/2;
  Phi=HalfDPhi;
  Scale=1;
}

void MakeHemiSphereDatabase()
{
  Horz=1;
  Vert=1;
  for(FacetNum=1; FacetNum<=LastFacet; FacetNum++)
  {
        SinPhi=Scale*SinD(Phi+HalfDPhi);
     CosPhi=Scale*CosD(Phi+HalfDPhi);
     AddVertex(SinPhi*CosD(Theta-HalfDTheta),
        SinPhi*SinD(Theta-HalfDTheta), CosPhi);
     AddVertex(SinPhi*CosD(Theta+HalfDTheta),
        SinPhi*SinD(Theta+HalfDTheta), CosPhi);
        SinPhi=Scale*SinD(Phi-HalfDPhi);
     CosPhi=Scale*CosD(Phi-HalfDPhi);
     AddVertex(SinPhi*CosD(Theta+HalfDTheta),
        SinPhi*SinD(Theta+HalfDTheta), CosPhi);
     AddVertex(SinPhi*CosD(Theta-HalfDTheta),
        SinPhi*SinD(Theta-HalfDTheta), CosPhi);
     Theta+=DTheta;
     VertexNumInFacet=1;
     ++Horz;
     if(Horz>HorzLoop)
     {
        Horz=1;
        ++Vert;
        Theta=HalfDTheta;
        Phi+=DPhi;
      }
  }
  EndCap();
}
```

```
/*
┌─────────────────────────────────────────┐
│              Main Program               │
└─────────────────────────────────────────┘
*/

void main()
{
  Facet=farcalloc(((MaxFacet+1)*(MaxVertexNumInFacet+1)),
   sizeof(int));
  InitVertexMaker();
  SetupHemiSphere(60, 45);
  MakeHemiSphereDatabase();
  SaveData("HMSPHERE.DAT");
  ExitGraphics();
  farfree(Facet);
}
```

Figure 9-5. Listing of Program to Generate Hemispheres

Generating the Data File for a Sphere

The program *Sphere.c* is used to generate the object data file for a sphere. This program is listed in Figure 9-6.

The program begins by calling *InitVertexMaker* to do the initialization necessary before making an object data file. It then calls the function *SetupSphere*. Two parameters are passed to this function. The first is the number of facets in a horizontal row projected onto the face of the hemisphere and the second is the number of facets in a vertical row. This program sets these values to 60 and 45 respectively, which are the maximum allowable values.

The function *SetupSphere* first sets starting values into the variables *VertexNum*, *VertexNumInFacet, Last Facet, LastVertexNumInFacet*, and *LastVertex* in the same way that these parameters were set up in the program described above. It then creates the parameters *DTheta* and *HalfDTheta* which represent angular increments horizontally around the perimeter of the sphere. The parameter *Theta* is then set to the starting angular position. The function then creates the parameters *DPhi* and

HalfDPhi which represent angular increments vertically on the sphere surface. Next, the parameter *Phi* is set to the starting angular position. The only difference between this function and the corresponding one for the hemisphere is that the vertical facets are made twice as large, so that they cover the full surface of the sphere vertically, instead of covering only half of\the vertical surface.

Getting back to the main program, the function *MakeSphereDataBase* is called next. This function is the same as the function of the same name used in generating the hemisphere earlier. When it is complete, we return to the main program, which then calls *SaveData* to create the sphere object data file (*Sphere.DAT*), and save all of the vertex and facet data to it. The program then returns to the text display mode and ends.

```
/* Sphere.c

                    Sphere Database Generator

               Program by Christopher D. Watkins

                 'C' Conversion by Larry Sharp

*/

#include "stdio.h"
#include "dos.h"
#include "conio.h"
#include "math.h"
#include "string.h"
#include "alloc.h"
#include "math.inc"
#include "graph.inc"
#include "model.inc"
#include "shpmk.inc"

int Theta, DTheta, HalfDTheta;
int Phi, DPhi, HalfDPhi;
int HorzLoop, VertLoop;
int Horz, Vert;
float SinPhi, CosPhi;
```

```
void SetupSphere(int Horizontal, int Vertical)
{
  VertexNum=1;
  VertexNumInFacet=1;
  HorzLoop=Horizontal;
  VertLoop=Vertical;
  LastFacet=HorzLoop*VertLoop;
  LastVertexNumInFacet=MaxVertexNumInFacet;
  LastVertex=LastFacet*LastVertexNumInFacet;
  DTheta=360/HorzLoop;
  HalfDTheta=DTheta/2;
  Theta=HalfDTheta;
  DPhi=180/VertLoop;
  HalfDPhi=DPhi/2;
  Phi=HalfDPhi;
}

void MakeSphereDatabase()
{
  Horz=1;
  Vert=1;
  for(FacetNum=1; FacetNum<=LastFacet; FacetNum++)
  {
    SinPhi=SinD(Phi+HalfDPhi);
    CosPhi=CosD(Phi+HalfDPhi);
    AddVertex(SinPhi*CosD(Theta-HalfDTheta),
   SinPhi*SinD(Theta-HalfDTheta), CosPhi);
    AddVertex(SinPhi*CosD(Theta+HalfDTheta),
   SinPhi*SinD(Theta+HalfDTheta), CosPhi);
       SinPhi=SinD(Phi-HalfDPhi);
    CosPhi=CosD(Phi-HalfDPhi);
    AddVertex(SinPhi*CosD(Theta+HalfDTheta),
   SinPhi*SinD(Theta+HalfDTheta), CosPhi);
    AddVertex(SinPhi*CosD(Theta-HalfDTheta),
   SinPhi*SinD(Theta-HalfDTheta), CosPhi);
    Theta+=DTheta;
    VertexNumInFacet=1;
    ++Horz;
    if(Horz>HorzLoop)
    {
```

```
        Horz=1;
        ++Vert;
        Theta=HalfDTheta;
        Phi+=DPhi;
      }
    }
  }

/*
    ┌──────────────────────────────────────────────┐
    │                 Main Program                 │
    └──────────────────────────────────────────────┘
*/

void main()
{
  Facet=farcalloc(((MaxFacet+1)*(MaxVertexNumInFacet+1)),
   sizeof(int));
  InitVertexMaker();
  SetupSphere(60, 45);
  MakeSphereDatabase();
  SaveData("SPHERE.DAT");
  ExitGraphics();
  farfree(Facet);
}
```

Figure 9-6. Program to Generate Spheres

Generating Data Files for Equations

The program *PlotEqns.c* is used to generate the object data files for a grid and for four different equations. Once you become familiar with the method used, it will be quite easy for you to adapt the program for other equations. The program is listed in Figure 9-7.

At the beginning of the program is a list of the values for the parameter *ObjF*, which is the name of the object file, and for the parameters *Span*, *Contour*, and *Offset* for the grid (*Grid.DAT*), and four different equations, depending on appropriate editing of this source file. In addition, for each is listed the function *zf*, which determines the value of *z* as a function of *x* and *y* for the particular case. For each run of the program, all of these sets of values except one are commented out.

The program begins by calling *InitVertexMaker* to do the initialization necessary before making an object data file. It then calls the function *SetupPlotEqn,* passing it the parameters for the left and right *x* boundaries (which are set to –*Span* and *Span*), the bottom and top *y* boundaries (which are set to –*Span* and *Span*), the number of facets in the horizontal direction (which is set to *Contour*), and the number of facets in the vertical direction (which is set to *Contour*).

The function *SetupPlotEqn* first sets starting values into the variables *VertexNum*, *VertexNumInFacet*, *Last Facet*, *LastVertexNumInFacet*, and *LastVertex* in the same way that these parameters were set up in the program described above. The function next creates scaling factors *sx*, *sy*, and *sz*. It then creates the parameters *Dx* and *HalfDx* which represent increments in the horizontal direction and *Dy* and *HalfDy* which represent increments in the vertical direction. The limits *Xlft*, *Ytop*, *Xrgt*, and *Ybot* which were passed to this function are then stored in global parameters *ix, iy*, *ex*, and *ey* respectively, completing the action of the function. Getting back to the main program, the function *MakePlotEqnDatabase* is called next. This function begins by setting *X* to *ix* and *Y* to *iy*. It then continues with a pair of nested *do* loops which are iterated until every value of *X* and *Y* is treated, thus covering all facets of the displayed object. At each iteration, for each of the four vertices of the facet, the value of *z* is computed and then the vertex is added to the vertex list.

The coordinates for each of the four vertices of a facet are clear from the program listing. The inner loop resets *VertexNumInFacet* to one and increases the value of *Y* for each iteration. When the maximum value is reached, the outer loop increases the value of *X* and resets *Y*. After all vertices have been treated, we return to the main program, which then calls *SaveData* to create the grid and equation object data file and save all of the vertex and facet data to it. The program then returns to the text display mode and ends.

```
/* PlotEqns.c

        Equation Plot and Grid Database Generator

          Program by Christopher D. Watkins

            'C' Conversion by Larry Sharp

*/

#include "stdio.h"
#include "dos.h"
#include "conio.h"
#include "math.h"
#include "string.h"
#include "alloc.h"
#include "math.inc"
#include "graph.inc"
#include "model.inc"
#include "shpmk.inc"

/*

                    Equations

*/


char ObjF[]="GRID.DAT";

#define Span 5
#define Contour 13
#define Offset 0.5

float zf()
{
  return(0.0);
}
```

```
/*
char ObjF[]="PLOTEQN1.DAT";

#define Span 5.0
#define Contour 58.0
#define Offset 0.0

float zf(float x, float y)
{
  float c;

  c=SqrFP(x)+SqrFP(y);
  return(75.0/(c+1.0));
}
*/

/*
char ObjF[]="PLOTEQN2.DAT";

#define Span 5.0
#define Contour 58.0
#define Offset 0.0

float zf(float x, float y)
{
  return(6.0*(cos(x*y*0.7)+1.0));
}
*/

/*
char ObjF[]="PLOTEQN3.DAT";

#define Span 5.0
#define Contour 58.0
#define Offset 0.0

float zf(float x, float y)
{
  float c;
```

```
  c=SqrFP(x)+SqrFP(y);
  return(20.0*(sin(sqrt(c)))+1.0);
}
*/

/*
char ObjF[]="PLOTEQN4.DAT";

#define Span 2.75
#define Contour 50.0
#define Offset 0.0

float zf(float x, float y)
{
  float c;

  c=SqrFP(x)+SqrFP(y)*0.65;
  return(10.0*(1.0+sqrt(c*0.5)+sin(SqrFP(c)*0.1)+sin(x*y)));
}
*/
/*************************************************************/

float Dx, HalfDx;
float Dy, HalfDy;
float x, y, z;
float sx, sy, sz;
float ix, iy;
float ex, ey;

void SetupPlotEqn(float Xlft, float Xrgt,
        float Ybot, float Ytop,
        int HorzContours, int VertContours,
        float offset)
{
  VertexNum=1;
  VertexNumInFacet=1;
  LastFacet=HorzContours*VertContours;
  LastVertexNumInFacet=MaxVertexNumInFacet;
  LastVertex=LastFacet*LastVertexNumInFacet;
  sx=200.0/100.0/(Xrgt-Xlft)*10.0/11.0;
```

```
    sy=200.0/100.0/(Ytop-Ybot)*10.0/11.0;
    sz=1.0/100.0;
    Dx=(Xrgt-Xlft)/(float)(HorzContours-1);
    Dy=(Ybot-Ytop)/(float)(VertContours-1);
    HalfDx=Dx/2.0/(offset+1.0);
    HalfDy=Dy/2.0/(offset+1.0);
    ix=Xlft;
    iy=Ytop;
    ex=Xrgt;
    ey=Ybot;
  }

  void MakePlotEqnDatabase()
  {
    FacetNum=0;
    x=ix;
    do
    {
      y=iy;
      do
      {
        ++FacetNum;
        z=zf((x-HalfDx), (y+HalfDy));
        AddVertex(sx*(x-HalfDx), sy*(y+HalfDy), sz*z);
        z=zf((x+HalfDx), (y+HalfDy));
        AddVertex(sx*(x+HalfDx), sy*(y+HalfDy), sz*z);
        z=zf((x+HalfDx), (y-HalfDy));
        AddVertex(sx*(x+HalfDx), sy*(y-HalfDy), sz*z);
        z=zf((x-HalfDx), (y-HalfDy));
        AddVertex(sx*(x-HalfDx), sy*(y-HalfDy), sz*z);
        VertexNumInFacet=1;
        y+=Dy;
      }
      while(y>=ey);
      x+=Dx;
    }
    while(x<=ex);
  }
```

```
/*
                        Main Program
*/

void main()
{
  Facet=farcalloc(((MaxFacet+1)*(MaxVertexNumInFacet+1)),
   sizeof(int));
  InitVertexMaker();
  SetupPlotEqn(-Span, Span, -Span, Span, Contour, Contour,
   Offset);
  MakePlotEqnDatabase();
  SaveData(ObjF);
  ExitGraphics();
  farfree(Facet);
}
```

Figure 9-7. Program To Create Equation Databases

Generating the Data File for a Toroid

The program *Toroid.c* is used to generate the object data file for a toroid. This program is listed in Figure 9-8.

The program begins by calling *InitVertexMaker* to do the initialization necessary before making an object data file. It then calls the function *SetupToroid*. Two parameters are passed to this function. The first is the number of facets in a horizontal row projected onto the face of the toroid and the second is the number of facets in a vertical row. This program sets these values to 60 and 60 respectively, which are the maximum allowable values.

The function *SetupToroid* first sets starting values into the variables *VertexNum*, *VertexNumInFacet*, *Last Facet*, *LastVertexNumInFacet*, and *LastVertex* in the same way that these parameters were set up in the program described above. It also sets the parameter *HorzLoop* and *VertLoop* to the maximum numbers of horizontal and vertical facets respectively that were passed to it. It then creates the parameters *DTheta* and *HalfDTheta* which represent angular increments horizontally around the base of the toroid. The parameter *Theta* is then set to the starting angular position. The function then creates the parameters *DPhi* and *HalfDPhi* which represent vertical increments vertically on the toroid surface. The parameter Phi is then set to the starting angular position.

Getting back to the main program, the function *MakeToroidDataBase* is called next. This function uses a nested pair of *do* loops to generate the vertices for every one of the facets that make up the toroid. The outer loop sets *Phi* to its starting values and then computes necessary sines and cosines for the current value of *Theta*. The inner loop computes the necessary sines and cosines of *Phi* multiplied by the radius. It then computes the *x*, *y*, and *z* coordinates for each of the four vertices that make up the facet and adds each vertex to the vertex list. It then increases *Phi* by *DPhi* and iterates again until the maximum value of the angle is reached, whereupon it returns to the outer loop. At the end of each iteration of the outer loop, *Theta* is increased by *DTheta* until the maximum value is reached, whereupon the loop and the function terminate. We then return to the main program, which then calls *SaveData* to create the toroid object data file and save all of the vertex and facet data to it. The program then returns to the text display mode and ends.

```
/* Toroid.c

                    Toroid Database Generator

                 Program by Christopher D. Watkins

                   'C' Conversion by Larry Sharp

*/

#include "stdio.h"
#include "dos.h"
#include "conio.h"
#include "math.h"
#include "string.h"
#include "alloc.h"
#include "math.inc"
#include "graph.inc"
```

```
#include "model.inc"
#include "shpmk.inc"

int Theta, DTheta, HalfDTheta;
int Phi, DPhi, HalfDPhi;
int HorzLoop, VertLoop;

void SetupToroid(int Horizontal, int Vertical)
{
  VertexNum==1;
  VertexNumInFacet=1;
  HorzLoop=Horizontal;
  VertLoop=Vertical;
  LastFacet=HorzLoop*VertLoop;
  LastVertexNumInFacet=MaxVertexNumInFacet;
  LastVertex=LastFacet*LastVertexNumInFacet;
  DTheta=360/HorzLoop;
  HalfDTheta=DTheta/2;
  Theta=HalfDTheta+45+45;
  DPhi=360/VertLoop;
  HalfDPhi=DPhi/2;
  Phi=HalfDPhi;
}

void MakeToroidDatabase(float Rho, float R)
{
  float CosThetaMinus, SinThetaMinus;
  float CosThetaPlus, SinThetaPlus;
  float RCosPhiMinus, RSinPhiMinus;
  float RCosPhiPlus, RSinPhiPlus;
  float x, y, z;

  FacetNum=0;
  do
  {
    Phi=HalfDPhi;
    CosThetaMinus=CosD(Theta-HalfDTheta);
    SinThetaMinus=SinD(Theta-HalfDTheta);
    CosThetaPlus=CosD(Theta+HalfDTheta);
    SinThetaPlus=SinD(Theta+HalfDTheta);
```

```
      do
      {
        RCosPhiMinus=R*CosD(Phi-HalfDPhi);
        RSinPhiMinus=R*SinD(Phi-HalfDPhi);
        RCosPhiPlus=R*CosD(Phi+HalfDPhi);
        RSinPhiPlus=R*SinD(Phi+HalfDPhi);
        ++FacetNum;
        x=(Rho+RCosPhiMinus)*CosThetaMinus;
        y=(Rho+RCosPhiMinus)*SinThetaMinus;
        z=RSinPhiMinus;
        AddVertex(x, y, z);
        x=(Rho+RCosPhiMinus)*CosThetaPlus;
        y=(Rho+RCosPhiMinus)*SinThetaPlus;
        z=RSinPhiMinus;
        AddVertex(x, y, z);
        x=(Rho+RCosPhiPlus)*CosThetaPlus;
        y=(Rho+RCosPhiPlus)*SinThetaPlus;
        z=RSinPhiPlus;
        AddVertex(x, y, z);
        x=(Rho+RCosPhiPlus)*CosThetaMinus;
        y=(Rho+RCosPhiPlus)*SinThetaMinus;
        z=RSinPhiPlus;
        AddVertex(x, y, z);
        VertexNumInFacet=1;
        Phi+=DPhi;
      }
      while(Phi<360+HalfDPhi);
      Theta+=DTheta;
    }
    while(Theta<360+HalfDTheta+90);
}

/*
┌──────────────────────────────────────────────────────────┐
│                      Main Program                         │
└──────────────────────────────────────────────────────────┘
*/
void main()
{
  Facet=farcalloc(((MaxFacet+1)*(MaxVertexNumInFacet+1)),
                                              sizeof(int));
```

```
    InitVertexMaker();
    SetupToroid(60, 60);
    MakeToroidDatabase(0.75, 0.25);
    SaveData("TOROID.DAT");
    ExitGraphics();
    farfree(Facet);
}
```

Figure 9-8. Program to Generate Toroids

Generating Data Files for Solids of Revolution

The program *SolOfRev.c* is used to generate the object data files for a number of solids of revolution. This program is listed in Figure 9-9.

Let us suppose that we have a two-dimensional figure that is symmetrical about an axis. Now suppose that we rotate this figure about the axis. The surface produced by the outline of the figure during rotation is a solid of revolution. All sorts of interesting figures can be produced by this technique. The *SolOfRev.c* program provides a technique for generating such solids as well as providing the data to generate a number of interesting object data files. Figure 9-10 shows a two-dimensional shape and the three-dimensional result of rotating it about the *z* axis.

The program begins by calling *InitVertexMaker* to do the initialization necessary before making an object data file. It then calls the function *SetupOfRevolution* . Two parameters are passed to this function. The first is the number of facets in a horizontal row around the circumference of the and the second is the number of facets in a vertical row. This program sets these values to 60 and 60 respectively, which are the maximum allowable values.

The function *SetupSolidOfRevolution* first sets starting values into the variables *VertexNum*, *VertexNumInFacet*, *Last Facet*, *LastVertexNumInFacet*, and *LastVertex* in the same way that these parameters were set up in the program described above. It also sets the parameters *HorzLoop* and *VertLoop* to the maximum numbers of horizontal and vertical facets, respectively, that were passed to it. It then creates the parameters *DTheta* and *HalfDTheta* which represent angular increments horizontally around the base of the toroid. The parameter *Theta* is then set to the starting angular position. Next, the function creates the parameters *DZ* and *HalfDZ* which represent vertical steps on the surface.

Getting back to the main program, the function *MakeOfRevolutionDatabase* is called next. This function first clears *RS* which will contain 60 values that determine the shape of the two dimensional figure that is to be rotated. Next, the function *RadialArray* is called. This function loads the array *RS* with the information needed to describe the two dimensional object and also sets up the name for the object data file. A number of versions of this function are given at the beginning of the listing, each describing a different shaped object. All but one are commented out; if you wish to create one particular object file, you should make sure that its version of this function is the only one *not* commented out. Alternately, you can think up your own version of the function to create a new shape.

Once the function *RadialArray* is complete, the function *DisplayRadialArray* is called. This function displays a silhouette of the desired solid in the lower right corner of the screen. Next, *MakeOfRevolution* uses a nested pair of *do* loops to generate the vertices for every one of the facets that make up the solid of revolution. The outer loop sets *I* to one and then computes necessary sines and cosines for the current value of *Theta* and the current value of *Zs*. The inner loop computes the necessary values for the *z* coordinate. It then computes the *x*, *y*, and *z* coordinates for each of the four vertices that make up the facet and adds each vertex to the vertex list. It then sets *VertexNumberInFacet* to one and increments *I*. When it has cycled through all values of *I*, it returns to the outer loop. At the end of each iteration of the outer loop, *Theta* is increased by *DTheta* until the maximum value is reached, whereupon the loop and the function terminate. We then return to the main program, which then calls *SaveData* to create the solid of revolution object data file and save all of the vertex and facet data to it. The program then returns to the text display mode and ends.

```
/* SolOfRev.c

            Solids of Revolution Database Generator

               Program by Christopher D. Watkins

                 'C' Conversion By Larry Sharp

*/
```

```
#include "stdio.h"
#include "dos.h"
#include "conio.h"
#include "math.h"
#include "string.h"
#include "alloc.h"
#include "math.inc"
#include "graph.inc"
#include "model.inc"
#include "shpmk.inc"

/*
                        Radial Arrays
*/

int I;
float RS[62];


char ObjF[]="LGBEADS.DAT";
void RadialArray()
{
  for(I=1; I<=59; I++)
    RS[I]=SinD(I*10)*0.5+0.5;
  RS[60]=0.05;
}


/*
char ObjF[]="BEADS.DAT";

void RadialArray()
{
  for(I=1; I<=60; I++)
    RS[I]=SinD((I-1)*9)*0.5;
}
*/
/*
```

```
char ObjF[]="FUNNELS.DAT";

void RadialArray()
{
  for(I=1; I<=60; I++)
    RS[I]=sin(sqrt(60.1-I)-0.5)*0.45+0.5;
}
*/

/*
char ObjF[]="MECHPART.DAT";

void RadialArray()
{
  for(I=1; I<=6; I++)
    RS[I]=(float)I/6*0.5+0.1;
  for(I=7; I<=20; I++)
    RS[I]=0.6;
  for(I=21; I<=32; I++)
    RS[I]=0.6+(float)(I-21)/32.0;
  for(I=33; I<=53; I++)
    RS[I]=1.0;
  for(I=54; I<=60; I++)
    RS[I]=0.1;
}
*/

/*
char ObjF[]="ROCKET.DAT";

void RadialArray()
{
  for(I=60; I>=53; I--)
    RS[I]=0.02;
  for(I=52; I>=47; I--)
    RS[I]=(float)(52-I)/52.0+0.05;
  for(I=46; I>=35; I--)
    RS[I]=0.16;
  for(I=34; I>=27; I--)
    RS[I]=(float)(34-I)/34.0+0.19;
```

```
  for(I=26; I>=5; I—)
    RS[I]=0.4;
  for(I=4; I>=1; I—)
    RS[I]=(float)(4-I)/22+0.4;
}
*/

/*
char ObjF[]="CHESPAWN.DAT";
void RadialArray()
{
  for(I=60; I>=44; I—)
    RS[I]=SinD((60-I)*9)*0.6;
  for(I=43; I>=11; I—)
    RS[I]=0.2;
  for(I=10; I>=1; I—)
    RS[I]=0.2+SinD((10-I)*12)*0.5;
}
*/

/*************************************************************/

void DisplayRadialArray()
{
  for(I=1; I<=60; I++)
    Draw(260-Round(60.0*RS[I]), 150-I, 260+Round(60.0*RS[I]),
      150-I, 35);
}

int Theta, DTheta, HalfDTheta;
float Zs, Dz, HalfDz;
int HorzLoop, VertLoop;

void SetupOfRevolution(int Horizontal, int Vertical)
{
  VertexNum=1;
  VertexNumInFacet=1;
  HorzLoop=Horizontal;
  VertLoop=Vertical;
  LastFacet=HorzLoop*(VertLoop-1);
```

```
    LastVertexNumInFacet=MaxVertexNumInFacet;
    LastVertex=LastFacet*LastVertexNumInFacet;
    DTheta=360/HorzLoop;
    HalfDTheta=DTheta/2;
    Theta=HalfDTheta+90;
    Dz=2.0/(float)VertLoop;
    HalfDz=Dz/2.0;
    Zs=HalfDz;
  }

  void MakeOfRevolutionDatabase()
  {
    float CosThetaMinus, SinThetaMinus;
    float CosThetaPlus, SinThetaPlus;
    float ZMinus, ZPlus, x, y, z;

    FacetNum=0;
    for(I=1; I<=60; I++)
      RS[I]=0.0;
    RadialArray();
    DisplayRadialArray();
    do
    {
      I=1;
      CosThetaMinus=CosD(Theta-HalfDTheta);
      SinThetaMinus=SinD(Theta-HalfDTheta);
      CosThetaPlus=CosD(Theta+HalfDTheta);
      SinThetaPlus=SinD(Theta+HalfDTheta);
      Zs=-1.0+HalfDz;
      do
      {
        ZMinus=Zs-HalfDz;
        ZPlus=Zs+HalfDz;
        ++FacetNum;
        x=CosThetaMinus*RS[I];
        y=SinThetaMinus*RS[I];
        z=ZMinus;
        AddVertex(x, y, z);
        x=CosThetaPlus*RS[I];
        y=SinThetaPlus*RS[I];
```

```
        z=ZMinus;
        AddVertex(x, y, z);
        x=CosThetaPlus*RS[I+1];
        y=SinThetaPlus*RS[I+1];
        z=ZPlus;
        AddVertex(x, y, z);
        x=CosThetaMinus*RS[I+1];
        y=SinThetaMinus*RS[I+1];
        z=ZPlus;
        AddVertex(x, y, z);
        VertexNumInFacet=1;
        ++I;
        Zs+=Dz;
      }
      while(I!=60);
      Theta+=DTheta;
    }
    while(Theta<(360+HalfDTheta+90));
}

/*
 ╔══════════════════════════════════════════════════════════════╗
 ║                        Main Program                          ║
 ╚══════════════════════════════════════════════════════════════╝
*/

void main()
{
  Facet=farcalloc(((MaxFacet+1)*(MaxVertexNumInFacet+1)),
   sizeof(int));
  InitVertexMaker();
  SetupOfRevolution(60, 60);
  MakeOfRevolutionDatabase();
  SaveData(ObjF);
  ExitGraphics();
  farfree(Facet);
}
```

Figure 9-9. Program to Generate Solids of Revolution

Figure 9-10. Profile of chess pawn used to generate solid of revolution.

Figure 9-11. Solid Rendering of Chess Pawn

CHAPTER 10

Creating a Scene File

You have now learned how to create data files for generic objects and how to display solid modeled scenes. Since some typical scene data files are supplied on the program disk and are listed in Appendix A, you probably have already produced some interesting scenes on your VGA display. However, you have not yet learned how to generate a scene file of your own so that you can allow your artistic talents full rein. This chapter will describe how to generate your own scene files using the program *ScnMaker.c*, which is listed in Figure 10-1.

Using the *ScnMaker.c* Program

Before we go into a detailed description of the *ScnMaker.c* program, we are going to guide you through how to use the program. As the program progresses, it displays various queries to which you must respond with entries. Although most of the information that you must enter has been described in previous sections, it isn't always easy to put together just what is meant and what is needed when a question appears on the screen. The program sometimes doesn't help too much. For example, if you are supposed to enter an integer and put in a floating point number instead, the program will quit with an error message and you will have to start over. Hopefully, this section will indicate what you have to decide before running the program and will help you to go through the program without errors.

```
/* ScnMaker.c

        Program for Generation of Scene Files for Model.c

              Program by Christopher D. Watkins

                'C' Conversion by Larry Sharp

*/

#include "stdio.h"
#include "dos.h"
#include "conio.h"
#include "string.h"
#include "math.inc"
#include "graph.inc"

/*

                    Keyboard Response Routines

   Response - returns true or false to a Y or N keyboard stroke
*/

#define MaxObjects 30

typedef char Name[20];

char Resp[6];

void Response()
{
  char c;

  strcpy(Resp, "\n");
  while((!(c=='Y')) && (!(c=='N')))
  {
    while(!(kbhit()));
    c=toupper(getch());
  }
```

```
  putch(c);
  if(c=='Y')
    strcpy(Resp, "true");
  else
    strcpy(Resp, "false");
  puts("");
}

void NumberResponse()
{
  char c;

  strcpy(Resp, "\n");
  while(!(isdigit(c)))
  {
    c=getch();
  }
  putch(c);
  Resp[0]=c;
}

/*
╔══════════════════════════════════════════════════════════════╗
║                       Save Scene Data                        ║
╚══════════════════════════════════════════════════════════════╝

   GetSceneFile - get name of scene file
   SaveScene    - save description of scene
*/

FILE *TextDiskFile;
Name SceneFile;

void GetSceneFile()
{
  int i;
  Byte x, y;

  printf("\nEnter File Name -> ");
  x=wherex();
```

```
    y=wherey();
    gets(SceneFile);
    if(!(strcmp(SceneFile, "")))
    {
      strcpy(SceneFile, "TEST");
      gotoxy(x, y);
      puts(SceneFile);
    }
    puts("");
    for(i=0; i<strlen(SceneFile); i++)
      SceneFile[i]=toupper(SceneFile[i]);
    strcat(SceneFile, ".SCN");
  }

  void SaveDescription(Name FileName)
  {
    char Descrip[81];
    int NumbResp;
    Boolean BoolResp;
    float R1, R2, R3, R4;
    int I1, I2, I3, I4;
    Name ObjectsName;
    int T, L1;

    TextDiskFile=fopen(FileName, "w+t");
    printf("Description of the Scene => ");
    gets(Descrip);
    fprintf(TextDiskFile, "%s\n\n", Descrip);
    printf("Perspective Display? ");
    Response();
    fprintf(TextDiskFile, "%s ", Resp);
    if(!(strcmp(Resp, "true")))
    {
      printf("(Mx, My, Mz, D) = ");
      scanf("%d %d %d %d", &I1, &I2, &I3, &I4);
      fprintf(TextDiskFile, "%3d %3d %3d %3d\n", I1, I2, I3, I4);
    }
    else
      fprintf(TextDiskFile, "0.0  0.0  0.0  0.0\n");
    printf("Direction for Viewing\n  Around the z-Axis = ");
```

```
scanf("%d", &NumbResp);
fprintf(TextDiskFile, "%d\n", NumbResp);
printf("  Off the z-Axis = ");
scanf("%d", &NumbResp);
fprintf(TextDiskFile, "%d\n", NumbResp);
printf("\nDirection for Light\n  Around the z-Axis = ");
scanf("%d", &NumbResp);
fprintf(TextDiskFile, "%d\n", NumbResp);
printf("  Off the z-Axis = ");
scanf("%d", &NumbResp);
fprintf(TextDiskFile, "%d\n", NumbResp);
printf("Vertical Sort of Objects? ");
Response();
fprintf(TextDiskFile, "%s\n", Resp);
printf
  ("Place Edge Reflectors at (x=-100, y=-100 and z=-100)? ");
Response();
fprintf(TextDiskFile, "%s\n", Resp);
printf("Place Edge Reflectors at (x=-100, y=-100
  and z=0)? ");
Response();
fprintf(TextDiskFile, "%s\n", Resp);
printf("\nNow add objects to the scene ->\n");
for(T=1; T<=MaxObjects; T++)
{
  printf("Enter the Objects Name => ");
  scanf("%s", &ObjectsName);
  strcat(ObjectsName, ".DAT");
  fprintf(TextDiskFile, "\n%s\n", ObjectsName);
  printf("Color of the Object => ");
  NumberResponse();
  fprintf(TextDiskFile, "%s\n", Resp);
  puts("");
  printf("Scale Factors (Sx Sy Sz) => ");
  scanf("%f %f %f", &R1, &R2, &R3);
  fprintf(TextDiskFile, "%4f %4f %4f\n", R1, R2, R3);
  printf("Rotate Factors (Rx Ry Rz) => ");
  scanf("%f %f %f", &R1, &R2, &R3);
  fprintf(TextDiskFile, "%4f %4f %4f\n", R1, R2, R3);
  printf("Translate Factors (Tx Ty Tz) =>" );
```

```
      scanf("%f %f %f", &R1, &R2, &R3);
      fprintf(TextDiskFile, "%4f %4f %4f\n", R1, R2, R3);
      printf("Reflect this Object in Mirrored Objects? ");
      Response();
      fprintf(TextDiskFile, "%s\n", Resp);
      printf("Allow this Object to be Sorted for Placement? ");
      Response();
      fprintf(TextDiskFile, "%s\n", Resp);
      printf("This Object is a Mirror? ");
      Response();
      fprintf(TextDiskFile, "%s\n", Resp);
      printf("Add another Object to Scene? ");
      Response();
      if(strcmp(Resp, "true"))
        goto L1;
      puts("");
    }
L1:
  fclose(TextDiskFile);
}

void main()
{
  clrscr();
  printf("Program to Generate a Scene File for Model\n\n");
  GetSceneFile();
  SaveDescription(SceneFile);
}
```

Figure 10-1. Listing of the *ScnMaker.c* Program

The program begins by displaying the following:

```
Program to Generate a Scene File for Model

Enter File Name =>
```

At this point, you need to enter an eight-character file name that is acceptable to DOS. This will be the name of your scene file. Don't enter an extension. The program will automatically supply the extension *.SCN*. If you just hit the *Ent* key, instead of entering a file name, the program will name the file *Test*. Next, the program displays:

```
Description of the Scene =>
```

At this point you can type in a line of description for the scene, which will be written to the disk file. This description serves to identify the context of the file, but is not actually used for anything. Next, the program displays:

```
Perspective Display?
```

You will normally want perspective in your scene, since it makes the scene more realistic by causing near objects to appear larger than far ones. If you decide that you want perspective, answer *Y*; otherwise answer *N*. If you selected perspective, the program will next ask you:

```
(Mx My Mz D) =
```

You now need to enter four integers, separated by spaces. The first three integers are the *x*, *y*, and z coordinates of the observer position and the fourth integer is the distance from the observer to the screen. A good place to start is with the values (0 0 500 500). The display will next show:

```
Direction for Viewing
    Around the z-Axis =
```

This is the first of two angles that define the direction in which the viewer is looking (which is not necessarily toward the center of the scene). An integer should be entered. Try 245 as a starting value. Next the display will show:

```
    Off of the z-Axis =
```

This is the second viewing angle. Again, an integer should be entered. A good trial value is 25. The display will then ask:

```
Direction of Light
    Around the z-Axis =
```

This is the first of two angles that determine the direction of the light source that illuminates the scene. The position of the light source will determine how the scene is lighted. Again an integer should be entered. A good trial value is 45. The display will then show:

```
Off the z-Axis =
```

This is the second light source angle. Again an integer should be entered. A good trial value is 45. You will remember that the angles are as defined in Figure 10-2. Next, the program will ask:

```
Vertical Sort of Objects?
```

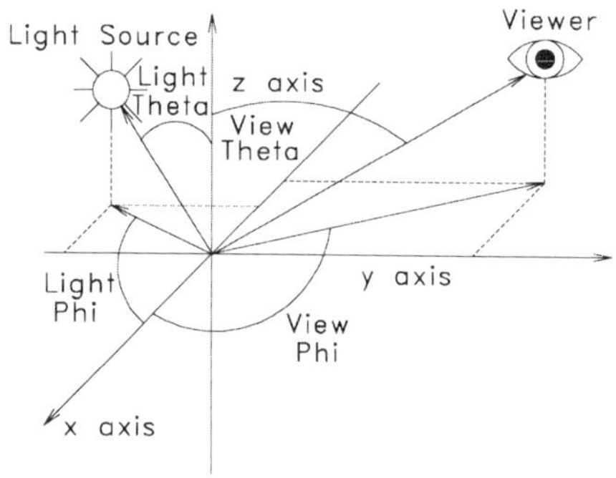

Figure 10-2. Viewer and Light Source Angles

If you want the objects to be sorted so that nearer objects will be written over farther objects, answer *Y*; otherwise answer *N*. The display will then show:

```
Place edge Reflectors at (x=-100, y=-100, and z=-100)?
```

If you respond *Y*, three walls consisting of mirror tiles will be generated at the coordinates shown. If you don't want these walls, respond *N*. The display will then show:

```
Place edge Reflectors at (x=-100, y=-100, and z=0)?
```

If you respond *Y*, three walls consisting of mirror tiles will be generated at the coordinates shown. If you don't want these walls, respond *N*. If you should happen to respond with a *Y* to both the above questions, the second response will override the first when the file is read and the walls will appear at the second location. The display will next show:

```
Now add objects to the scene ->

Enter the Object's Name =>
```

At this point, you must type in the name of an object data file, without the extension. (Note that if you type in the name of the object file incorrectly or if you type in the name of a non-existent object file, the program will save it to the disk file and go right ahead as if nothing were wrong. It is only when you come to create a scene using this data file that you will obtain an error message and have the program bomb out.) The program will then ask:

```
Color Of the Object?
```

You need to respond to this query by entering an integer from 0 to 7, representing colors as shown in Table 10-1. The 256 color palette is set up so that it contains 35 shades of each of the colors from 1 to 7 as well as black. The color you select for the object is the basic color; which of the shades is chosen for each facet will depend upon the position and lighting of the facet. Next the display will show:

```
Scale Factors (Sx Sy Sz) =>
```

Each object is normally sized at about 1 x 1 x 1. This is a very small object on the screen. You can scale up the object to any size you desire, with independent scalings for each of the three coordinates. Do this by entering scaling factors for *x*, *y*, and z. These may be real numbers having up to four places for the non-decimal part of the number and up to four decimal places. The three numbers should be separated by spaces. The scaling is approximately in screen coordinates. The screen is 320 by 200 pixels, so an object scaled up to this size will fill the entire screen. The display will then show:

Rotate factors (Rx Ry Rz) =>

Number	Color
0	Black
1	Blue
2	Green
3	Cyan
4	Red
5	Magenta
6	Brown
7	Gray

Table 10-1. Color Assignments

These represent the rotation of the object, from its nominal position, about the *x*, *y*, and z axes. Each is a real number and is an angle in degrees. If you don 't want any rotation, you can enter

```
0.0  0.0  0.0
```

The display will next show:

```
Translate Factors (Tx Ty Tz) =>
```

These enable you to specify that the object be moved from its nominal position at the center of the screen. You may enter three real numbers, separated by spaces, which represent translation amounts in the *x*, *y*, and z directions. Remember that the screen is 320 by 200 pixels. If you translate much farther than this, the object will likely be off the screen altogether. The display will now ask:

```
Reflect this Object in Mirrored Objects?
```

You will normally want to answer *Y* to this, as an object that doesn't reflect in mirrors is a very peculiar object indeed. The display will then ask:

```
Allow this Object to be Sorted for Placement?
```

Again, the usual answer is *Y* unless you are creating background walls or floors. The display will then ask:

```
This Object is a Mirror?
```

You answer *Y* or *N* to this according to your desires. The display will then ask:

```
Add another Object to Scene?
```

If you answer *Y* to this, the program will loop through all of the queries about an object again, giving you the opportunity to add another object to the scene. If you answer *N*, the program will terminate, saving the scene file.

Keyboard Response Routines

Before describing the main program, let's take a look at the functions that are used to obtain a response from the keyboard. First let's look at the function R*esponse*. This is the same as the function of the same name described in Chapter 7. This function is designed to obtain a response to a question and to make sure that it is either a *Y* or an *N*. It does this by means of two nested *do* loops. The inner loop keeps trying to read a key from the keyboard until the response is other than a null, indicating that a key has been pressed. Then the character received from the keyboard is converted to a capital letter. If it is a *Y* or an *N*, the outer loop terminates; otherwise the loops continue to iterate until an acceptable response is received. Note that whenever *Response* is called in a program, nothing can happen until you type in either *Y*, *y*, *N*, or *n*. When a correct response is received, if it is *Y* the function returns *true*; otherwise, it returns *false*.

Next, let's look at the function *NumberResponse*. This is basically the same in operation as the function described above. The principal difference is that instead of demanding a response of *Y*, *y*, *N*, or *n*, the function requires that one of the number keys from 0 to 9 be pressed. When this occurs, the function converts the ASCII character received from the keyboard to a number from 0 to 9 and returns this number.

The *ScnMaker.c* Program

The *ScnMaker.c* program begins by clearing the screen and then displaying a title. It then calls the function *GetSceneFile*. This function asks for the file name to be entered, and then stores the cursor position. If only the *Ent* key is hit, it names the file *Test*, returns to the stored cursor position and writes *Test* to the screen. It then returns to the main program, which calls the function *SaveScene*.

This function begins by appending the extension *.SCN* to the file name. It then opens a text file having the assigned name for writing. Next, the function writes out to the display, asking for a description of the scene. It reads in a line of text and writes it out to the disk file. It then asks if a perspective display is desired. It writes the response from the keyboard to the disk file. If the response was *Y* (Boolean *true*), the function asks for the parameters *MX*, *My*, *Mz*, and *D*. When these are entered, in the form of three digit integers separated by spaces and followed by the *Ent* key, they are written to the disk file . If perspective was not selected, four zeroes are written to the disk file instead of asking for these parameters. Next, the function asks for the viewing direction around the *z* axis. It reads the keyboard response and writes it to the disk file. Next, the function asks for the viewing direction off of the *z* axis. It reads the keyboard response and writes it to the disk file. Next, the function asks for the light direction around the z axis. It reads the keyboard response and writes it to the disk file. Next, the function asks for the viewing direction off of the *z* axis. It reads the keyboard response and writes it to the disk file. The function then asks if a vertical sort of objects is to be made. It writes the Boolean result obtained from Response to the disk file. The function then asks if edge reflectors are to be placed at (*–100, –100, –100*). It writes the Boolean result obtained from Response to the disk file. The function then asks if edge reflectors are to be placed at (*–100, –100, 0*). It writes the Boolean result obtained from *Response* to the disk file. The function then writes to the display, *Now add objects to the scene ->*. It then begins a *for* loop that iterates once for each of the possible 40 objects that may make up a scene. Within this loop, the function first asks for the name of the object file. It reads this from the keyboard, appends the extension *.DAT* and writes the result to the disk file. It then asks for the object color and writes the return from *NumberResponse* (a number from 0 to 9) to the disk file. It then asks for scale factors and writes the three real numbers that are returned to the disk file. It then asks for rotation factors and writes the three real numbers that are returned to the disk file. It then asks for translate factors and writes the three real numbers that are returned to the disk file. The function then asks if this object should be reflected in mirrored objects. It writes the Boolean result obtained from Response to the disk file. The function then asks if this object may be sorted. It writes the Boolean result obtained from *Response* to the disk file. The function then asks if this object is a mirror. It writes the Boolean result obtained from *Response* to the disk file.

Finally, the function asks if another object should be added to the scene. If the answer is no, the function leaves the loop, closes the disk file, and the entire program ends. Otherwise another iteration of the loop takes place.

Part III

Z BUFFERING AND HORIZON RENDERING

CHAPTER 11

Z Buffering Theory and Database Structure

Z-buffering is a technique for rendering a picture of a three-dimensional scene that makes use of a file that contains a height or *z* value for every point in the scene. If we were to display this file using *x* and *y* to define the pixel location and a color to represent the height, we would have an interesting plasma-like display reminiscent of a contour map. To create a representation of a three-dimensional scene in two-dimensions, we project each point onto the two-dimensional viewing screen. We start with the points farthest from the viewer and then process points nearer and nearer to the viewer. This automatically writes near data over far data, automatically yielding on the display only that data that would actually be seen if this were a photograph. For each point, we compute the color resulting from ambient light, the light impinging on the object at that point, Phong shading, and reflections. The result is the color and intensity for that point.

We need to treat one other problem; although we have an array of points in the original file that are all adjacent to each other, when we project this to the viewing screen, there may be gaps between the adjacent points, consisting of pixels that have no assigned color. We interpolate between the colors of the nearest points to assign colors for these pixels.

The difference between this technique and the solid modeling technique is that here we have an array that defines the entire scene, whereas in the solid modeling technique, we had arrays of facets for every object in the scene.

The file that contains the variables, constants, and functions that are responsible for the file and structure of the z-buffering program is called *Render.Inc*. It is listed in Figure 11-1.

```
/* Render.Inc
╔══════════════════════════════════════════════════════════╗
║                Declare Constants and Variables           ║
╚══════════════════════════════════════════════════════════╝

   HeightBufferScalingFactor - scales height for integer
      manipulation
*/

#define MaxRes 160  /* 160x160 pixels - actually we have memory
                      for 173x173 */

int Height[MaxRes+1][MaxRes+1];
int Scaling;
int MaxHeight;
int Res;

void HeightBufferScalingFactor()
{
  Scaling=32767/MaxHeight;
}

/*
╔══════════════════════════════════════════════════════════╗
║         Clear, Load and Save Height Buffer Data          ║
╚══════════════════════════════════════════════════════════╝

   ClearHeightBuffer - clears all heights to zero
   SaveHeightBuffer  - saves height buffer
   LoadHeightBuffer  - loads height buffer
   GetObjectFile     - get filename
   GetObjectColor    - text representation of color
*/

typedef char Name[32];

FILE *TextDiskFile;
Name ObjectFile;

void ClearHeightBuffer()
{
```

```
  int i, j;

  for(i=0; i<=MaxRes; i++)
  {
    for(j=0; j<=MaxRes; j++)
      Height[i][j]=0;
  }
}

void SaveHeightBuffer(Name FileName)
{
  int i, j;

  strcat(FileName, ".DAT");
  TextDiskFile=fopen(FileName, "w+b");
  if(ferror(TextDiskFile))
  {
    ungetch(32);
    ExitGraphics();
    printf("Can't open file!\n");
    getch();
    exit(1);
  }
  putw(Res, TextDiskFile);
  putw(Scaling, TextDiskFile);
  for(i=0; i<=Res; i++)
  {
    for(j=0; j<=Res; j++)
      putw(Height[i][j], TextDiskFile);
  }
  fclose(TextDiskFile);
}

void LoadHeightBuffer(Name FileName)
{
  int i, j;

  strcat(FileName, ".DAT");
  printf("\nLoading %s\n", FileName);
  TextDiskFile=fopen(FileName, "r+b");
```

```
    Res=getw(TextDiskFile);
    Scaling=getw(TextDiskFile);
    for(i=0; i<=Res; i++)
    {
      for(j=0; j<=Res; j++)
        Height[i][j]=getw(TextDiskFile);
    }
    fclose(TextDiskFile);
  }

  void GetObjectFile()
  {
    int i;
    Byte x, y;

    printf("\nEnter File Name -> ");
    x=wherex();
    y=wherey();
    gets(ObjectFile);
    if(!(strcmp(ObjectFile, "")))
    {
      strcpy(ObjectFile, "MOUNTAIN");
      gotoxy(x, y);
      puts(ObjectFile);
    }
    puts("");
    for(i=0; i<strlen(ObjectFile); i++)
      ObjectFile[i]=toupper(ObjectFile[i]);
  }

  void GetObjectColor(int C)
  {
    switch(C)
    {
      case 0 : puts("Black"); break;
      case 1 : puts("Blue"); break;
      case 2 : puts("Green"); break;
      case 3 : puts("Cyan"); break;
      case 4 : puts("Red"); break;
      case 5 : puts("Magenta"); break;
```

```
        case 6 : puts("Brown/Yellow"); break;
        case 7 : puts("Grey"); break;
    }
}
```

Figure 11-1. Listing of the Render.Inc File

The file begins by defining a few constants, the most important of which is *MaxRes*, which represents the maximum resolution of a square picture produced by the z-buffering technique. Because we want to include the entire array of points defining the picture in a single array, we are limited to a total of less than 32K points. A convenient size that gives us a little memory to spare is 160 by 160 pixels, so *MaxRes* is defined to be 160. Next, the *Height* array, which contains all of the picture information, is defined. This is an array of *MaxRes* by *MaxRes* or 160 by 160 pixels.

Scale Factors

The first function in this file is *HeightBufferScalingFactor*. It defines the scaling factor for height to be 32767 divided by the maximum height. The maximum height is the greatest height of any point in the data file for a particular scene. The division is performed so that when actual height information is multiplied by the scaling factor, the resulting information will never be greater than the maximum value that can be handled by an integer.

Clearing, Loading, and Saving Height Data

The next routines considered in the listing are those that are involved with clearing, loading, and saving the height data. The first of these functions, *ClearHeightBuffer*, clears the *Height* buffer. It uses a pair of nested *for* loops to set every member of the *Height* array to zero.

In Chapter 14, we are going to learn how to generate, examine and modify the databases for various z-buffered scenes. Here, we are going to assume that a height file already exists, and that we are going to load it back into the working program, or, alternately, that we have already stored such data in the program and want to save it to a disk file.

The function *LoadHeightBuffer* is passed the name of the data file for a z-buffered scene, not including the extension. It adds the extension *.DAT* to the file name and then displays, "Loading filename", where filename is actually the name of the desired data file. It then opens the file for reading and resets it to the beginning. Next, the function reads the resolution, *Res* and the scale factor, *Scaling*. Then a pair of nested *for* loops are used to read each height integer and store it in the *Height* array. After all height values are read, the file is closed and the function terminates.

The *SaveHeightBuffer* function works just the opposite of the above. It is passed the name of a file of z-buffered scene data and first writes, "Saving filename", where *filename* is actually the name of the file. It then opens this as a binary file for writing. Next, the *Res* and *Scaling* variables are written to the file. The function then begins a pair of nested *for* loops which iterate once for each member of the *Height* array. At each iteration, an integer from the *Height* array is written to the file. When these loops are complete, the file is closed and the function terminates.

Getting an Object File

The *GetObjectFile* function permits the user to enter the name of the file containing height data for the desired scene to be operated upon by the z-buffering function. The function begins by displaying, "Enter File Name => ", on the screen. Next, it saves the cursor position. It then reads a line of data typed in by the user on the keyboard into the variable *ObjectFile*. This name appears on the screen as it is typed. If the user only hits the *Enter* key, the object file name *Mountain* is selected by default, the cursor is repositioned and this name is displayed on the screen. The function then calls the function *MakeUpCase*. This function simply changes the file name to all capital letters. This ends the *GetObjectFile* function.

Displaying the Object Color Name

The function *GetObjectColor* is passed a color number from 0 to 7 in the parameter *C*. It then displays the proper name for the selected color (Black, Blue, and so on) on the screen.

CHAPTER 12

The DesMake.c Description File Maker

The program that creates an image using the z-buffering techniques is called *Render.EXE.* The source code file for this program is named *Render.c*. It is discussed in Chapter 13 of this book.

The *Render.EXE* program uses control information stored in a file created by a separate program *DesMake.EXE.* The program *DesMake.EXE* is the subject of this chapter.

When we run the *Render.EXE* program to generate a z-buffered scene, there are several options built into the program which are selected by reading a *.Des* file tailored particularly for that scene. These options are set up by compiling and running the *DesMake.c* file before running the *Render.EXE* file. The content of this program and the files that it makes are relatively simple. The source to this program is in the file *DesMake.c*, which is listed in Figure 12-1.

Keyboard Response Routines

First let's look at the function *Response.* This function is designed to obtain a response to a question and to make sure that it is either a *Y* or an *N*. It does this by means of two nested *do* loops. The inner loop keeps trying to read a key from the keyboard until the response is other than a null, indicating that a key has been pressed. Then the character received from the keyboard is converted to a capital letter. If it is a *Y* or an *N*, the outer loop terminates; otherwise the loops continue to iterate until an acceptable response is received. Note that whenever *Response* is called in a program, nothing can happen until you type in either *Y*, *y*, *N*, or *n*. When a correct response is received, if it is *Y* the function returns *true*; otherwise, it returns *false*.

Now, let's look at the function *NumberResponse*. This function is very much like the *Response* function except that the permissible responses are the numbers from 0 to 9. These numbers are returned as ASCII characters. When an acceptable one is received, it is converted to an integer, which is returned by the function.

```
/* DesMake.c

   Program for Generation of Description Files for Render.c

               Program by Christopher D. Watkins

                 'C' Conversion by Larry Sharp

*/

#include "stdio.h"
#include "dos.h"
#include "conio.h"
#include "math.h"
#include "string.h"
#include "math.inc"
#include "graph.inc"
#include "render.inc"

/*

                    Keyboard Response Routines

   Response - returns true or flase to a Y or N keyboard stroke
   NumberResponse - returns a 0 to 9 based on keyboard stroke

*/

char NumbResp[6];

void Response()
{
  char c;
```

```
  strcpy(NumbResp, "\n");
  while((!(c=='Y')) && (!(c=='N')))
  {
    while(!(kbhit()));
    c=toupper(getch());
  }
  putch(c);
  if(c=='Y')
    strcpy(NumbResp, "true");
  else
    strcpy(NumbResp, "false");
}

void NumberResponse()
{
  char c;

  strcpy(NumbResp, "\n");
  while(!(isdigit(c)))
  {
    c=getch();
  }
  putch(c);
  NumbResp[0]=c;
}

/*
```

Save Description Data

```
   SaveDescription - saves description of object
*/

void SaveDescription(Name FileName)
{
  int NDiv, i;

  strcat(FileName, ".DES");
  TextDiskFile=fopen(FileName, "w+t");
```

```
printf("Display in Half Scale? ");
Response();
fprintf(TextDiskFile, "%s\n", NumbResp);
printf("\nDisplay the Ground? ");
Response();
fprintf(TextDiskFile, "%s\n", NumbResp);
for(i=0; i<8; i++)
{
  printf("\nColor #%d is ", i);
  GetObjectColor(i);
}
puts("");
if(strcmp(NumbResp, "Y"))
{
  printf("Ground Color (1-7) = ");
  NumberResponse();
  fprintf(TextDiskFile, "%s\n", NumbResp);
}
else
  fprintf(TextDiskFile, "%s\n", "0");
printf("\nNumber of Height Divisions = ");
NumberResponse();
fprintf(TextDiskFile, "%s\n", NumbResp);
printf("\nEnter Color for each Division : \n");
NDiv=atoi(NumbResp);
for(i=1; i<=NDiv; i++)
{
  printf("Color for %d / %d (1-7) = ", i, NDiv);
  NumberResponse();
  fprintf(TextDiskFile, "%s\n", NumbResp);
  puts("");
}
printf("Top Color (1-7) = ");
NumberResponse();
fprintf(TextDiskFile, "%s\n", NumbResp);
printf("\nSpread of Normal Calculation = ");
NumberResponse();
fprintf(TextDiskFile, "%s\n", NumbResp);
printf("\nDirecton of Light\nAround the z-Axis = ");
gets(NumbResp);
```

```
    fprintf(TextDiskFile, "%s\n", NumbResp);
    printf("\n    off the z-Axis = ");
    gets(NumbResp);
    fprintf(TextDiskFile, "%s\n", NumbResp);
    printf("Tilt of the xy-Plane = ");
    gets(NumbResp);
    fprintf(TextDiskFile, "%s\n", NumbResp);
    printf("\nY Offset = ");
    gets(NumbResp);
    fprintf(TextDiskFile, "%s\n", NumbResp);
    fclose(TextDiskFile);
}

void main()
{
    clrscr();
    printf("Program to Generate a Description File for an
      Object\n\n");
    GetObjectFile();
    SaveDescription(ObjectFile);
}
```

Figure 12-1. Listing of the DesMaker.c File

The Main Function

The main function begins by displaying the heading "Program to Generate a Description File for an Object", followed by a blank line. Next, *GetObject* is called to ask for and read in the desired file name (without an extension). The extension *.DES* is added to this file name. The file is then opened for writing. Next, function *SaveDescription* displays, "Display in Half Scale?" and waits for a "*Y*" or "*N*" response from the user. This is stored in the file as a Boolean *true* or *false*. If it is *true* all of the coordinates will be divided by two to display a half-scale image; otherwise, the coordinates will be unchanged and a full-scale image will be created. The program then displays, "Display the Ground?". Again, a Boolean response is transmitted from the user to the file. If the response is *true*, all ground level points in the display will be shown in color; otherwise they will not be painted in.

The program then displays a chart of color names and calls *GetObjectColor* to obtain a color number from the user. If in the above step the ground coloring option was selected, the user-entered color is stored in the file as the color for the ground and is also written out to the display. If the option was not selected, a zero is stored in the file, regardless of what color the user may have chosen.

The program then asks for the number of height divisions. The rendering program is set up so that the overall height range of the scene may be divided into any desired number of equal sections from 1 to 6. Each of these sections may then be assigned a color, and then when the point on the scene being displayed is within a particular section, the selected color will be used, with the shade depending upon the lighting conditions. The program next asks for the color for each division and enters it in the file. Finally, the program asks for the top color and stores the resulting entry in the file. Next, the program asks, "Spread of Normal Calculation = ", and stores the user response in the file. If the spread is zero, a single normal vector is calculated for each pixel and used in the light intensity computations. This the mode used for most scenic displays.

However, in some cases of fractal displays, the surface of the fractal object is so rough that the usual normal technique does not produce an acceptable-looking surface. For such scenes, a number may be entered for the spread, and that number of additional normals, surrounding the pixel in each direction, will be computed and averaged to obtain the normal value, giving a smoother and more pleasing surface.

The program now turns its attention to the light direction and asks for and records the direction of the light source around the z-axis and off the z-axis. The tilt of the x-y plane is then requested and stored in the file. Next the y offset is requested and stored in the file. These last two terms effectively define the position from which the scene is being viewed. This completes the description file and the program terminates.

A number of description and scene data files are furnished as part of the program disk. The contents of the description files and the plate or figure number where the scene is shown in the book are given in Figure 12-2. Information about how to make up the files of scene data is described in Chapter 14.

Item	HmSphere	Bowl	HmToroid	PlotEqn1
Plate Number				16
Half Scale?	Y	Y	Y	N
Display Grnd?	Y	Y	Y	Y
Ground Color	1	1	1	2
No. of Ht. Div	5	5	5	1
Color for Div 1	2	2	2	2
Color for Div 2	3	3	3	
Color for Div 3	4	4	4	
Color for Div 4	5	5	5	
Color for Div 5	6	6	6	
Color for Div 6				
Top Color	7	7	7	2
Normal Spread	0	0	0	0
LightDirection Around z-axis	-30	-30	-35	45
Light Direction Off z-axis	45	45	45	60
Tilt of xy-plane	35	35	35	23
Y offset	60	0	0	0

Figure 12-2. Description File Contents

Item	PlotEqn2	PlotEqn3	PlotEqn4	MagnFlds
Plate Number				
Half Scale?	N	N	N	Y
Display Grnd?	Y	Y	Y	Y
Ground Color	1	1	1	1
No. of Ht. Div	1	1	1	5
Color for Div 1	1	1	1	2
Color for Div 2				3
Color for Div 3				4
Color for Div 4				5
Color for Div 5				6
Color for Div 6				
Top Color	1	1	1	7
Normal Spread	0	0	0	0
Light Direction Around z-axis	45	45	45	45
Light Direction Off z-axis	60	60	60	45
Tilt of xy-plane	23	23	23	35
Y offset	0	0	0	0

Figure 12-2. Description File Contents (continued)

Item	Mountain	Mountan1	Mountan2	CPM1
Plate Number	Fig. 15-2	Fig. 15-3	Fig. 15-4	17
Half Scale?	N	N	N	N
Display Grnd?	Y	Y	Y	Y
Ground Color	7	7	7	0
No. of Ht. Div	1	1	1	1
Color for Div 1	7	7	7	1
Color for Div 2				
Color for Div 3				
Color for Div 4				
Color for Div 5				
Color for Div 6				
Top Color	7	7	7	0
Normal Spread	0	0	0	0
Light Direction Around z-axis	-35	-35	-35	-35
Light Direction Off z-axis	60	60	60	40
Tilt of xy-plane	30	30	90	18
Y offset	0	0	0	70

Figure 12-2. Description File Contents (continued)

Item	CPM2	CPMJ1	CPMJ2	Dragon / Drag2	RevSolid / RevSol2	Plasma	CPM12
Plate Number	18	19	20	21	22	24	25
Half Scale?	N	N	N	Y	Y	Y	N
Display Grnd?	Y	Y	Y	N	N	Y	Y
Ground Color	0	0	0	0	0	0	0
No. of Ht. Div	1	1	1	1	1	1	1
Color for Div 1	5	3	1	2	3	7	1
Color for Div 2							
Color for Div 3							
Color for Div 4							
Color for Div 5							
Color for Div 6							
Top Color	7	7	5	2	3	7	0
Normal Spread	0	0	0	0	1	1	0
Light Direction Around z-axis	-144	-35	-35	0	160	-25	-35
Light Direction Off z-axis	70	40	40	75	65	80	40
Tilt of xy-plane	18	22	22	90	90	15	25
Y offset	140	70	70	0	0	0	30

Figure 12-2. Description File Contents (continued)

CHAPTER 13

The Z-Buffer Rendering Program

Before we go into the details of how to create databases to be rendered by the z-buffering technique, we are going to look at the details of the rendering program itself. We'll assume that we have an array of data, contained in a two-dimensional 160-by-160 array, where each array position represents a particular x and y position and the contents of that member of the array represents the height of the scene at that point. The program that performs the rendering operation is called *Render.c*. It is listed in Figure 13-1. The program and the associated functions are described in the following paragraphs.

Screen Functions

This set of functions is concerned with making sure that each pixel on the screen is displayed with the proper color and intensity. If we are in the half-scale mode, this is relatively simple.

If you look at the function *Pixel*, you will note that in the half-scale mode, when the function is passed a pair of coordinates (x,y), it simply takes these as the coordinates of the pixel (reversing the y value so that increasing values of y move upward on the screen, rather than the perverse usual mapping of the screen that makes y increase in a downward direction). The function has also been passed the intensity and using that and the current color, calls *PutPixel* (described in Chapter 2) to paint the pixel on the screen with the proper shade of color.

Observe, however, that the process becomes much more complicated for the full-scale mode, because there are points on the screen that are between data points of the z-buffered array, so that interpolation is required. If you really want to know exactly how this works in detail, you'll have to trace through every step of the code, which is rather difficult and convoluted. Here, we're just going to give an overall picture.

```
/* Render.c

                    Z-buffer Rendering Package

                 Program by Christopher D. Watkins

                  'C' Conversion by Larry Sharp


   The data is in an integer valued (MaxRes+1 x MaxRes+1 x
        32768) cube where an integer height value is stored in
        a cell at (x, y)
   The height value is then scaled to fit into the unit cube

   tilt = 0 for side view and tilt = 90 for top view
   looking from top view  : x-axis is right while y-axis is up
   looking from side view : x-axis is right while y-axis is in
*/

#include "stdio.h"
#include "stdlib.h"
#include "dos.h"
#include "conio.h"
#include "math.h"
#include "string.h"
#include "math.inc"
#include "graph.inc"
#include "render.inc"

/*

                          Toggle Switch


   InitGround - allows Height[i][j] = 0 to be plotted
   InitScale  - show image at half scale
*/
```

```
Boolean ShowGround;

void InitGround(Boolean Ground)
{
  if(Ground)
    ShowGround=true;
  else
    ShowGround=false;
}

Boolean HalfScale;

void InitScale(Boolean HlfScl)
{
  if(HlfScl)
    HalfScale=true;
  else
    HalfScale=false;
}


/*
╔══════════════════════════════════════════════════════════════╗
║                       Screen Functions                       ║
╚══════════════════════════════════════════════════════════════╝

Pixel       - the place interpolated pixels routine
   InitPixBuf - intialize the pixel buffer
*/

#define MaxBufs 3
typedef Byte PixBuffer[(MaxRes*2)+1];
typedef PixBuffer PixBuf[MaxBufs+1];

PixBuf PixBufColor;
PixBuf PixBufInten;
PixBuf NullPixBuf;
int TwoMaxRes;

void ClearPixBuf(int Buf1, int Buf2)
{
```

```
  Byte i;
  Word j, k;

  j=MaxRes*2;
  for(i=Buf1; i<=Buf2; i++)
  {
    for(k=0; k<=j; k++)
    {
      PixBufColor[i][k]=NullPixBuf[i][k];
      PixBufInten[i][k]=NullPixBuf[i][k];
    }
  }
}

void CopyPixBuf(int Buf1, int Buf2)
{
  Word i;
  Word j;

  j=MaxRes*2;
  for(i=0; i<=j; i++)
  {
    PixBufColor[Buf2][i]=PixBufColor[Buf1][i];
    PixBufInten[Buf2][i]=PixBufInten[Buf1][i];
  }
}

void InterpolateX(int buf, int buf1, int buf2)
{
  int i;

  for(i=0; i<=TwoMaxRes; i++)
  {
    if(random(2)==1)
      PixBufColor[buf][i]=PixBufColor[buf1][i];
    else
      PixBufColor[buf][i]=PixBufColor[buf2][i];
    PixBufInten[buf][i]=(PixBufInten[buf1][i]+
        PixBufInten[buf2][i])/2;
  }
}
```

```
void InterpolateY(int buf)
{
  int i, k;

  for(i=0; i<MaxRes; i++)
  {
    k=i*2;
    if(random(2)==1)
      PixBufColor[buf][k+1]=PixBufColor[buf][k];
    else
      PixBufColor[buf][k+1]=PixBufColor[buf][k+2];
    PixBufInten[buf][k+1]=(PixBufInten[buf][k] +
PixBufInten[buf][k+2])/2;
  }
}

void InterpolatePixBuf()
{
  InterpolateY(1);
  InterpolateY(3);
  InterpolateX(2, 1, 3);
}

int OldCol, YOffset;

void DisplayPixBuf(int buf1, int buf2)
{
  int buf, row, x, yc;

  x=(OldCol-1)*2-1;
  yc=MaxY+YOffset;
  for(buf=buf1; buf<=buf2; buf++)
  {
    for(row=0; row<=TwoMaxRes; row++)
    {
      if(!(PixBufColor[buf][row]==0))
        PutPixel((buf+x), (yc-row), PixBufColor[buf][row],
            PixBufInten[buf][row]);
    }
  }
}
```

```
int ColNum;
int RowNum;
Byte BufNum;
Byte MaxBuf;
Boolean FoundFirstCol;
Byte DisplayColor;

void Pixel(int x, int y, Byte Inten)
{
  if(HalfScale)
    PutPixel(x, 199-y, DisplayColor, Inten);
  else
  {
    ColNum=x;
    RowNum=2*y;
    if(ShowGround)
    {
      if(ColNum>0)
        BufNum=MaxBuf;
      else
      {
        if(ColNum==0)
      BufNum=1;
      }
    }
    else
    {
      if(FoundFirstCol)
        BufNum=MaxBuf;
      else
      {
        if(ColNum>0)
        {
          OldCol=ColNum;
          BufNum=1;
          FoundFirstCol=true;
        }
      }
    }
    if(ColNum==2)
    {
```

```
      if(OldCol==1)
      {
        InterpolatePixBuf();
        DisplayPixBuf(1, MaxBuf);
        OldCol=ColNum;
        CopyPixBuf(MaxBuf, 1);
        ClearPixBuf(2, MaxBuf);
        return;
      }
    }
    if(OldCol==ColNum-1)
    {
      InterpolatePixBuf();
      DisplayPixBuf(2, MaxBuf);
      OldCol=ColNum;
      CopyPixBuf(MaxBuf, 1);
      ClearPixBuf(2, MaxBuf);
      return;
    }
    PixBufColor[BufNum][RowNum]=DisplayColor;
    PixBufInten[BufNum][RowNum]=Inten;
  }
}

void InitPixBuf()
{
  int i, j;

  randomize();
  OldCol=1;
  TwoMaxRes=2*MaxRes;
  FoundFirstCol=false;
  for(i=1; i<=MaxBufs; i++)
  {
    for(j=0; j<=TwoMaxRes; j++)
      NullPixBuf[i][j]=0;
  }
  if(HalfScale)
    MaxBuf=1;
  else
```

```
    MaxBuf=MaxBufs;
  ClearPixBuf(1, MaxBufs);
}

/*
 ┌─────────────────────────────────────────────────────────────┐
 │              Viewer and Light Source Vectors                │
 └─────────────────────────────────────────────────────────────┘

   Viewer              - the viewer unit vector
   InitLightDirection  - set the light direction
   GetLightVector      - the light direction unit vector
*/

TDA View;
float SinViewPhi;
float CosViewPhi;

float VPhi;
float Vx, Vy, Vz;

void GetViewVector()
{
  Vx=0.0;
  Vy=-CosViewPhi;
  Vz=SinViewPhi;
  Vec(Vx, Vy, Vz, View);
}
void Viewer(float DPhi)
{
  VPhi=Radians(DPhi);
  SinViewPhi=sin(VPhi);
  CosViewPhi=cos(VPhi);
  GetViewVector();
}

float LightPhi;
float LightTheta;

void InitLightDirection(float Phi, float Theta)
{
```

```
  LightPhi=Phi;
  LightTheta=Theta;
}

TDA Light;

void GetLightVector()
{
  float Phi, Theta;
  float x, y, z;

  Phi=Radians(LightPhi);
  Theta=Radians(LightTheta);
  x=sin(Theta)*cos(Phi);
  y=sin(Theta)*sin(Phi);
  z=cos(Theta);
  Vec(x, y, z, Light);
}

/*

                    The Illumination Model

   InitSpread - choose the spread for the normal calculation
   Intensity  - calculate the intensity of a pixel
*/

#define Ambient 0.15
#define DifRfl 0.45
#define SpcRfl 0.40
#define Gloss 2

int Spread;
float CosTheta;
float CosAlpha;
TDA SrfNorm;
TDA Ref;
```

```
void InitSpread(int SpreadOfCalc)
{
  Spread=SpreadOfCalc;
}

int i1, j1;

void GetNormal()
{
  float dx, dy, dz;

  if(j1-1<0)
    Vec(0.0, 0.0, 1.0, SrfNorm);
  else
  {
    dx=(float)(Height[i1][j1]-Height[i1+1][j1])/(float)
Scaling;
    dy=(float)(Height[i1][j1-1]-Height[i1][j1])/(float)
Scaling;
    dz=1.0/(float)(Res-1);
    Vec(dx, dy, dz, SrfNorm);
    VecNormalize(SrfNorm);
  }
}

void GetSurfaceNormalVector(int i, int j, int Spread)
{
  TDA SrfNormSum;
  int Cells;

  VecNull(SrfNormSum);
  Cells=Sqr(2*Spread+1);
  for(i1=(i-Spread); i1<=(i+Spread); i1++)
  {
    for(j1=(j-Spread); j1<=(j+Spread); j1++)
    {
      GetNormal();
      VecAdd(SrfNormSum, SrfNorm, SrfNormSum);
    }
  }
```

```
  VecScalMult(1.0/(float) Cells, SrfNormSum, SrfNorm);
}

void GetReflectedVector()
{
  float TwoCosTheta;
  TDA temp;

  TwoCosTheta=2.0*CosTheta;
  VecScalMult(TwoCosTheta, SrfNorm, temp);
  VecNormalize(temp);
  VecSub(temp, Light, Ref);
  VecNormalize(Ref);
}

int Intensity(int i, int j)
{
  GetSurfaceNormalVector(i, j, Spread);
  CosTheta=VecDot(SrfNorm, Light);
  if(CosTheta<0.0)
    return(Round(MaxInten*Ambient));
  else
  {
    GetReflectedVector();
    CosAlpha=VecDot(View, Ref);
    return(Round(MaxInten*(Ambient+DifRfl*CosTheta+SpcRfl*
        pow(CosAlpha, Gloss))));
  }
}

/*
```

Load Description Data

```
   LoadDescription - load description of object
*/

#define MaxDiv 6
```

```
int NumHgtDiv;
int GroundColor;
int HeightColor[MaxDiv+1];
int TopColor;
int HeightLimit[MaxDiv+1];

typedef char Strg[10];

Boolean Bool(Strg B)
{
  if(!(strcmp(B, "false")))
    return(false);
  else
    return(true);
}

void LoadDescription(Name FileName)
{
  char B[10];
  int I1, I2;
  int i;
  float fi1, fi2;

  strcpy(B, "\n");
  strcat(FileName, ".DES");
  TextDiskFile=fopen(FileName, "r+t");
  puts("");
  fscanf(TextDiskFile, "%s", &B);
  InitScale(Bool(B));
  if(Bool(B))
    printf("Scale=Half\n\n");
  else
    printf("Scale=Full\n\n");
  fscanf(TextDiskFile, "%s", &B);
  InitGround(Bool(B));
  if(!(Bool(B)))
    printf("Ground coloring off\n");
```

```
    fgets(B, 9, TextDiskFile);
    I1=atoi(fgets(B, 9, TextDiskFile));
    GroundColor=I1;
    if(ShowGround)
    {
      printf("Ground Color = ");
      GetObjectColor(I1);
    }
    NumHgtDiv=atoi(fgets(B, 9, TextDiskFile));
    for(i=1; i<=NumHgtDiv; i++)
    {
      I2=atoi(fgets(B, 9, TextDiskFile));
      HeightColor[i]=I2;
      printf("Color below %d / %d = ", i, NumHgtDiv);
      GetObjectColor(I2);
    }
    I1=atoi(fgets(B, 9, TextDiskFile));
    TopColor=I1;
    printf("Top Color = ");
    GetObjectColor(I1);
    puts("");
    I1=atoi(fgets(B, 9, TextDiskFile));
    InitSpread(I1);
    printf("Normal Calculation Spread = %d\n\n", I1);
    fi1=atof(fgets(B, 9, TextDiskFile));
    fi2=atof(fgets(B, 9, TextDiskFile));
    InitLightDirection(fi1, fi2);
    printf("Light Direction is %4f around the z-Axis and\n", fi1);
    printf("%4f off of the z-Axis\n\n", fi2);
    fi1=atof(fgets(B, 9, TextDiskFile));
    Viewer(fi1);
    GetLightVector();
    printf("Tilt of xy-Plane = %4f  \n\n", fi1);
    I1=atoi(fgets(B, 9, TextDiskFile));
    YOffset=I1;
    printf("Y Offset = %d\n", I1);
    fclose(TextDiskFile);
}
```

```
/*
 ┌──────────────────────────────────────────────────────────────┐
 │                   Display the Height Field                   │
 └──────────────────────────────────────────────────────────────┘

   DisplayHeightField - calculate pixel positions and interpo-
        late intensities
*/

int Max;
int II, JJ;
int p0, p1;
int horizon;
int Pix;
int OldPix;
int NewPix;
int PP;

void Interpolate()
{
  float h;

  h=(float)(PP-p0)/(p1-p0);
  Pix=Round((h*OldPix+(1.0-h)*NewPix));
  Pixel(II, PP, Pix);
  --PP;
}

void AboveHorizon()
{
  OldPix=Intensity(II, JJ);
  Pixel(II, p1, OldPix);
  PP=p1-1;
  if((ShowGround) && (PP>horizon))
  {
    NewPix=Intensity(II, JJ-1);
    while(PP>horizon)
      Interpolate();
  }
  horizon=p1;
}
```

```
int Proj(float y, float z)
{
  return(Round(Res*(y*SinViewPhi+z*CosViewPhi)));
}

void DisplayHeightField()
{
  int n;
  int L1, L2;

  for(n=1; n<=NumHgtDiv; n++)
    HeightLimit[n]=n*(Max/NumHgtDiv);
  for(II=(0+Spread); II<=((Res-1)-Spread); II++)
  {
    p0=Proj(0.0, (float) Height[II][0]/Scaling);
    horizon=p0;
    for(JJ=(1+Spread); JJ<=((Res-1)-Spread); JJ++)
    {
      if(Height[II][JJ]==0)
      {
        if(ShowGround)
            DisplayColor=GroundColor;
        else
            goto L1;
      }
      else
      {
        for(n=1; n<=NumHgtDiv; n++)
        {
            if(Height[II][JJ]<HeightLimit[n])
            {
                DisplayColor=HeightColor[n];
                goto L2;
            }
        }
        DisplayColor=TopColor;
      }
L2:
      p1=Proj((float) JJ/(Res-1), (float)
        Height [II][JJ]/Scaling);
```

```
      if(p1>horizon)
        AboveHorizon();
      p0=p1;
L1:;
    }
  }
}

void FindMax()
{
  int i, j;
  Max=0;
  for(i=0; i<=MaxRes; i++)
  {
    for(j=0; j<=MaxRes; j++)
    {
      if(Height[i][j]>Max)
        Max=Height[i][j];
    }
  }
}

/*
╔══════════════════════════════════════════════════════════╗
║           Place the Special Add-Ons to the Screen        ║
╚══════════════════════════════════════════════════════════╝

   PlaceAddOnsToScreen - special additions such as lightning
    and moons
*/

#include "addons.inc"

void PlaceAddOnsToScreen(Name ObjectFile)
{
  if(!(strcmp(ObjectFile, "CPM1")))
  {
    JuliaSet(0.0, 1.0, 0, Res/3, Res, Res, BLUE);
    MapJuliaSetToSphere(-0.15652, -1.03225, -3*Res/4, -Res/2,
    35, 90, 90, MAGENTA);
```

```
  }
  if(!(strcmp(ObjectFile, "CPM2")))
  {
    JuliaSet(0.0, 1.0, 0, Res/3, Res, Res, RED);
    MapJuliaSetToSphere(-0.15652, -1.03225, -3*Res/4, -Res/2,
    35, 90, 90, BLUE);
  }
  if(!(strcmp(ObjectFile, "CPMJ1")))
  {
    JuliaSet(0.0, 1.0, 0, Res/3, Res, Res, LIGHTGRAY);
    MapJuliaSetToSphere(-0.15652, -1.03225, -3*Res/4, -Res/2,
    35, 90, 90, YELLOW);
  }
  if(!(strcmp(ObjectFile, "CPMJ2")))
  {
    Sky(0, 0, Res, Res, CYAN);
    MapJuliaSetToSphere(-0.15652, -1.03225, -3*Res/4, -Res/2,
    35, 90, 90, MAGENTA);
  }
}

/*
                          Main Program
*/

Name OF2;

void main()
{
  Title();
  printf("z-Buffer Rendering System\n\n");
  ClearHeightBuffer();
  GetObjectFile();
  strcpy(OF2, ObjectFile);
  LoadDescription(ObjectFile);
  printf("\nHit any key....");
  getch();
  InitPixBuf();
```

```
    strcpy(ObjectFile, OF2);
    LoadHeightBuffer(ObjectFile);
    InitGraphics();
    InitPalette2(Color);
    SetPalette(Color);
    FindMax();
    strcpy(ObjectFile, OF2);
    PlaceAddOnsToScreen(ObjectFile);
    DisplayHeightField();
    ExitGraphics();
}
```

Figure 13-1. Listing of *Render.c* File

There are three buffers called *PixBufColor* for storing pixel color and three called *PixBufInten* for storing pixel intensity. In the full-scale mode, instead of writing pixel data to the screen, information is stored in one pair of these buffers, until a full column of picture data is accumulated. The buffers are rotated so that data for the two latest columns is always available. Each time that a new column of data has been accumulated, the function calls *InterpolatePixBuf* to perform interpolation. The interpolation functions determine the color and intensity for each pixel to be written to the screen at locations between data points by randomly selecting between the colors and intensities of adjacent data points from the data stored in the buffer pairs. The resulting data for a column is then displayed on the screen. The functions involved in this process are *CopyPixBuf, InterpolatePixBuf, InterpolateY, InterpolateX,* and *DisplayPixBuf.*

The Illumination Model

The illumination model determines the intensity of the color at any given data point. This is accomplished by the function *Intensity*. This function has passed to it the parameters *i* and *j*, which are the *x* and *y* coordinates of the point whose light intensity is being determined. The function begins by zeroing *SrfNormSum*, which stores the surface normal vector summation for the designated point. Next, the function looks at *Spread*, which tells how many adjacent points are to be used in computing the surface normal vector. For each point, the function computes the coordinates of the surface normal vector and adds that vector to *SrfNormSum*. When all of the normals have been computed, the sum is divided by the number of points utilized to obtain an average, which is *SrfNorm*, the surface normal vector.

Next, the function finds the angle theta between the light source and the surface normal vector. If the cosine of this angle is less than zero, none of the light from the light source is reflected from the point, so the intensity is set to that of ambient light. Otherwise, the function determines the Phong shading reflection, which is found by raising the cosine of alpha to the power defined for the glossiness. This cosine is that of the angle between the viewer position vector and a reference vector which is the normalized difference between the light source vector and the angle at which light is reflected off of the point.

The function then determines the intensity of light at the point, which is the sum of the ambient light, the diffused light factor multiplied by the cosine of theta, and the specular reflection factor multiplied by the cosine of alpha raised to the glossiness power.

Loading the Description Data

Before we can go through the rendering process, we need to load data from the description file to set up the rendering parameters. These parameters have already been described in the previous chapter. Here, we will describe how they are transferred to the data base for the rendering program. The function *LoadDescription* performs the loading function.

Before it is listed, however, the function *Bool* is listed. This function returns a Boolean variable which is *false* if the string "FALSE" is passed to the function and *true* otherwise. The function *LoadDescription* is passed a filename as a parameter. It begins by appending the extension *.DES* to this file name. It then opens and resets the file. It next reads the scale parameter from the file and sets *HalfScale* to true and writes "Scale=Half" to the screen if the parameter is true. Otherwise it sets *HalfScale* to *false* and writes "Scale=Full" to the screen.

Next, the function reads and converts to Boolean the parameter that determines whether the ground is to be colored. It sets the parameter *ShowGround* to this Boolean value, and if it was false displays on the screen "Ground Coloring Off".

Then, the function reads the number of height divisions from the file and enters this value into *NumHgtDiv*. The function enters a loop which it iterates for the number of height divisions specified, reading the color for each from the file, saving it in the proper member of the array *HeightColor* and then displaying the color on the screen.

Next, the top color is read from the file, saved in *TopColor*, and displayed on the screen. In a similar manner, the parameters *Spread*, *LightPhi*, and *LightTheta* are read and displayed. The tilt of the *xy* plane is read as an angle in degrees, converted to radians, and the sine and cosine of the angle found and stored. These are used to find the *View* vector. Using the light and view information, the light vector is computed. Finally, the function reads the *y* offset from the file, saves it in *YOffset* and then displays it on the screen.

The *Render.c* Program

We're not quite through with all of the associated functions yet, but let's pause long enough to get an overview by looking at the main function of *Render.c*. This function begins by clearing the height buffer. It then gets the name of the desired data file from the user. It calls *LoadDescription* to obtain the various parameter values from the associated *.DES* file. It then zeroes out all of the pixel intensity and color buffers. Then the function calls *LoadHeightBuffer* to get all of the picture height information from the appropriate *.DAT* file. Next, *PlaceAddOnsToScreen* is called with the file name as a parameter to permit any added displays to be painted to the screen. When this is complete, the function *DisplayHeightField* is called to display the main scene. Finally, the program exits from the graphics mode and terminates.

Displaying the Height Field

A scene consists of a principal three-dimensional scene, plus some special effects which we call "AddOns." *AddOns* will be discussed in the next section. (Note that most of the z-buffered pictures don't have any *AddOns*.)

In this section, we shall describe the function *DisplayHeightField*, which converts the z-buffer array to a depiction of a three-dimensional scene. The *DisplayHeightField* function begins by determining from the parameter *NumHgtDiv* the number of height divisions that have been specified and determining the height for each of these divisions. The function next enters a *for* loop which iterates once for each column of the display. At the start of each iteration, the function calls *Proj*, which computes the proper row for the projection of the initial value of *y* and its corresponding height value onto the two-dimensional screen. The parameter horizon is then set to this value.

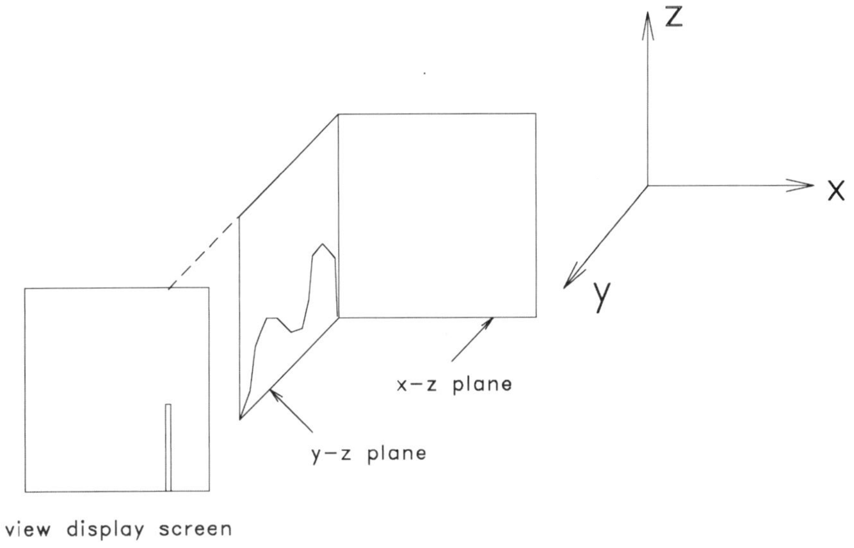

Figure 13-2. Geometry for Z-Buffer Projection

Next, the function enters an inner *for* loop which iterates once for each row in the column. If the height for the current column and row is zero and *ShowGround* is false, the loop proceeds to the next iteration; if *ShowGround* is true, the parameter *DisplayColor* is set to the ground color. Alternately, if the height is greater than zero, the function determines which height division the height is in, and sets *DisplayColor* accordingly. The function then calls *Proj*, which computes the proper row for the projection of the current value of *y* and its corresponding height value onto the two-dimensional screen. The geometry is shown in Figure 13-2. A *y-z* plane slice of the three-dimensional space is projected onto the screen as a single line having the maximum height of the object for that slice. If this value is greater than the value of horizon, the function calls *AboveHorizon*. This function paints a pixel on the screen, and if there were pixels left out between the current pixel and the last pixel that was painted to the screen, it interpolates to find the intensity of the intermediate pixels and paints them to the screen also. It then stores the value of the current pixel as *OldPix* for reference the next time the function is run. The two *for* loops in *DisplayHeightField* then continue to iterate until all of the pixels which make up the display have been painted on the screen.

Placing AddOns on the Screen

We promised to describe how the various *AddOns* are added to the picture. If you look at the function *PlaceAddOnsToScreen*, you'll note that it is only operative for four of the data files that create z-buffered pictures. These are *CPM1, CPM2, CPMJ1,* and *CPMJ2*. For each of these particular files, certain functions are called which create specialized displays. These specialized functions are included in the file *AddOns.Inc*, which is listed in Figure 13-3. This file is incorporated into the main source file *Render.c* by use of an *include* directive.

```
/* AddOns.Inc

        Special Effects for z-Buffered Scene Creation

         Original Material by Christopher D. Watkins

               'C' Conversion by Larry Sharp

   JuliaSet              - plot a Julia set (lighting)
   MapJuliaSetToSphere - map a Julia set on to a sphere (moon
                              with dendrite)
   Ground                - checkerboard ground
   Sky                   - blend a sky color from the horizon to
                              the zenith
*/
```

```
void PutDitheredSphere(int xx, int yy, int r,
                int LocX, int LocY,
                Byte Color, Byte Intensity)
{
  float Xc, Yc, Zc;
  int Xp, Yp;
  float Theta, Phi;

  Theta=Radians(yy);
  Phi=Radians(xx);
  Xc=r*sin(Theta)*cos(Phi);
  Yc=r*sin(Theta)*sin(Phi);
  Zc=r*cos(Theta);
  MapCoordinates(Xc, Yc, Zc, &Xp, &Yp);
  PutPixel(Xp+LocX, Yp+LocY, Color, Intensity);
}

void PlotSphrPix(int LocX, int LocY, int x, int y, int r, Byte
Color, Byte Intensity)
{
  x*=2;
  y*=2;
  PutDitheredSphere(x, y, r, LocX, LocY, Color, Intensity);
  PutDitheredSphere(x+1, y, r, LocX, LocY, Color, Intensity);
  PutDitheredSphere(x, y+1, r, LocX, LocY, Color, Intensity);
  PutDitheredSphere(x+1, y+1, r, LocX, LocY, Color, Intensity);
}

/*
   ┌──────────────────────────────────────────────┐
   │                Julia Set Images              │
   └──────────────────────────────────────────────┘

   JuliaSet            - plot a Julia set
   MapJuliaSetToSphere - map a Julia set on to a sphere
*/

int Iterate(float p, float q, float xo, float yo)
{
  int MaxIntens=MaxInten-5;
```

```
  float DivBndSqr=100.0;
  float xn, yn;
  int Iters, A;

  Iters=0;
A:
  xn=SqrFP(xo)-SqrFP(yo)+p;
  yn=2*xo*yo+q;
  xo=xn;
  yo=yn;
  ++Iters;
  if((SqrFP(xn)+SqrFP(yn))>DivBndSqr)
    return(Iters);
  if(Iters==MaxIntens)
    return(0);
  goto A;
}

Boolean SphrPix;

void Scan(float p, float q,
          float xmin, float ymin,
          float xmax, float ymax,
          int LocX, int LocY, int Rad,
          int ResX, int ResY, int Color)
{
  float dx, dy;
  int x, y;
  float xo, yo;
  int Inten;

  dx=(xmax-xmin)/(ResX-1);
  dy=(ymax-ymin)/(ResY-1);
  for(x=0; x<=((ResX-1) >> 1); x++)
  {
    for(y=0; y<ResY; y++)
    {
      xo=xmin+x*dx;
      yo=ymin+y*dy;
```

```
        Inten=Iterate(p, q, xo, yo);
        Inten+=5;
        if(SphrPix)
        {
          if(HalfScale)
          {
              PlotSphrPix(LocX, 3*Res/8+LocY, x, y, Rad, Color,
                                                          Inten);
              PlotSphrPix(LocX, 3*Res/8+LocY, ResX-1-x, ResY-1-y,
                                              Rad, Color, Inten);
          }
          else
          {
              PlotSphrPix(LocX, LocY, x, y, Rad, Color, Inten);
              PlotSphrPix(LocX, LocY, ResX-1-x, ResY-1-y, Rad,
                                                   Color,  Inten);
          }
        }
        else
        {
          if(HalfScale)
          {
              PutPixel(LocX+x, LocY+y, Color, Inten);
              PutPixel(LocX+ResX-1-x, LocY+ResY-1-y, Color,
                                                          Inten);
          }
          else
          {
              PutPixel(LocX+x*2, LocY+y, Color, Inten);
              PutPixel(LocX+x*2+1, LocY+y, Color, Inten);
              PutPixel(LocX+(ResX-1-x)*2, LocY+ResY-1-y, Color,
                                                          Inten);
              PutPixel(LocX+(ResX-1-x)*2+1, LocY+ResY-1-y, Color,
                                                          Inten);
          }
        }
      }
    }
  }
```

```
void JuliaSet(float p, float q, int LocX, int LocY, int ResX,
                                            int ResY,int Color)
{
  SphrPix=false;
  LocX+=MaxX/2-ResX;
  LocY+=MaxY/2-ResY;
  Scan(p, q, -1.4, -1.4, 1.4, 1.4, LocX, LocY, 0, ResX, ResY,
                                                        Color);
}

void MapJuliaSetToSphere(float p, float q, int LocX, int LocY,
    int Rad, int ResX, int ResY, int Color)
{
  SphrPix=true;
  InitPlotting(180, 0);
  InitPerspective(false, 0, 0, 0, 0);
  Scan(p, q, -2.2, -2.2, 2.2, 2.2, LocX, LocY, Rad, ResX, ResY,
                                                        Color);
}

Byte CalcSky(TDA Dir)
{
  float Small=1E-03;
  float HorInten=0.25;
  float ZenInten=1.00;
  float sin2, cos2;
  float x2, y2, z2;

  x2=SqrFP(Dir[0]);
  y2=SqrFP(Dir[1]);
  z2=SqrFP(Dir[2]);
  if(z2==0)
    z2-Small;
  sin2=z2/(x2+y2+z2);
  cos2=1.0-sin2;
  return(Round((cos2*HorInten+sin2*ZenInten)*MaxInten));
}

void Sky(int LocX, int LocY,
     int ResX, int ResY,
```

```
        Byte Color)
{
  int i, j;
  TDA Dir;
  TDIA Tmp, Eye;
  int HalfResX;
  int HalfResY;
  int EyeDist;
  int OffX;
  int OffY;
  Byte Inten;

  HalfResX=ResX/2;
  HalfResY=ResY/2;
  OffX=0;
  OffY=-HalfResY-HalfResY/2-HalfResY/4;
  EyeDist=-HalfResY;
  VecInt(OffX, OffY, EyeDist, Eye);
  for(i=0; i<ResX; i++)
  {
    for(j=0; j<ResY; j++)
    {
      VecInt(i-HalfResX, j-HalfResY, 0, Tmp);
      VecSubInt(Tmp, Eye, Dir);
      VecNormalize(Dir);
      Inten=CalcSky(Dir);
      if(HalfScale)
        PutPixel(LocX+i, LocY+j+HalfResY, Color, Inten);
      else
      {
        PutPixel(LocX+i*2, LocY+j*2, Color, Inten);
        PutPixel(LocX+i*2+1, LocY+j*2, Color, Inten);
        PutPixel(LocX+i*2, LocY+j*2+1, Color, Inten);
        PutPixel(LocX+i*2+1, LocY+j*2+1, Color, Inten);
      }
    }
  }
}
```

Figure 13-3. Listing of *AddOns.Inc* File

Julia Set Images

The Julia set is a plot of the iterated equation:

$$z_n = z^2_{n-1} + c \qquad \text{(Equation 13-1)}$$

where c is a complex number that is held fixed for a particular Julia set while the complex number z_0 (the initial value of z) is varied over the range of the screen, with the real part plotted horizontally and the imaginary part plotted vertically.

Figure 13-4 is a chart of various values of c with a description of the kind of Julia set that results for each.

c = p + iq	**ACP = attractive cycle period**	
p	q	Description
0.31	0.04	
-0.11	0.6557	JSet ACP=3 before decay into Cantor set
-0.194	0.6557	after decay into Cantor set
-0.12	0.74	
0.0	1.0	lightning dendrite
-0.74543	0.11301	seahorse valley c-value
-1.25	0.0	parabolic case c>1.25 ACP=2, c<1.25 ACP=4
-0.481762	-0.531657	
-0.39054	-0.58679	
-0.15652	-1.03225	dendrite with beads (secondary MSet)
0.11031	-0.67037	Fatou dust
0.27334	0.00742	parabolic case small c ACP=20

Figure 13-4. Types of Julia Set

Now look at function *Scan*. It begins by determining the incremental values of x and y for the specified display resolution. It then enters a pair of nested *for* loops which iterate over the whole range of x and y for the desired display. At each iteration of the inner loop, the initial values of x and y (the real and imaginary parts of z_0 in the equation are set to the coordinates for that point in the display). The function then calls *Iterate* to perform the actual iteration of the equation. This function repeats the iteration of the equation until the sum of the squares of x and y is greater than 100. When this occurs, the *Inten* parameter is set to the number of iterations and the function terminates. If the number of iterations becomes equal to the maximum intensity level without the above condition occurring, the function sets *Inten* to zero and the function terminates.

Back in the *Scan* function, the intensity is increased by 5. For an ordinary Julia set at half-scale display, this intensity is then plotted to the screen at the designated location and in the designated color. For an ordinary Julia set at full-scale, the intensity is plotted to four pixels which form a square at the desired location.

If the parameter *SphrPix* is true, the Julia set is projected onto the surface of a sphere. The code to do this is the same as that for plotting pixels to the screen for the ordinary Julia set, except that instead of plotting each pixel its information is passed in a call to the function *PlotSphrPix*. This function is passed the coordinates for the lower left corner of the display area, the coordinates of the current point in the display, the radius of a sphere, and the pixel color and intensity. It starts by multiplying the point coordinates by two and then calls *PutDitheredSphere* to paint four pixels to the screen—the designated point and three surrounding it in a square. The *PutDitheredSphere* function converts the coordinates of the point to angles on the sphere and then determines from them the x, y, and z coordinates of the point on the sphere. It then calls *MapCoordinates* to convert this three-dimensional information to the appropriate pixel location on the two-dimensional screen. The pixel is painted to the screen with *PutPixel*. This completes the *PutDitheredSphere*, *PlotSphrPix*, and *Scan* functions.

Now let's look at the *JuliaSet* function which is responsible for generating the Julia set. This function is passed the parameters p and q which are the parameters for the Julia set, *LocX* and *LocY*, which are the center of the desired display area, *ResX* and *ResY*, which are the size of the desired display in pixels, and *Color*, which is the desired display color. The function sets *SphrPix* to false so that the Julia set will not be mapped onto a sphere. It then changes *LocX* and *LocY* to the bottom left corner of the desired display area. It then calls *Scan* to generate the Julia set display. The function *MapJuliaSetToSphere* is just the same as this except that it first sets *SphrPix* to true to cause the Julia set to be mapped to a sphere, and then calls *InitPlotting* and *InitPerspective* (described in Chapter 2) to set up for converting the three-dimensional information to a two-dimensional display.

Creating a Blended Sky

Another of the specialized functions is *Sky*, which creates a sky color that is blended from horizon to zenith. This function creates a set of coordinates for the eye position of a viewer; then for each position on the screen it creates a vector from the eye position to that position and then normalizes this vector. It then calls *CalcSky*, which finds the squares of the cosine and sine of the angle of this normalized vector to the *xy* plane. The sky intensity at that point is then set to be the horizon intensity (0.25) multiplied by the cosine squared of the angle plus the zenith intensity (1.0) multiplied by the sine squared of the angle. This completes *CalcSky*. The *Sky* function then paints the proper pixels on the screen with the designated color and the just-computed intensity.

CHAPTER 14

Creating and Working with Z-Buffer Databases

You now know how we produce a scene, given that we have a database containing an array which consists of a grid of equally spaced points in the *x-y* plane and the height associated with each. But up to this point we have said nothing about how to create such arrays. In this chapter, we will look at how to generate, examine, and modify databases for such shapes as hemispheres, hemitoroids, the solution of various equations, and the plotting of magnetic fields. In the next chapter we will consider how to generate databases for scenes containing fractals that create mountains, Julia and Mandelbrot sets, dragons, and solids of revolution.

Generating the Database for a Hemisphere

Figure 14-1 is a listing of the program *HmSphere.c*, which is used to generate the database for painting a hemisphere on the screen using z-buffering. The program begins by clearing the screen. It then displays, "Creating Hemisphere Height Buffer". It then calls *ClearHeightBuffer*. This function (described in Chapter 11), clears the array in which all of the height data is to be temporarily stored. Next, the program sets the parameter *Res* (the picture resolution) to the value of *MaxRes* (160). The object data file is then named *HmSphere*. The program then calls the function *CreateHemisphereHeightBuffer*. This function begins by determining *Offset*, which determines where the location of the object will be in the *x-y* plane. This is set to be exactly in the center of the plane. The radius for the hemisphere, *R*, is now set to one less than the distance from the center to the edge of the plane.

Next, the function calls *HeightBufferScalingFactor* (described in Chapter 11), to determine the proper scaling factor for the height values. The function next enters a *for* loop, which is iterated for every integer angle *Phi* from 0 to 89. This is the number of passes required to move around a quarter of the hemisphere in one degree steps. Because the hemisphere is symmetrical, at each step four points can be computed to cover the four quarters, thus completing data for the hemisphere.

Within the loop, the function begins by computing the radius times the cosine of the angle and the radius times the sine of the angle for each of four angles 90 degrees apart. (These values are computed separately, but actually the sines and cosines of the last three angles are very simply related to the first angle, so that you might want to try achieving a small speed up by computing the last three angles by simple trigonometric relations, instead of recalculating.) The two values that have just been computed are actually the *x* and *y* coordinates of the points on a circle that forms the base of the hemisphere. The function now enters a second, nested *for* loop, which iterates for integer steps of the height angle *theta* from 0 to 90 degrees. At each step, the *x*, *y*, and *z* coordinates of a point on the surface of the hemisphere are computed for each of the four quarters of the hemisphere. These are all converted to integers, and at the location (*x*,*y*) in the *Height* array, the value of the height *z* is stored. After the loops have finished iterating, the function returns to the main program, which then calls *SaveHeightBuffer* (described in Chapter 11) to save the data to a disk file called *HmSphere.DAT*.

```
/* HmSphere.c

            Generate Hemisphere Database

          Program by Christopher D. Watkins

            'C' Conversion by Larry Sharp

*/


#include "stdio.h"
#include "dos.h"
#include "conio.h"
#include "math.h"
#include "string.h"
```

```
#include "math.inc"
#include "graph.inc"
#include "render.inc"

void CreatHemiSphereHeightBuffer()
{
  int x, y, r, Offset, z;
  int PhiR, ThetaR;
  float Phi, Theta;
  float RSinPhi1, RCosPhi1;
  float RSinPhi2, RCosPhi2;
  float RSinPhi3, RCosPhi3;
  float RSinPhi4, RCosPhi4;
  float SinTheta, CosTheta;

  Offset=Res/2;
  r=Offset-1;
  MaxHeight=r;
  HeightBufferScalingFactor();
  for(PhiR=0; PhiR<=89; PhiR++)
  {
    Phi=Radians(PhiR);
    RCosPhi1=r*cos(Phi);
    RSinPhi1=r*sin(Phi);
    Phi=Radians(PhiR+90);
    RCosPhi2=r*cos(Phi);
    RSinPhi2=r*sin(Phi);
    Phi=Radians(PhiR+180);
    RCosPhi3=r*cos(Phi);
    RSinPhi3=r*sin(Phi);
    Phi=Radians(PhiR+270);
    RCosPhi4=r*cos(Phi);
    RSinPhi4=r*sin(Phi);
    for(ThetaR=0; ThetaR<=90; ThetaR++)
    {
      Theta=Radians(ThetaR);
      CosTheta=cos(Theta);
      SinTheta=sin(Theta);
      z=Round(CosTheta*Scaling)/2;
      x=Round(SinTheta*RCosPhi1)+Offset;
```

```
        y=Round(SinTheta*RSinPhi1)+Offset;
        Height[x][y]=z;
        x=Round(SinTheta*RCosPhi2)+Offset;
        y=Round(SinTheta*RSinPhi2)+Offset;
        Height[x][y]=z;
        x=Round(SinTheta*RCosPhi3)+Offset;
        y=Round(SinTheta*RSinPhi3)+Offset;
        Height[x][y]=z;
        x=Round(SinTheta*RCosPhi4)+Offset;
        y=Round(SinTheta*RSinPhi4)+Offset;
        Height[x][y]=z;
      }
    }
}

/*
                         Main Program
*/

void main()
{
  clrscr();
  printf("Creating Hemisphere Height Buffer\n");
  ClearHeightBuffer();
  Res=MaxRes;
  CreatHemiSphereHeightBuffer();
  strcpy(ObjectFile, "HMSPHERE");
  SaveHeightBuffer(ObjectFile);
}
```

Figure 14-1. Listing of Program to Generate a Hemisphere

Generating the Database for a Hemitoroid

The main program for creating the database for a hemitoroid is listed in Figure 14-2. It is just the same as the main program for generating a hemisphere, except for the message it displays on the screen and the fact that it calls the function *CreateHemiToroidHeightBuffer* instead of *CreateHemiSphereHeightBuffer*. This function is passed two parameters, *Rho* and *R*. The parameter *Rho* (0.75) is multiplied by half the display resolution to obtain a new *Rho* which is the radius of the doughnut; the parameter *R* (0.25) is multiplied by half the display resolution to obtain a new *R*, which is the radius of the doughnut cross-section.

The function begins an outer *for* loop just like the function for the sphere, iterating for angle *ThetaR* from 0 to 89 to do one-quarter of the circle formed by the half-doughnut on the base plane. At each iteration the coordinates of four points on this circle are computed. Then an inner *for* loop is entered which iterates for angle *PhiR* from 0 to 180. In creating the hemisphere data, the inner loop swept through a quarter-circle in height at a constant radius from the center of base circle. For the hemitoroid, the inner loop sweeps through a half circle at a constant radius from the point on the circumference of the base circle. At each step, the *x*, *y*, and *z* coordinates of a point on the surface of the hemitoroid are computed for each of the four quarters of the hemitoroid. These are all converted to integers, and at the location (*x*,*y*) in the *Height* array, the value of the height *z* is stored.

After the loops have finished iterating, the function returns to the main program, which then calls *SaveHeightBuffer* (described in Chapter 11) to save the data to a disk file called *HmToroid.DAT*.

```
/* HmToroid.c

            Generate HemiToroid Database

*/

#include "stdio.h"
#include "dos.h"
#include "conio.h"
#include "math.h"
#include "string.h"
#include "math.inc"
#include "graph.inc"
#include "render.inc"

#define ZScale 1.0
```

```
char ObjF[]="HMTOROID";

/*
#define ZScale 2.0

char ObjF[]="BOWL";
*/

void CreatHemiToroidHeightBuffer(float Rho, float r)
{
  int ThetaR, PhiR;
  int x, y, z, Offset;
  float Theta, Phi;
  float CosTheta1, SinTheta1;
  float RhoCosTheta1, RhoSinTheta1;
  float CosTheta2, SinTheta2;
  float RhoCosTheta2, RhoSinTheta2;
  float CosTheta3, SinTheta3;
  float RhoCosTheta3, RhoSinTheta3;
  float CosTheta4, SinTheta4;
  float RhoCosTheta4, RhoSinTheta4;
  float RCosPhi, RSinPhi;
  float Zfactor;

  Rho=Rho * (float) Res/2;
  r=r * (float) Res/2;
  Offset=Res/2;
  MaxHeight=Round(r*2);
  HeightBufferScalingFactor();
  Zfactor=ZScale*MaxHeight/4;
  for(ThetaR=0; ThetaR<=89; ThetaR++)
  {
    Theta=Radians(ThetaR);
    CosTheta1=cos(Theta);
    SinTheta1=sin(Theta);
    RhoCosTheta1=Rho*CosTheta1;
    RhoSinTheta1=Rho*SinTheta1;
    Theta=Radians(ThetaR+90);
    CosTheta2=cos(Theta);
    SinTheta2=sin(Theta);
```

```
    RhoCosTheta2=Rho*CosTheta2;
    RhoSinTheta2=Rho*SinTheta2;
    Theta=Radians(ThetaR+180);
    CosTheta3=cos(Theta);
    SinTheta3=sin(Theta);
    RhoCosTheta3=Rho*CosTheta3;
    RhoSinTheta3=Rho*SinTheta3;
    Theta=Radians(ThetaR+270);
    CosTheta4=cos(Theta);
    SinTheta4=sin(Theta);
    RhoCosTheta4=Rho*CosTheta4;
    RhoSinTheta4=Rho*SinTheta4;
    for(PhiR=0; PhiR<=180; PhiR++)
    {
      Phi=Radians(PhiR);
      RCosPhi=r*cos(Phi);
      RSinPhi=r*sin(Phi);
      z=Round(RSinPhi*Zfactor);
      x=Round(RCosPhi*CosTheta1+RhoCosTheta1)+Offset;
      y=Round(RCosPhi*SinTheta1+RhoSinTheta1)+Offset;
      Height[x][y]=z;
      x=Round(RCosPhi*CosTheta2+RhoCosTheta2)+Offset;
      y=Round(RCosPhi*SinTheta2+RhoSinTheta2)+Offset;
      Height[x][y]=z;
      x=Round(RCosPhi*CosTheta3+RhoCosTheta3)+Offset;
      y=Round(RCosPhi*SinTheta3+RhoSinTheta3)+Offset;
      Height[x][y]=z;
      x=Round(RCosPhi*CosTheta4+RhoCosTheta4)+Offset;
      y=Round(RCosPhi*SinTheta4+RhoSinTheta4)+Offset;
      Height[x][y]=z;
    }
  }
}
/*
+==========================================================+
|                       Main Program                       |
+==========================================================+
*/

void main()
{
```

```
    clrscr();
    printf("Creating HemiToroid Height Buffer\n");
    ClearHeightBuffer();
    Res=MaxRes;
    CreatHemiToroidHeightBuffer(0.75, 0.25);
    strcpy(ObjectFile, ObjF);
    SaveHeightBuffer(ObjectFile);
}
```

Figure 14-2. Listing of Program to Generate a Bowl or Hemitoroid

You will note at the beginning of this file that there are two sets of constants given. For the first, the parameter *Zscale* is set to 1.0 and the name of the object data file, *ObjF* is set to *HmToroid*. This produces the database file that we have just described. Following that is another set of values for the same constants, in which the parameter *Zscale* is set to 2.0 and the name of the object data file, *ObjF* is set to *Bowl*. This set of constants has been commented out. If you remove the /* and */ that are commenting out this set of constants and instead use them to comment out the first set of values, the database for a bowl-shaped object will be created.

Generating the Database for Equations

A single program is used to generate database files for four different equations. The source file for this program is *PlotEqn.c*. It is listed in Figure 14-3.

At the beginning of the file listing, you will see a section for each of the four equations, which contains the name of the object data file for the particular equation, the span of the equation (which determines the magnification needed for the equation to fill the screen), and the necessary function to plot the values of *z*, given a particular set of values for *x* and *y*. The equations are the same as those used in the solid modeling program. They are:

$$z=\frac{75}{x^2+y^2+1} \qquad \text{(Equation 14-1)}$$

$$z=6\ (\cos(xy)+1) \qquad \text{(Equation 14-2)}$$

$z=20\ (\sin(\sqrt{x^2+y^2})+1)$ (Equation 14-3)

$z=10(1+\sqrt{x^2+y^2}+\sin(0.1(x^2+y^2)^2)+\sin(xy))$ (Equation 14-4)

The above information for each of the four equations is commented out. To run the program, you will need to select a single set of equation information and remove the comment indicators surrounding it (/* and */) so that the program can be run to generate that database.

The program begins by clearing the screen and then displaying, "Creating Equation Plot Height Buffer". The function *ClearHeightBuffer* is then called to clear the height buffer. The resolution of the display is set to 160. The name of the object data file is set to that contained in *ObjF*. The program then calls *InitPerspective, InitPlotting*, and *InitGraphics* to prepare for generating a graphics display. (These were not needed in the previously described programs, because the information was not displayed; it was only transferred to the data file. In this program, we are going to display the data as it is created, so that you can correct any mistakes and try again until you are satisfied that the right information is going to the file.) Next, the program calls a function which is named *CreateEquationPlotHeightBuffer*. This function begins by clearing the height buffer and determining the height scaling factor. It then sets up the increments for increasing adjacent values of x and y. The function then enters a pair of nested *for* loops, which together iterate through every member of the height buffer array. At each iteration, the values of x and y are determined. The appropriate equation function is then used to determine the height (z), which is rounded off to an integer. If the height is less than zero, the function returns to the text mode, displays, "Adjust the equation: z value less than zero", delays for two seconds, and then halts the computer. You then have to restart and change the equation parameters in your editor before recompiling and running the program again.

If the height value is not less than zero, it is stored in the proper member of the height array and then projected to two dimensions and plotted on the screen with the function *CartesianPlot3D*. The color of the pixel plotted is a function of the height, modulo 255, so as not to exceed the color range of the VGA mode being used. These colors bear no real relation to the lighting of the object (which requires running of

Render.EXE) but they do show the figure shape for study and reference. Once all of the members of the height buffer array have been filled, the function returns to the main program, where the function *SaveHeightBuffer* saves the array to the object data file specified.

```
/* PlotEqn.c

              Generate Equation Plot Database

*/

#include "stdio.h"
#include "dos.h"
#include "conio.h"
#include "math.h"
#include "string.h"
#include "math.inc"
#include "graph.inc"
#include "render.inc"

/*

                         Equations

*/

/*
#define Span 5

char ObjF[]="PLOTEQN1";

float zf(float x, float y)
{
  float c;

  c=SqrFP(x)+SqrFP(y);
  return(75.0/(c+1.0));
}
*/
```

```
/*
#define Span 5

char ObjF[]="PLOTEQN2";

float zf(float x, float y)
{
  return(6.0*(cos(x*y)+1.0));
}
*/

/*
#define Span 5

char ObjF[]="PLOTEQN3";

float zf(float x, float y)
{
  float c;

  c=SqrFP(x)+SqrFP(y);
  return(20.0*(sin(sqrt(c))+1.0));
}
*/


#define Span 2.75

char ObjF[]="PLOTEQN4";

float zf(float x, float y)
{
  float c;

  c=SqrFP(x)+SqrFP(y);
  return(10.0*(1.0+sqrt(c)+sin(SqrFP(c)*0.1)+sin(x*y)));
}


/*
```

```
******************************************************************/

void CreatEquationPlotHeightBuffer(float Xlft, float Xrgt,
                  float Ybot, float Ytop)
{
  int ix, iy, iz;
  float x, y;
  float dx, dy;

  MaxHeight=Res;
  HeightBufferScalingFactor();
  dx=(Xrgt-Xlft)/(Res-1);
  dy=(Ytop-Ybot)/(Res-1);
  for(ix=0; ix<Res; ix++)
  {
    x=Xlft+ix*dx;
    for(iy=0; iy<Res; iy++)
    {
      y=Ybot+iy*dy;
      iz=Round(zf(x, y));
      if(iz<0)
      {
        ExitGraphics();
        printf
            ("Adjust the equation : z value less than zero\n");
        delay(2000);
        exit(1);
      }
      Height[ix][iy]=iz;
      CartesianPlot3D(ix-Res/2, iy-Res/2, iz, (iz*MaxCol)%255);
    }
  }
}

/*
 ╔══════════════════════════════════════════════════════════════╗
 ║                         Main Program                         ║
 ╚══════════════════════════════════════════════════════════════╝
*/

void main()
{
```

```
    clrscr();
    printf("Creating Equation Plot Height Buffer\n\n");
    ClearHeightBuffer();
    Res=MaxRes;
    InitPerspective(false, 0, 0, 500, 500);
    InitPlotting(240, 18);
    InitGraphics();
    CreatEquationPlotHeightBuffer(-Span, Span, -Span, Span);
    strcpy(ObjectFile, ObjF);
    SaveHeightBuffer(ObjectFile);
    ExitGraphics();
}
```

Figure 14-3. Listing of Program to Generate Plots of Equations

Generating a Magnetic Field Database

The program *MagnFlds.c*, shown in Figure 14-4, generates the database for the magnetic fields produced by two parallel wires, one having a current of 100 amperes passing through it in one direction and the other having a current of 40 amperes passing through it in the opposite direction.

The main program begins by clearing the screen and displaying, "Creating Magnetic Field Height Buffer". It then calls *ClearHeightBuffer* to clear the height buffer array. The display resolution is set to maximum (160) and the object data file named *MagnFlds*. Then the function *Parameters* is called. This function simply sets the values of the parameters used in the magnetic field equation. Next, *InitGraphics* is called to enter the graphics mode. (We are going to create a simple two-dimensional display of the field.) Next, the program calls the function *CreateMagneticField*. This function begins by setting the maximum height and the scaling factor. It then enters a pair of nested *for* loops which iterate once for every combination of *x* and *y* in the height array. At each point, the function computes the strength of the magnetic field and stores it as height in the proper member of the height array. It then plots a pixel to the screen at the *x-y* location, using the height to designate the color and intensity information.

After all members of the array are computed, stored, and plotted, the function returns to the main program, which calls *SaveHeightBuffer* to store the height array data in a database file. It then leaves the graphics mode and terminates.

Finding the Highest and Lowest Points in the Height Array

It may well be that after you have created a data file of height data and used the *Render.c* program to display it, you find that either the variation in height over the display is too small, so that the display is uninteresting, or else the variation is too great and the program cannot handle it. Rather than try to guess how parameters need to be modified to bring the height data into the proper range, it is useful to have a program which will extract the highest and lowest values from the object database file. The program *FindLmts.c*, which is listed in Figure 14-5, performs this task.

This program first clears the display screen and then displays, "Find Locations of Highest and Lowest Points". Next, it calls *GetObjectFile*, which asks you, "Enter File Name => ". You then need to enter an object database file name without the extension. (The program will automatically add the extension *.DAT*.) The program then calls *ClearHeightBuffer*, which clears the height buffer array. Next, it calls *LoadHeightBuffer*, which displays, "Loading nnnn.DAT" (where *nnnn* is the name of the database file that you specified) and then loads the file into the height array. The program then enters a pair of nested *for* loops which together scan every member of the height array. At each loop iteration, the current height value is compared with the contents of *B* (which begins at 0) and *C* (which begins at 32767). If the current value is larger than *B*, it is used to replace *B* and its coordinates saved; if it is smaller than *C*, it is used to replace *C* and its coordinates saved. When the loops are finished, *B* contains the highest value in the array and *C* contains the lowest. The program then displays:

```
High Point is (x1,y1) = B
Low Point is (x2,y2) = C
```

where *B* is actually the value of the high point, and (*x1*,*y1*) are actually the values of its coordinates and *C* is actually the value of the low point, and (*x2*,*y2*) are actually the values of its coordinates. The program continues to loop, displaying this data, until a key is pressed.

```
 /* MagnFlds.c

  Generate Magnetic Fields Database

*/

#include "stdio.h"
#include "dos.h"
#include "conio.h"
#include "math.h"
#include "string.h"
#include "math.inc"
#include "graph.inc"
#include "render.inc"

int Xa, Ya, Xb, Yb;
float Ia, Ib;
float k;

void Parameters()
{
  Xa=Round((float) Res*0.34);
  Ya=Round((float) Res*0.60);
  Xb=Round((float) Res*0.68);
  Yb=Round((float) Res*0.40);
  Ia=100.0;
  Ib=-40.0;
  k=2E-07;
}

void CreatMagneticFieldHeightBuffer()
{
  int x, y;
  float Da, Db;
  float Hgt, b;
  Byte Inten;
  int z;

  MaxHeight=Res/2-1;
  HeightBufferScalingFactor();
```

```
    for(x=0; x<=Res; x++)
    {
      for(y=0; y<=Res; y++)
      {
        Da=sqrt(Sqr(Xa-x)+Sqr(Ya-y));
        Db=sqrt(Sqr(Xb-x)+Sqr(Yb-y));
        if((Da!=0.0) && (Db!=0.0))
              b=k*(Ia/Da+Ib/Db);
        else
              b=0.0;
        Hgt=fabs(b*1E+08+0.5);
        z=Round(Hgt*0.25);
        Height[x][y]=z;
        Inten=Round(Hgt)&255;
        PutPixel(x, 199-y, Inten/MaxCol, Inten%MaxInten);
      }
    }
  }

  /*
  ┌──────────────────────────────────────────────┐
  │                 Main Program                 │
  └──────────────────────────────────────────────┘
  */

  void main()
  {
    clrscr();
    printf("Creating Magnetic Field Height Buffer\n");
    ClearHeightBuffer();
    Res=MaxRes;
    Parameters();
    InitGraphics();
    CreatMagneticFieldHeightBuffer();
    strcpy(ObjectFile, "MAGNFLDS");
    SaveHeightBuffer(ObjectFile);
    ExitGraphics();
  }
```

Figure 14-4. Listing of Program to Generate Magnetic Fields Data

Viewing a Slice of the Database

In analyzing a three-dimensional function that is to be displayed with the z-buffering technique, it is useful to be able to view a cross-section of the displayed data. The program *ViewSlic.c*, which is listed in Figure 14-6, will either allow you to specify a particular value for the *x* coordinate and then draw a picture of the value of *z* for every *y* or it will let you specify a particular value for the *y* coordinate and then draw a picture of the value of *z* for every *x*. The program begins by clearing the screen and then displaying, "Display Slice of z-buffer data." Next, it calls *GetObjectFile*, which asks you, "Enter File Name => ". You then need to enter an object database file name without the extension. (The program will automatically add the extension *.DAT*.) The program then calls *ClearHeightBuffer*, which clears the height buffer array. Next, it calls *LoadHeightBuffer*, which displays, "Loading nnnn.DAT" (where *nnnn* is the name of the database file that you specified) and then loads the file into the height array. The program then enters a *do* loop which is iterated as long as the value of *Sl* is either *0* or *1*. The program then displays, "Xslice=0 or Yslice=1 =>". If you want a display of the *xz* plane for a particular value of *y*, you enter a 0. If you want a display of the *yz* plane for a particular value of *x*, you enter a 1. If you want to quit the program, you enter anything else. The character that is entered becomes the value of *Sl*. Next, if the value of *Sl* is one, the program displays, "Choose a slice in X =>". You then enter a number for the value of *x* at which the slice is to be taken. The program then starts the graphics mode and calls the function *TestHeightBufferYZPlane* to compute and display the slice profile. Then the program enters a waiting loop until a key is pressed. If the value of *Sl* is zero, the program displays, "Choose a slice in Y =>". You then enter a number for the value of *y* at which the slice is to be taken. The program then starts the graphics mode and calls the function *TestHeightBufferXZPlane* to compute and display the slice profile. Then the program enters a waiting loop until a key is pressed. After either of these actions takes place (or neither, depending upon which key was entered to set the value of *Sl*) the program calls *ExitGraphics* to leave the graphics mode and return to the text mode. Then if *Sl* was 0 or 1, the program returns to the beginning of the *Repeat* loop, providing the opportunity to select another slice for viewing. If *SL* has any other value, the program terminates.

```
/* FindLmts.c

        Program to find highest and lowest z-values

*/

#include "stdio.h"
#include "dos.h"
#include "conio.h"
#include "math.h"
#include "string.h"
#include "math.inc"
#include "graph.inc"
#include "render.inc"

int i, j;
int a, b, c;
int x1, y1;
int x2, y2;

void main()
{
  clrscr();
  printf("Find Locations of Highest and Lowest Points\n");
  ClearHeightBuffer();
  GetObjectFile();
  LoadHeightBuffer(ObjectFile);
  b=0;
  c=32767;
  for(i=0; i<=Res; i++)
  {
    for(j=0; j<=Res; j++)
    {
      a=Height[i][j];
      if(a>b)
      {
        x1=i;
        y1=j;
        b=a;
      }
```

```
      if(a<c)
      {
        x2=i;
        y2=j;
        c=a;
      }
    }
  }
  printf("\nHigh Point is (%d, %d) = %d\n", x1, y1, b);
  printf("Low Point is (%d, %d) = %d\n\n\n", x2, y2, c);
  puts("Hit any key to exit.");
  getch();
}
```

Figure 14-5. Listing of Program to Find Highest and Lowest Values in Array

```
/* ViewSlic.c

             Program to display slices of the database

*/

#include "stdio.h"
#include "stdlib.h"
#include "dos.h"
#include "conio.h"
#include "math.h"
#include "string.h"
#include "math.inc"
#include "graph.inc"
#include "render.inc"

int Max;

void TestHeightBufferXZPlane(int Slice)
{
  int i, j;

  j=Slice;
```

```
    for(i=0; i<Res; i++)
      PutPixel(i, Round(MaxY-100*Height[i][j]/Max), MaxCol,
          MaxInten);
}

void TestHeightBufferYZPlane(int Slice)
{
  int i, j;

  i=Slice;
  for(j=0; j<Res; j++)
    PutPixel(j, Round(MaxY-100*Height[i][j]/Max), MaxCol,
        MaxInten);
}

void FindMax()
{
  int i, j;

  Max=0;
  for(i=0; i<=MaxRes; i++)
  {
    for(j=0; j<=MaxRes; j++)
    {
      if(Height[i][j]>Max)
            Max=Height[i][j];
    }
  }
}

/*
╔══════════════════════════════════════════════════════════════╗
║                        Main Program                          ║
╚══════════════════════════════════════════════════════════════╝
*/

void main()
{
  int Slice;
  int Sl;
```

```
    clrscr();
    printf("Display Slice of z-Buffer Data\n");
    ClearHeightBuffer();
    GetObjectFile();
    LoadHeightBuffer(ObjectFile);
    FindMax();
    do
    {
      clrscr();
      printf("Xslice = 0 or Yslice = 1 or Quit = -1 => ");
      scanf("%d", &Sl);
      if(Sl>=0)
      {
        printf("\nChoose a Slice =>");
        scanf("%d", &Slice);
        InitGraphics();
        if(Sl==1)
          TestHeightBufferYZPlane(Slice);
        else
          TestHeightBufferXZPlane(Slice);
        ExitGraphics();
      }
    }
    while(Sl!=-1);
}
```

Figure 14-6. Program to View Slice of Height Buffer

The function *TestHeightBufferXZPlane* takes the heights for all of the *y* values in the height buffer at the value of *x* taken as the slice point, scales them, and plots them to the screen in bright white. The scaling is done over a range of 100 pixels, by dividing the height values by the maximum height value and then multiplying the result by 100. The same process occurs for the function *TextHeightBufferYZPlane*, except that the function takes the heights for all of the x values in the height buffer at the value of y taken as the slice point, scales them, and plots them to the screen in bright white.

Removing Discontinuous Zeroes

Sometimes the height array database contains erroneous isolated points that are recorded at zero height. These points are not part of a realistic definition of the surface and therefore need to be corrected before the database is sent to the rendering program. The program *Smooth.c*, which is listed in Figure 14-7, performs this operation. The program first clears the display screen and then displays, "z-Buffer Data Correction Program". Next, it calls *GetObjectFile*, which asks you, "Enter File Name => ". You then need to enter an object database file name without the extension. (The program will automatically add the extension *.DAT*.) The program then calls *ClearHeightBuffer*, which clears the height buffer array.

Next, it calls *LoadHeightBuffer*, which displays, "Loading nnnn.DAT" (where *nnnn* is the name of the database file that you specified) and then loads the file into the height array. Next, it displays the line, "Correcting Height Buffer". It then enters a pair of nested *for* loops which iterate once for ever member of the height array. If a member of the array is found to contain zero height and neither of the points in the columns on either side of it is zero, the height is set to the average of the values of the two adjacent points. The entire function is then repeated, except that each point is this time checked against points in the rows on each side. The program then calls *SaveHeightBuffer* to save the corrected height array as the new database file.

```
/* Smooth.c

    Program to remove discontinuous zeroes from the data

*/

#include "stdio.h"
#include "stdlib.h"
#include "dos.h"
#include "conio.h"
#include "math.h"
#include "string.h"
#include "math.inc"
#include "graph.inc"
#include "render.inc"
```

```
int i, j, a, b, c;
Name OF2;

void main()
{
  clrscr();
  printf("z-Buffer Data correction Program\n\n");
  ClearHeightBuffer();
  GetObjectFile();
  strcpy(OF2, ObjectFile);
  LoadHeightBuffer(ObjectFile);
  printf("\nCorrecting Height Buffer\n");
  for(j=0; j<=Res; j++)
  {
    for(i=1; i<Res; i++)
    {
      a=Height[i][j];
      b=Height[i-1][j];
      c=Height[i+1][j];
      if((a==0) && (b!=0) && (c!=0))
        Height[i][j]=(b+c)/2;
    }
  }
  for(i=0; i<=Res; i++)
  {
    for(j=1; j<Res; j++)
    {
      a=Height[i][j];
      b=Height[i][j-1];
      c=Height[i][j+1];
      if((a==0) && (b!=0) && (c!=0))
        Height[i][j]=(b+c)/2;
    }
  }
  strcpy(ObjectFile, OF2);
  SaveHeightBuffer(ObjectFile);
}
```

Figure 14-7 Listing of program *Smooth.c*

CHAPTER 15

Fractal Programs to Generate Databases

In this chapter we shall look at some methods for using fractals to generate interesting databases for rendering by the z-buffering method. Some types of fractals produce pictures that are very similar to things found in nature. We shall generate several fractal mountains that look very similar to the real thing. We shall also convert the traditional Mandelbrot and Julia sets into three-dimensional representations, resulting in some unusual and hauntingly familiar scenes. We shall find a program that generates cloud-like plasmas that can be converted into realistic looking mountains. Finally, we'll look at creating three-dimensional dragons and solids of revolution in the quaternions.

Generating Fractal Mountains

The program and source code is in the file *Mountain.c*, which is listed in Figure 15-1. It is used to generate fractal mountain databases. The program begins by displaying:

```
                Mountain Scene Generator
                    By Chris Watkins
```

Next the function *ClearHeightBuffer* is called to zero the array of height data. The program then calls the function *Initialization*. This function determines the value of *Points* (which is 2 raised to the *NumberLevels* (7) power. It then determines the value of *Space* (which is 2 raised to the *MaximumLevel - NumberLevels* (0) power. It then sets *MaxHeight* to the value of *Roughness* (100) and calls the function *HeightBufferScalingFactor* to determine the proper scaling factor for the height data. The function then returns to the main program. The program then calls the function *CalculateFractalHeights* to calculate all of the data to fill the height array.

```
/* Mountain.c

                    Fractal Landscape Generator

                 Program by Christopher D. Watkins

                   'C' Conversion by Larry Sharp

*/

#include "stdio.h"
#include "stdlib.h"
#include "dos.h"
#include "conio.h"
#include "math.h"
#include "string.h"
#include "math.inc"
#include "graph.inc"
#include "render.inc"

#define NumberLevels 7
#define MaximumLevel 7
#define Roughness  100

int Points, Space;

void Initialization()
{
  int i;

  randomize();
  Points=1;
  for(i=1; i<=NumberLevels; i++)
    Points*=2;
  Space=1;
  for(i=1; i<=(MaximumLevel-NumberLevels); i++)
```

```
    Space*=2;
  MaxHeight=Roughness;
  HeightBufferScalingFactor();
}

int Hgt(int i, int j)
{
  return(Height[i*Space][j*Space]);
}

int ii, jj, kk;
int Deviation;
int HalfDeviation;
int Skip, Offset;

void InterpolateHeight(int i, int j, int i0, int j0, int i1,
int j1)
{
  float r;

  r=(float)(random(32766))/32767;
  Height[i*Space][j*Space]=(Hgt(i0, j0)+Hgt(i1, j1))/
    2+Round(r*Deviation-HalfDeviation);
}

void AssignHeightsAlongX()
{
  int x, y;

  jj=0;
  do
  {
    ii=Offset;
    do
    {
      InterpolateHeight(ii, jj, ii-Offset, jj, ii+Offset, jj);
      x=Points-ii;
      y=Points-jj;
      InterpolateHeight(x, y, x+Offset, y, x-Offset, y);
```

```
      ii+=Skip;
    }
    while(ii<=Points);
    jj+=Skip;
  }
  while(jj<=Points);
}

void AssignHeightsAlongY()
{
  int x, y;

  ii=Points;
  do
  {
    jj=Offset;
    do
    {
      InterpolateHeight(ii, jj, ii, jj+Offset, ii, jj-Offset);
      x=Points-ii;
      y=Points-jj;
      InterpolateHeight(x, y, x, y-Offset, x, y+Offset);
      jj+=Skip;
    }
    while(jj<=ii);
    ii-=Skip;
  }
  while(ii>0);
}

void AssignHeightsAlongDiagonal()
{
  int x, y;
  int l;

  ii=0;
  do
  {
    jj=Offset;
```

```
    kk=Points-ii;
    do
    {
      l=ii+jj;
      InterpolateHeight(l, jj, l-Offset, jj-Offset, l+Offset,
        jj+Offset);
      x=Points-l;
      y=Points-jj;
      InterpolateHeight(x, y, x+Offset, y+Offset, x-Offset,
        y-Offset);
      jj+=Skip;
    }
    while(jj<=kk);
    ii+=Skip;
  }
  while(ii<Points);
}

void CalculateFractalHeights()
{
  int n;

  HalfDeviation=Roughness;
  Offset=Points;
  for(n=1; n<=NumberLevels; n++)
  {
    Deviation=HalfDeviation;
    HalfDeviation=Deviation/2;
    Skip=Offset;
    Offset=Skip/2;
    printf("\nPass Level %d -> ", n);
    AssignHeightsAlongX();
    printf(" X");
    AssignHeightsAlongY();
    printf(" Y");
    AssignHeightsAlongDiagonal();
    printf(" Diag\n");
  }
```

```
  puts("");
}

void ZeroHeightBufferBelowWaterLevel()
{
  int i, j;

  for(i=0 ; i<=Res; i++)
  {
    for(j=0 ; j<=Res; j++)
    {
      if(Height[i][j]<0)
    Height[i][j]=0;
    }
  }
}

/*
╔══════════════════════════════════════════════════════════════╗
║                        Main Program                          ║
╚══════════════════════════════════════════════════════════════╝
*/

void main()
{
  Title();
  printf("Mountain Scene Generator\n\nBy Chris Watkins\n\n");
  ClearHeightBuffer();
  Initialization();
  Res=Points;
  CalculateFractalHeights();
  ZeroHeightBufferBelowWaterLevel();
  strcpy(ObjectFile, "MOUNTAIN");
  SaveHeightBuffer(ObjectFile);
  ExitGraphics();
}
```

Figure 15-1. Listing of Program to Generate Mountain Databases

This function starts with a *for* loop that iterates once for each level from one up to the specified number of levels. At each level, the loop begins by setting the values for *Deviation, HalfDeviation, Skip*, and *Offset*. The function then displays on the screen, "Pass Level", followed by the number of the level being processed. The function then interpolates in x .

What is happening here, is that, at the first level, a point is selected at the center of the top line of the picture and its height is made to be the average of the heights of the points at the two ends of the line plus a random height factor. The same process is then applied to the point at the center of the bottom line of the array. The function then interpolates in y, using the same process, but determining the height for points at midway in the first and last columns, using the average height of the points at the ends of the column plus a random factor. Finally the same process takes place to determine the height of a point in the center of the display, using the average of the heights of points on the opposite ends of a diagonal through the center, plus a random factor.

At the next level of the *for* loop, the spacings are changed, so that the heights are computed for points midway between each pair of points that was computed at the previous level. This process is repeated at each level, so that when the *for* loop is finally complete, heights have been computed for all of the members of the height array. Each height is related to the heights of the points around it, but also includes a random roughness factor.

The main program then calls *SaveHeightBuffer*, which saves the height array to a disk file database called *Mountain.DAT*. Figures 15-2, 15-3, and 15-4 show pictures of typical mountains produced by rendering the databases created with this program, using the z-buffering rendering technique.

Because of the use of random numbers in this program, and because the function *Randomize* was called during initialization to assure that different random numbers are used at each pass through the program, a new and unique mountain scene will be produced from each run of the program. However, each time you run the program, the new database file will be written out as *Mountain.DAT* overwriting the previous data in the file. Therefore, if you have a mountain scene that you particularly want to keep, you should rename the *Mountain.DAT* file to something else before you run the *Mountain.EXE* file again.

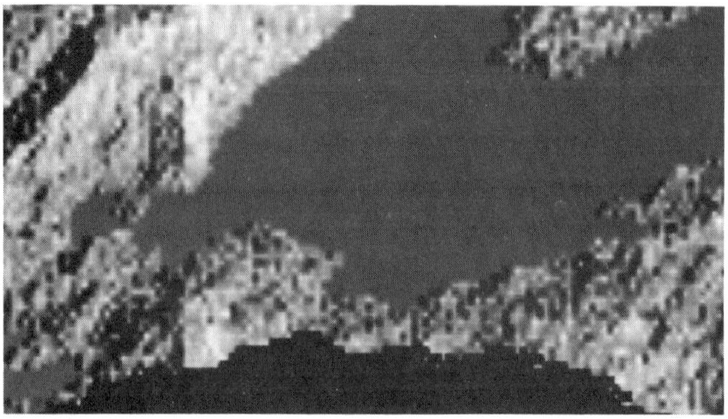

Figure 15-2. Fractal Mountain Created by Z-Buffering

Mountains from Plasmas

The *plasma.c* program listed in Figure 15-5 selects four randomly colored points at the corners of a display area. It then chooses a color for the midpoint between each pair of points, based on the average of the two endpoint colors plus a random factor. This subdivision process continues until every pixel within the display area has been colored. The resulting display is a plasma-like effect. The colors then cycle until a key is pressed. The original display is saved to provide a height buffer file for running of the z-buffering render program. The result of z-buffering is a mountain-like display. Plate 23 is a plasma display while Plate 24 is a mountain created by rendering the plasma data with the z-buffering technique.

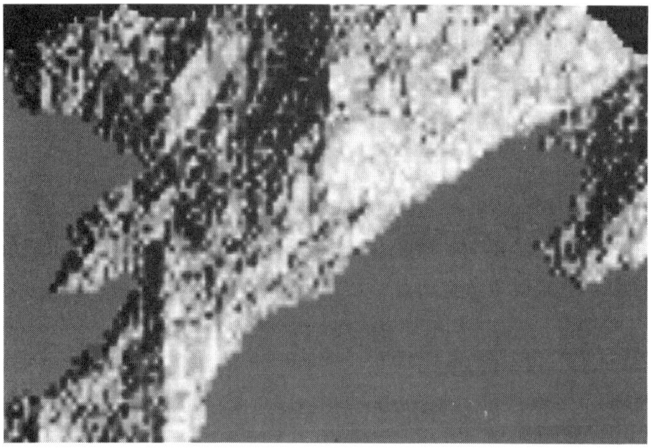

Figure 15-3. Another Fractal Mountain Created by Z-Buffering

Three-Dimensional Mandelbrot Sets

The program *CPM.c* creates the database for a three-dimensional Mandelbrot set. The program is listed in Figure 15-6. The program begins with two sets of constants, for creating two different Mandelbrot set databases. One is presently commented out. If you want to run this one, remove the comment indicators (/* and */) from around the second set of constants and put them around the first set of constants instead.

The main program clears the screen, sets up some initial parameters, and then calls *InitGraphics* to enter the graphics mode. The program then calls *ClearHeightBuffer* to zero out the height array. Next the program enters two nested *for* loops to iterate for every point on the two-dimensional display. For each iteration of the inner loop, a *while* loop is run which iterates for the iterated Mandelbrot equation as many times as were specified by *Iter* or until the square of the xy vector becomes greater than 20000. The equations in this loop are the same as were given for the Mandelbrot set in Chapter 3. However, at the end of the *while* loop, instead of directly plotting a color that is a function of the number of iterations, the program uses the exiting values of x^2 and y^2 to compute the value of *MSetPot*. This value is the continuous potential of the point with respect to the set in the same sense that the potential of an electric field is calculated. It can also be scaled and used as a height for a three-dimensional display. The program computes this height for the appropriate member of the height array. It also plots a point to the screen in the appropriate color for a two-dimensional display for reference as to how the plot is proceeding.

The continuous potential method yields a potential that is smallest right at the boundary of the Mandelbrot set and gets larger and larger as the distance of the point from the set boundary increases. This would produce a three-dimensional display in which the set itself was down in a hole, with sides that sloped sharply down to it. The display is more interesting if the set is a plateau on top of a mountain, with the sides sloping upward. To achieve this effect, after the nested loops are complete, the program calls the function *InverseHeightBuffer*. This function first determines the maximum height that is stored in the buffer, and then subtracts every member of the height array from it to create a new value for the member. As a result, the Mandelbrot set itself is at the maximum height and the points that previously were highest are now at zero.

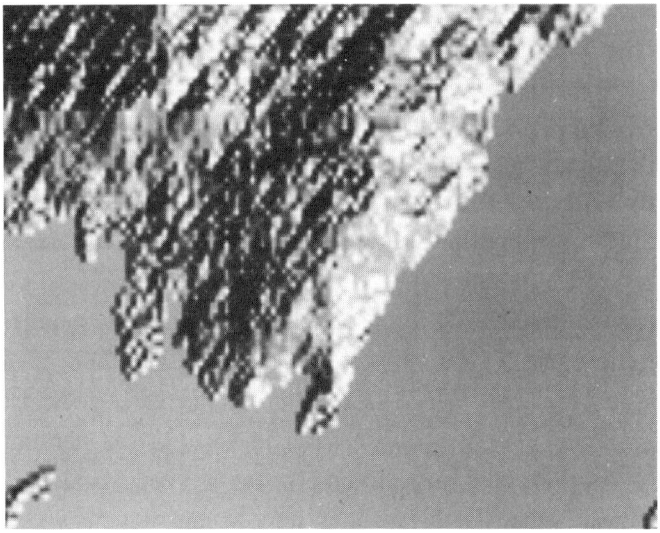

Figure 15-4. A Third Fractal Mountain Created by Z-Buffering

The program then calls *SaveHeightBuffer*, which stores the height array in a database file. Plates 17 and 18 are scenes generated with the Mandelbrot set program and the z-buffering technique. Two scenes generated from the Mandelbrot set program using the z-buffering technique are shown in Plates 17 and 18.

```
/* Plasma.c

        Plasma Generator by Christopher D. Watkins

*/

#include "stdio.h"
#include "stdlib.h"
#include "dos.h"
#include "conio.h"
#include "math.h"
#include "string.h"
#include "math.inc"
#include "graph.inc"
#include "render.inc"
```

```
#define mcol 63

void InitPalette3(PaletteRegister Color)
{
  Byte i;

  Color[0].Red=0;
  Color[0].Grn=Round(mcol/85);
  Color[0].Blu=mcol;
  for(i=1; i<=85; i++)
  {
    Color[i].Red=0;
    Color[i].Grn=Round((i*mcol)/85);
    Color[i].Blu=Round(((86-i)*mcol)/85);
    Color[i+85].Red=Round((i*mcol)/85);
    Color[i+85].Grn=Round(((86-i)*mcol)/85);
    Color[i+85].Blu=0;
    Color[i+170].Red=Round(((86-i)*mcol)/85);
    Color[i+170].Grn=0;
    Color[i+170].Blu=Round((i*mcol)/85);
  }
}

void UpdateHeight(int x, int y, int Color)
{
  Plot(x, y, Color&255);
  Height[Res-x][Res-y]=Color >> 1;
}

void NewCol(int xa, int ya, int x, int y, int xb, int yb)
{
  int Color;

  Color=abs(xa-xb)+abs(ya-yb);
  Color=random(Color<<1)-Color;
  Color+=(GetPixel(xa, ya)+GetPixel(xb, yb)+1) >> 1;
  if(Color<1)
    Color=1;
  else
  {
```

```
    if(Color>255)
      Color=255;
  }
  if(GetPixel(x, y)==0)
    UpdateHeight(x, y, Color);
}

void SubDivide(int x1, int y1, int x2, int y2)
{
  int x, y, Color;
  if(!((x2-x1<2) && (y2-y1<2)))
  {
    x=(x1+x2)>>1;
    y=(y1+y2)>>1;
    NewCol(x1, y1, x, y1, x2, y1);
    NewCol(x2, y1, x2, y, x2, y2);
    NewCol(x1, y2, x, y2, x2, y2);
    NewCol(x1, y1, x1, y, x1, y2);
    Color=(GetPixel(x1, y1)+GetPixel(x2, y1)+GetPixel(x2,y2) +
                                   GetPixel(x1, y2)+2)>>2;
    UpdateHeight(x, y, Color);
    SubDivide(x1, y1, x, y);
    SubDivide(x, y1, x2, y);
    SubDivide(x, y, x2, y2);
    SubDivide(x1, y, x, y2);
  }
}

/*
╔══════════════════════════════════════════════════════════════╗
║                         Main Program                         ║
╚══════════════════════════════════════════════════════════════╝
*/

PaletteRegister PalArray;

void main()
{
  ClearHeightBuffer();
  Res=MaxRes;
  MaxHeight=Res;
```

```
    HeightBufferScalingFactor();
    InitGraphics();
    InitPalette3(PalArray);
    SetPalette(PalArray);
    randomize();
    UpdateHeight(0, 0, 255);
    UpdateHeight(Res, 0, 255);
    UpdateHeight(Res, Res, 1);
    UpdateHeight(0, Res, 1);
    SubDivide(0, 0, Res, Res);
    strcpy(ObjectFile, "PLASMA");
    SaveHeightBuffer(ObjectFile);
    while(!(kbhit()))
    {
      CyclePalette(PalArray);
    }
    ExitGraphics();
}
```

Figure 15-5. Listing of *Plasma.c* Program

Three-Dimensional Julia Sets

The program *CPMJ.c* creates the database for a three-dimensional Julia set. The program is listed in Figure 15-7. The program begins with two sets of constants, for creating two different Julia set databases. One is presently commented out. If you want to run this one, remove the comment designators from around the second set of constants and put them around the first set of constants instead.

The program is very similar to that for the Mandelbrot set, except that the variables used in the iterated equation are different.

The main program clears the screen, sets up some initial parameters, and then calls *InitGraphics* to enter the graphics mode. The program then calls *ClearHeightBuffer* to zero out the height array. Next, the program enters two nested *for* loops to iterate for every point on the two-dimensional display. For each iteration of the inner loop, a *while* loop is run which iterates for the iterated Julia set equation as many times as were specified by *Iter* or until the square of the *xy* vector becomes greater than 20000. (The equations in this loop are the same as given for the

Mandelbrot set in Chapter 3.) However, at the end of the *while* loop, instead of directly plotting a color that is a function of the number of iterations, the program uses the exiting values of x^2 and y^2 to compute the value of *MSetPot.* This value is the continuous potential of the point with respect to the set in the same sense that the potential of an electric field is calculated. It can also be scaled and used as a height for a three-dimensional display. The program computes this height for the appropriate member of the height array. It also plots a point to the screen in the appropriate color for a two-dimensional display for reference as to how the plot is proceeding.

The continuous potential method yields a potential that is smallest right at the boundary of the Julia set and gets larger and larger as the distance of the point from the set boundary increases. This would give a three-dimensional display in which the set itself was down in a hole, with sides that sloped sharply down to it. The display is more interesting if the set is a plateau on top of a mountain, with the sides sloping upward. To achieve this effect, after the nested loops are complete, the program calls the function *InverseHeightBuffer.* This function is a duplicate of the same function described above for the Mandelbrot set. The program then calls *SaveHeightBuffer,* which stores the height array in a database file. Scenes created with the Julia set program and z-buffering are shown in Plates 19 and 20.

```
/* CPM.c

    The Continuous Potential Method for the Mandelbrot Set

*/

#include "stdio.h"
#include "dos.h"
#include "conio.h"
#include "math.h"
#include "string.h"
#include "math.inc"
#include "graph.inc"
#include "render.inc"

/*
   125 iterations maximum
```

```
*/

#define XMin -2.50
#define XMax  1.35
#define YMin -1.80
#define YMax  1.80
#define Iter  32
#define Scal  32767

char ObjF[]="CPM1";
/*
#define XMin -0.19
#define XMax -0.13
#define YMin  1.01
#define YMax  1.06
#define Iter  125
#define Scal  3276700

char ObjF[]="CPM2";
*/

float MSetPot(float cx, float cy, int MaxIter, int *Iters)
{
  float x, y;
  float x2, y2;
  float temp;

  x=cx;
  x2=SqrFP(x);
  y=cy;
  y2=SqrFP(y);
  *Iters=0;
  while((*Iters<MaxIter) && (x2+y2<20000.0))
  {
    temp=cx+x2-y2;
    y=cy+2*x*y;
    y2=SqrFP(y);
    x=temp;
    x2=SqrFP(x);
    ++*Iters;
```

```
  }
  if(*Iters<MaxIter)
    return(0.5*log10(x2+y2)/pow(2, *Iters));
  else
    return(0.0);
}

void MSetCPM(int nx, int ny, int MaxIter, float Xmin, float
Xmax, float Ymin, float Ymax)
{
  int ix, iy;
  int Iters;
  float cx, cy;
  float dx, dy;

  dx=(Xmax-Xmin)/(nx-1);
  dy=(Ymax-Ymin)/(ny-1);
  for(iy=0; iy<ny; iy++)
  {
    cy=Ymin+iy*dy;
    for(ix=0; ix<nx; ix++)
    {
      cx=Xmin+ix*dx;
      Height[ix][iy]=Round(MSetPot(cx, cy, MaxIter,
                                              &Iters)*Scal);
      PutPixel(ix, iy, (Iters/7), (Iters%35));
    }
  }
}

void InverseHeightBuffer()
{
  int i, j;
  int Max;

  Max=0;
  for(i=0; i<=MaxRes; i++)
  {
    for(j=0; j<=MaxRes; j++)
    {
      if(Height[i][j]>Max)
```

```
      Max=Height[i][j];
      }
    }
    for(i=0; i<=MaxRes; i++)
    {
      for(j=0; j<=MaxRes; j++)
      {
        Height[i][j]=Max-Height[i][j];
      }
    }
}

/*
┌──────────────────────────────────────────┐
│               Main Program               │
└──────────────────────────────────────────┘
*/

void main()
{
  clrscr();
  Scaling=32767;
  Res=MaxRes;
  InitGraphics();
  ClearHeightBuffer();
  MSetCPM(Res, Res, Iter, XMin, XMax, YMin, YMax);
  InverseHeightBuffer();
  strcpy(ObjectFile, ObjF);
  SaveHeightBuffer(ObjectFile);
  ExitGraphics();
}
```

Figure 15-6. Listing of Program to Generate Three-Dimensional Mandelbrot Sets

Fractals Using Quaternions

A quaternion is very similar to a three dimensional vector, except that it has the strange characteristic that multiplication of quaternions does not follow the commutative law. For most types of numbers, the expression:

$$a \times b = b \times a \qquad \text{(Equation 15-1)}$$

In other words the order in which the numbers are multiplied doesn't matter; we get the same result no matter what order is used. This is known as the commutative law. For quaternions, this is not true. In fact, we find that if a and b are quaternions then:

$$ab = -(ba) \qquad \text{(Equation 15-2)}$$

With this introduction, lets look at just what quaternions are. We may define a quaternion as consisting of a scalar q_0, and a three-dimensional vector having components q_1, q_2, and q_3, directed along the mutually orthogonal axes identified by the unit vectors *i*, *j*, and *k*. These vectors follow the rules for vector cross products in a right-hand coordinate system, namely:

$$\begin{array}{ll} ij = k & ji = -k \\ jk = i & kj = -i \\ ki = j & ik = -j \end{array} \qquad \text{(Equation 15-3)}$$

and

$$ijk = i^2 = j^2 = k^2 = -1 \qquad \text{(Equation 15-4)}$$

We can write the quaternion as:

$$Q = q_0 + iq_1 + jq_2 + kq_3 \qquad \text{(Equation 15-5)}$$

or alternately as:

$$Q = q_0 + \underline{q} \qquad \text{(Equation 15-6)}$$

where the underlining means that the variable is a three dimensional vector, or in other words:

$$\underline{q} = iq_1 + jq_2 + kq_3 \qquad \text{(Equation 15-7)}$$

```
/* CPMJ.c

      The Continuous Potential Method for the Julia Set

   c  =  p     +     q  i        ACP = attractive cycle period

       p           q
     -----       -----
      0.31        0.04      -
     -0.11        0.6557    -  JSet  ACP=3  before decay into
                                                    Cantor set
     -0.194       0.6557    -  after decay into Cantor set
     -0.12        0.74      -
      0.0         1.0       -  lightning dendrite
     -0.74543     0.11301   -  seahorse valley c-value
     -1.25        0.0       -  parabolic case  c>1.25 ACP=2, c<1.25
                                                         ACP=4
     -0.481762   -0.531657  -
     -0.39054    -0.58679   -
     -0.15652    -1.03225   -  dendrite with beads (secondary MSet)
      0.11031    -0.67037   -  Fatou dust
      0.27334     0.00742   -  parabolic case  small c  ACP=20

   125 iterations maximum
*/

#include "stdio.h"
#include "dos.h"
#include "conio.h"
#include "math.h"
#include "string.h"
#include "math.inc"
#include "graph.inc"
#include "render.inc"

#define cp    -0.12
#define cq     0.74
#define XMin  -1.4
```

```
#define XMax  1.4
#define YMin -1.4
#define YMax  1.4
#define Iter  32
#define Scal  32767

char ObjF[]="CPMJ1";

/*
#define cp    0.31
#define cq    0.04
#define XMin -1.4
#define XMax  1.4
#define YMin -1.4
#define YMax  1.4
#define Iter  32
#define Scal  32767

char ObjF[]="CPMJ2";
*/

int Iters;

float JSetPot(float p, float q, float cx, float cy, int
MaxIter)
{
  float x, y;
  float x2, y2;
  float temp;

  x=cx;
  x2=SqrFP(x);
  y=cy;
  y2=SqrFP(y);
  Iters=0;
  while((Iters<MaxIter) && (x2+y2<20000.0))
  {
    temp=p+x2-y2;
    y=q+2*x*y;
    y2=SqrFP(y);
```

```
    x=temp;
    x2=SqrFP(x);
    ++Iters;
  }
  if(Iters<MaxIter)
    return(0.5*log10(x2+y2)/pow(2, Iters));
  else
    return(0.0);
}

void JSetCPM(int nx, int ny, int MaxIter,
         float p, float q,
         float Xmin, float Xmax,
         float Ymin, float Ymax)
{
  int ix, iy;
  float cx, cy;
  float dx, dy;
  int z;

  dx=(Xmax-Xmin)/(nx-1);
  dy=(Ymax-Ymin)/(ny-1);
  for(ix=0; ix<=((nx-1)/2); ix++)
  {
    cx=Xmin+ix*dx;
    for(iy=0; iy<ny; iy++)
    {
      cy=Ymin+iy*dy;
      z=Round(JSetPot(p, q, cx, cy, MaxIter)*Scal);
      Height[ix][iy]=z;
      Height[Res-1-ix][Res-1-iy]=z;
      PutPixel(ix, 199-iy, Iters/7, Iters%35);
      PutPixel((Res-1-ix), 199-(Res-1-iy), Iters/7, Iters%35);
    }
  }
}

void InverseHeightBuffer()
{
  int i, j;
  int Max;
```

```
  Max=0;
  for(i=0; i<=MaxRes; i++)
  {
    for(j=0; j<=MaxRes; j++)
    {
      if(Height[i][j]>Max)
    Max=Height[i][j];
    }
  }
  for(i=0; i<=MaxRes; i++)
  {
    for(j=0; j<=MaxRes; j++)
    {
      Height[i][j]=Max-Height[i][j];
    }
  }
}

/*
                         Main Program
*/

void main()
{
  clrscr();
  Scaling=32767;
  Res=MaxRes;
  InitGraphics();
  ClearHeightBuffer();
  JSetCPM(Res, Res, Iter, cp, cq, XMin, XMax, YMin, YMax);
  InverseHeightBuffer();
  strcpy(ObjectFile, ObjF);
  SaveHeightBuffer(ObjectFile);
  ExitGraphics();
}
```

Figure 15-7. Listing of Program to Generate Three-Dimensional Julia Sets

Quaternions have interesting uses in transforming three-dimensional systems (for example in transforming from coordinate system of a space shuttle to earth coordinate system without encountering singularities) and also can be used in iterative equations to create strange four-dimensional fractals. Of course, we're really in deep trouble when we try to display a four-dimensional figure on a two-dimensional screen, so what we usually do is compute the data for a three-dimensional slice of the figure and then use the usual methods for projecting this onto the two-dimensional screen.

Quaternion Mathematics

Quaternion addition and subtraction can be done on a component by component basis just like vectors are added and subtracted. Quaternion multiplication gets a little more complicated. Suppose we have two quaternions, *P* and *Q*. The product is:

$$PQ = p_0q_0 + p_0\underline{q} + q_0\underline{p} + i^2p_1q_1 + j^2p_2q_2 + k^2p_3q_3$$
$$+ ip_1(jq_2 + kq_3) + jp_2(iq_1 + kq_3) + kp_3(iq_1 + jq_2)$$
$$= p_0q_0 + p_0\underline{q} + q_0\underline{p} - (\underline{p}\cdot\underline{q}) + \underline{p} \times \underline{q} \qquad \text{(Equation 15-8)}$$

where $\underline{p}\cdot\underline{q}$ and $\underline{p} \times \underline{q}$ are the vector dot product and vector cross product respectively as defined in any text on vector analysis. If you take a close look at this expression, you will see that it has two scalar terms (which may be summed to give one scalar) and three three-dimensional vector terms (which may be summed to give one three-dimensional vector). The result then consists of a scalar and a three dimensional vector (which is a quaternion) so that the product of two quaternions is a quaternion. Now, note that since one of these terms is not commutative ($\underline{p} \times \underline{q} = -\underline{q} \times \underline{p}$), the quaternion multiplication is also not commutative.

We won't go into any further detail on quaternion mathematics, except to say that we need a complete set of functions for performing these operations before we begin any serious programming with quaternions. Such a set of functions is provided in the file *Quater.Inc,* which is listed in Figure 15-8. The functions are fairly self-explanatory; by examining them in detail you ought to get a good idea of what is involved in each operation. The file *Quater.Inc* will be incorporated within the principal program file *Quater.c* by means of an include directive.

Generating Quaternion Fractal Databases

The file *Quater.c*, which is listed in Figure 15-9, includes the main program and functions for generating databases for quaternion fractals. The main program is relatively simple. It begins by calling the function *Parameters* to establish some initial parameters. It then sets the maximum height and calls *HeightBufferScalingFactor* to determine the scaling factor for the height values. Next, it calls *ScanSpace* which does all of the work necessary to fill the height array with height values. The program finally calls *SaveHeightBuffer* to save the height data to a disk database file.

The function *Parameters* first sets the text color to yellow and the background to blue. It then clears the display screen and displays ten lines of data about the quaternion generator. Next, it calls *ClearHeightBuffer* to zero the height array. Next it calls the function *QSetCons*. This function sets up a number of constants needed by the program. There are two versions of this function, one to generate a shape that is similar to the two-dimensional dragon curves—it's data is stored in the file *Dragon.DAT*—and the other to generate a shape that is similar to two-dimensional Julia sets. This version creates the data file *RevSolid.DAT*. As shown, the version for the dragon is commented out; if you want to create this database, remove the comment symbols (/* and */) and place them around the alternate version of the function instead. The *Parameters* function then sets up scale factors in the x, y, and z directions and offsets in the x and y directions.

The function *ScanSpace* begins by calling *MaxDepthOfRecursion*. We are going to use a recursive technique to determine height values, and this function determines the number of recursions that are needed to get from the stated display size down to a pixel level of resolution. The resulting number is displayed on the screen, and is stored in the parameter *MaxDepth*. *ScanSpace* then computes the change on x and y that is required for each increment in the height array, and the change in z for each increment of height that is allowed. The function then enters a pair of nested *do* loops which iterate once for every member of the height array. Within these loops, the function sets up the initial value for the quaternion P (at the farthest z) and then calls *Iterate*. This function repeatedly calls *Func* (which performs one iteration of the quaternion equation) until either the maximum number of iterations is achieved, or the magnitude of the quaternion exceeds a predetermined level.

When *Iterate* returns to *ScanSpace*, if the maximum number of iterations was not reached, we are done and the proper height value is determined. In this case, we call *UpdateHeight* which places the height data in the proper member of the height array. If the maximum number of iterations was reached, the function is run again for the nearest *z*. If the maximum number of iterations was reached we are done and the proper height value is determined, so we again call *UpdateHeight* to place the height data in the proper member of the height array. If neither of the above conditions occurred, we call *RecursiveCalc*.

This function sets up new limits for the beginning and ending *z* values and runs *Iterate* to perform the tests all over again, either terminating when the correct height value is found or running *RecursiveCalc* again, until the function finally zeroes in on the correct height value. When all of this has been done for one slice of data (a column), we display "Slice # nn", where *nn* is the column number, and then increment *Slice*, set *X* to a new value, and proceed through the loop again, until the entire height array has been filled and the function returns to the main program.

Plate 21 shows a quaternion dragon produced by the z-buffering technique. Plate 22 shows a solid of revolution generated with quaternions and rendered by the z-buffering technique.

Smearing Height Data

Sometimes, particularly in the case of quaternion and fractal height arrays, the discontinuities between adjacent points in the array are just too violent to make believable displays. For such cases, the program *Smear.c* may be used to modify the data in the *Height* array. This acts as a sort of box filter, which takes each point in the array and replaces it by the average of itself and every adjacent point. This smooths out any violent irregularities in the data. The *Smear.c* program is listed in Figure 15-10. Plate 25 shows a Mandelbrot set scene from the same program as Plate 17, but with smearing added.

```
/* Quater.c

                    Quaternion Mathematics Routines

  QAdd         - quaternion addition
  QSubtract    - quaternion subtraction
  QMultiply    - quaternion multiplication
  QDivide      - quaternion division
  QSquareRoot  - quaternion square root
  QSquare      - quaternion square

  Q = R + Ai + Bj + Ck = q[0] + q[1]i + q[2]j + q[3]k

*/

void QAdd(FDA p, FDA q, FDA r)            /* r=p+q */
{
  r[0]=p[0]+q[0];
  r[1]=p[1]+q[1];
  r[2]=p[2]+q[2];
  r[3]=p[3]+q[3];
}

void QSubtract(FDA p, FDA q, FDA r)       /* r=p-q */
{
  r[0]=p[0]-q[0];
  r[1]=p[1]-q[1];
  r[2]=p[2]-q[2];
  r[3]=p[3]-q[3];
}

void QMultiply(FDA p, FDA q, FDA r)       /* r=p*q */
{
  r[0]=p[0]*q[0]-p[1]*q[1]-p[2]*q[2]-p[3]*q[3];
  r[1]=p[0]*q[1]-p[1]*q[0]-p[2]*q[3]-p[3]*q[2];
  r[2]=p[0]*q[2]-p[2]*q[0]-p[3]*q[1]-p[1]*q[3];
  r[3]=p[0]*q[3]-p[3]*q[0]-p[1]*q[2]-p[2]*q[1];
}
```

```
void QDivide(FDA p, FDA q, FDA r)          /* r=p/q */
{
  FDA t, s;
  float a;

  q[1]=-q[1];
  q[2]=-q[2];
  q[3]=-q[3];
  QMultiply(p, q, t);
  QMultiply(q, q, s);
  a=1.0/s[0];
  r[0]=t[0]*a;
  r[1]=t[1]*a;
  r[2]=t[2]*a;
  r[3]=t[3]*a;
}

void QSquareRoot(FDA q, FDA s)
{
  float len, l, m;
  float a, b;
  FDA r;

  len=sqrt(SqrFP(q[0])+SqrFP(q[1])+SqrFP(q[2]));
  l=1.0/len;
  r[0]=q[0]*1.0;
  r[1]=q[1]*1.0;
  r[2]=q[2]*1.0;
  r[3]=0.0;
  m=1.0/sqrt(SqrFP(r[0])+SqrFP(r[1]));
  a=sqrt((1.0+r[2])/2.0);
  b=sqrt((1.0-r[2])/2.0);
  s[0]=sqrt(len)*b*r[0]*m;
  s[1]=sqrt(len)*b*r[1]*m;
  s[2]=sqrt(len)*a;
  s[3]=q[3];
}

void QSquare(FDA q, FDA r)          /* r=q^2 */
{
```

```
  float a;

  a=2.0*q[0];
  r[0]=SqrFP(q[0])-SqrFP(q[1])-SqrFP(q[2])-SqrFP(q[3]);
  r[1]=a*q[1];
  r[2]=a*q[2];
  r[3]=a*q[3];
}
```

Figure 15-8. Listing of Quaternion Mathematics Routines

```
/* Quater.c

            Quaternion Fractal Generator
               (rough approximation)
              f(q) = q * q * lambda

       Iteration of the Forward Equation in
                Quaternion Space

            By Christopher D. Watkins

           'C' Conversion by Larry Sharp

*/

#include "stdio.h"
#include "stdlib.h"
#include "dos.h"
#include "conio.h"
#include "math.h"
#include "string.h"
#include "math.inc"
#include "graph.inc"
#include "render.inc"
#include "quater.inc"

FDA q, l;
int DivergenceBoundary;
```

```
int MaximumIterations;
float XLeft, XRight;
float YBottom, YTop;
float ZBack, ZFront;

/*
    Constants for Quaternion Generator
*/


char ObjF[]="DRAGON";

void QSetCons()
{
  q[0]=0.0;
  q[1]=0.0;
  q[2]=0.0;
  q[3]=0.0;
  l[0]=0.2809;
  l[1]=0.53;
  l[2]=0.0;
  l[3]=0.0;
  DivergenceBoundary=4;
  MaximumIterations=100;
  XLeft=-1.3;
  XRight=1.3;
  YBottom=-1.3;
  YTop=1.3;
  ZBack=0.0;
  ZFront=1.3;
}

/*
char ObjF[]="REVSOLID";

void QSetCons()
{
  q[0]=0.0;
```

```
  q[1]=0.0;
  q[2]=0.0;
  q[3]=0.0;
  l[0]=-1.0;
  l[1]=0.0;
  l[2]=0.0;
  l[3]=0.0;
  DivergenceBoundary=4;
  MaximumIterations=100;
  XLeft=-1.8;
  XRight=1.8;
  YBottom=-1.8;
  YTop=1.8;
  ZBack=0.0;
  ZFront=1.8;
}
*/

float XScale, YScale, ZScale;
float XOffset, YOffset;

void Parameters()
{
  int tmp;

  textcolor(YELLOW);
  textbackground(BLUE);
  clrscr();
  printf("Quaternion Generator\n\n");
  printf ("approximation\n\n");
  printf("Equation : f(q)=lambda+q*q\n\n");
  printf("lambda   : quaternion constant for a particular
                                          fractal curve\n\n");
  printf("q        : quaternion variable seeded as
                                             0+0i+0j+0k\n\n");
  printf("The fractal surface is realized by examination of
                                                    the\n");
  printf("divergence properties of the equation in quaternion
                                               space\n\n");
```

```
  ClearHeightBuffer();
  QSetCons();
  XScale=(float) Res/(XRight-XLeft);
  XOffset=-XScale*XLeft;
  YScale=(float) Res/(YBottom-YTop);
  YOffset=-YScale*YTop;
  tmp=Res*Scaling;
  ZScale=(float) tmp/(ZFront-ZBack);
}

void Func(FDA Q, FDA NQ)
{
  QSquare(Q, Q);
  QAdd(Q, 1, NQ);
}

void Iterate(FDA p, int *NumberOfIterations)
{
  FDA nq;
  float tmp;

  Func(p, q);
  *NumberOfIterations=0;
  do
  {
    Func(q, nq);
    ++*NumberOfIterations;
    q[0]=nq[0];
    q[1]=nq[1];
    q[2]=nq[2];
    q[3]=nq[3];
    tmp=SqrFP(nq[0])+SqrFP(nq[1]);
  }
  while((SqrFP(nq[0])+SqrFP(nq[1])<DivergenceBoundary) &&
                    (*NumberOfIterations!=MaximumIterations));
}

Byte MaxDepth;
FDA p;
```

```
float X, Y, Z;
int NumOfIters;

void UpdateHeight(float x, float y, float z)
{
  int PlotX, PlotY, PlotZ;

  PlotX=Round(XScale*x+XOffset);
  PlotY=Round(YScale*y+YOffset);
  PlotZ=Round(ZScale*z);
  Height[PlotX][PlotY]=PlotZ;
}

void CalculateMaxDepthOfRecursion()
{
  float k;

  k=(float) Res*0.5;
  MaxDepth=0;
  while(k>=1.0)
  {
    k*=0.5;
    ++MaxDepth;
  }
  printf("Recursion Depth based on Resolution is %d\n",
    MaxDepth);
}

void RecursiveCalc(float Zrec, float Delta, int Depth)
{
  Z=Zrec;
  if(Depth!=MaxDepth)
  {
    p[0]=X;
    p[1]=Y;
    p[2]=Z;
    p[3]=0.0;
    Iterate(p, &NumOfIters);
    if(NumOfIters<MaximumIterations)
```

```
      Z-=Delta;
    else
      Z+=Delta;
    RecursiveCalc(Z, Delta*0.5, Depth+1);
  }
}

void ScanSpace()
{

  float dx, dy, dz;
  int Slice;
  float Zseed, DZseed;
  int Done;

  CalculateMaxDepthOfRecursion();
  dx=(XRight-XLeft)/(float) Res;
  dy=(YBottom-YTop)/(float) Res;
  dz=(ZFront-ZBack);
  Zseed=dz*0.5;
  DZseed=Zseed*0.5;
  Slice=0;
  X=XLeft;
  do
  {
    Y=YTop;
    do
    {
      Z=ZBack;
      p[0]=X;
      p[1]=Y;
      p[2]=Z;
      p[3]=0.0;
      Iterate(p, &NumOfIters);
      if(NumOfIters<MaximumIterations)
        goto Done;
      Z=ZFront;
      p[0]=X;
      p[1]=Y;
```

```
        p[2]=Z;
        p[3]=0.0;
        Iterate(p, &NumOfIters);
        if(!(NumOfIters<MaximumIterations))
          goto Done;
        RecursiveCalc(Zseed, DZseed, 0);
Done:
        UpdateHeight(X, Y, Z);
        Y+=dy;
      }
      while(!(Y<YBottom));
      gotoxy(1, 20);
      printf("Slice # %d\n", Slice);
      ++Slice;
      X+=dx;
    }
    while(!(X>XRight));
  }

  /*
  ┌──────────────────────────────────────────┐
  │               Main Program               │
  └──────────────────────────────────────────┘
  */

  void main()
  {
    Res=MaxRes;
    MaxHeight=Res;
    HeightBufferScalingFactor();
    Parameters();
    ScanSpace();
    strcpy(ObjectFile, ObjF);
    SaveHeightBuffer(ObjectFile);
  }
```

Figure 15-9. Listing of Program to Generate Quaternion Database

```
/* Smear.c

    Smear Algorithm (Box Filter of Sort) for Smoothing Data

                  Program by Larry Sharp

*/

#include "stdio.h"
#include "stdlib.h"
#include "dos.h"
#include "conio.h"
#include "math.h"
#include "string.h"
#include "math.inc"
#include "graph.inc"
#include "render.inc"

/*

         Program to Smear Data (Box Filter of Sort)

*/

int i, j, d, d1, d2, d3, d4, d5, d6, d7, d8, d9;
Name OF2;

void main()
{
  clrscr();
  printf("z-Buffer Data correction Program\n\n");
  ClearHeightBuffer();
  GetObjectFile();
  strcpy(OF2, ObjectFile);
  LoadHeightBuffer(ObjectFile);
  printf("\nCorrecting Height Buffer\n");

  for(j=1; j<Res; j++)
```

```
    {
      for(i=1; i<Res; i++)
      {
        d1=Height[i][j];
        d2=Height[i-1][j];
        d3=Height[i+1][j];
        d4=Height[i][j-1];
        d5=Height[i][j+1];
        d6=Height[i-1][j-1];
        d7=Height[i+1][j+1];
        d8=Height[i-1][j+1];
        d9=Height[i+1][j-1];
        d=(d1+d1+d3+d4+d5+d6+d7+d8+d9)/9;
        Height[i][j]=d;
      }
    }

    strcpy(ObjectFile, OF2);
    SaveHeightBuffer(ObjectFile);
  }
```

Figure 15-10. Program to Smear Z-Buffering Data

Part IV

RAY TRACING

CHAPTER 16

Ray Tracing Fundamentals

Ray tracing creates a two-dimensional picture of a three-dimensional world. It does this by using a computer process that is just the opposite of what a camera does in taking a picture. When a picture is taken with a camera the light from every point in a scene is projected to the camera lens and then to a film (the viewing screen) where a permanent record is made. With ray tracing we trace a ray from the viewer's eye to the screen and then on to whatever object in the scene it first hits. If the object is reflective, we continue tracing until we have accounted for every source of light that contributes to the color of the object at the point of intersection with the ray. The resulting color is then transferred to the viewing screen at the point where the ray intersected it. When we do this for every point on the viewing screen, we have a realistic two-dimensional picture of the scene, complete with shadows and reflections.

The limitation of this technique is that we must be able to specify the scene in terms of primitive objects (spheres, parallelograms, triangles, fractals, and so forth) which can be described by fairly simple mathematical equations. These, together with patterns to be projected on surfaces, light sources, and the position of the observer provide the information that is needed to define a scene so that the ray tracer will be able to trace every beam of light, creating all of the complex shadows and reflections that make up a real life scene. The results are scenes of breathtaking realism.

To see how this works in more detail, let's begin by postulating a scene made up of various primitive objects and light sources. An observer, stationed at a specified point in the coordinate system, is looking at this scene. He observes the scene through a translucent screen. Each tiny point on the screen (corresponding to a pixel on a color monitor display) appears to have some color associated with it; the color actually is the color of the ray of light that intersects the screen and projects onward to the observer's eye. This is the way a camera works, but it is inefficient for the computer to construct light rays from objects because millions of rays that are projected from each object in the scene do not intersect the screen and then continue to the viewer's eye, so they are not really needed for picture creation. Therefore, we project the light ray backwards from observer to screen and then in a straight line to the nearest object. This way, we consider only those rays that are essential for the picture.

The color of the ray at the intersection with this object is the color that it appears to have on the screen; we shall build a file of color data in which we assign that pixel on the screen to the light ray color. The color of the ray at the object intersection is not something that can be determined casually, since it often depends not only on the inherent color of the object, but also upon what happens to the light ray before it reaches the object. If the light is totally emitted by the object, and is of a specified color, our problem is solved. This seldom is the case, however. More often, the object is illuminated by external light sources or by ambient light, or both. If the surface is transmitting a color from within a partially transparent object, or reflecting a color from somewhere else, or changing a color that is originally projected by a light source, we have to follow the path of the light ray back toward the light sources and sum the various color contributions to determine the actual ray color at the object intersection. This is a very complex task, but not beyond the capabilities of our PC's.

Figure 16-1 shows the geometry of a simple ray-traced scene. This is a simple example that shows you how the process works. Now look at Figure 16-2, where a few additional objects and light sources have been added, together with shadows and some reflections. Already things are beginning to get more complex. When you consider that a realistic scene may contain thousands of objects, you begin to get an idea of the magnitude of the problem which faces the computer. Fortunately, however, in specifying the scene, we only have to enumerate the primitive objects of which it is composed. All of the complicated interactions of light and shadow are performed by the computer program.

It turns out that we can perform all of these ray tracing tasks within the constraints of an IBM PC or compatible in a reasonable amount of time, so if we have the proper software, we are in the picture-generating business. We are constrained, however, by the fact we must define a scene in terms of some primitive geometric objects. Each of these objects has its own unique properties that we must know in order to perform ray tracing computations. For example, the normal for a sphere is different from the normal for a triangle. The point of intersection of the light ray and a sphere requires a particular set of calculations. The calculations of the intersection of the light ray with a parallelogram are the same for all parallelograms but different from those for a sphere.

We begin to note a couple of important facts. First, the computer operations are computation intensive. Second, the methodology is highly suggestive of object oriented programming. In other words, our orientation in creating the program is to specify things that are to be done to various objects, and let the programming language handle the mechanics whereby it sorts out which type of object is being referred to for each operation and behaves appropriately for that object. Since we are trying to create code that will work without too many modifications in most recent versions of C, we have not made use of the latest object-oriented capabilities of Turbo C++ or Borland C++. If you have one of these compilers, you may want to try your hand at modifying the ray tracing program to work in an object-oriented mode. To begin with, however, try running the program in its original state and become familiar with how to specify scenes that the ray tracer translates into life-like pictures.

Compiler Memory Model

All of the programs described in this book up to this point can be compiled and run using the *small* memory model of any of the Borland family of C compilers. This model uses a 64K segment of memory for the program and another 64K segment of memory for data.

The ray tracing programs that are to be described in the following chapters need a great deal more memory. For them to compile and run without errors, you'll need to use the *large* memory model. Usually the compiler is set up to use the *small* memory model by default. To change to the large model, using Borland C compilers (Borland C++, Turbo C++, or Turbo C), type Alternate-o. From the menu that appears select *Compiler*. From the sub-menu select *Code Generation*. From the new menu that appears, go to the section headed *Model* and select *Large*.

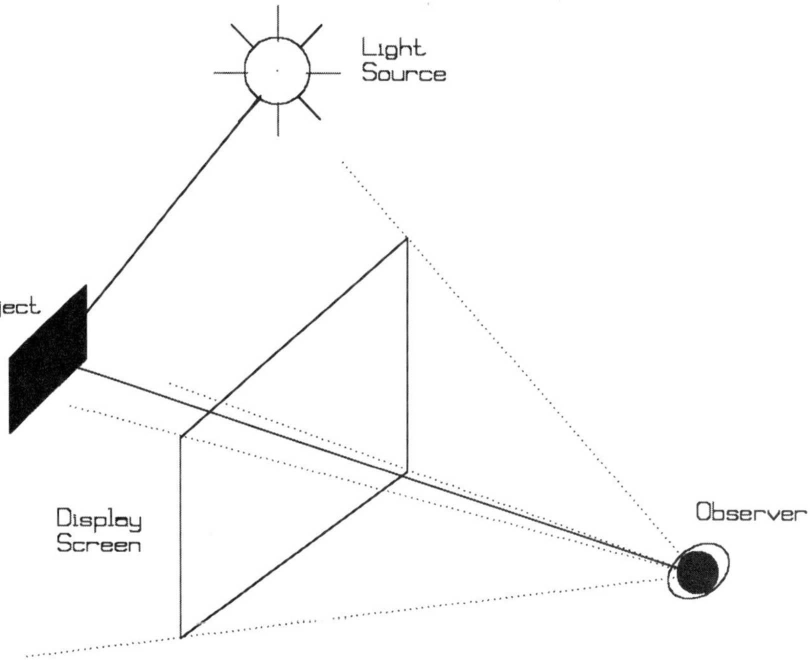

Figure 16-1. Ray Tracing Geometry

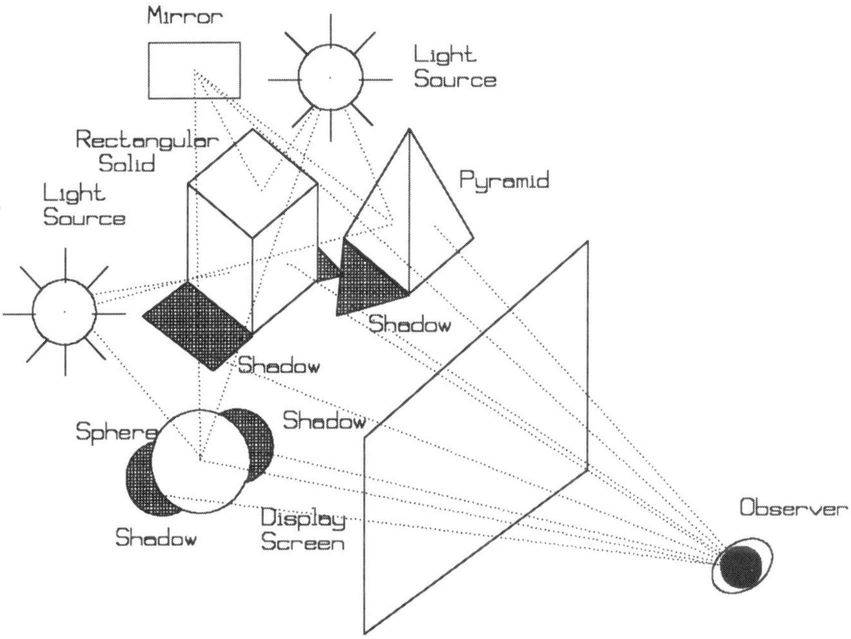

Figure 16-2. More Complicated Scene For Ray Tracing

CHAPTER 17

High Resolution Graphics

Using ray tracing and a little ingenuity in how we decide to display the picture, we can produce very realistic scenes using the 320-by-200-pixel-by-256-color mode of the VGA card. However, if you really want to see breathtaking graphics, you must produce ray-traced pictures using one of the extended modes that are now available with some VGA cards. We are using the Power-Graph ERGO-VGA card made by:

STB Systems, Inc.
P. O. Box 850957
Richardson, Texas 75085-0957

This top-quality card has given us excellent results with no problems or failures. The card uses the Tseng Laboratories ET4000 graphics chip set and 1 megabyte of memory to produce a number of extended display modes. These are shown in Table 17-1.

The mode that we use for ray tracing is mode 56, which is 1024-by-768-pixels-by-256 colors. It is remarkably easy to program, but requires that some modifications be made to the *Math.Inc* and *Graph.Inc* files that were described in Chapters 1 and 2. The new versions of these programs are listed in Figures 17-1 and 17-2 respectively. Most of the modifications are fairly simple and obvious. The most important thing to look at is the procedure *Plot.*

Plotting a point to the screen in the normal 256-color VGA mode was very simple; you simply compute the offset from the base display memory address by counting the number of bytes required to get to the location of the desired pixel (at one byte per pixel) and then write out the color data to that address. With the high-resolution mode, things are a little more complex, since all of the memory required to define a high-resolution display will not fit within the memory address space allocated by the IBM PC memory scheme.

Mode	Type	Resolution Characters	Resolution Pixels	Colors	Horizontal Frequency
0,1	Text	40 x 25	320 x 200	16	31.5 KHz
2,3	Text	80 x 25	640 x 200	16	31.5 KHz
4,5	Graphics	40 x 25	320 x 200	4	31.5 KHz
6	Graphics	80 x 25	640 x 200	2	31.5 KHz
7	Text	80 x 25	720 x 350	4	31.5 KHz
8	Text	132 x 25	1056 x 350	16	31.5 KHz
10	Text	132 x 44	1056 x 616	16	31.5 KHz
13	Graphics	40 x 25	320 x 200	16	31.5 KHz
14	Graphics	80 x 25	640 x 200	16	31.5 KHz
15	Graphics	80 x 25	640 x 350	2	31.5 KHz
16	Graphics	80 x 25	640 x 350	16	31.5 KHz
17	Graphics	80 x 30	640 x 480	2	31.5/38.0 KHz
18	Graphics	80 x 30	640 x 480	16	31.5/38.0 KHz
19	Graphics	40 x 25	320 x 200	256	31.5 KHz
34	Text	132 x 44	1056 x 616	16	31.5 KHz
35	Text	132 x 25	1056 x 350	16	31.5 KHz
36	Text	132 x 28	1056 x 400	16	31.5 KHz
41	Graphics	100 x 43	800 x 600	16	35.5/45.0 KHz
45	Graphics	80 x 25	640 x 350	256	31.5 KHz
46	Graphics	80 x 30	640 x 480	256	31.5/38.0 KHz
48	Graphics	100 x 43	800 x 600	256	35.5/45.0 KHz
55	Graphics	128 x 54	1024 x 768	16	35.5/48/57 KHz

Table 17-1. Display Modes for PowerGraph ERGO Extended VGA

Mode	Type	Resolution Characters	Resolution Pixels	Colors	Horizontal Frequency
56	Graphics	128 x 54	1024 x 768	256	35.5/48/57 KHz
106	Graphics	100 x 43	800 x 600	16	35.5/45.0 KHz
120	Graphics	80 x 25	640 x 400	256	31.5 KHz

Table 17-1. Display Modes for PowerGraph ERGO Extended VGA (continued)

Consequently, this memory is accessed through a 64K window; a page register on the VGA board is used to keep track of which part of the display memory is being accessed through the window. Thus, the new *Plot* procedure computes the memory address offset in the same way as the old function, except that it is found in modulo 64K so as to be sure to fit within the window. Then the procedure computes a page number, which is sent to the register in the VGA which stores page numbers in order to select the proper memory segment. The color is then written out to the memory location as before.

As you can see, the penalty for using a high-resolution display is minimal. If you want to speed up this procedure a bit, you can save the previous page number and not output to the page number register unless the new page number is different from the previous one.

One other thing to note is that the pixels in the 1024 x 768 mode are square, whereas in the 320 x 200 mode they are not. In other words, with a 3 x 4 screen aspect ratio, the horizontal distance per pixel with 1024 pixels in a row is the same as the vertical distance per pixel with 768 pixels in a column. This is not true of the 320 x 200 mode, where the width of a pixel is greater than its height. Thus in the high resolution mode, when drawing circles, for example, no adjustment in the radius needs to be made to obtain a true circle. In the low-resolution mode, however, the radius used in computing the horizontal direction must be different from that used in the vertical direction; otherwise you will get an oval instead of a circle. Because of this, you will see corrections at various places in the graphics routines to take this problem into account.

```
{ Math2.Inc

                     Mathematical Functions

          Original Material by Christopher D. Watkins

                 'C' Conversion by Larry Sharp

   Radians    - converts degrees to radians
   Degrees    - converts radians to degrees
   CosD       - cosine in degrees
   SinD       - sine in degrees
   Power      - power a^n
   Log        - log base 10
   Exp10      - exp base 10
   Sign       - negative=-1  positive=1  null=0
   IntSign    - negative=-1  positive=1  null=0
   IntSqrt    - integer square root
   IntPower   - integer power a^n
*/

#define Ln10 2.30258509299405E+000
#define OneOverLn10 0.43429448190325E+000
#define Pi 3.1415927
#define PiOver180 1.74532925199433E-002
#define PiUnder180 5.72957795130823E+001

typedef unsigned char      Byte;
typedef unsigned int       Word;
typedef enum {false, true} Boolean;

int Round(float x)
{
  return((int)(x+0.5));
}

int Trunc(float x)
{
  return((int)(x));
}
```

```
float Frac(float x)
{
  int y;

  y=((int)(x));
  return(x-y);
}
float SqrFP(float x)
{
  return(x*x);
}

int Sqr(int x)
{
  return(x*x);
}

float Radians(float Angle)
{
  return(Angle*PiOver180);
}

float Degrees(float Angle)
{
  return(Angle*PiUnder180);
}

float CosD(float Angle)
{
  return(cos(Radians(Angle)));
}

float SinD(float Angle)
{
  return(sin(Radians(Angle)));
}

float Power(float Base, int Exponent)
{
  float BPower;
```

```
  int   t;
  if(Exponent==0)
    return(1);
  else
  {
    BPower=1.0;
    for(t=1; t<=Exponent; t++)
    {
      BPower*=Base;
    }
    return(BPower);
  }
}

float Log(float x)
{
  return(log(x)*OneOverLn10);
}

float Exp10(float x)
{
  return(exp(x*Ln10));
}

float Sign(float x)
{
  if(x<0)
    return(-1);
  else
  {
    if(x>0)
      return(1);
    else
    {
      return(0);
    }
  }
}
```

```
int IntSign(int x)
{
  if(x<0)
    return(-1);
  else
  {
    if(x>0)
      return(1);
    else
    {
      return(0);
    }
  }
}

int IntSqrt(int x)
{
  int OddInt, OldArg, FirstSqrt;

  OddInt=1;
  OldArg=x;
  while(x>=0)
  {
    x-=OddInt;
    OddInt+=2;
  }
  FirstSqrt=OddInt >> 1;
  if(Sqr(FirstSqrt)-FirstSqrt+1 > OldArg)
    return(FirstSqrt-1);
  else
    return(FirstSqrt);
}

int IntPower(int Base, int Exponent)
{
  if(Exponent==0)
    return(1);
  else
    return(Base*IntPower(Base, Exponent-1));
}
```

```
/*
┌──────────────────────────────────────────────────────────────┐
│                  Vector and Matrix Routines                  │
└──────────────────────────────────────────────────────────────┘

   Vec           - Make Vector
   VecInt        - Make Integer Vector
   UnVec         - Get Components of vector
   UnVecInt      - Get Components of Integer Vector
   VecDot        - Vector Dot Product
   VecCross      - Vector Cross Product
   VecLen        - Vector Length
   VecNormalize  - Vector Normalize
   VecMatxMult   - Vector Matrix Multiply
   VecSub        - Vector Subtraction
   VecSubInt     - Vector Subtraction Integer
   VecAdd        - Vector Addition
   VecAdd3       - Vector Addition
   VecCopy       - Vector Copy
   VecLinComb    - Vector Linear Combination
   VecScalMult   - Vector Scalar Multiple
   VecScalMultI  - Vector Scalar Multiple
   VecScalMultInt- Vector Scalar Multiple and Rounding
   VecAddScalMult- Vector Add Scalar Multiple
   VecNull       - Vector Null
   VecNullInt    - Vector Null Integer
   VecElemMult   - Vector Element Multiply
*/

typedef float TDA[3];
typedef int   TDIA[3];
typedef float FDA[4];
typedef float Matx4x4[4][4];

void Vec(float r, float s, float t, TDA A)
{
  A[0]=r;
  A[1]=s;
  A[2]=t;
}
```

```
void VecInt(int r, int s, int t, TDIA A)
{
  A[0]=r;
  A[1]=s;
  A[2]=t;
}

void UnVec(TDA A, float *r, float *s, float *t)
{
  *r=A[0];
  *s=A[1];
  *t=A[2];
}

void UnVecInt(TDIA A, int *r, int *s, int *t)
{
  *r=A[0];
  *s=A[1];
  *t=A[2];
}

float VecDot(TDA A, TDA B)
{
  return(A[0]*B[0] + A[1]*B[1] + A[2]*B[2]);
}

void VecCross(TDA A, TDA B, TDA C)
{
  C[0]=A[1]*B[2] - A[2]*B[1];
  C[1]=A[2]*B[0] - A[0]*B[2];
  C[2]=A[0]*B[1] - A[1]*B[0];
}

float VecLen(TDA A)
{
 return(sqrt(SqrFP(A[0])+SqrFP(A[1])+SqrFP(A[2])));
}

void VecNormalize(TDA A)
{
  float dist,invdist;
```

```
  dist=VecLen(A);
  if(!(dist==0.0))
  {
    invdist=1.0/dist;
    A[0]*=invdist;
    A[1]*=invdist;
    A[2]*=invdist;
  }
  else
  {
    puts("Zero-Length Vectors cannot be Normalized");
    exit(1);
  }
}

void VecMatxMult(FDA A, Matx4x4 Matrix, FDA B)
{
  int mRow, mCol;

  for(mCol=0; mCol<4; mCol++)
  {
    B[mCol]=0;
    for(mRow=0; mRow<4; mRow++)
      B[mCol]+=A[mRow]*Matrix[mRow][mCol];
  }
}

void VecSub(TDA A, TDA B, TDA C)
{
  C[0]=A[0]-B[0];
  C[1]=A[1]-B[1];
  C[2]=A[2]-B[2];
}

void VecSubInt(TDIA A, TDIA B, TDA C)
{
  C[0]=A[0]-B[0];
  C[1]=A[1]-B[1];
  C[2]=A[2]-B[2];
}
```

```
void VecAdd(TDA A, TDA B, TDA C)
{
  C[0]=A[0]+B[0];
  C[1]=A[1]+B[1];
  C[2]=A[2]+B[2];
}

void VecAdd3(TDA A, TDA B, TDA C, TDA D)
{
  D[0]=A[0]+B[0]+C[0];
  D[1]=A[1]+B[1]+C[1];
  D[2]=A[2]+B[2]+C[2];
}

void VecCopy(TDA A, TDA B)
{
  Byte i;

  for(i=0; i<3; i++)
  {
     B[i]=A[i];
  }
}

void VecLinComb(float r, TDA A, float s, TDA B, TDA C)
{
  C[0]=r*A[0]+s*B[0];
  C[1]=r*A[1]+s*B[1];
  C[2]=r*A[2]+s*B[2];
}

void VecScalMult(float r, TDA A, TDA B)
{
  B[0]=r*A[0];
  B[1]=r*A[1];
  B[2]=r*A[2];
}

void VecScalMultI(float r, TDIA A, TDA B)
{
```

```
  B[0]=r*A[0];
  B[1]=r*A[1];
  B[2]=r*A[2];
}

void VecScalMultInt(float r, TDA A, TDIA B)
{
  B[0]=Round(r*A[0]);
  B[1]=Round(r*A[1]);
  B[2]=Round(r*A[2]);
}

void VecAddScalMult(float r, TDA A, TDA B, TDA C)
{
  C[0]=r*A[0]+B[0];
  C[1]=r*A[1]+B[1];
  C[2]=r*A[2]+B[2];
}

void VecNull(TDA A)
{
  A[0]=0.0;
  A[1]=0.0;
  A[2]=0.0;
}

void VecNullInt(TDIA A)
{
  A[0]=0;
  A[1]=0;
  A[2]=0;
}

void VecElemMult(float r, TDA A, TDA B, TDA C)
{
  C[0]=r*A[0]*B[0];
  C[1]=r*A[1]*B[1];
  C[2]=r*A[2]*B[2];
}
```

```
/*
    Affine Transformation Routines

   ZeroMatrix        - zeros the elements of a 4x4 matrix
   Translate3D       - make translation matrix
   Scale3D           - make scaling matrix
   Rotate3D          - make rotation matrix
   ZeroAllMatricies  - zeros all matrices used in transformation
   Multiply3DMatricies- multiply 2 4x4 matricies
   PrepareMatrix     - prepare the transformation matrix
                                                    (Tm=S*R*T)
   PrepareInvMatrix  - prepare the inverse transformation matrix
   Transform         - multiply a vertex by the transformation
                                                        matrix
*/

void ZeroMatrix(Matx4x4 A)
{
  int i, j;

  for(i=0; i<4; i++)
  {
    for(j=0; j<4; j++)
      A[i][j]=0.0;
  }
}

void Translate3D(float tx, float ty, float tz, Matx4x4 A)
{
  int i;

  ZeroMatrix(A);
  for(i=0; i<4; i++)
    A[i][i]=1.0;
  A[0][3]=-tx;
  A[1][3]=-ty;
  A[2][3]=-tz;
}
```

```
void Scale3D(float sx, float sy, float sz, Matx4x4 A)
{
  ZeroMatrix(A);
  A[0][0]=sx;
  A[1][1]=sy;
  A[2][2]=sz;
  A[3][3]=1.0;
}

void Rotate3D(int m, float Theta, Matx4x4 A)
{
  int   m1, m2;
  float c, s;

  ZeroMatrix(A);
  A[m-1][m-1]=1.0;
  A[3][3]=1.0;
  m1=(m % 3)+1;
  m2=(m1 % 3);
  m1-=1;
  c=CosD(Theta);
  s=SinD(Theta);
  A[m1][m1]=c;
  A[m1][m2]=s;
  A[m2][m2]=c;
  A[m2][m1]=-s;
}

void Multiply3DMatricies(Matx4x4 A, Matx4x4 B, Matx4x4 C)
{

  int   i, j, k;
  float ab;

  for(i=0; i<4; i++)
  {
    for(j=0; j<4; j++)
    {
      ab=0;
      for(k=0; k<4; k++)
```

```
      ab+=A[i][k]*B[k][j];
      C[i][j]=ab;
    }
  }
}

void MatCopy(Matx4x4 a, Matx4x4 b)
{
  Byte i, j;

  for(i=0; i<4; i++)
  {
    for(j=0; j<4; j++)
      b[i][j]=a[i][j];
  }
}

void PrepareMatrix(float Tx, float Ty, float Tz,
           float Sx, float Sy, float Sz,
           float Rx, float Ry, float Rz,
           Matx4x4 XForm)
{
  Matx4x4 M1, M2, M3, M4, M5, M6, M7, M8, M9;

  Scale3D(Sx, Sy, Sz, M1);
  Rotate3D(1, Rx, M2);
  Rotate3D(2, Ry, M3);
  Rotate3D(3, Rz, M4);
  Translate3D(Tx, Ty, Tz, M5);
  Multiply3DMatricies(M2, M1, M6);
  Multiply3DMatricies(M3, M6, M7);
  Multiply3DMatricies(M4, M7, M8);
  Multiply3DMatricies(M5, M8, M9);
  MatCopy(M9, XForm);
}

void PrepareInvMatrix(float Tx, float Ty, float Tz,
          float Sx, float Sy, float Sz,
          float Rx, float Ry, float Rz,
          Matx4x4 XForm)
{
```

```
  Matx4x4 M1, M2, M3, M4, M5, M6, M7, M8, M9;

  Scale3D(Sx, Sy, Sz, M1);
  Rotate3D(1, Rx, M2);
  Rotate3D(2, Ry, M3);
  Rotate3D(3, Rz, M4);
  Translate3D(Tx, Ty, Tz, M5);
  Multiply3DMatricies(M4, M5, M6);
  Multiply3DMatricies(M3, M6, M7);
  Multiply3DMatricies(M2, M7, M8);
  Multiply3DMatricies(M1, M8, M9);
  MatCopy(M9, XForm);
}

void Transform(TDA A, Matx4x4 M, TDA B)
{
  B[0]=M[0][0]*A[0]+M[0][1]*A[1]+M[0][2]*A[2]+M[0][3];
  B[1]=M[1][0]*A[0]+M[1][1]*A[1]+M[1][2]*A[2]+M[1][3];
  B[2]=M[2][0]*A[0]+M[2][1]*A[1]+M[2][2]*A[2]+M[2][3];
}
```

Figure 17-1. Listing of the Math2.Inc File

```
/* Graph2.Inc

                    Video Graphics Array Driver

   Plot          - place pixel to screen
   ClearPallete  - clear palette register
   SetPalette    - set palette register
   InitPalette1  - 64 levels of grey, red, green and blue
   InitPalette2  - 7 colors with 35 intensities each
   CyclePalette  - cycle through palette
   Circle        - circle draw routine
   Draw          - line draw routine
   InitGraphics  - initialize graphics
   WaitForKey    - wait for key press
```

```
   ExitGraphics  - sound and wait for keypress before exiting
                                                        graphics
   Title         - set up text screen colors
*/

union  REGS reg;
struct SREGS inreg;

void SetMode(int Mode)

{
  reg.h.ah=0;
  reg.h.al=Mode;
  int86(0x10,&reg,&reg);
}

#define MaxXres 1024
#define MaxYres 768
#define MaxX (MaxXres-1)
#define MaxY (MaxYres-1)

int     XRes, YRes;
int     PreCalcY[MaxY+1];
Boolean HighRes;

void PreCalc()
{
  int j;

  for(j=0; j<=MaxY; j++)
    PreCalcY[j]=0;
  if(HighRes)
  {
    for(j=0; j<=767; j++)
      PreCalcY[j]=1024*j;
  }
  else
  {
    for(j=0; j<=199; j++)
      PreCalcY[j]=320*j;
```

```
    }
  }

  void Plot(int x, int y, Byte color)

  {
    Word Offset, Page;
    char far *address;

    if(!((x<0) || (y<0) || (x>MaxX) || (y>MaxY)))
    {
      if(HighRes)
      {
        Offset=PreCalcY[y]+x;
        Page=y/64;
        outport(0x3CD, Page|64);
        address=(char far *) (0xA0000000L + Offset);
        *address=color;
      }
      else
      {
        Offset = PreCalcY[y] + x;
        address = (char far *)  (0xA0000000L + Offset);
        *address = color;
      }
    }
  }

  typedef struct
  {
    Byte Red;
    Byte Grn;
    Byte Blu;
  }
  RGB;

  typedef RGB PaletteRegister[255];
  PaletteRegister Color;

  void ClearPalette(PaletteRegister Color)
```

```
{ Word i;

  for(i=0; i<=255; i++)
  {
    Color[i].Red=0;
    Color[i].Grn=0;
    Color[i].Blu=0;
  }
}

void SetPalette(PaletteRegister Hue)
{
  reg.x.ax=0x1012;
  segread(&inreg);
  inreg.es=inreg.ds;
  reg.x.bx=0;
  reg.x.cx=256;
  reg.x.dx=(int)&Hue[0];
  int86x(0x10,&reg,&reg,&inreg);
}

void InitPalette(PaletteRegister Color)
{
  Word i;

  for(i=0; i<64; i++)
  {
    Color[i].Red=i;
    Color[i].Grn=i;
    Color[i].Blu=i;
  }

  for(i=64; i<128; i++)
  {
    Color[i].Red=i-64;
    Color[i].Grn=0;
    Color[i].Blu=0;
  }

  for(i=128; i<192; i++)
```

```
    {
      Color[i].Red=0;
      Color[i].Grn=i-128;
      Color[i].Blu=0;
    }

    for(i=192; i<=255; i++)
    {
      Color[i].Red=0;
      Color[i].Grn=0;
      Color[i].Blu=i-192;
    }
}

void InitPalette2(PaletteRegister Color)
{
    Word i;

    for(i=0; i<36; i++)
    {
      Color[i].Red=0;
      Color[i].Grn=0;
      Color[i].Blu=Round(1.8*i);
    }

    for(i=36; i<72; i++)
    {
      Color[i].Red=0;
      Color[i].Grn=Round(1.8*(i-36));
      Color[i].Blu=0;
    }

    for(i=72; i<108; i++)
    {
      Color[i].Red=0;
      Color[i].Grn=Round(1.8*(i-72));
      Color[i].Blu=Round(1.8*(i-72));
    }

    for(i=108; i<144; i++)
    {
```

```
    Color[i].Red=Round(1.8*(i-108));
    Color[i].Grn=0;
    Color[i].Blu=0;
  }

  for(i=144; i<180; i++)
  {
    Color[i].Red=Round(1.8*(i-144));
    Color[i].Grn=0;
    Color[i].Blu=Round(1.8*(i-144));
  }

  for(i=180; i<216; i++)
  {
    Color[i].Red=Round(1.8*(i-180));
    Color[i].Grn=Round(1.8*(i-180));
    Color[i].Blu=0;
  }

  for(i=216; i<252; i++)
  {
    Color[i].Red=Round(1.8*(i-216));
    Color[i].Grn=Round(1.8*(i-216));
    Color[i].Blu=Round(1.8*(i-216));
  }
}

void CyclePalette(PaletteRegister Hue)
{
  Word i;
  RGB  tmp;

  tmp=Hue[0];
  for(i=1; i<=255; i++)
    Hue[i-1]=Hue[i];
  Hue[255]=tmp;
  SetPalette(Hue);
}

void Swap(int *first, int *second)
{
```

```
  int temp;

  temp=*first;
  *first=*second;
  *second=temp;
}

void Circle(Word x, Word y, Word radius, Byte color)
{
  int a, af, b, bf, target, r2, asp;

  if(HighRes)
    asp=100;
  else
    asp=120;
  target=0;
  a=radius;
  b=0;
  r2=Sqr(radius);
  while(a>=b)
   {
    b=Round(sqrt(r2-Sqr(a)));
    Swap(&target,&b);
    while(b<target)
     {
      af=(asp*a) / 100;
      bf=(asp*b) / 100;
      Plot(x+af, y+b, color);
      Plot(x+bf, y+a, color);
      Plot(x-af, y+b, color);
      Plot(x-bf, y+a, color);
      Plot(x-af, y-b, color);
      Plot(x-bf, y-a, color);
      Plot(x+af, y-b, color);
      Plot(x+bf, y-a, color);
      ++b;
     }
    -a;
   }
 }
```

```
void Draw(int xx1, int yy1, int xx2, int yy2, Byte color)
{
  int LgDelta, ShDelta, Cycle, LgStep, ShStep, dtotal;

  LgDelta=xx2-xx1;
  ShDelta=yy2-yy1;
  if(LgDelta<0)
  {
    LgDelta=-LgDelta;
    LgStep=-1;
  }
  else
    LgStep=1;
  if(ShDelta<0)
  {
    ShDelta=-ShDelta;
    ShStep=-1;
  }
  else
    ShStep=1;
  if(ShDelta<LgDelta)
  {
    Cycle=LgDelta >> 1;
    while(xx1 != xx2)
    {
      Plot(xx1, yy1, color);
      Cycle+=ShDelta;
      if(Cycle>LgDelta)
       {
    Cycle-=LgDelta;
    yy1+=ShStep;
       }
      xx1+=LgStep;
    }
    Plot(xx1, yy1, color);
  }
  else
  {
    Cycle=ShDelta >> 1;
    Swap(&LgDelta, &ShDelta);
```

```
      Swap(&LgStep, &ShStep);
      while(yy1 != yy2)
      {
        Plot(xx1, yy1, color);
        Cycle+=ShDelta;
        if(Cycle>LgDelta)
        {
      Cycle-=LgDelta;
      xx1+=ShStep;
        }
        yy1+=LgStep;
      }
      Plot(xx1, yy1, color);
    }
  }
  void InitGraphics(Byte Mode)
  {
    switch(Mode)
    {
      case 19 : HighRes=false;
            XRes=320;
            YRes=200;
            break;
      case 56 : HighRes=true;
            XRes=1024;
            YRes=768;
            break;
      default :
           printf("Mode %d is not a valid graphics
              mode\n\n",Mode);
            puts("Hit any key to exit");
            getch();
            exit(1);
            break;
    }
    PreCalc();
    SetMode(Mode);
    ClearPalette(Color);
    InitPalette2(Color);
    SetPalette(Color);
  }
```

```
void WaitForKey()
{
  char k;

  while(!(k=getch()));
}

void ExitGraphics()
{
  sound(1000);
  delay(500);
  nosound();
  WaitForKey();
  SetMode(3);
}

void Title()
{
  textcolor(YELLOW);
  textbackground(BLUE);
  clrscr();
}


/*
 ╔════════════════════════════════════════════════════════╗
 ║           Three Dimensional Plotting Routines          ║
 ╚════════════════════════════════════════════════════════╝

   InitPlotting        - rotation and tilt angles
   InitPerspective     - observer location and distances
   MapCoordinates      - maps 3D space onto the 2D screen
   CartesianPlot       - plot a cartesian system point
   CylindricalPlot3D   - plot a cylindrical system point
   SphericalPlot3D     - plot a spherical system point
   DrawLine3D          - plots a line from 3D coordinates
*/

int   CentreX, CentreY;
int   Angl, Tilt;
float CosA, SinA;
```

```
float CosB, SinB;
float CosACosB, SinASinB;
float CosASinB, SinACosB;

void InitPlotting(int Ang, int Tlt)
{
  CentreX=MaxX/2;
  CentreY=MaxY/2;
  Angl=Ang;
  Tilt=Tlt;
  CosA=CosD(Angl);
  SinA=SinD(Angl);
  CosB=CosD(Tilt);
  SinB=SinD(Tilt);
  CosACosB=CosA*CosB;
  SinASinB=SinA*SinB;
  CosASinB=CosA*SinB;
  SinACosB=SinA*CosB;
}

Boolean PerspectivePlot;
float   Mx, My, Mz, ds;

void InitPerspective(Boolean Perspective, float x, float y,
float z, float m)
{
  PerspectivePlot=Perspective;
  Mx=x;
  My=y;
  Mz=z;
  ds=m;
}

void MapCoordinates(float X, float Y, float Z, int *Xp, int
*Yp)
{
  float Xt, Yt, Zt;

  Xt=(Mx+X*CosA-Y*SinA);
```

```
  Yt=(My+X*SinASinB+Y*CosASinB+Z*CosB);
  if(PerspectivePlot)
  {
    Zt=Mz+X*SinACosB+Y*CosACosB-Z*SinB;
    *Xp=CentreX+Round(ds*Xt/Zt);
    *Yp=CentreY-Round(ds*Yt/Zt);
  }
  else
  {
    *Xp=CentreX+Round(Xt);
    *Yp=CentreY-Round(Yt);
  }
}

void CartesianPlot3D(float X, float Y, float Z, Byte Color)
{
  int Xp, Yp;

  MapCoordinates(X, Y, Z, &Xp, &Yp);
  Plot(Xp, Yp, Color);
}

void CylindricalPlot3D(float Rho, float Theta, float Z, Byte
Color)
{
  float X, Y;

  Theta=Radians(Theta);
  X=Rho*cos(Theta);
  Y=Rho*sin(Theta);
  CartesianPlot3D(X, Y, Z, Color);
}

void SphericalPlot3D(float R, float Theta, float Phi, Byte
Color)
{
  float X, Y, Z;

  Theta=Radians(Theta);
```

```
  Phi=Radians(Phi);
  X=R*sin(Theta)*cos(Phi);
  Y=R*sin(Theta)*sin(Phi);
  Z=R*cos(Theta);
  CartesianPlot3D(X, Y, Z, Color);
}

void DrawLine3D(TDA Pnt1, TDA Pnt2, Byte Color)
{
  int   Xp1, Yp1;
  int   Xp2, Yp2;
  float x1, y1, z1;
  float x2, y2, z2;

  UnVec(Pnt1, &x1, &y1, &z1);
  UnVec(Pnt2, &x2, &y2, &z2);
  MapCoordinates(x1, y1, z1, &Xp1, &Yp1);
  MapCoordinates(x2, y2, z2, &Xp2, &Yp2);
  Draw(Xp1, Yp1, Xp2, Yp2, Color);
}

/*
```

Pixel

```
   PutPixel - plots pixel
   GetPixel - gets pixel

   Color 1 - Blue
     2 - Green
     3 - Cyan
     4 - Red
     5 - Magenta
     6 - Brown/Yellow
     7 - Gray Scale

   Intensity levels (0..35) for each color
*/
```

```
#define MaxCol   7
#define MaxInten 35

void PutPixel(int x, int y, Byte Color, Byte Intensity)
{
  Byte Col;

  if(Intensity>MaxInten)
    abort();
  Col=((MaxInten+1)*(Color-1)+Intensity) & 255;
  Plot(x, y, Col);
}

int GetPixel(int x, int y)
{
  reg.x.ax=3328;
  reg.x.dx=y;
  reg.x.cx=x;
  int86(0x10,&reg,&reg);
  return(reg.x.ax&255);
}

/*
          Setup of Coordinate Axes and Color Palette

   PutAxisAndPalette - toggle for Axis and Palette
   AxisAndPalette    - places Axis and Color Palette on screen
*/

Boolean DrawAxisAndPalette;

void PutAxisAndPalette(Boolean PlaceOnScreen)
{
  if(PlaceOnScreen)
    DrawAxisAndPalette=true;
  else
```

```
    DrawAxisAndPalette=false;
}

void DisplayAxis()
{
  int x, y, z;

  for(x=-100; x<101; x++)
  {
    CartesianPlot3D(x, 0, 0, 35);
    CartesianPlot3D(100, 0, 0, 251);
  }
  for(y=-100; y<101; y++)
  {
    CartesianPlot3D(0, y, 0, 71);
    CartesianPlot3D(0, 100, 0,251);
  }
  for(z=-100; z<101; z++)
  {
    CartesianPlot3D(0, 0, z, 107);
    CartesianPlot3D(0, 0, 100, 251);
  }
}

void DisplayPalette()
{
  int  X, Y;
  Byte Color;
  Byte Intensity;

  for(Color=1; Color<=MaxCol; Color++)
  {
    for(Intensity=0; Intensity<=MaxInten; Intensity++)
     {
       for(X=0; X<4; X++)
       {
     for(Y=0; Y<4; Y++)
       PutPixel(X+5*Color, 190-Y-5*Intensity, Color, Intensity);
       }
```

```
      }
    }
  }

  void AxisAndPalette()
  {
    if(DrawAxisAndPalette)
    {
      DisplayAxis();
      DisplayPalette();
    }
  }
```

Figure 17-2. Listing of the *Graph2.Inc* File

CHAPTER 18

Defining a Scene: The .RT File

Before we can begin ray tracing, we need somehow to define the scene upon which we are to be operating. This is done by means of a file ending with the extension *.RT*. This is a text file, so you can create one on your standard text editor, as long as it has an ASCII output (one that doesn't include any weird control sequences). However, the order in which things are specified, and what should appear on each line, are constrained.

Figure 18-1 lists all of the *.RT* files that have been created for scenes thus far. Once you try out these scenes and get an idea of how they are created, you may branch out and create scenes of your own, which can be made up of the primitive objects defined in the appropriate files. We're going to describe the makeup of a typical *.RT* file in the section that follows. Later, in Chapter 19, we'll describe how the ray tracing program makes use of this file, which will give you a better idea of the constraints involved.

Formatting Constraints

The files that are listed in this chapter are all text files that are read into the ray tracing program using C's *fscanf* function. This makes it easy to create and process the files, but it requires that the arrangement of elements and the positioning of the various elements on a line be set rigidly. The categories that you see flush with the left-hand margin are object definitions that can occur in the file in any order. However, once you have specified one of these objects, certain numerical values and/or names must occur at the exact positions where they are shown. We'll go into depth on the first file; *Stack.RT*. Keep in mind, however, that the problems and reasoning are similar for all the files.

The first parameter that is specified is *STATS*. Note that on the following five lines are specified the parameters *OUTFILE*, *XRES*, *YRES*, *XPITCH*, and *YPITCH*. When the program reads this file, it takes the string (of no more than 30 characters) beginning at column 14 of the first line below *STATS* and sets it up as the name of the output file. Similarly, the eight characters beginning at column 14 of the next line will be the integer value for x resolution; the eight characters beginning at column 14 on the next line will be the integer value of *y* resolution; the eight characters beginning at column 14 on the next line will be the floating point value for the x pitch (a scalar which is somewhat like the inverse of the focal length); and the eight characters beginning at column 14 on the next line will be the floating point value for the *y* pitch. It doesn't make any difference what you call these; if you made the first line *XRES* the output would still be the name for the output file. So don't get mixed up as to what lines things should go on; use one of the sample files as a template. Similarly, be sure to start your inputs at column 14. If you do not start your inputs there then the numbers stored by the program may be something different than you think.

The next category that is listed is *ENVIRONMENT*. There are four weighting factors here that are used to determine when a ray is no longer making a significant contribution to the overall light plus a depth factor that indicates how many recursions should take place to continue tracing the ray before it is no longer significant. You'll note that all of the sample files use the same values for these parameters. Until you have studied the ray tracing program very carefully and have a good understanding of how these factors interact, leave them alone.

The next category is *OBSERVER*. The first parameter here is the focal length. Unfortunately, this doesn't relate directly to any similar values for lenses. However, the principle is the same. Large focal lengths give telephoto effects, with a narrow angular view and much distance compression. Small focal lengths give large angle coverage (the wide angle effect) and considerable distortion. The value of 1.0 used in most of the example files is too wide an angle. A value of about 3.2 seems to be good. However, note that as you change the focal length, the coverage changes, so you may have to move the observer position to compensate. The parameters that follow are the observer position vector, the observer rotation angle, and the observer tilt angle. These all have a substantial effect upon the appearance of the scene.

The next category is *SKY*. It has two vector parameters, defining the color of the sky at the horizon and at the zenith. If your scene doesn't include any sky, you don't need to worry about this one.

The next category is *AMBIENTLIGHT*. It has a single parameter, the ambient light intensity color vector. Ambient light is not a major contributor, so you probably don't need to worry about it too much.

The next category is *LAMP*. You need one of these for each light source (including the sun or moon if you're outdoors). Its parameters are the vector marking the position of the light source, the radius of the light source, and the color vector indicating the red, green, and blue components of the light source.

The next category is *MATERIAL*. You'll need one of these for every different type of material that you plan to define. Its first parameter is a material-type name, to which you can assign whatever you wish. The second parameter is the name of a texture. This may be any of the following existing textures, *SMOOTH, CHECKER, GRIT, MARBLE, WOOD,* and *SHEETROCK*. The texture name is followed by three color vectors defining the colors of the ambient, diffuse and spectral reflections from the material. This is followed by the glossiness factor, which is the power used in the shading model.

The remainder of each file is dedicated to the definition of the primitive objects which make up the scene. For the *SPHERE*, for example, all that is needed is the location of the center of the sphere, its radius, and the material of which it is made. Looking at the sample files, you'll see what parameters are needed to define each of the other primitive objects.

```
Sphere Stack

By Larry Sharp

Pictured in Plate 26
```

```
STATS
   OUTFILE = Stack.CPR
   XRES    = 1024
   YRES    = 768
   XPITCH  = 1.000
   YPITCH  = 1.000


ENVIRONMENT
   LOCLWGT =    0.800     0.800     0.800
   REFLWGT =    0.200     0.200     0.200
   MINWGT  =    0.030     0.030     0.030
   MAXWGT  =    1.000     1.000     1.000
   RDEPTH  =    5


OBSERVER
   FLENGTH =    3.200
   OBSPOS  =    0.000  -750.000   200.000
   ROTATE  =    0.000
   TILT    =    4.500


SKY
   HORCOL  =    0.600     0.700     1.000
   ZENCOL  =    0.500     0.500     0.500


AMBIENTLIGHT
   INTENS  =    0.100     0.100     0.100


MATERIAL
   TYPE    - ITALIANMARBLE
   TEXTURE = MARBLE
   AMBRFL  =    0.100     0.100     0.100
   DIFRFL  =    0.700     0.700     0.700
   SPCRFL  =    0.200     0.200     0.200
   GLOSS   =   10.000
```

```
MATERIAL
   TYPE    = OAKWOOD
   TEXTURE = WOOD
   AMBRFL  =     0.200    0.200    0.200
   DIFRFL  =     0.700    0.400    0.300
   SPCRFL  =     0.100    0.100    0.100
   GLOSS   =     5.000


MATERIAL
   TYPE    = MIRROR
   TEXTURE = SMOOTH
   AMBRFL  =     0.000    0.000    0.000
   DIFRFL  =     0.700    0.700    0.700
   SPCRFL  =     0.300    0.300    0.300
   GLOSS   =    50.000


MATERIAL
   TYPE    = CHROME
   TEXTURE = SMOOTH
   AMBRFL  =     0.100    0.100    0.100
   DIFRFL  =     0.100    0.100    0.100
   SPCRFL  =     0.600    0.600    0.600
   GLOSS   =    30.000


MATERIAL
   TYPE    = BRASS
   TEXTURE = SMOOTH
   AMBRFL  =     0.100    0.100    0.100
   DIFRFL  =     0.300    0.300    0.300
   SPCRFL  =     0.600    0.500    0.250
   GLOSS   =    30.000


MATERIAL
   TYPE    = WATER
   TEXTURE = GRIT
   AMBRFL  =     0.100    0.100    0.300
```

```
   DIFRFL  =    0.100    0.300    0.300
   SPCRFL  =    0.100    0.100    0.400
   GLOSS   =    3.000


MATERIAL
   TYPE    = PLASTICTILE
   TEXTURE = CHECKER
   AMBRFL  =    0.100    0.100    0.100
   DIFRFL  =    0.700    0.700    0.700
   SPCRFL  =    0.200    0.200    0.200
   GLOSS   =    4.000
CHECK
   TILE1   =    1.000    0.000    0.000
   TILE2   =    0.200    0.200    0.200
   TILE    =    0.07


GROUND
   MATL    = WATER


LAMP
   LOC     = 1000.000 -999.000 1000.000
   RADIUS  =  700.000
   INTENS  =    1.000    1.000    0.900


SPHERE
   LOC     = -100.000    0.000   50.000
   RADIUS  =   50.000
   MATL    = MIRROR


SPHERE
   LOC     =    0.000    0.000   50.000
   RADIUS  =   50.000
   MATL    = BRASS
```

```
SPHERE
   LOC     =  100.000    0.000   50.000
   RADIUS  =   50.000
   MATL    = CHROME


SPHERE
   LOC     =  -50.000    0.000  136.000
   RADIUS  =   50.000
   MATL    = ITALIANMARBLE


SPHERE
   LOC     =   50.000    0.000  136.000
   RADIUS  =   50.000
   MATL    = OAKWOOD


SPHERE
   LOC     =    0.000    0.000  222.000
   RADIUS  =   50.000
   MATL    = PLASTICTILE
```

```
Marbles on Wood

By Christopher D. Watkins

Pictured in Plate 27
```

```
STATS
   OUTFILE = Marbles.CPR
   XRes    = 1024
   YRes    = 768
   XPitch  = 1.000
   YPitch  = 1.000
```

```
ENVIRONMENT
   LOCLWGT =     0.800     0.800     0.800
   REFLWGT =     0.200     0.200     0.200
   MINWGT  =     0.030     0.030     0.030
   MAXWGT  =     1.000     1.000     1.000
   RDEPTH  =     5


OBSERVER
   FLENGTH =     3.200
   OBSPOS  =   -50.000  -400.000   110.000
   ROTATE  =    16.000
   TILT    =     5.000


SKY
   HORCOL  =     0.600     0.700     1.000
   ZENCOL  =     0.500     0.500     0.500


AMBIENTLIGHT
   INTENS  =     0.700     0.700     0.700


MATERIAL
   TYPE    = ITALIANMARBLE
   TEXTURE = WOOD
   AMBRFL  =     0.100     0.100     0.100
   DIFRFL  =     0.700     0.700     0.700
   SPCRFL  =     0.200     0.200     0.200
   GLOSS   =    10.000


MATERIAL
   TYPE    = OAKWOOD
   TEXTURE = WOOD
   AMBRFL  =     0.200     0.200     0.200
   DIFRFL  =     0.700     0.400     0.300
   SPCRFL  =     0.100     0.100     0.100
   GLOSS   =     5.000
```

```
GROUND
   MATL    = OAKWOOD


SPHERE
   LOC     =    0.000    0.000   50.000
   RADIUS  =   50.000
   MATL    = ITALIANMARBLE


SPHERE
   LOC     =  140.000    0.000   50.000
   RADIUS  =   50.000
   MATL    = ITALIANMARBLE


SPHERE
   LOC     =  70.000  150.000   50.000
   RADIUS  =  50.000
   MATL    =  ITALIANMARBLE


LAMP
   LOC     = 1000.000 -999.000 1000.000
   RADIUS  =  700.000
   INTENS  =    1.000    1.000    0.900
```

Office Scene By Christopher D. Watkins Pictured in Plate 28

```
STATS
   OUTFILE = OFFICE.CPR
   XRES    = 160
   YRES    = 100
   XPITCH  = 1.000
   YPITCH  = 1.000
```

```
ENVIRONMENT
   LOCLWGT =    0.750    0.750    0.750
   REFLWGT =    0.250    0.250    0.250
   MINWGT  =    0.030    0.030    0.030
   MAXWGT  =    1.000    1.000    1.000
   RDEPTH  =    5


OBSERVER
   FLENGTH =    1.000
   OBSPOS  =    0.000 -340.000  140.000
   ROTATE  =    0.000
   TILT    =    7.000


SKY
   HORCOL  =    0.000    0.000    0.000
   ZENCOL  =    0.000    0.000    0.000


AMBIENTLIGHT
   INTENS  =    0.200    0.200    0.200


MATERIAL
   TYPE    = MATTEWALL
   TEXTURE = SHEETROCK
   AMBRFL  =    0.500    0.500    0.500
   DIFRFL  =    0.500    0.500    0.500
   SPCRFL  =    0.000    0.000    0.000
   GLOSS   =    0.000


MATERIAL
   TYPE    = CHROME
   TEXTURE = SMOOTH
   AMBRFL  =    0.100    0.100    0.100
   DIFRFL  =    0.100    0.100    0.100
   SPCRFL  =    0.800    0.800    0.800
   GLOSS   =   40.000
```

```
MATERIAL
   TYPE    = BRASS
   TEXTURE = SMOOTH
   AMBRFL  =    0.100    0.100    0.100
   DIFRFL  =    0.300    0.300    0.300
   SPCRFL  =    0.600    0.500    0.250
   GLOSS   =   25.000


MATERIAL
   TYPE    = MIRROR
   TEXTURE = SMOOTH
   AMBRFL  =    0.100    0.100    0.100
   DIFRFL  =    0.200    0.200    0.200
   SPCRFL  =    0.700    0.700    0.700
   GLOSS   =   20.000


MATERIAL
   TYPE    = ITALIANMARBLE
   TEXTURE = MARBLE
   AMBRFL  =    0.200    0.200    0.200
   DIFRFL  =    0.600    0.600    0.600
   SPCRFL  =    0.200    0.200    0.200
   GLOSS   =   10.000


MATERIAL
   TYPE    = OAKWOOD
   TEXTURE = WOOD
   AMBRFL  =    0.200    0.200    0.200
   DIFRFL  =    0.700    0.400    0.300
   SPCRFL  =    0.100    0.100    0.100
   GLOSS   =    5.000


{ floor }

GROUND
   MATL    = OAKWOOD
```

```
{ end wall }

PARALLELOGRAM
   LOC      = -300.000  300.000    0.000
   V1       =  600.000    0.000    0.000
   V2       =    0.000    0.000  400.000
   MATL     = MATTEWALL


{ left wall }

PARALLELOGRAM
   LOC      = -300.000 -300.000    0.000
   V1       =    0.000  600.000    0.000
   V2       =    0.000    0.000  400.000
   MATL     = MATTEWALL


{ right wall }

PARALLELOGRAM
   LOC      =  300.000  300.000    0.000
   V1       =    0.000 -600.000    0.000
   V2       =    0.000    0.000  400.000
   MATL     = MATTEWALL


{ back wall }

PARALLELOGRAM
   LOC      =  300.000 -350.000    0.000
   V1       = -600.000    0.000    0.000
   V2       =    0.000    0.000  400.000
   MATL     = MIRROR


{ ceiling }

PARALLELOGRAM
   LOC      = -300.000  300.000  400.000
```

```
   V1      =  600.000    0.000    0.000
   V2      =    0.000 -600.000    0.000
   MATL    = MATTEWALL


{ table }

BOX
   LOC     = -150.000 -100.000   80.000
   V1      =  300.000    0.000    0.000
   V2      =    0.000  200.000    0.000
   V3      =    0.000    0.000   20.000
   MATL    = ITALIANMARBLE


{ table stand }

BOX
   LOC     = -125.000  -75.000    0.000
   V1      =  250.000    0.000    0.000
   V2      =    0.000  150.000    0.000
   V3      =    0.000    0.000   80.000
   MATL    = ITALIANMARBLE


{ lamp on table }

CIRCLE
   LOC     =  125.000   75.000  100.000
   V1      =    1.000    0.000    0.000
   V2      =    0.000    1.000    0.000
   RADIUS  =   25.000
   MATL    = CHROME


CYLINDER
   LOC     =  125.000   75.000  101.000
   DIRECT  =    0.000    0.000    1.000
   RADIUS  =   15.000
   HEIGHT  =   18.000
   MATL    = CHROME
```

```
LAMP
   LOC      =  125.000   75.000  145.000
   RADIUS   =   25.000
   INTENS   =    0.800    0.800    0.800


{ orb on table }

SPHERE
   LOC      = -125.000   75.000  120.000
   RADIUS   =   20.000
   MATL     = BRASS


{ pyramid on table }

PYRAMID
   LOC      = -125.000  -70.000  100.000
   V1       =   20.000    0.000    0.000
   V2       =    0.000   20.000    0.000
   HEIGHT   =   40.000
   MATL     = CHROME


{ box on table }

BOX
   LOC      =  120.000  -70.000  100.000
   V1       =   20.000    0.000    0.000
   V2       =    0.000   20.000    0.000
   V3       =    0.000    0.000   20.000
   MATL     = MIRROR


{ mirror on wall }

PARALLELOGRAM
   LOC      = -150.000  299.000  125.000
   V1       =  300.000    0.000    0.000
   V2       =    0.000    0.000  150.000
   MATL     = MIRROR
```

```
{ lamp on ceiling }

LAMP
   LOC     =    0.000     0.000  395.000
   RADIUS  =   15.000
   INTENS  =    0.700     0.700    0.700
```

```
Lakeside Park

By Christopher D. Watkins

Pictured in Plate 29
```

```
STATS
   OUTFILE = Park.CPR
   XRES    =  1024
   YRES    =   768
   XPITCH  = 1.000
   YPITCH  = 1.000


ENVIRONMENT
   LOCLWGT =    0.700     0.700    0.700
   REFLWGT =    0.300     0.300    0.300
   MINWGT  =    0.030     0.030    0.030
   MAXWGT  =    1.000     1.000    1.000
   RDEPTH  =    5


OBSERVER
   FLENGTH =    1.300
   OBSPOS  =  -45.000 -250.000  100.000
   ROTATE  =   20.000
   TILT    =   10.000
```

```
SKY
   HORCOL  =    0.600    0.700    1.000
   ZENCOL  =    0.500    0.500    0.500


AMBIENTLIGHT
   INTENS  =    0.150    0.150    0.150


MATERIAL
   TYPE    = GRASS
   TEXTURE = GRIT
   AMBRFL  =    0.200    0.200    0.200
   DIFRFL  =    0.600    0.800    0.250
   SPCRFL  =    0.000    0.000    0.000
   GLOSS   =    0.000


MATERIAL
   TYPE    = CEMENT
   TEXTURE = GRIT
   AMBRFL  =    0.200    0.200    0.200
   DIFRFL  =    0.800    0.800    0.800
   SPCRFL  =    0.000    0.000    0.000
   GLOSS   =    0.000


MATERIAL
   TYPE    = LIGHTCEMENT
   TEXTURE = SHEETROCK
   AMBRFL  =    0.100    0.100    0.100
   DIFRFL  =    0.900    0.900    0.900
   SPCRFL  =    0.000    0.000    0.000
   GLOSS   =    0.000


MATERIAL
   TYPE    = WATER
   TEXTURE = GRIT
   AMBRFL  =    0.100    0.100    0.300
```

```
   DIFRFL  =    0.100    0.300    0.300
   SPCRFL  =    0.100    0.100    0.400
   GLOSS   =    3.000


MATERIAL
   TYPE    = LAKEWATER
   TEXTURE = GRIT
   AMBRFL  =    0.100    0.100    0.200
   DIFRFL  =    0.100    0.200    0.200
   SPCRFL  =    0.100    0.100    0.300
   GLOSS   =    2.000


MATERIAL
   TYPE    = BLACKANODIZED
   TEXTURE = SMOOTH
   AMBRFL  =    1.000    1.000    1.000
   DIFRFL  =    0.000    0.000    0.000
   SPCRFL  =    0.000    0.000    0.000
   GLOSS   =    0.000


MATERIAL
   TYPE    = MILKWHITEGLASS
   TEXTURE = SMOOTH
   AMBRFL  =    0.500    0.500    0.500
   DIFRFL  =    0.400    0.400    0.400
   SPCRFL  =    0.100    0.100    0.100
   GLOSS   =    4.000


MATERIAL
   TYPE    = MIRROR
   TEXTURE = SMOOTH
   AMBRFL  =    0.100    0.100    0.100
   DIFRFL  =    0.200    0.200    0.200
   SPCRFL  =    0.700    0.700    0.700
   GLOSS   =   30.000
```

```
GROUND
   MATL     = GRASS


{ sun }

LAMP
   LOC      = 1000.000 -999.000 1000.000
   RADIUS   =  700.000
   INTENS   =    1.000    1.000    0.900


{ birdbath }

CYLINDER
   LOC      =    0.000    0.000    0.000
   DIRECT   =    0.000    0.000    1.000
   RADIUS   =   80.000
   HEIGHT   =   25.000
   MATL     = CEMENT


RING
   LOC      =    0.000    0.000   25.000
   V1       =    1.000    0.000    0.000
   V2       =    0.000    1.000    0.000
   RAD1     =   70.000
   RAD2     =   80.000
   MATL     = CEMENT


CYLINDER
   LOC      =    0.000    0.000   25.000
   DIRECT   =    0.000    0.000    1.000
   RADIUS   =   70.000
   HEIGHT   =   20.000
   MATL     = CEMENT
```

```
RING
   LOC     =    0.000    0.000   45.000
   V1      =    1.000    0.000    0.000
   V2      =    0.000    1.000    0.000
   RAD1    =   65.000
   RAD2    =   70.000
   MATL    = CEMENT


CIRCLE
   LOC     =    0.000    0.000   44.500
   V1      =    1.000    0.000    0.000
   V2      =    0.000    1.000    0.000
   RADIUS  =   68.000
   MATL    = WATER


CYLINDER
   LOC     =    0.000    0.000   45.000
   DIRECT  =    0.000    0.000    1.000
   RADIUS  =    6.000
   HEIGHT  =   28.000
   MATL    = CEMENT


CONE
   LOC     =    0.000    0.000   60.000
   DIRECT  =    0.000    0.000   -1.000
   RADIUS  =   40.000
   HEIGHT  =   15.000
   MATL    = CEMENT


CIRCLE
   LOC     =    0.000    0.000   74.000
   V1      =    1.000    0.000    0.000
   V2      =    0.000    1.000    0.000
   RADIUS  =   39.000
   MATL    = WATER
```

```
{ lake water }

PARALLELOGRAM
   LOC      = -999.000  750.000    1.000
   V1       = 9999.000    0.000    0.000
   V2       =    0.000 5000.000    0.000
   MATL     = LAKEWATER


{ sidewalk }

PARALLELOGRAM
   LOC      = -299.000  160.000    1.500
   V1       = 1999.000    0.000    0.000
   V2       =    0.000   80.000    0.000
   MATL     = LIGHTCEMENT


{ streetlamps }

CYLINDER
   LOC      = -200.000  250.000    0.000
   DIRECT   =    0.000    0.000    1.000
   RADIUS   =    6.000
   HEIGHT   =  100.000
   MATL     = BLACKANODIZED


SPHERE
   LOC      = -200.000  250.000  115.000
   RADIUS   =   15.000
   MATL     = MILKWHITEGLASS


CYLINDER
   LOC      =  100.000  250.000    0.000
   DIRECT   =    0.000    0.000    1.000
   RADIUS   =    6.000
   HEIGHT   =  100.000
   MATL     = BLACKANODIZED
```

```
SPHERE
   LOC      =  100.000  250.000  115.000
   RADIUS   =   15.000
   MATL     = MILKWHITEGLASS


CYLINDER
   LOC      =  400.000  250.000    0.000
   DIRECT   =    0.000    0.000    1.000
   RADIUS   =    6.000
   HEIGHT   =  100.000
   MATL     = BLACKANODIZED


SPHERE
   LOC      =  400.000  250.000  115.000
   RADIUS   =   15.000
   MATL     = MILKWHITEGLASS


CYLINDER
   LOC      =  700.000  250.000    0.000
   DIRECT   =    0.000    0.000    1.000
   RADIUS   =    6.000
   HEIGHT   =  100.000
   MATL     = BLACKANODIZED


SPHERE
   LOC      =  700.000  250.000  115.000
   RADIUS   =   15.000
   MATL     = MILKWHITEGLASS


{ park bench }

CYLINDER
   LOC      =  400.000  120.000    0.000
   DIRECT   =    0.000    0.000    1.000
   RADIUS   =   10.000
   HEIGHT   =   35.000
   MATL     = CEMENT
```

```
CYLINDER
   LOC     =  500.000  120.000    0.000
   DIRECT  =    0.000    0.000    1.000
   RADIUS  =   10.000
   HEIGHT  =   35.000
   MATL    = CEMENT


BOX
   LOC     =  380.000   90.000   35.000
   V1      =  140.000    0.000    0.000
   V2      =    0.000   60.000    0.000
   V3      =    0.000    0.000    5.000
   MATL    = CEMENT


{ garbage can }

CYLINDER
   LOC     =  200.000  120.000    0.000
   DIRECT  =    0.000    0.000    1.000
   RADIUS  =   16.000
   HEIGHT  =   35.000
   MATL    = CEMENT


{ city }

BOX
   LOC     =  790.000 9999.000    0.000
   V1      =  450.000    0.000    0.000
   V2      =    0.000  450.000    0.000
   V3      =    0.000    0.000 2200.000
   MATL    = CEMENT


CYLINDER
   LOC     = 4500.000 9999.000    0.000
   DIRECT  =    0.000    0.000    1.000
   RADIUS  =  510.000
```

```
   HEIGHT  = 1500.000
   MATL    = MIRROR
```

Water Molecule
By Christopher D. Watkins
Pictured in Plate 30

```
STATS
   OUTFILE = Molecule.CPR
   XRES    = 1024
   YRES    = 768
   XPITCH  = 1.000
   YPITCH  = 1.000


ENVIRONMENT
   LOCLWGT =    0.800     0.800     0.800
   REFLWGT =    0.200     0.200     0.200
   MINWGT  =    0.030     0.030     0.030
   MAXWGT  =    1.000     1.000     1.000
   RDEPTH  =    2


OBSERVER
   FLENGTH =    3.500
   OBSPOS  =  425.000  -850.000   300.000
   ROTATE  =  -25.000
   TILT    =    8.000


SKY
   HORCOL  =    0.600     0.700     1.000
   ZENCOL  =    0.500     0.500     0.500
```

```
AMBIENTLIGHT
   INTENS  =    0.100     0.100     0.100


MATERIAL
   TYPE    = BLUEMIRROR
   TEXTURE = SMOOTH
   AMBRFL  =    0.100     0.100     0.100
   DIFRFL  =    0.200     0.200     0.500
   SPCRFL  =    0.100     0.100     0.400
   GLOSS   =   30.000


MATERIAL
   TYPE    = REDMIRROR
   TEXTURE = SMOOTH
   AMBRFL  =    0.100     0.100     0.100
   DIFRFL  =    0.500     0.200     0.200
   SPCRFL  =    0.400     0.100     0.100
   GLOSS   =   30.000


MATERIAL
   TYPE    = CHROME
   TEXTURE = SMOOTH
   AMBRFL  =    0.000     0.000     0.000
   DIFRFL  =    0.250     0.250     0.250
   SPCRFL  =    0.750     0.750     0.750
   GLOSS   =   40.000


MATERIAL
   TYPE    = BRASS
   TEXTURE = SMOOTH
   AMBRFL  =    0.100     0.100     0.100
   DIFRFL  =    0.300     0.300     0.300
   SPCRFL  =    0.600     0.500     0.250
   GLOSS   =   30.000
```

```
MATERIAL
   TYPE    = WATER
   TEXTURE = GRIT
   AMBRFL  =    0.100    0.100    0.300
   DIFRFL  =    0.100    0.300    0.300
   SPCRFL  =    0.100    0.100    0.400
   GLOSS   =    3.000


GROUND
   MATL    = WATER


LAMP
   LOC     = 1000.000 -999.000 1000.000
   RADIUS  =  700.000
   INTENS  =    1.000    1.000    0.900


{ molecule (108_ between H-O bonds) }

SPHERE
   LOC     =    0.000  300.000  130.000
   RADIUS  =   50.000
   MATL    = REDMIRROR


SPHERE
   LOC     =    0.000  300.000  280.000
   RADIUS  =   25.000
   MATL    = BLUEMIRROR


SPHERE
   LOC     =  142.650  300.000   83.650
   RADIUS  =   25.000
   MATL    = BLUEMIRROR
```

```
CYLINDER
   LOC     =    0.000  300.000  130.000
   DIRECT  =    0.000    0.000    1.000
   RADIUS  =   12.000
   HEIGHT  =  150.000
   MATL    = CHROME


CYLINDER
   LOC     =    0.000  300.000  130.000
   DIRECT  =    0.951    0.000   -0.309
   RADIUS  =   12.000
   HEIGHT  =  150.000
   MATL    = CHROME


{ H of H2O }

SPHERE
   LOC     = -100.000    0.000   50.000
   RADIUS  =   15.000
   MATL    = BRASS


CYLINDER
   LOC     = -100.000    0.000   50.000
   DIRECT  =    0.000    0.000    1.000
   RADIUS  =   15.000
   HEIGHT  =  100.000
   MATL    = BRASS


SPHERE
   LOC     = -100.000    0.000  150.000
   RADIUS  =   15.000
   MATL    = BRASS


CYLINDER
   LOC     = -100.000    0.000  100.000
```

```
   DIRECT  =    1.000     0.000     0.000
   RADIUS  =   15.000
   HEIGHT  =   50.000
   MATL    = BRASS


SPHERE
   LOC     =  -50.000     0.000    50.000
   RADIUS  =   15.000
   MATL    = BRASS


CYLINDER
   LOC     =  -50.000     0.000    50.000
   DIRECT  =    0.000     0.000     1.000
   RADIUS  =   15.000
   HEIGHT  =  100.000
   MATL    = BRASS


SPHERE
   LOC     =  -50.000     0.000   150.000
   RADIUS  =   15.000
   MATL    = BRASS


{ 2 of H2O }

SPHERE
   LOC     =    0.000     0.000    90.000
   RADIUS  =   10.000
   MATL    = BRASS


SPHERE
   LOC     =   50.000     0.000    90.000
   RADIUS  =   10.000
   MATL    = BRASS
```

```
SPHERE
   LOC     =    0.000    0.000   60.000
   RADIUS  =   10.000
   MATL    = BRASS


SPHERE
   LOC     =   50.000    0.000   60.000
   RADIUS  =   10.000
   MATL    = BRASS


SPHERE
   LOC     =    0.000    0.000   30.000
   RADIUS  =   10.000
   MATL    = BRASS


SPHERE
   LOC     =   50.000    0.000   30.000
   RADIUS  =   10.000
   MATL    = BRASS


CYLINDER
   LOC     =    0.000    0.000   90.000
   DIRECT  =    1.000    0.000    0.000
   RADIUS  =   10.000
   HEIGHT  =   50.000
   MATL    = BRASS


CYLINDER
   LOC     =    0.000    0.000   60.000
   DIRECT  =    1.000    0.000    0.000
   RADIUS  =   10.000
   HEIGHT  =   50.000
   MATL    = BRASS
```

```
CYLINDER
   LOC     =    0.000    0.000   30.000
   DIRECT  =    1.000    0.000    0.000
   RADIUS  =   10.000
   HEIGHT  =   50.000
   MATL    = BRASS


CYLINDER
   LOC     =   50.000    0.000   60.000
   DIRECT  =    0.000    0.000    1.000
   RADIUS  =   10.000
   HEIGHT  =   30.000
   MATL    = BRASS


CYLINDER
   LOC     =    0.000    0.000   30.000
   DIRECT  =    0.000    0.000    1.000
   RADIUS  =   10.000
   HEIGHT  =   30.000
   MATL    = BRASS


{ 0 of H20 }

SPHERE
   LOC     =  100.000    0.000   50.000
   RADIUS  =   15.000
   MATL    = BRASS


CYLINDER
   LOC     =  100.000    0.000   50.000
   DIRECT  =    0.000    0.000    1.000
   RADIUS  =   15.000
   HEIGHT  =  100.000
   MATL    = BRASS
```

```
SPHERE
   LOC      =  100.000    0.000  150.000
   RADIUS   =   15.000
   MATL     = BRASS


CYLINDER
   LOC      =  100.000    0.000  150.000
   DIRECT   =    1.000    0.000    0.000
   RADIUS   =   15.000
   HEIGHT   =   50.000
   MATL     = BRASS


CYLINDER
   LOC      =  100.000    0.000   50.000
   DIRECT   =    1.000    0.000    0.000
   RADIUS   =   15.000
   HEIGHT   =   50.000
   MATL     = BRASS


SPHERE
   LOC      =  150.000    0.000   50.000
   RADIUS   =   15.000
   MATL     = BRASS


CYLINDER
   LOC      =  150.000    0.000   50.000
   DIRECT   =    0.000    0.000    1.000
   RADIUS   =   15.000
   HEIGHT   =  100.000
   MATL     = BRASS


SPHERE
   LOC      =  150.000    0.000  150.000
   RADIUS   =   15.000
   MATL     = BRASS
```

```
Pyramid

By Christopher D. Watkins

Pictured in Plate 31
```

```
STATS
  OUTFILE = Pyramid.CPR
  XRES    = 1024
  YRES    =  768
  XPITCH  = 1.000
  YPITCH  = 1.000


ENVIRONMENT
  LOCLWGT =    0.800    0.800    0.800
  REFLWGT =    0.200    0.200    0.200
  MINWGT  =    0.030    0.030    0.030
  MAXWGT  =    1.000    1.000    1.000
  RDEPTH  =    5


OBSERVER
  FLENGTH =    3.000
  OBSPOS  =  250.000  950.000  280.000
  ROTATE  =  195.000
  TILT    =    8.000


SKY
  HORCOL  =    0.600    0.700    1.000
  ZENCOL  =    0.500    0.500    0.500


AMBIENTLIGHT
  INTENS  =    0.100    0.100    0.100
```

```
MATERIAL
   TYPE    = ITALIANMARBLE
   TEXTURE = MARBLE
   AMBRFL  =     0.100     0.100     0.100
   DIFRFL  =     0.700     0.700     0.700
   SPCRFL  =     0.200     0.200     0.200
   GLOSS   =    10.000


MATERIAL
   TYPE    = OAKWOOD
   TEXTURE = WOOD
   AMBRFL  =     0.200     0.200     0.200
   DIFRFL  =     0.700     0.400     0.300
   SPCRFL  =     0.100     0.100     0.100
   GLOSS   =     5.000


MATERIAL
   TYPE    = MIRROR
   TEXTURE = SMOOTH
   AMBRFL  =     0.000     0.000     0.000
   DIFRFL  =     0.700     0.700     0.700
   SPCRFL  =     0.300     0.300     0.300
   GLOSS   =    50.000


MATERIAL
   TYPE    = CHROME
   TEXTURE = SMOOTH
   AMBRFL  =     0.100     0.100     0.100
   DIFRFL  =     0.100     0.100     0.100
   SPCRFL  =     0.600     0.600     0.600
   GLOSS   =    30.000


MATERIAL
   TYPE    = BRASS
   TEXTURE = SMOOTH
```

```
   AMBRFL  =    0.100     0.100     0.100
   DIFRFL  =    0.300     0.300     0.300
   SPCRFL  =    0.600     0.500     0.250
   GLOSS   =   20.000


MATERIAL
   TYPE    = WATER
   TEXTURE = GRIT
   AMBRFL  =    0.100     0.100     0.300
   DIFRFL  =    0.100     0.300     0.300
   SPCRFL  =    0.100     0.100     0.400
   GLOSS   =    3.000


MATERIAL
   TYPE    = PLASTICTILE
   TEXTURE = CHECKER
   AMBRFL  =    0.100     0.100     0.100
   DIFRFL  =    0.700     0.700     0.700
   SPCRFL  =    0.200     0.200     0.200
   GLOSS   =    4.000
CHECK
   TILE1   =    1.000     0.000     0.000
   TILE2   =    0.200     0.200     0.200
   TILE    =    0.005


GROUND
   MATL    = PLASTICTILE


LAMP
   LOC     = -300.000   300.000   100.000
   RADIUS  =   60.000
   INTENS  =    0.700     0.800     0.900
```

```
{ sun }

LAMP
   LOC     = 1000.000  999.000 1000.000
   RADIUS  =  700.000
   INTENS  =    1.000    1.000    0.900


{ support lamp }

LAMP
   LOC     = -300.000  300.000  100.000
   RADIUS  =   80.000
   INTENS  =    0.600    0.700    0.900


{ first level }

PYRAMID
   LOC     = -150.000 -150.000    0.000
   V1      =  100.000    0.000    0.000
   V2      =    0.000  100.000    0.000
   HEIGHT  =  100.000
   MATL    = MIRROR


PYRAMID
   LOC     =  -50.000 -150.000    0.000
   V1      =  100.000    0.000    0.000
   V2      =    0.000  100.000    0.000
   HEIGHT  =  100.000
   MATL    = ITALIANMARBLE


PYRAMID
   LOC     =   50.000 -150.000    0.000
   V1      =  100.000    0.000    0.000
   V2      =    0.000  100.000    0.000
   HEIGHT  =  100.000
   MATL    = CHROME
```

```
PYRAMID
   LOC      = -100.000  -50.000    0.000
   V1       =  100.000    0.000    0.000
   V2       =    0.000  100.000    0.000
   HEIGHT   =  100.000
   MATL     = ITALIANMARBLE


PYRAMID
   LOC      =    0.000  -50.000    0.000
   V1       =  100.000    0.000    0.000
   V2       =    0.000  100.000    0.000
   HEIGHT   =  100.000
   MATL     = OAKWOOD


PYRAMID
   LOC      =  -50.000   50.000    0.000
   V1       =  100.000    0.000    0.000
   V2       =    0.000  100.000    0.000
   HEIGHT   =  100.000
   MATL     = MIRROR


{ second level }

PYRAMID
   LOC      = -100.000 -100.000  100.000
   V1       =  100.000    0.000    0.000
   V2       =    0.000  100.000    0.000
   HEIGHT   =  100.000
   MATL     = OAKWOOD


PYRAMID
   LOC      =    0.000 -100.000  100.000
   V1       =  100.000    0.000    0.000
   V2       =    0.000  100.000    0.000
   HEIGHT   =  100.000
   MATL     = BRASS
```

```
PYRAMID
   LOC      =  -50.000     0.000  100.000
   V1       =  100.000     0.000    0.000
   V2       =    0.000   100.000    0.000
   HEIGHT   =  100.000
   MATL     = ITALIANMARBLE


{ third level }

PYRAMID
   LOC      =  -50.000   -50.000  200.000
   V1       =  100.000     0.000    0.000
   V2       =    0.000   100.000    0.000
   HEIGHT   =  100.000
   MATL     = WATER
```

Planets By Larry Sharp and Christopher D. Watkins Pictured in Plate 32

```
STATS
   OUTFILE = Planets.CPR
   XRES    = 1024
   YRES    =  768
   XPITCH  = 1.000
   YPITCH  = 1.000


ENVIRONMENT
   LOCLWGT =    0.800     0.800     0.800
   REFLWGT =    0.200     0.200     0.200
   MINWGT  =    0.030     0.030     0.030
   MAXWGT  =    1.000     1.000     1.000
   RDEPTH  =    1
```

```
OBSERVER
   FLENGTH =    3.200
   OBSPOS  =    0.000  -750.000  300.000
   ROTATE  =    0.000
   TILT    =   10.000


SKY
   HORCOL  =    0.000     0.000     0.000
   ZENCOL  =    0.000     0.000     0.000


AMBIENTLIGHT
   INTENS  =    0.900     0.900     0.900


MATERIAL
   TYPE    = ICEANDROCK
   TEXTURE = GRIT
   AMBRFL  =    0.150     0.150     0.150
   DIFRFL  =    0.850     0.850     0.850
   SPCRFL  =    0.000     0.000     0.000
   GLOSS   =    0.000


MATERIAL
   TYPE    = PLANET1
   TEXTURE = SHEETROCK
   AMBRFL  =    0.200     0.200     0.200
   DIFRFL  =    0.800     0.700     0.500
   SPCRFL  =    0.000     0.000     0.000
   GLOSS   =    0.000


MATERIAL
   TYPE    = PLANET2
   TEXTURE = SHEETROCK
   AMBRFL  =    0.200     0.200     0.200
   DIFRFL  =    0.700     0.800     0.700
   SPCRFL  =    0.000     0.000     0.000
   GLOSS   =    0.000
```

```
MATERIAL
   TYPE    = PLANET3
   TEXTURE = SHEETROCK
   AMBRFL  =     0.150    0.150    0.150
   DIFRFL  =     0.500    0.600    0.700
   SPCRFL  =     0.000    0.000    0.000
   GLOSS   =     0.000


MATERIAL
   TYPE    = MOON1
   TEXTURE = SHEETROCK
   AMBRFL  =     0.200    0.200    0.200
   DIFRFL  =     0.800    0.800    0.800
   SPCRFL  =     0.000    0.000    0.000
   GLOSS   =     0.000


MATERIAL
   TYPE    = STAR
   TEXTURE = SHEETROCK
   AMBRFL  =     0.500    0.500    0.500
   DIFRFL  =     0.350    0.350    0.500
   SPCRFL  =     0.000    0.000    0.000
   GLOSS   =     0.000


MATERIAL
   TYPE    = REDGIANT
   TEXTURE = SHEETROCK
   AMBRFL  =     0.500    0.500    0.500
   DIFRFL  =     0.500    0.350    0.350
   SPCRFL  =     0.000    0.000    0.000
   GLOSS   =     0.000


MATERIAL
   TYPE    = BLUEDWARF
   TEXTURE = SHEETROCK
```

```
   AMBRFL  =    0.500     0.500     0.500
   DIFRFL  =    0.300     0.300     0.500
   SPCRFL  =    0.000     0.000     0.000
   GLOSS   =    0.000


{ Sun }

LAMP
   LOC     = 1000.000 -999.000 1000.000
   RADIUS  =  700.000
   INTENS  =    1.000     1.000     0.900


{ Stars }

SPHERE
   LOC     = -100.000  250.000  255.000
   RADIUS  =    3.000
   MATL    = STAR


SPHERE
   LOC     = -130.000  250.000  295.000
   RADIUS  =    2.000
   MATL    = BLUEDWARF


SPHERE
   LOC     = -290.000  250.000  300.000
   RADIUS  =    2.000
   MATL    = BLUEDWARF


SPHERE
   LOC     =  -65.000  250.000  180.000
   RADIUS  =    3.000
   MATL    = STAR
```

```
SPHERE
   LOC     = -170.000  250.000  184.000
   RADIUS  =    4.000
   MATL    = REDGIANT


SPHERE
   LOC     =   50.000  250.000  215.000
   RADIUS  =    3.000
   MATL    = STAR


SPHERE
   LOC     =   70.000  250.000  255.000
   RADIUS  =    3.000
   MATL    = STAR


SPHERE
   LOC     =   20.000  250.000  245.000
   RADIUS  =    2.000
   MATL    = BLUEDWARF


SPHERE
   LOC     =  130.000  250.000  175.000
   RADIUS  =    3.000
   MATL    = STAR


{ Saturn }

SPHERE
   LOC     =    0.000    0.000  100.000
   RADIUS  =   80.000
   MATL    = PLANET1


RING
   LOC     =    0.000    0.000  100.000
   V1      =    1.000    0.000    0.000
```

```
   V2      =    0.000    1.000    0.000
   RAD1    =  100.000
   RAD2    =  110.000
   MATL    = ICEANDROCK


RING
   LOC     =    0.000    0.000  100.000
   V1      =    1.000    0.000    0.000
   V2      =    0.000    1.000    0.000
   RAD1    =  115.000
   RAD2    =  124.000
   MATL    = ICEANDROCK


RING
   LOC     =    0.000    0.000  100.000
   V1      =    1.000    0.000    0.000
   V2      =    0.000    1.000    0.000
   RAD1    =  130.000
   RAD2    =  145.000
   MATL    = ICEANDROCK


RING
   LOC     =    0.000    0.000  100.000
   V1      =    1.000    0.000    0.000
   V2      =    0.000    1.000    0.000
   RAD1    =  160.000
   RAD2    =  170.000
   MATL    = ICEANDROCK


RING
   LOC     =    0.000    0.000  100.000
   V1      =    1.000    0.000    0.000
   V2      =    0.000    1.000    0.000
   RAD1    =  176.000
   RAD2    =  183.000
   MATL    = ICEANDROCK
```

```
RING
   LOC      =    0.000    0.000  100.000
   V1       =    1.000    0.000    0.000
   V2       =    0.000    1.000    0.000
   RAD1     =  191.000
   RAD2     =  207.000
   MATL     = ICEANDROCK


RING
   LOC      =    0.000    0.000  100.000
   V1       =    1.000    0.000    0.000
   V2       =    0.000    1.000    0.000
   RAD1     =  212.000
   RAD2     =  215.000
   MATL     = ICEANDROCK


RING
   LOC      =    0.000    0.000  100.000
   V1       =    1.000    0.000    0.000
   V2       =    0.000    1.000    0.000
   RAD1     =  219.000
   RAD2     =  224.000
   MATL     = ICEANDROCK


RING
   LOC      =    0.000    0.000  100.000
   V1       =    1.000    0.000    0.000
   V2       =    0.000    1.000    0.000
   RAD1     =  229.000
   RAD2     =  235.000
   MATL     = ICEANDROCK
```

```
RING
   LOC     =    0.000    0.000  100.000
   V1      =    1.000    0.000    0.000
   V2      =    0.000    1.000    0.000
   RAD1    =  240.000
   RAD2    =  250.000
   MATL    = ICEANDROCK


{ Moon of Saturn }

SPHERE
   LOC     = -300.000   300.000  125.000
   RADIUS  =   10.000
   MATL    = MOON1


{ Uranus }

SPHERE
   LOC     =  300.000  1000.000  200.000
   RADIUS  =   80.000
   MATL    = PLANET2


{ Neptune }

SPHERE
   LOC     =  450.000  3400.000  150.000
   RADIUS  =   80.000
   MATL    = PLANET3
```

Figure 18-1. Listing of *.RT* Data Files for Typical Scenes

CHAPTER 19

The Ray Tracing Program

The ray tracing program is *Raytrace.exe*, and it is produced by the source file *raytrace.c*. It reads in one of the scene description (*.RT*) files and operates upon it to produce a *.CPR* file which contains red, green, and blue color information for every pixel which makes up the picture. This program is listed in Figure 19-1. It will be described in detail in this chapter.

At the same time that the scene is being ray traced, a monochrome display (in shades of gray) is being created on the display screen. This will give you an idea of how the full-color display will look, so that if there are problems with your scene description, you can go ahead and make the necessary modifications without having to run the separate program *Display.exe* (produced from the source file *Display.c*), to see what the finished image will look like.

The detailed color information in the *.CPR* file is operated upon by the *Display.c* program, to produce a full-color picture upon the display screen. You need to run this program to see the full capability of ray tracing to produce a pleasing color picture. The source file to *Display.exe* will be described in Chapter 21.

Ray Tracing Overview

The easiest way to achieve an overall understanding of how the ray tracing program works is to start at the end of the listing with the main program. First, however, let's take a quick look at some of the constants and variables that are defined at the beginning of the program.

The first of these is *ReflectiveLamps*. This is a boolean constant which indicates whether the lamps in the program will reflect light from their surface. Obviously, if your light source is supposed to be the sun, it is far too bright to reflect any other light sources, so you should set this constant to *false*. However, for much less intense light sources, it is quite possible that they will reflect part of the light cast upon them, in which case you would set the constant to *true*.

```
/* Raytrace.c

        Recursive Ray Tracing Program

        Renders Reflective Objects

        Program by Christopher D. Watkins

        "C" Conversion by Larry Sharp

*/

#include "stdio.h"
#include "stdlib.h"
#include "dos.h"
#include "conio.h"
#include "alloc.h"
#include "math.h"
#include "string.h"
#include "math2.inc"
#include "graph2.inc"

/*

        Declare Constants and Variables

*/
#define ReflectiveLamps true
#define DistEffect 0.3

typedef char Name[32];

Name OutputFile;     /* Stats */
float XPitch, YPitch;

TDA LoclWgt;         /* Environment */
TDA ReflWgt;
```

```
TDA MinWgt;
TDA MaxWgt;
int MaxDepth;

float FocalLength;       /* Observer */
TDA ObsPos;
float ObsRotate;
float ObsTilt;
TDA ViewDir;
TDA U, V;

TDA HorCol;              /* Sky Horizon to Zenith Coloration */
TDA ZenCol;

TDA Tile1;               /* Checkerboard tiling coloration */
TDA Tile2;
float Tile;

#define MaxMaterial 10   /* Maximum Types of Materials */

typedef struct {
  Name MType;
  Name Textur;
  TDA  AmbRfl;
  TDA  DifRfl;
  TDA  SpcRfl;
  float Gloss;
} MaterialList;

MaterialList Matl[MaxMaterial+1];

TDA AmbIntens;

#define MaxTexture  6

#define Smooth      1
#define Checker     2
#define Grit        3
#define Marbl       4
#define Wood        5
```

```
#define Sheetrock          6

#define MaxShapeType       9

#define Ground             0

#define Lamp               1
#define Triangle           2
#define Parallelogram      3
#define Circles            4
#define Ring               5
#define Sphere             6
#define Quadratic          7
#define Cone               8
#define Cylinder           9

#define MaxLamp            15
#define MaxTriangle        30
#define MaxParallelogram 40
#define MaxCircles         20
#define MaxRing            20
#define MaxSphere          30
#define MaxQuadratic       5
#define MaxCone            15
#define MaxCylinder        15

typedef struct {
  int MtlNum;
  int TexNum;
} GroundList;

typedef struct {
  TDA Loc;
  float Rad;
  float RadSqr;
  TDA Intens;
} LampList;

typedef struct {
  TDA Loc;
```

```
  TDA v1;
  TDA v2;
  TDA Norm;
  float NdotLoc;
  int MtlNum;
  int TexNum;
} TriangleList;

typedef struct {
  TDA Loc;
  TDA v1;
  TDA v2;
  TDA Norm;
  float NdotLoc;
  int MtlNum;
  int TexNum;
}  ParallelogramList;

typedef struct {
  TDA Loc;
  TDA v1;
  TDA v2;
  TDA Norm;
  float NdotLoc;
  float Radius;
  int MtlNum;
  int TexNum;
}  CircleList;

typedef struct {
  TDA Loc;
  TDA v1;
  TDA v2;
  TDA Norm;
  float NdotLoc;
  float Rad1;
  float Rad2;
  int MtlNum;
  int TexNum;
}  RingList;
```

```
typedef struct {
  TDA Loc;
  float Rad;
  float RadSqr;
  int MtlNum;
  int TexNum;
} SphereList;

typedef struct {
  TDA Loc;
  TDA Direct;
  float cos1;
  float sin1;
  float cos2;
  float sin2;
  float c1;
  float c2;
  float c3;
  float c4;
  float c5;
  float xmin;
  float xmax;
  float ymin;
  float ymax;
  float zmin;
  float zmax;
  int MtlNum;
  int TexNum;
} QuadraticList;

typedef QuadraticList ConeList;

typedef QuadraticList CylinderList;

int ObjCnt[MaxShapeType+1];

GroundList Gnd;
LampList Lmp[MaxLamp+1];
TriangleList Tri[MaxTriangle+1];
ParallelogramList Para[MaxParallelogram+1];
```

```
CircleList Cir[MaxCircles+1];
RingList Rng[MaxRing+1];
SphereList Sphr[MaxSphere+1];
QuadraticList Quad[MaxQuadratic+1];
ConeList Con[MaxCone+1];
CylinderList Cyl[MaxCylinder+1];

FILE *DiskFile;
FILE *TextDiskFile;

/*

                    Clear all variables

   ClearMemory - clear all variables

*/

void ClearQuadratic(QuadraticList *List)
{
  VecNull(List->Loc);
  VecNull(List->Direct);
  List->cos1=0.0;
  List->sin1=0.0;
  List->cos2=0.0;
  List->sin2=0.0;
  List->c1=0.0;
  List->c2=0.0;
  List->c3=0.0;
  List->c4=0.0;
  List->c5=0.0;
  List->xmin=0.0;
  List->xmax=0.0;
  List->ymin=0.0;
  List->ymax=0.0;
  List->zmin=0.0;
  List->zmax=0.0;
  List->MtlNum=0;
  List->TexNum=0;
}
```

```
void ClearMemory()
{
  int i;

  strcpy(OutputFile, "");
  XRes=0;
  YRes=0;
  XPitch=0.0;
  YPitch=0.0;
  VecNull(LoclWgt);
  VecNull(ReflWgt);
  VecNull(MinWgt);
  VecNull(MaxWgt);
  MaxDepth=0;
  FocalLength=0.0;
  VecNull(ObsPos);
  ObsRotate=0.0;
  ObsTilt=0.0;
  VecNull(ViewDir);
  VecNull(U);
  VecNull(V);
  VecNull(HorCol);
  VecNull(ZenCol);
  VecNull(Tile1);
  VecNull(Tile2);
  Tile=0.0;
  for(i=0; i<=MaxMaterial; i++)
  {
    strcpy(Matl[i].MType, "");
    strcpy(Matl[i].Textur, "");
    VecNull(Matl[i].AmbRfl);
    VecNull(Matl[i].DifRfl);
    VecNull(Matl[i].SpcRfl);
    Matl[i].Gloss=0.0;
  }

  VecNull(AmbIntens);
  ObjCnt[Ground]=1;
  for(i=1; i<=MaxShapeType; i++)
    ObjCnt[i]=0;
```

```
Gnd.MtlNum=0;
Gnd.TexNum=0;
for(i=0; i<=MaxLamp; i++)
{
  VecNull(Lmp[i].Loc);
  Lmp[i].Rad=0.0;
  Lmp[i].RadSqr=0.0;
  VecNull(Lmp[i].Intens);
}
for(i=0; i<=MaxTriangle; i++)
{
  VecNull(Tri[i].Loc);
  VecNull(Tri[i].v1);
  VecNull(Tri[i].v2);
  VecNull(Tri[i].Norm);
  Tri[i].NdotLoc=0.0;
  Tri[i].MtlNum=0;
  Tri[i].TexNum=0;
}
for(i=0; i<=MaxParallelogram; i++)
{
  VecNull(Para[i].Loc);
  VecNull(Para[i].v1);
  VecNull(Para[i].v2);
  VecNull(Para[i].Norm);
  Para[i].NdotLoc=0.0;
  Para[i].MtlNum=0;
  Para[i].TexNum=0;
}
for(i=0; i<=MaxCircles; i++)
{
  VecNull(Cir[i].Loc);
  VecNull(Cir[i].v1);
  VecNull(Cir[i].v2);
  VecNull(Cir[i].Norm);
  Cir[i].NdotLoc=0.0;
  Cir[i].Radius=0.0;
  Cir[i].MtlNum=0;
  Cir[i].TexNum=0;
}
```

```
  for(i=0; i<=MaxRing; i++)
  {
    VecNull(Rng[i].Loc);
    VecNull(Rng[i].v1);
    VecNull(Rng[i].v2);
    VecNull(Rng[i].Norm);
    Rng[i].NdotLoc=0.0;
    Rng[i].Rad1=0.0;
    Rng[i].Rad2=0.0;
    Rng[i].MtlNum=0;
    Rng[i].TexNum=0;
  }
  for(i=0; i<=MaxSphere; i++)
  {
    VecNull(Sphr[i].Loc);
    Sphr[i].Rad=0.0;
    Sphr[i].RadSqr=0.0;
    Sphr[i].MtlNum=0;
    Sphr[i].TexNum=0;
  }
  for(i=0; i<=MaxQuadratic; i++)
    ClearQuadratic(&Quad[i]);
  for(i=0; i<=MaxCone; i++)
    ClearQuadratic(&Con[i]);
  for(i=0; i<=MaxCylinder; i++)
    ClearQuadratic(&Cyl[i]);
}

/*
 ____________________________________________________________
|                                                            |
|                      Load an *.RT File                     |
|____________________________________________________________|
*/

int MtlCount;    /* Number of Materials Loaded */

void GetViewDir(float Angl, float Tilt, TDA View, TDA U, TDA V)
{
  float Phi, Theta;
  float x, y, z;
```

```
  Phi=Radians(Angl);
  Theta=Radians(Tilt);
  x=cos(Theta)*sin(Phi);
  y=cos(Theta)*cos(Phi);
  z=-sin(Theta);
  Vec(x, y, z, View);
  x=cos(Phi);
  y=-sin(Phi);
  z=0.0;
  Vec(x, y, z, U);
  x=sin(Theta)*sin(Phi);
  y=sin(Theta)*cos(Phi);
  z=cos(Theta);
  Vec(x, y, z, V);
}

char Buf1[256], Buf2[256], Buf3[256], Buf4[256], Buf5[256];
int dummy;
Name MtlName;

void Clear_Buffers()
{
  strset(Buf1, 0);
  strset(Buf2, 0);
  strset(Buf3, 0);
  strset(Buf4, 0);
  strset(Buf5, 0);
}

void LoadTDA(TDA A)
{
  Clear_Buffers();
  fscanf(TextDiskFile, "%s %s %s %s %s", Buf1, Buf2, Buf3,
                                          Buf4, Buf5);
  A[0]=atof(Buf3);
  A[1]=atof(Buf4);
  A[2]=atof(Buf5);
}

void LoadReal(float *a)
{
```

```
  Clear_Buffers();
  fscanf(TextDiskFile, "%s %s %s", Buf1, Buf2, Buf3);
  *a=atof(Buf3);
}

void LoadInteger(int *a)
{
  Clear_Buffers();
  fscanf(TextDiskFile, "%s %s %s", Buf1, Buf2, Buf3);
  *a=atof(Buf3);
}

void LoadText(Name a)
{
  Clear_Buffers();
  fscanf(TextDiskFile, "%s %s %s", Buf1, Buf2, Buf3);
  strcpy(a, Buf3);
}

void GetMatlNum(char Mat[], int *MatNum)
{
  int i;

  for(i=1; i<=MtlCount; i++)
  {
    if(!(strcmp(Matl[i].MType, Mat)))
      *MatNum=i;
  }
}

void GetTexNum(char Tex[], int *TexNum)
{
     if(!(strcmp(Tex, "SMOOTH")))
         *TexNum=Smooth;
     else
     {
         if(!(strcmp(Tex, "CHECKER")))
         *TexNum=Checker;
         else
         {
```

```
        if(!(strcmp(Tex, "GRIT")))
                *TexNum=Grit;
        else
        {
                if(!(strcmp(Tex, "MARBLE")))
                    *TexNum=Marble;
                else
                {
                    if(!(strcmp(Tex, "WOOD")))
                        *TexNum=Wood;
                    else
                    {
                        if(!(strcmp(Tex, "SHEETROCK")))
                        *TexNum=Sheetrock;
                    }
                }
        }
        }
    }
}

void OrientQuadratic(QuadraticList *List)
{
    float Temp;
    TDA NewDirect;

    VecNormalize(List->Direct);
    Temp=SqrFP(List->Direct[0])+SqrFP(List->Direct[2]);
    if(Temp==0.0)
        List->cos1=1.0;
    else
        List->cos1=List->Direct[2]/sqrt(Temp);
    List->sin1=sqrt(1.0-SqrFP(List->cos1));
    NewDirect[0]=List->Direct[0]*List->cos1 -
        List->Direct[2]*List->sin1;
    NewDirect[1]=List->Direct[1];
    NewDirect[2]=List->Direct[0]*List->sin1 +
        List->Direct[2]*List->cos1;
    Temp=SqrFP(NewDirect[1])+SqrFP(NewDirect[2]);
```

```
    if(Temp==0.0)
        List->cos2=1.0;
    else
        List->cos2=NewDirect[1]/sqrt(Temp);
    List->sin2=sqrt(1.0-SqrFP(List->cos2));
}

void GetData(Name FileName)
{
  float Rad, Hgt;
  TDA   ShapeLoc, TempLoc, vec1, vec2, vec3;
  int   MtlNumber, TexNumber;
  int TDF;

  MtlCount=0;
  TextDiskFile=fopen(FileName, "r");
  TDF=fileno(TextDiskFile);
  do
  {
    Clear_Buffers();
    fscanf(TextDiskFile, "%s", Buf1);
    if(ferror(TextDiskFile))
    {
      printf("Error!!!!!\n");
      getch();
      exit(1);
    }
    if(!(strcmp(Buf1, "STATS")))
    {
      LoadText(OutputFile);
      LoadInteger(&XRes);
      LoadInteger(&YRes);
      LoadReal(&XPitch);
      LoadReal(&YPitch);
    }
    if(!(strcmp(Buf1, "ENVIRONMENT")))
    {
      LoadTDA(LoclWgt);
      LoadTDA(ReflWgt);
      LoadTDA(MinWgt);
```

```
   LoadTDA(MaxWgt);
   LoadInteger(&MaxDepth);
  }
 if(!(strcmp(Buf1, "OBSERVER")))
  {
   LoadReal(&FocalLength);
   LoadTDA(ObsPos);
   LoadReal(&ObsRotate);
   LoadReal(&ObsTilt);
   GetViewDir(ObsRotate, ObsTilt, ViewDir, U, V);
  }
 if(!(strcmp(Buf1, "SKY")))
  {
   LoadTDA(HorCol);
   LoadTDA(ZenCol);
  }
 if(!(strcmp(Buf1, "CHECK")))
  {
   LoadTDA(Tile1);
   LoadTDA(Tile2);
   LoadReal(&Tile);
  }
 if(!(strcmp(Buf1, "MATERIAL")))
  {
   MtlCount+=1;
   LoadText(Matl[MtlCount].MType);
   LoadText(Matl[MtlCount].Textur);
   LoadTDA(Matl[MtlCount].AmbRfl);
   LoadTDA(Matl[MtlCount].DifRfl);
   LoadTDA(Matl[MtlCount].SpcRfl);
   LoadReal(&Matl[MtlCount].Gloss);
  }
 if(!(strcmp(Buf1, "AMBIENTLIGHT")))
   LoadTDA(AmbIntens);
 if(!(strcmp(Buf1, "GROUND")))
  {
   LoadText(MtlName);
   GetMatlNum(MtlName, &Gnd.MtlNum);
   GetTexNum(Matl[Gnd.MtlNum].Textur, &Gnd.TexNum);
  }
```

```
}
if(!(strcmp(Buf1, "LAMP")))
{
  ObjCnt[Lamp]+=1;
  LoadTDA(Lmp[ObjCnt[Lamp]].Loc);
  LoadReal(&Lmp[ObjCnt[Lamp]].Rad);
  Lmp[ObjCnt[Lamp]].RadSqr=SqrFP(Lmp[ObjCnt[Lamp]].Rad);
  LoadTDA(Lmp[ObjCnt[Lamp]].Intens);
}
if(!(strcmp(Buf1, "TRIANGLE")))
{
  ObjCnt[Triangle]+=1;
  LoadTDA(Tri[ObjCnt[Triangle]].Loc);
  LoadTDA(Tri[ObjCnt[Triangle]].v1);
  LoadTDA(Tri[ObjCnt[Triangle]].v2);
  VecCross(Tri[ObjCnt[Triangle]].v1,
  Tri[ObjCnt[Triangle]].v2, Tri[ObjCnt[Triangle]].Norm);
  VecNormalize(Tri[ObjCnt[Triangle]].Norm);
  Tri[ObjCnt[Triangle]].NdotLoc =
  VecDot(Tri[ObjCnt[Triangle]].Norm,
  Tri[ObjCnt[Triangle]].Loc);
  LoadText(MtlName);
  GetMatlNum(MtlName, &Tri[ObjCnt[Triangle]].MtlNum);
  GetTexNum(Matl[Tri[ObjCnt[Triangle]].MtlNum].Textur,
    &Tri[ObjCnt[Triangle]].TexNum);
}
if(!(strcmp(Buf1, "PARALLELOGRAM")))
{
    ObjCnt[Parallelogram]+=1;
    LoadTDA(Para[ObjCnt[Parallelogram]].Loc);
    LoadTDA(Para[ObjCnt[Parallelogram]].v1);
    LoadTDA(Para[ObjCnt[Parallelogram]].v2);
    VecCross(Para[ObjCnt[Parallelogram]].v1,
    Para[ObjCnt[Parallelogram]].v2,
    Para[ObjCnt[Parallelogram]].Norm);
    VecNormalize(Para[ObjCnt[Parallelogram]].Norm);
    Para[ObjCnt[Parallelogram]].NdotLoc =
    VecDot(Para[ObjCnt[Parallelogram]].Norm,
    Para[ObjCnt[Parallelogram]].Loc);
  LoadText(MtlName);
 GetMatlNum(MtlName, &Para[ObjCnt[Parallelogram]].MtlNum);
```

```
      GetTexNum
(Matl[Para[ObjCnt[Parallelogram]].MtlNum].Textur,
&Para[ObjCnt[Parallelogram]].TexNum);
    }
    if(!(strcmp(Buf1, "CIRCLE")))
    {
      ObjCnt[Circles]+=1;
      LoadTDA(Cir[ObjCnt[Circles]].Loc);
      LoadTDA(Cir[ObjCnt[Circles]].v1);
      VecNormalize(Cir[ObjCnt[Circles]].v1);
      LoadTDA(Cir[ObjCnt[Circles]].v2);
      VecNormalize(Cir[ObjCnt[Circles]].v2);
      VecCross(Cir[ObjCnt[Circles]].v1,
      Cir[ObjCnt[Circles]].v2, Cir[ObjCnt[Circles]].Norm);
      VecNormalize(Cir[ObjCnt[Circles]].Norm);
      Cir[ObjCnt[Circles]].NdotLoc =
      VecDot(Cir[ObjCnt[Circles]].Norm,
      Cir[ObjCnt[Circles]].Loc);
      LoadReal(&Cir[ObjCnt[Circles]].Radius);
      LoadText(MtlName);
      GetMatlNum(MtlName, &Cir[ObjCnt[Circles]].MtlNum);
      GetTexNum(Matl[Cir[ObjCnt[Circles]].MtlNum].Textur,
        &Cir[ObjCnt[Circles]].TexNum);
    }
    if(!(strcmp(Buf1, "RING")))
    {
      ObjCnt[Ring]+=1;
      LoadTDA(Rng[ObjCnt[Ring]].Loc);
      LoadTDA(Rng[ObjCnt[Ring]].v1);
      VecNormalize(Rng[ObjCnt[Ring]].v1);
      LoadTDA(Rng[ObjCnt[Ring]].v2);
      VecNormalize(Rng[ObjCnt[Ring]].v2);
      VecCross(Rng[ObjCnt[Ring]].v1, Rng[ObjCnt[Ring]].v2,
        Rng[ObjCnt[Ring]].Norm);
        VecNormalize(Rng[ObjCnt[Ring]].Norm);
      Rng[ObjCnt[Ring]].NdotLoc=VecDot(Rng[ObjCnt[Ring]].Norm,
        Rng[ObjCnt[Ring]].Loc);
      LoadReal(&Rng[ObjCnt[Ring]].Rad1);
      LoadReal(&Rng[ObjCnt[Ring]].Rad2);
      LoadText(MtlName);
```

```
    GetMatlNum(MtlName, &Rng[ObjCnt[Ring]].MtlNum);
    GetTexNum(Matl[Rng[ObjCnt[Ring]].MtlNum].Textur,
      &Rng[ObjCnt[Ring]].TexNum);
  }
  if(!(strcmp(Buf1, "SPHERE")))
  {
    ObjCnt[Sphere]+=1;
    LoadTDA(Sphr[ObjCnt[Sphere]].Loc);
    LoadReal(&Sphr[ObjCnt[Sphere]].Rad);
    Sphr[ObjCnt[Sphere]].RadSqr =
      SqrFP(Sphr[ObjCnt[Sphere]].Rad);
    LoadText(MtlName);
    GetMatlNum(MtlName, &Sphr[ObjCnt[Sphere]].MtlNum);
    GetTexNum(Matl[Sphr[ObjCnt[Sphere]].MtlNum].Textur,
      &Sphr[ObjCnt[Sphere]].TexNum);
  }
  if(!(strcmp(Buf1, "QUADRATIC")))
  {
    ObjCnt[Quadratic]+=1;
    LoadTDA(Quad[ObjCnt[Quadratic]].Loc);
    LoadTDA(Quad[ObjCnt[Quadratic]].Direct);
    OrientQuadratic(&Quad[ObjCnt[Quadratic]]);
    LoadReal(&Quad[ObjCnt[Quadratic]].c1);
    LoadReal(&Quad[ObjCnt[Quadratic]].c2);
    LoadReal(&Quad[ObjCnt[Quadratic]].c3);
    LoadReal(&Quad[ObjCnt[Quadratic]].c4);
    LoadReal(&Quad[ObjCnt[Quadratic]].c5);
    LoadReal(&Quad[ObjCnt[Quadratic]].xmin);
    LoadReal(&Quad[ObjCnt[Quadratic]].xmax);
    LoadReal(&Quad[ObjCnt[Quadratic]].ymin);
    LoadReal(&Quad[ObjCnt[Quadratic]].ymax);
    LoadReal(&Quad[ObjCnt[Quadratic]].zmin);
    LoadReal(&Quad[ObjCnt[Quadratic]].zmax);
    LoadText(MtlName);
    GetMatlNum(MtlName, &Quad[ObjCnt[Quadratic]].MtlNum);
    GetTexNum(Matl[Quad[ObjCnt[Quadratic]].MtlNum].Textur,
      &Quad[ObjCnt[Quadratic]].TexNum);
  }
  if(!(strcmp(Buf1, "CONE")))
  {
```

```
    ObjCnt[Cone]+=1;
    LoadTDA(Con[ObjCnt[Cone]].Loc);
    LoadTDA(Con[ObjCnt[Cone]].Direct);
    OrientQuadratic(&Con[ObjCnt[Cone]]);
    LoadReal(&Rad);
    LoadReal(&Hgt);
    Con[ObjCnt[Cone]].xmin=-Rad;
    Con[ObjCnt[Cone]].zmin=-Rad;
    Con[ObjCnt[Cone]].ymin=-Hgt;
    Con[ObjCnt[Cone]].xmax=Rad;
    Con[ObjCnt[Cone]].zmax=Rad;
    Con[ObjCnt[Cone]].ymax=0.0;
    Con[ObjCnt[Cone]].c1=SqrFP(Rad);
    Con[ObjCnt[Cone]].c2=-SqrFP(Con[ObjCnt[Cone]].c1);
    Con[ObjCnt[Cone]].c3=SqrFP(Hgt);
    Con[ObjCnt[Cone]].c1 =Con[ObjCnt[Cone]].c1*
      Con[ObjCnt[Cone]].c3;
    Con[ObjCnt[Cone]].c3=Con[ObjCnt[Cone]].c1;
    Con[ObjCnt[Cone]].c4=0.0;
    Con[ObjCnt[Cone]].c5=0.0;
    LoadText(MtlName);
    GetMatlNum(MtlName, &Con[ObjCnt[Cone]].MtlNum);
    GetTexNum(Matl[Con[ObjCnt[Cone]].MtlNum].Textur,
      &Con[ObjCnt[Cone]].TexNum);
  }
  if(!(strcmp(Buf1, "CYLINDER")))
  {
    ObjCnt[Cylinder]+=1;
    LoadTDA(Cyl[ObjCnt[Cylinder]].Loc);
    LoadTDA(Cyl[ObjCnt[Cylinder]].Direct);
    OrientQuadratic(&Cyl[ObjCnt[Cylinder]]);
    LoadReal(&Rad);
    LoadReal(&Hgt);
    Cyl[ObjCnt[Cylinder]].xmin=-Rad;
    Cyl[ObjCnt[Cylinder]].zmin=-Rad;
    Cyl[ObjCnt[Cylinder]].ymin=0.0;
    Cyl[ObjCnt[Cylinder]].xmax=Rad;
    Cyl[ObjCnt[Cylinder]].zmax=Rad;
    Cyl[ObjCnt[Cylinder]].ymax=Hgt;
    Cyl[ObjCnt[Cylinder]].c1=1.0;
```

```
    Cyl[ObjCnt[Cylinder]].c2=0.0;
    Cyl[ObjCnt[Cylinder]].c3=1.0;
    Cyl[ObjCnt[Cylinder]].c4=SqrFP(Rad);
    Cyl[ObjCnt[Cylinder]].c5=0.0;
    LoadText(MtlName);
    GetMatlNum(MtlName, &Cyl[ObjCnt[Cylinder]].MtlNum);
    GetTexNum(Matl[Cyl[ObjCnt[Cylinder]].MtlNum].Textur,
          &Cyl[ObjCnt[Cylinder]].TexNum);
  }
  if(!(strcmp(Buf1, "BOX")))
  {
    LoadTDA(ShapeLoc);
    LoadTDA(vec1);
    LoadTDA(vec2);
    LoadTDA(vec3);
    LoadText(MtlName);
    GetMatlNum(MtlName, &MtlNumber);
    GetTexNum(Matl[MtlNumber].Textur, &TexNumber);
    ObjCnt[Parallelogram]+=1;
    VecCopy(ShapeLoc, Para[ObjCnt[Parallelogram]].Loc);
    VecCopy(vec1, Para[ObjCnt[Parallelogram]].v1);
    VecCopy(vec3, Para[ObjCnt[Parallelogram]].v2);
    VecCross(Para[ObjCnt[Parallelogram]].v1,
          Para[ObjCnt[Parallelogram]].v2,
          Para[ObjCnt[Parallelogram]].Norm);
    VecNormalize(Para[ObjCnt[Parallelogram]].Norm);
    Para[ObjCnt[Parallelogram]].NdotLoc =
          VecDot(Para[ObjCnt[Parallelogram]].Norm,
          Para[ObjCnt[Parallelogram]].Loc);
    Para[ObjCnt[Parallelogram]].MtlNum=MtlNumber;
    Para[ObjCnt[Parallelogram]].TexNum=TexNumber;
    ObjCnt[Parallelogram]+=1;
    VecCopy(ShapeLoc, Para[ObjCnt[Parallelogram]].Loc);
    VecCopy(vec3, Para[ObjCnt[Parallelogram]].v1);
    VecCopy(vec1, Para[ObjCnt[Parallelogram]].v2);
    VecCross(Para[ObjCnt[Parallelogram]].v1,
          Para[ObjCnt[Parallelogram]].v2,
          Para[ObjCnt[Parallelogram]].Norm);
    VecNormalize(Para[ObjCnt[Parallelogram]].Norm);
    Vec(0.0, vec2[1], 0.0, TempLoc);
```

```
VecAdd(TempLoc, Para[ObjCnt[Parallelogram]].Loc,
          Para[ObjCnt[Parallelogram]].Loc);
Para[ObjCnt[Parallelogram]].NdotLoc =
          VecDot(Para[ObjCnt[Parallelogram]].Norm,
          Para[ObjCnt[Parallelogram]].Loc);
Para[ObjCnt[Parallelogram]].MtlNum=MtlNumber;
Para[ObjCnt[Parallelogram]].TexNum=TexNumber;
ObjCnt[Parallelogram]+=1;
VecCopy(ShapeLoc, Para[ObjCnt[Parallelogram]].Loc);
VecCopy(vec3, Para[ObjCnt[Parallelogram]].v1);
VecCopy(vec2, Para[ObjCnt[Parallelogram]].v2);
VecCross(Para[ObjCnt[Parallelogram]].v1,
          Para[ObjCnt[Parallelogram]].v2,
          Para[ObjCnt[Parallelogram]].Norm);
VecNormalize(Para[ObjCnt[Parallelogram]].Norm);
Para[ObjCnt[Parallelogram]].NdotLoc =
          VecDot(Para[ObjCnt[Parallelogram]].Norm,
          Para[ObjCnt[Parallelogram]].Loc);
Para[ObjCnt[Parallelogram]].MtlNum=MtlNumber;
Para[ObjCnt[Parallelogram]].TexNum=TexNumber;
ObjCnt[Parallelogram]+=1;
VecCopy(ShapeLoc, Para[ObjCnt[Parallelogram]].Loc);
VecCopy(vec2, Para[ObjCnt[Parallelogram]].v1);
VecCopy(vec3, Para[ObjCnt[Parallelogram]].v2);
VecCross(Para[ObjCnt[Parallelogram]].v1,
          Para[ObjCnt[Parallelogram]].v2,
          Para[ObjCnt[Parallelogram]].Norm);
VecNormalize(Para[ObjCnt[Parallelogram]].Norm);
Vec(vec1[0], 0.0, 0.0, TempLoc);
VecAdd(TempLoc, Para[ObjCnt[Parallelogram]].Loc,
          Para[ObjCnt[Parallelogram]].Loc);
Para[ObjCnt[Parallelogram]].NdotLoc =
          VecDot(Para[ObjCnt[Parallelogram]].Norm,
          Para[ObjCnt[Parallelogram]].Loc);
Para[ObjCnt[Parallelogram]].MtlNum=MtlNumber;
Para[ObjCnt[Parallelogram]].TexNum=TexNumber;
ObjCnt[Parallelogram]+=1;
VecCopy(ShapeLoc, Para[ObjCnt[Parallelogram]].Loc);
VecCopy(vec2, Para[ObjCnt[Parallelogram]].v1);
VecCopy(vec1, Para[ObjCnt[Parallelogram]].v2);
```

```
     VecCross(Para[ObjCnt[Parallelogram]].v1,
           Para[ObjCnt[Parallelogram]].v2,
           Para[ObjCnt[Parallelogram]].Norm);
     VecNormalize(Para[ObjCnt[Parallelogram]].Norm);
     Para[ObjCnt[Parallelogram]].NdotLoc =
           VecDot(Para[ObjCnt[Parallelogram]].Norm,
           Para[ObjCnt[Parallelogram]].Loc);
     Para[ObjCnt[Parallelogram]].MtlNum=MtlNumber;
     Para[ObjCnt[Parallelogram]].TexNum=TexNumber;
     ObjCnt[Parallelogram]+=1;
     VecCopy(ShapeLoc, Para[ObjCnt[Parallelogram]].Loc);
     VecCopy(vec1, Para[ObjCnt[Parallelogram]].v1);
     VecCopy(vec2, Para[ObjCnt[Parallelogram]].v2);
     VecCross(Para[ObjCnt[Parallelogram]].v1,
           Para[ObjCnt[Parallelogram]].v2,
           Para[ObjCnt[Parallelogram]].Norm);
     VecNormalize(Para[ObjCnt[Parallelogram]].Norm);
     Vec(0.0, 0.0, vec3[2], TempLoc);
     VecAdd(TempLoc, Para[ObjCnt[Parallelogram]].Loc,
           Para[ObjCnt[Parallelogram]].Loc);
     Para[ObjCnt[Parallelogram]].NdotLoc =
           VecDot(Para[ObjCnt[Parallelogram]].Norm,
           Para[ObjCnt[Parallelogram]].Loc);
     Para[ObjCnt[Parallelogram]].MtlNum=MtlNumber;
     Para[ObjCnt[Parallelogram]].TexNum=TexNumber;
    }
   if(!(strcmp(Buf1, "PYRAMID")))
    {
      LoadTDA(ShapeLoc);
      LoadTDA(vec1);
      LoadTDA(vec2);
      LoadReal(&Hgt);
      LoadText(MtlName);
      GetMatlNum(MtlName, &MtlNumber);
      GetTexNum(Matl[MtlNumber].Textur, &TexNumber);
      ObjCnt[Parallelogram]+=1;
      VecCopy(ShapeLoc, Para[ObjCnt[Parallelogram]].Loc);
      VecCopy(vec2, Para[ObjCnt[Parallelogram]].v1);
      VecCopy(vec1, Para[ObjCnt[Parallelogram]].v2);
      VecCross(Para[ObjCnt[Parallelogram]].v1,
```

```
        Para[ObjCnt[Parallelogram]].v2,
        Para[ObjCnt[Parallelogram]].Norm);
VecNormalize(Para[ObjCnt[Parallelogram]].Norm);
Para[ObjCnt[Parallelogram]].NdotLoc =
        VecDot(Para[ObjCnt[Parallelogram]].Norm,
        Para[ObjCnt[Parallelogram]].Loc);
Para[ObjCnt[Parallelogram]].MtlNum=MtlNumber;
Para[ObjCnt[Parallelogram]].TexNum=TexNumber;
ObjCnt[Triangle]+=1;
VecCopy(ShapeLoc, Tri[ObjCnt[Triangle]].Loc);
VecCopy(vec1, Tri[ObjCnt[Triangle]].v1);
Vec(0.5*vec1[0], 0.5*vec2[1], Hgt,
        Tri[ObjCnt[Triangle]].v2);
VecCross(Tri[ObjCnt[Triangle]].v1,
        Tri[ObjCnt[Triangle]].v2,
        Tri[ObjCnt[Triangle]].Norm);
VecNormalize(Tri[ObjCnt[Triangle]].Norm);
Tri[ObjCnt[Triangle]].NdotLoc =
        VecDot(Tri[ObjCnt[Triangle]].Norm,
        Tri[ObjCnt[Triangle]].Loc);
Tri[ObjCnt[Triangle]].MtlNum=MtlNumber;
Tri[ObjCnt[Triangle]].TexNum=TexNumber;
ObjCnt[Triangle]+=1;
Tri[ObjCnt[Triangle]].Loc[0]=ShapeLoc[0]+vec1[0];
Tri[ObjCnt[Triangle]].Loc[1]=ShapeLoc[1]+vec2[1];
Tri[ObjCnt[Triangle]].Loc[2]=ShapeLoc[2];
VecScalMult(-1.0, vec1, Tri[ObjCnt[Triangle]].v1);
Vec(-0.5*vec1[0], -0.5*vec2[1], Hgt,
        Tri[ObjCnt[Triangle]].v2);
VecCross(Tri[ObjCnt[Triangle]].v1,
        Tri[ObjCnt[Triangle]].v2,
        Tri[ObjCnt[Triangle]].Norm);
VecNormalize(Tri[ObjCnt[Triangle]].Norm);
Tri[ObjCnt[Triangle]].NdotLoc =
        VecDot(Tri[ObjCnt[Triangle]].Norm,
        Tri[ObjCnt[Triangle]].Loc);
Tri[ObjCnt[Triangle]].MtlNum=MtlNumber;
Tri[ObjCnt[Triangle]].TexNum=TexNumber;
ObjCnt[Triangle]+=1;
Tri[ObjCnt[Triangle]].Loc[0]=ShapeLoc[0]+vec1[0];
```

```
      Tri[ObjCnt[Triangle]].Loc[1]=ShapeLoc[1]+vec2[1];
      Tri[ObjCnt[Triangle]].Loc[2]=ShapeLoc[2];
      Vec(-0.5*vec1[0], -0.5*vec2[1], Hgt,
            Tri[ObjCnt[Triangle]].v1);
      VecScalMult(-1.0, vec2, Tri[ObjCnt[Triangle]].v2);
      VecCross(Tri[ObjCnt[Triangle]].v1,
            Tri[ObjCnt[Triangle]].v2,
            Tri[ObjCnt[Triangle]].Norm);
      VecNormalize(Tri[ObjCnt[Triangle]].Norm);
      Tri[ObjCnt[Triangle]].NdotLoc =
            VecDot(Tri[ObjCnt[Triangle]].Norm,
            Tri[ObjCnt[Triangle]].Loc);
      Tri[ObjCnt[Triangle]].MtlNum=MtlNumber;
      Tri[ObjCnt[Triangle]].TexNum=TexNumber;
      ObjCnt[Triangle]+=1;
      VecCopy(ShapeLoc, Tri[ObjCnt[Triangle]].Loc);
      Vec(0.5*vec1[0], 0.5*vec2[1], Hgt,
            Tri[ObjCnt[Triangle]].v1);
      VecCopy(vec2, Tri[ObjCnt[Triangle]].v2);
      VecCross(Tri[ObjCnt[Triangle]].v1,
            Tri[ObjCnt[Triangle]].v2,
            Tri[ObjCnt[Triangle]].Norm);
      VecNormalize(Tri[ObjCnt[Triangle]].Norm);
      Tri[ObjCnt[Triangle]].NdotLoc =
            VecDot(Tri[ObjCnt[Triangle]].Norm,
            Tri[ObjCnt[Triangle]].Loc);
      Tri[ObjCnt[Triangle]].MtlNum=MtlNumber;
      Tri[ObjCnt[Triangle]].TexNum=TexNumber;
    }
  }
  while((Buf1[0]!=0) && (Buf1[0]!=0));
  fclose(TextDiskFile);
}

/*

      Calculate Directions of Reflected Rays

   CalcDirofReflRay - calculate the direction of a reflected ray
*/
```

```
void CalcDirofReflRay(TDA Dir, TDA SrfNrm, TDA ReflRay)
{
  float Tmp;

  Tmp=-2.0*VecDot(Dir, SrfNrm);
  VecAddScalMult(Tmp, SrfNrm, Dir, ReflRay);
}

/*
```

Intersection of Ray with Objects

```
   GetIntrPt  - find the intersection point given a point,
                                       direction and dist
   GetSrfNrm  - find the surface normal given the point of
                                             intersection
   Intersect  - determine if an object has been hit by a ray
   ShootRay   - check ray intersect against all objects and
                                           return closest

*/

void GetIntrPt(TDA Pt, TDA Dir, float Dist, TDA IntrPt)
{
  VecAddScalMult(Dist, Dir, Pt, IntrPt);
}

void Rotate(TDA vect,
        float cos1, float sin1,
        float cos2, float sin2,
        TDA result)
{
  float temp;

  result[0]=vect[0]*cos1-vect[2]*sin1;
  temp=vect[0]*sin1+vect[2]*cos1;
  result[1]=-vect[1]*cos2+temp*sin2;
  result[2]=-vect[1]*sin2-temp*cos2;
}
```

```
void RevRotate(TDA vect,
          float cos1, float sin1,
          float cos2, float sin2,
          TDA result)
{
  float temp;

  result[1]=vect[1]*cos2-vect[2]*sin2;
  temp=vect[1]*sin2+vect[2]*cos2;
  result[0]=-vect[0]*cos1+temp*sin1;
  result[2]=-vect[0]*sin1-temp*cos1;
}

void QuadraticSrfNrm(TDA IntrPt, TDA SrfNrm, QuadraticList
        *List)
{
  TDA NewPos, NewPos2, NewDir;
  float temp;

  VecSub(IntrPt, List->Loc, NewPos);
  VecCopy(NewPos, NewPos2);
  if((List->Direct[0]==0.0) && (List->Direct[1]==1.0) &&
        (List->Direct[2]==0.0))
  {
    SrfNrm[0]=List->c1*NewPos[0];
    SrfNrm[1]=List->c2*NewPos[1];
    SrfNrm[2]=List->c3*NewPos[2];
  }
  else
  {
    Rotate(NewPos2, List->cos1, List->sin1, -List->cos2,
         List->sin2, NewPos);
    NewDir[0]=List->c1*NewPos[0];
    NewDir[1]=List->c2*NewPos[1];
    NewDir[2]=List->c3*NewPos[2];
    RevRotate(NewDir, -List->cos1, List->sin1, -List->cos2,
         List->sin2, SrfNrm);
  }
  VecNormalize(SrfNrm);
}
```

```
void GetSrfNrm(int Shp, int Obj, TDA IntrPt, TDA SrfNrm)
{
  switch(Shp)
  {
    case Ground:
         Vec(0.0, 0.0, 1.0, SrfNrm);
         break;
    case Lamp:
         VecSub(IntrPt, Lmp[Obj].Loc, SrfNrm);
         VecNormalize(SrfNrm);
         break;
    case Triangle:
         VecCopy(Tri[Obj].Norm, SrfNrm);
         break;
    case Parallelogram:
         VecCopy(Para[Obj].Norm, SrfNrm);
         break;
    case Circles:
         VecCopy(Cir[Obj].Norm, SrfNrm);
         break;
    case Ring:
         VecCopy(Rng[Obj].Norm, SrfNrm);
         break;
    case Sphere:
         VecSub(IntrPt, Sphr[Obj].Loc, SrfNrm);
         VecNormalize(SrfNrm);
         break;
    case Quadratic:
         QuadraticSrfNrm(IntrPt, SrfNrm, &Quad[Obj]);
         break;
    case Cone:
         QuadraticSrfNrm(IntrPt, SrfNrm, &Con[Obj]);
         break;
    case Cylinder:
         QuadraticSrfNrm(IntrPt, SrfNrm, &Cyl[Obj]);
         break;
  }
}

#define Small 1E-03
```

```
TDA I_IntrPoint;
TDA I_delta;
float I_dot;
float I_pos1, I_pos2;
FDA I_gu, I_gv;
TDA I_Temp;
float I_b, I_c, I_t;
float I_disc, I_sroot;
float I_rad;
float I_t1, I_t2;

void SetUpTriangle(Byte p1, Byte p2, int Obj)
{
  I_gu[0]=-I_delta[p1];
  I_gv[0]=-I_delta[p2];
  I_gu[1]=Tri[Obj].v1[p1]-I_delta[p1];
  I_gv[1]=Tri[Obj].v1[p2]-I_delta[p2];
  I_gu[2]=Tri[Obj].v2[p1]-I_delta[p1];
  I_gv[2]=Tri[Obj].v2[p2]-I_delta[p2];
}

void SetUpParallelogram(Byte p1, Byte p2, int Obj)
{
  I_gu[0]=-I_delta[p1];
  I_gv[0]=-I_delta[p2];
  I_gu[1]=Para[Obj].v1[p1]-I_delta[p1];
  I_gv[1]=Para[Obj].v1[p2]-I_delta[p2];
  I_gu[2]=Para[Obj].v2[p1]+Para[Obj].v1[p1]-I_delta[p1];
  I_gv[2]=Para[Obj].v2[p2]+Para[Obj].v1[p2]-I_delta[p2];
  I_gu[3]=Para[Obj].v2[p1]-I_delta[p1];
  I_gv[3]=Para[Obj].v2[p2]-I_delta[p2];
}

Boolean EvenCrossings(int Sides)
{
    Byte i, j;
    Word crossings;
    crossings=0;
    for(i=0; i<Sides; i++)
    {
```

```
        j=(i+1) % Sides;
        if(((I_gv[i]<0) && (I_gv[j]>=0)) || ((I_gv[j]<0) &&
            (I_gv[i]>=0)))
        {
            if((I_gu[i]>=0) && (I_gu[j]>=0))
                ++crossings;
            else
            {
                if((I_gu[i]>=0) || (I_gu[j]>=0))
                {
                    if((I_gu[i]-I_gv[i]*(I_gu[j]-I_gu[i]) /
                        (I_gv[j]-I_gv[i]))>0)
                        ++crossings;
                }
        }
        }
    }
    if((crossings%2)==0)
        return(true);
    else
        return(false);
}

float QuadraticIntersectionCheck()
{
    float intersection;

    if((!(I_t1>Small)) && (!(I_t2>Small)))
        intersection=-1.0;
    else
    {
        if(I_t1>I_t2)
        {
        if(I_t2<Small)
            I_t2=I_t1;
        }
        else
        {
        if(I_t1>Small)
            I_t2=I_t1;
        }
```

```
        intersection=I_t2;
    }
    return(intersection);
}

Boolean PointOutofBounds(TDA Point, QuadraticList *List)
{
  if((Point[0]<List->xmin) || (Point[0]>List->xmax) ||
     (Point[1]<List->ymin) || (Point[1]>List->ymax) ||
     (Point[2]<List->zmin) || (Point[2]>List->zmax))
    return(true);
  else
    return(false);
}

float QuadraticShapes(QuadraticList *List, TDA Pt, TDA Dir)
{
  int i;
  TDA NewLoc, NewLoc2, NewDir;
  float a, disc;
  TDA loc2, loc1;
  float intersection, temp;

  VecSub(Pt, List->Loc, NewLoc);
  VecCopy(NewLoc, NewLoc2);
  if((List->Direct[0]==0.0) && (List->Direct[1]==1.0) &&
            (List->Direct[2]==0.0))
    VecCopy(Dir, NewDir);
  else
  {
    Rotate(Dir, List->cos1, List->sin1, List->cos2, List->sin2,
     NewDir);
    Rotate(NewLoc2, List->cos1, List->sin1, List->cos2,
            List->sin2, NewLoc);
  }
  if(List->c5==0.0)
  {
    I_c=-List->c4+List->c1*SqrFP(NewLoc[0])+
         List->c2*SqrFP(NewLoc[1])+
         List->c3*SqrFP(NewLoc[2]);
```

```
    I_b=2.0*(List->c1*NewLoc[0]*NewDir[0]+
          List->c2*NewLoc[1]*NewDir[1]+
          List->c3*NewLoc[2]*NewDir[2]);
             a=List->c1*SqrFP(NewDir[0])+
             List->c2*SqrFP(NewDir[1])+
             List->c3*SqrFP(NewDir[2]);
  }
  else
  {
    I_c=-List->c4+List->c1*SqrFP(NewLoc[0])-
          List->c5*NewLoc[1]+
          List->c3*SqrFP(NewLoc[2]);
    I_b=2.0*(List->c1*NewLoc[0]*NewDir[0]-
          List->c5*NewDir[1]+
          List->c3*NewLoc[2]*NewDir[2]);
             a=List->c1*SqrFP(NewDir[0])+
             List->c3*SqrFP(NewDir[2]);
  }
  disc=SqrFP(I_b)-4.0*a*I_c;
  if(disc<0.0)
    intersection=-1.0;
  else
  {
    I_sroot=sqrt(disc);
    I_t2=(-I_b+I_sroot)/(a+a);
    GetIntrPt(NewLoc, NewDir, I_t2, loc2);
    if(PointOutofBounds(loc2, List))
      I_t2=-1.0;
    I_t1=(-I_b-I_sroot)/(a+a);
    GetIntrPt(NewLoc, NewDir, I_t1, loc1);
    if(PointOutofBounds(loc1, List))
      I_t1=-1.0;
    intersection=QuadraticIntersectionCheck();
  }
  return(intersection);
}

float Intersect(TDA Pt, TDA Dir, int Shp, int Obj)
{
  float intersection;
```

```
switch(Shp)
{
  case Ground:
      if(Dir[2]==0.0)
          intersection=-1.0;
      else
      {
          I_t=-Pt[2]/Dir[2];
          if(I_t>Small)
              intersection=I_t;
          else
              intersection=-1.0;
      }
      break;
  case Lamp:
      VecSub(Lmp[Obj].Loc, Pt, I_Temp);
      I_b=VecDot(Dir, I_Temp)*-2.0;
      I_c=VecDot(I_Temp, I_Temp)-Lmp[Obj].RadSqr;
      I_disc=SqrFP(I_b)-4.0*I_c;
      if(!(I_disc>0.0))
          intersection=-1.0;
      else
      {
          I_sroot=sqrt(I_disc);
          I_t1=(-I_b-I_sroot)*0.5;
          I_t2=(-I_b+I_sroot)*0.5;
          intersection=QuadraticIntersectionCheck();
      }
      break;
  case Triangle:
      I_dot=VecDot(Tri[Obj].Norm, Dir);
      if(fabs(I_dot)<Small)
          intersection=-1.0;
      else
      {
          I_pos1=Tri[Obj].NdotLoc;
          I_pos2=VecDot(Tri[Obj].Norm, Pt);
          I_t=(I_pos1-I_pos2)/I_dot;
          GetIntrPt(Pt, Dir, I_t, I_IntrPoint);
          VecSub(I_IntrPoint, Tri[Obj].Loc, I_delta);
```

```
            if((fabs(Tri[Obj].Norm[0])>fabs(Tri[Obj].Norm[1]))
            && (fabs(Tri[Obj].Norm[0]) >
                        fabs(Tri[Obj].Norm[2])))
                 SetUpTriangle(1, 2, Obj);
            else
            {
                if(fabs(Tri[Obj].Norm[1])> =
                        fabs(Tri[Obj].Norm[2]))
                SetUpTriangle(0, 2, Obj);
                 else
                SetUpTriangle(0, 1, Obj);
            }
        }
        if(EvenCrossings(3))
            intersection=-1.0;
        else
            intersection=I_t;
        break;
    case Parallelogram:
        I_dot=VecDot(Para[Obj].Norm, Dir);
        if(fabs(I_dot)<Small)
            intersection=-1.0;
        else
        {
            I_pos1=Para[Obj].NdotLoc;
            I_pos2=VecDot(Para[Obj].Norm, Pt);
            I_t=(I_pos1-I_pos2)/I_dot;
            GetIntrPt(Pt, Dir, I_t, I_IntrPoint);
            VecSub(I_IntrPoint, Para[Obj].Loc, I_delta);
            if((fabs(Para[Obj].Norm[0]) >
            fabs(Para[Obj].Norm[1])) &&
                 (fabs(Para[Obj].Norm[0]) >
            fabs(Para[Obj].Norm[2])))
                 SetUpParallelogram(1, 2, Obj);
            else
            {
                if(fabs(Para[Obj].Norm[1]) >=
                    fabs(Para[Obj].Norm[2]))
                    SetUpParallelogram(0, 2, Obj);
                 else
```

```
                SetUpParallelogram(0, 1, Obj);
            }
        }
        if(EvenCrossings(4))
            intersection=-1.0;
        else
            intersection=I_t;
        break;
    case Circles:
        I_dot=VecDot(Cir[Obj].Norm, Dir);
        if(fabs(I_dot)<Small)
            intersection=-1.0;
        else
        {
            I_pos1=Cir[Obj].NdotLoc;
            I_pos2=VecDot(Cir[Obj].Norm, Pt);
            I_t=(I_pos1-I_pos2)/I_dot;
            GetIntrPt(Pt, Dir, I_t, I_IntrPoint);
            VecSub(I_IntrPoint, Cir[Obj].Loc, I_delta);
            I_rad=sqrt(VecDot(I_delta, I_delta));
            if(I_rad>Cir[Obj].Radius)
                intersection=-1.0;
            else
                intersection=I_t;
        }
        break;
    case Ring:
        I_dot=VecDot(Rng[Obj].Norm, Dir);
        if(fabs(I_dot)<Small)
            intersection=-1.0;
        else
        {
            I_pos1=Rng[Obj].NdotLoc;
            I_pos2=VecDot(Rng[Obj].Norm, Pt);
            I_t=(I_pos1-I_pos2)/I_dot;
            GetIntrPt(Pt, Dir, I_t, I_IntrPoint);
            VecSub(I_IntrPoint, Rng[Obj].Loc, I_delta);
            I_rad=sqrt(VecDot(I_delta, I_delta));
            if((I_rad<Rng[Obj].Rad1) || (I_rad>Rng[Obj].Rad2))
                intersection=-1.0;
```

```
            else
                intersection=I_t;
        }
        break;
    case Sphere:
        VecSub(Sphr[Obj].Loc, Pt, I_Temp);
        I_b=VecDot(Dir, I_Temp)*-2.0;
        I_c=VecDot(I_Temp, I_Temp)-Sphr[Obj].RadSqr;
        I_disc=SqrFP(I_b)-4.0*I_c;
        if(!(I_disc>0.0))
            intersection=-1.0;
        else
        {
            I_sroot=sqrt(I_disc);
            I_t1=(-I_b-I_sroot)*0.5;
            I_t2=(-I_b+I_sroot)*0.5;
            intersection=QuadraticIntersectionCheck();
        }
        break;
    case Quadratic:
        intersection=QuadraticShapes(&Quad[Obj], Pt, Dir);
        break;
    case Cone:
        intersection=QuadraticShapes(&Con[Obj], Pt, Dir);
        break;
    case Cylinder:
        intersection=QuadraticShapes(&Cyl[Obj], Pt, Dir);
        break;
  }
  return(intersection);
}

Boolean ShootRay(TDA Start, TDA Dir, int *Shp, int *Obj, float
    *Dist)
{
    int ShapeNum;
    int ObjectNum;
    float NewDist;
    Boolean ObjHit;

    *Shp=-1;
```

```
    *Obj=-1;
    *Dist=-1.0;
    ObjHit=false;
    for(ShapeNum=0; ShapeNum<=MaxShapeType; ShapeNum++)
    {
        for(ObjectNum=1; ObjectNum<=ObjCnt[ShapeNum];
            ObjectNum++)
        {
        if((ShapeNum==0) && (!(Gnd.MtlNum==0)))
                NewDist=Intersect(Start, Dir, Ground, 0);
        else
                NewDist=Intersect(Start, Dir, ShapeNum,
        ObjectNum);
        if(NewDist>Small)
        {
                if(*Dist==-1.0)
                {
                    ObjHit=true;
                    *Dist=NewDist;
                    *Shp=ShapeNum;
                    *Obj=ObjectNum;
                }
                else
                {
                    if(NewDist<*Dist)
                    {
                        *Dist=NewDist;
                        *Shp=ShapeNum;
                        *Obj=ObjectNum;
                    }
                }
        }
        }
    }
    return(ObjHit);
}
```

```
/*

  Calculate Contribution of Local Color Model at Intersection

   GetLoclCol - calculate ambient, diffuse, reflection and
                                          specular reflection

*/

#define  MaxNoise 28

Word NoiseMatrix[MaxNoise][MaxNoise][MaxNoise];

void InitNoise()
{
  Byte x, y, z;
  Byte i, j, k;

  randomize();
  for(x=0; x<=MaxNoise-1; x++)
  {
    for(y=0; y<=MaxNoise-1; y++)
    {
      for(z=0; z<=MaxNoise-1; z++)
      {
        NoiseMatrix[x][y][z] = random(12000);
        if(x==MaxNoise-1)
      i=0;
    else
      i=x;
    if(y==MaxNoise-1)
      j=0;
    else
      j=y;
    if(z==MaxNoise-1)
      k=0;
    else
      k=z;
    NoiseMatrix[x][y][z]=NoiseMatrix[i][j][k];
```

```
        }
      }
    }
  }

  int Noise(float x, float y, float z)
  {

  /* harmonic and random functions combined to create a noise
  function based on Perlin's (1985) noise function - ideasfound
  in Alan Watt's -
      Fundamentals of Three-Dimensional Computer Graphics */

    Byte ix, iy, iz;
    float ox, oy, oz;
    int p000, p001;
    int p010, p011;
    int p100, p101;
    int p110, p111;
    int p00, p01;
    int p10, p11;
    int p0, p1;
    int d00, d01;
    int d10, d11;
    int d0, d1;
    int d;

    x=fabs(x);
    y=fabs(y);
    z=fabs(z);
    ix=Trunc(x)%MaxNoise;
    iy=Trunc(y)%MaxNoise;
    iz=Trunc(z)%MaxNoise;
    ox=Frac(x);
    oy=Frac(y);
    oz=Frac(z);
    p000=NoiseMatrix[ix][iy][iz];
    p001=NoiseMatrix[ix][iy][iz+1];
    p010=NoiseMatrix[ix][iy+1][iz];
    p011=NoiseMatrix[ix][iy+1][iz+1];
```

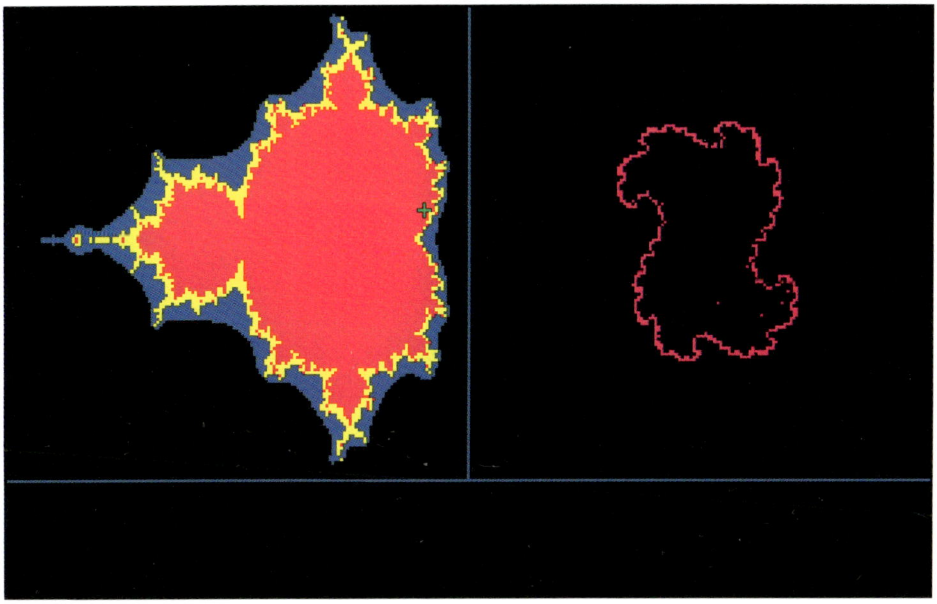

Plate 1. Walking About the Mandelbrot Set

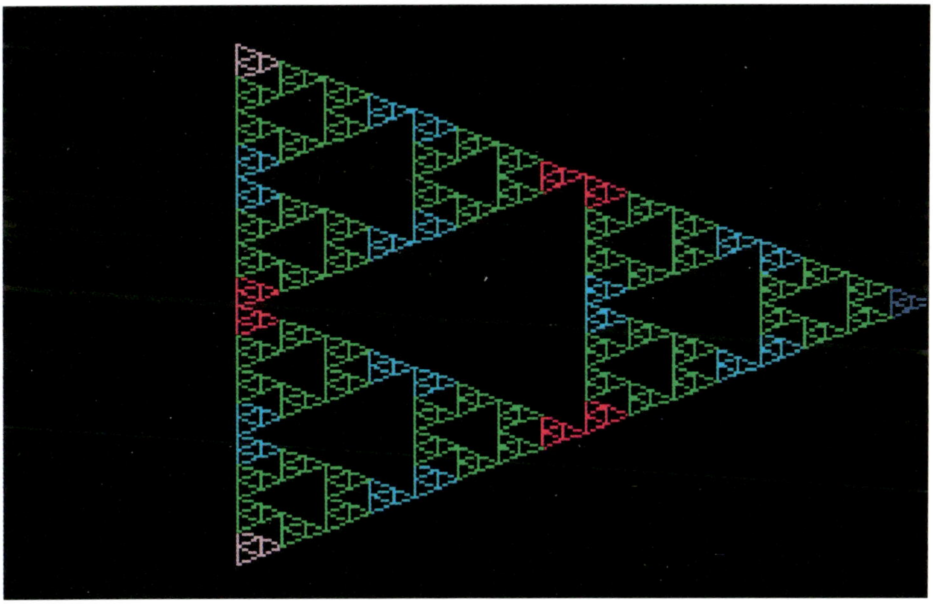

Plate 2. The Sierpinski Triangle

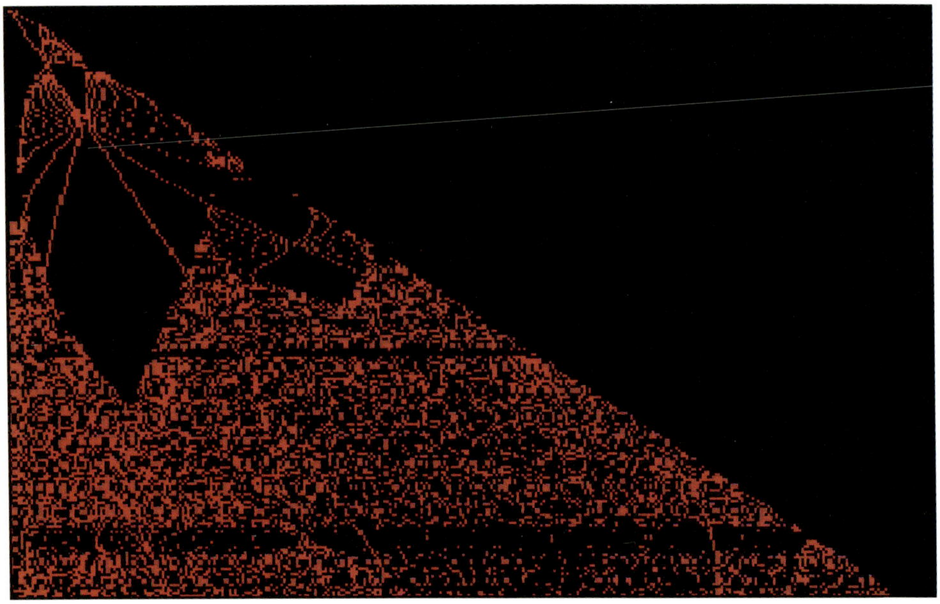

Plate 3. Bifurcation Diagram

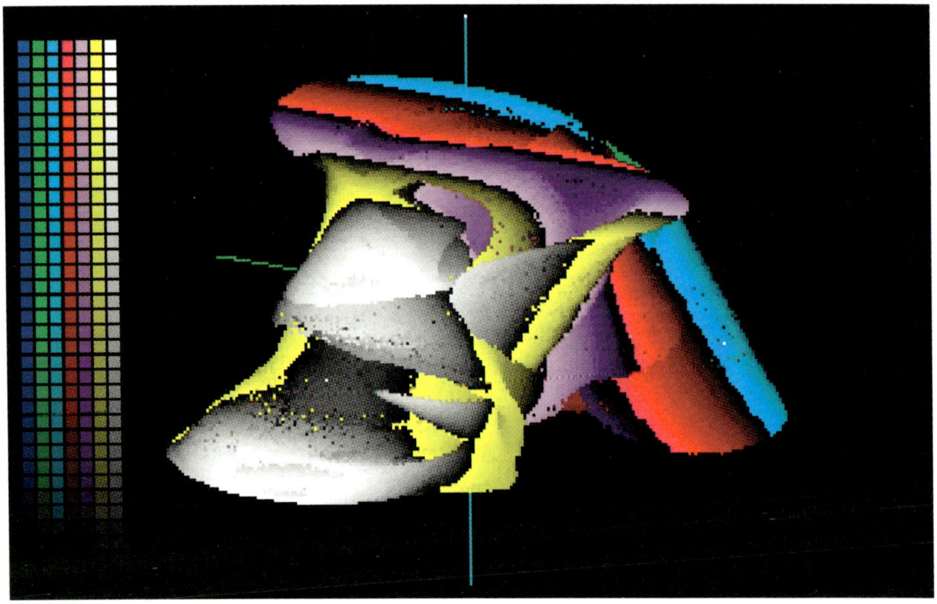

Plate 4. A Strange Attractor in Three Dimensions

Plate 5. 3-D Modeled Cube

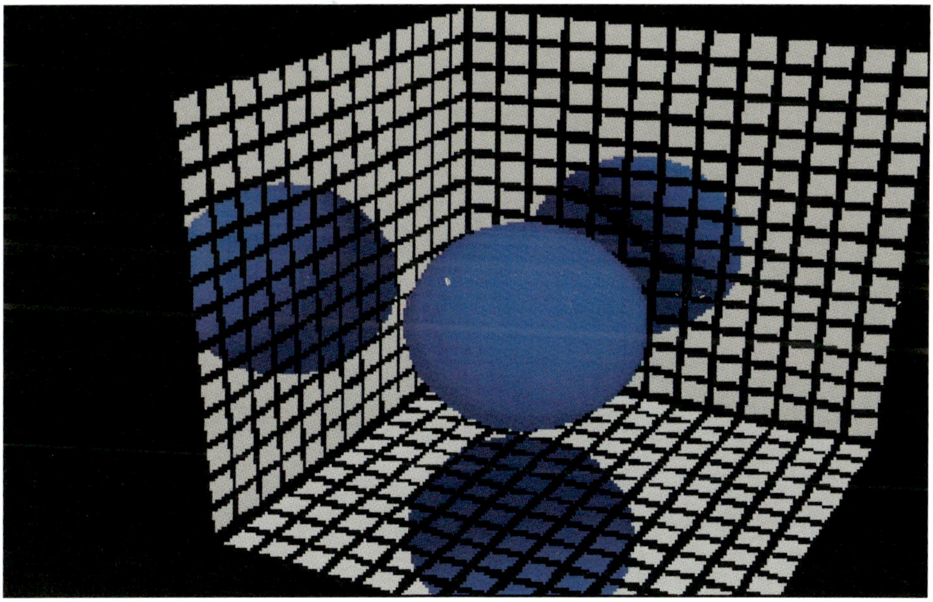

Plate 6. 3-D Modeled Sphere with Mirrored Walls

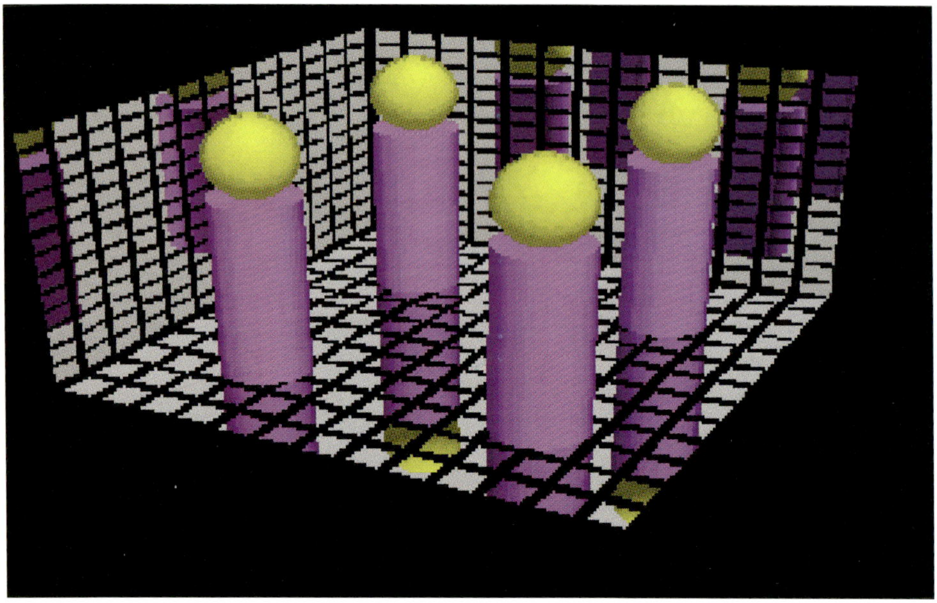

Plate 7. 3-D Modeled Columns with Spheres on Top

Plate 8. 3-D Modeled Well Scene

Plate 9. 3-D Modeled Collection of Solid Shapes

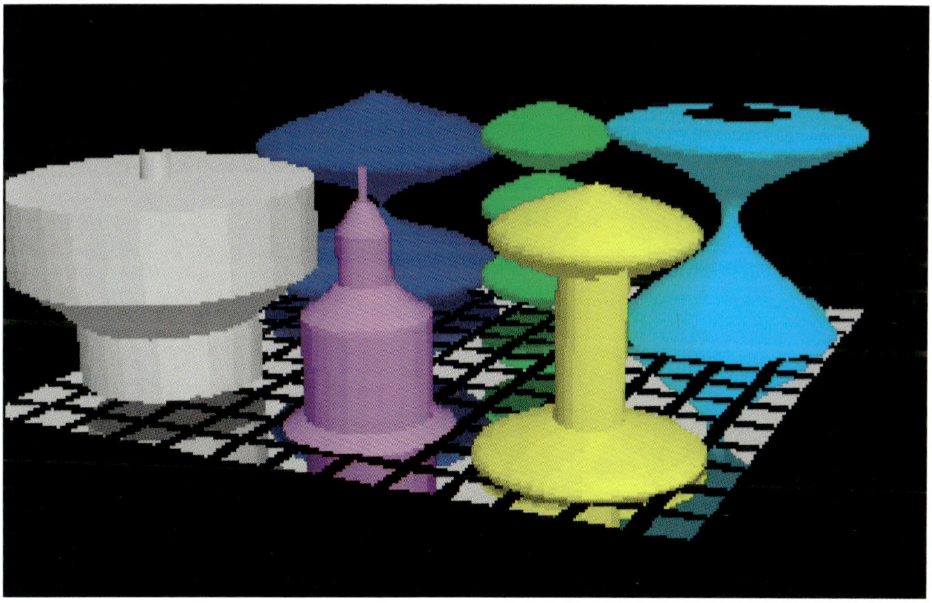

Plate 10. 3-D Modeled Collection of Solids of Revolution

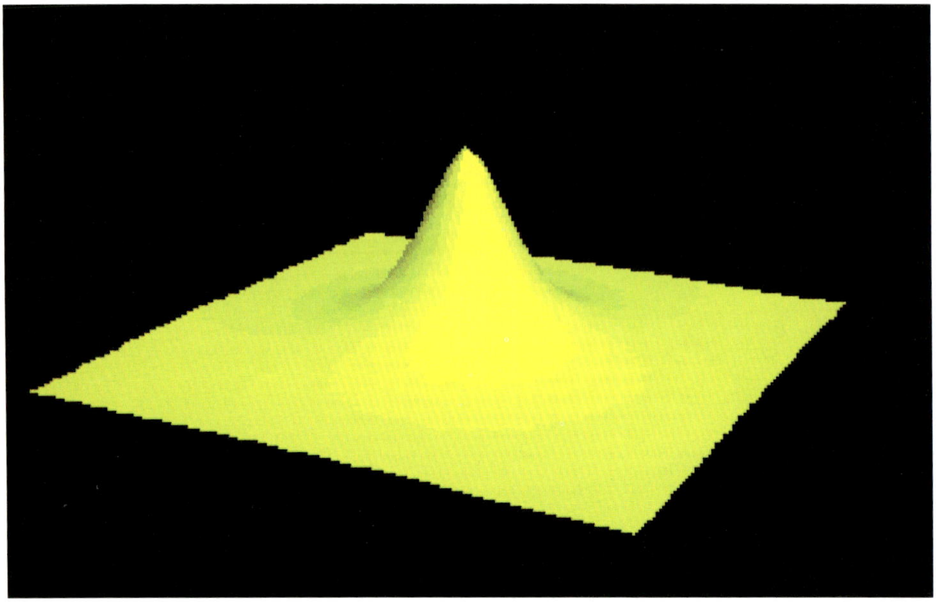

Plate 11. 3-D Modeled Equation Plot of $z=75/(x^2+y^2+1)$

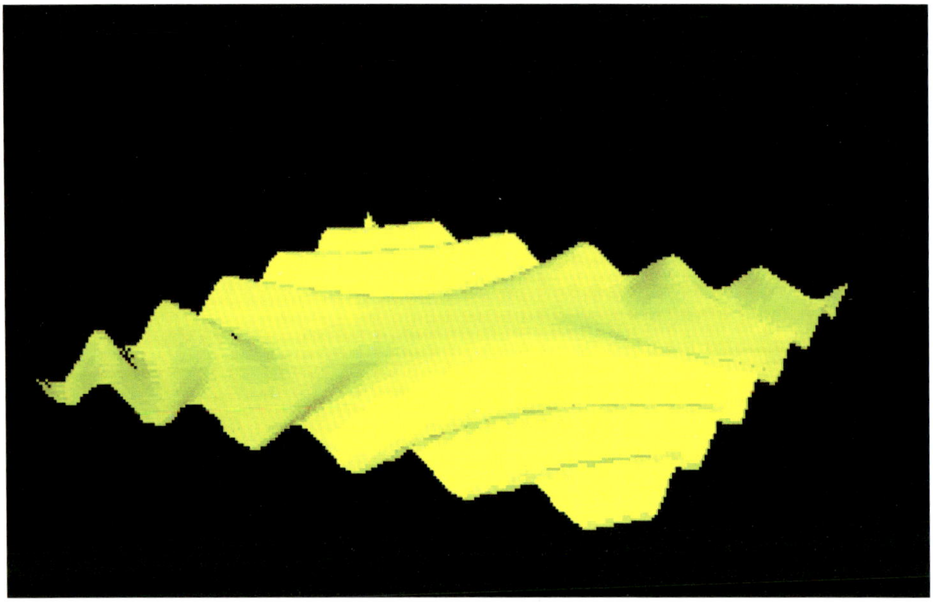

Plate 12. 3-D Modeled Equation Plot of $z=6(\cos(xy)+1)$

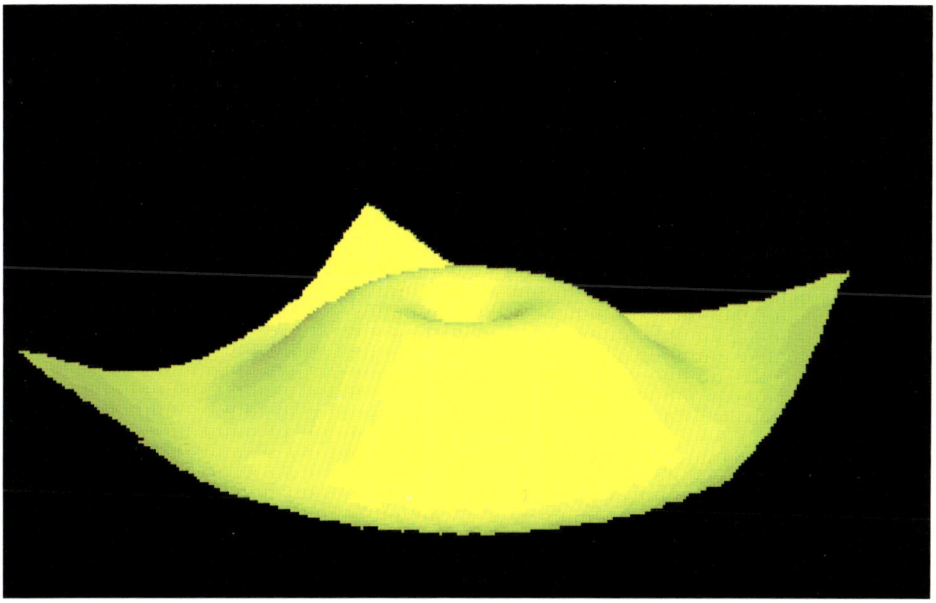

Plate 13. 3-D Modeled Equation Plot of $z=20(\sin(\sqrt{(x^2+y^2)}))$

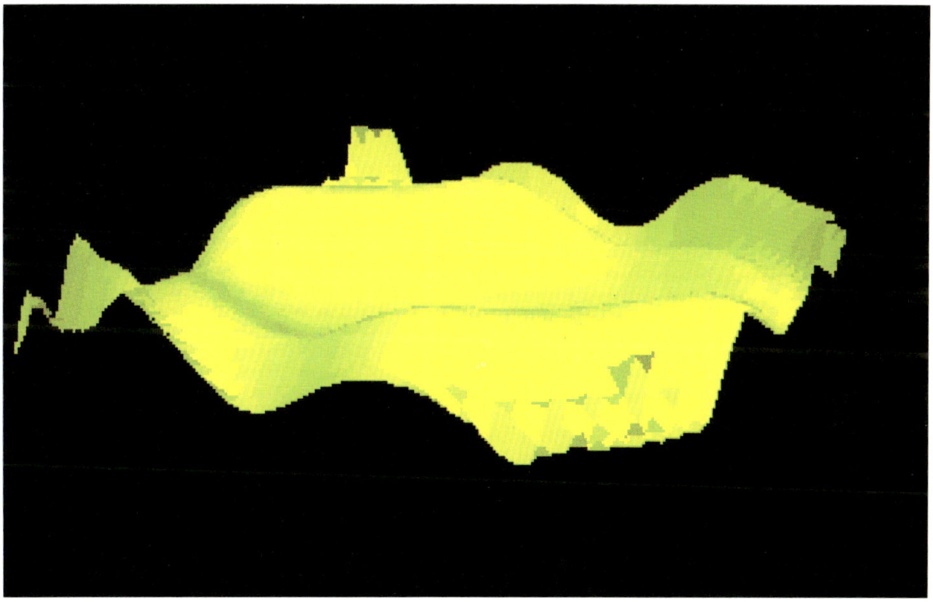

Plate 14. 3-D Modeled Equation Plot of $z=10(1+\sqrt{(x^2+y^2)}+\sin(0.1(x^2+y^2))+\sin(xy))$

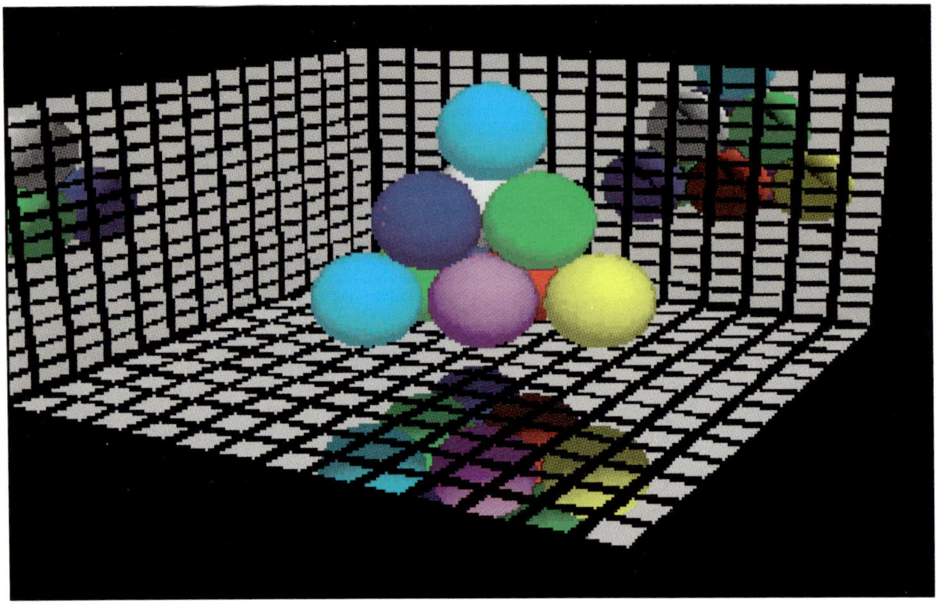

Plate 15. 3-D Modeled Stacked Spheres

Plate 16. Z-Buffered Equation Plot of $z=75/(x^2+y^2+1)$

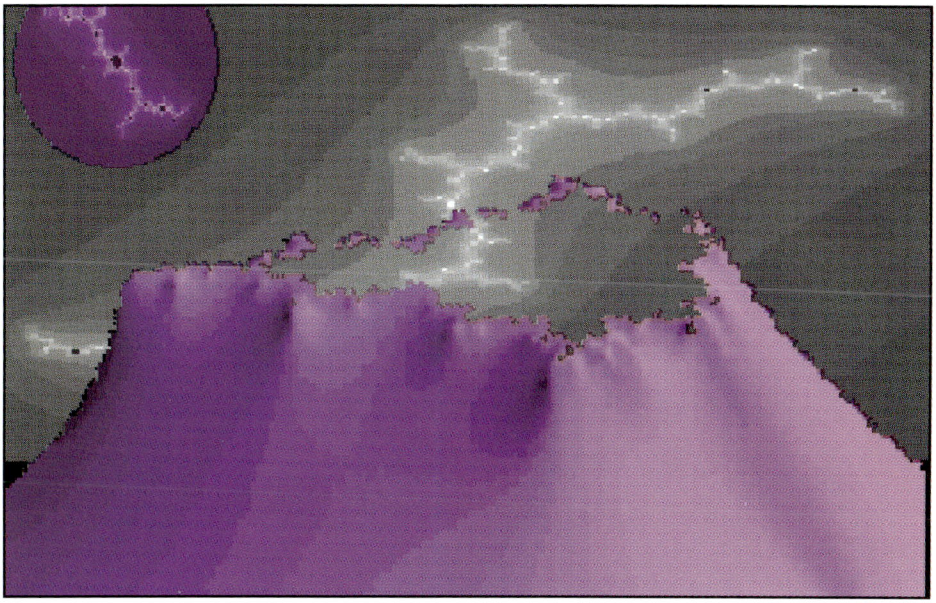

Plate 17. Z-Buffered Three-Dimensional Mandelbrot Set

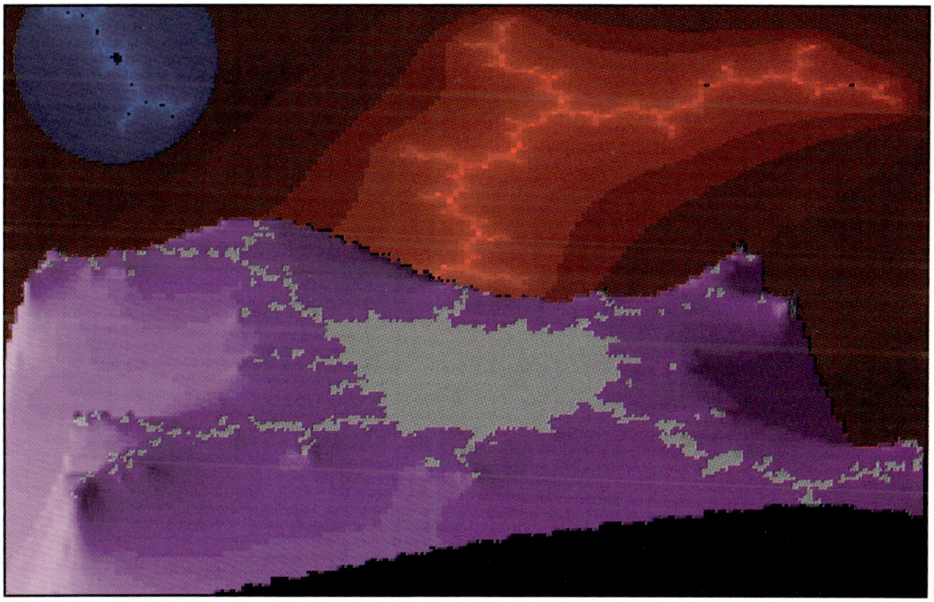

Plate 18. Z-Buffered Three-Dimensional Mandelbrot Set

Plate 19. Z-Buffered Three-Dimensional Julia Set

Plate 20. Z-Buffered Three-Dimensional Julia Set

Plate 21. Z-Buffered Quaternion, Unsmoothed / Smoothed

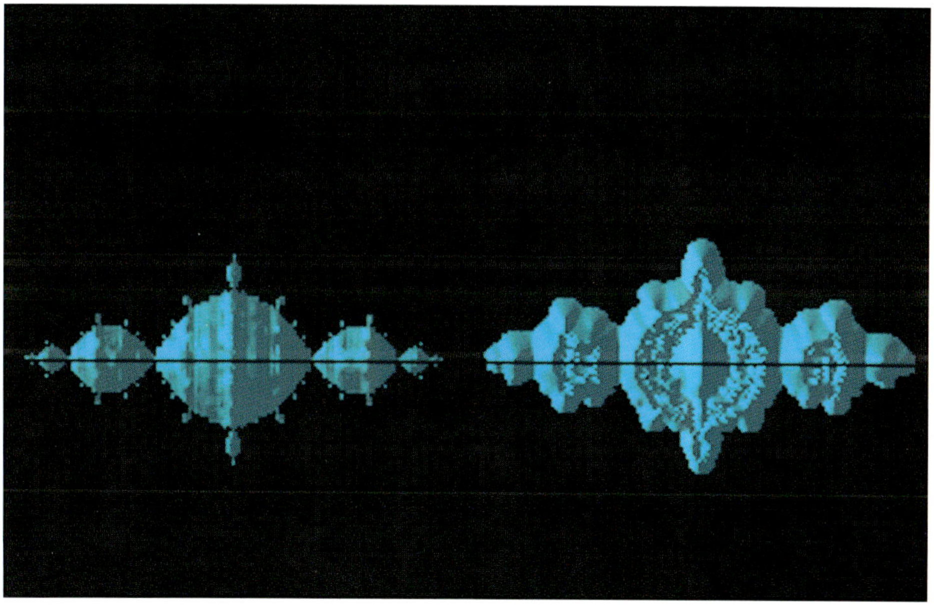

Plate 22. Z-Buffered Quaternion, Unsmoothed / Smoothed

Plate 23. Color Representing Mountain Elevations

Plate 24. Z-Buffered Plasma Mountains

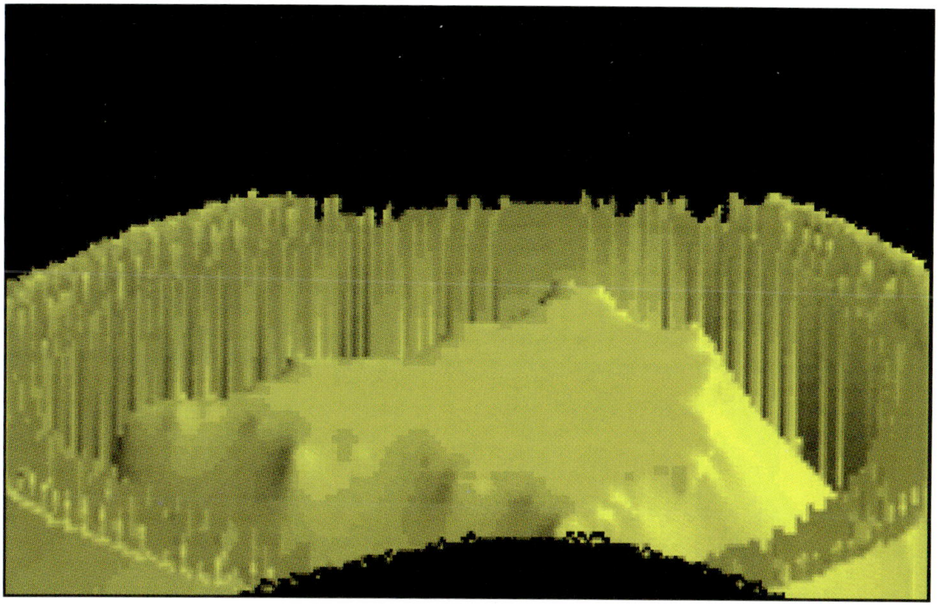

Plate 25. Smoothed z-Buffered Mandelbrot Set

Plate 26. Stack of Textured Spheres

Plate 27. Marbles on Wood Floor

Plate 28. Office Scene

Plate 29. Daytime Scene of Lakeside Park

Plate 30. Water Molecule

Plate 31. Stack of Textured Pyramids

Plate 32. Saturn, Uranus and Neptune

```
  p100=NoiseMatrix[ix+1][iy][iz];
  p101=NoiseMatrix[ix+1][iy][iz+1];
  p110=NoiseMatrix[ix+1][iy+1][iz];
  p111=NoiseMatrix[ix+1][iy+1][iz+1];
  d00=p100-p000;
  d01=p101-p001;
  d10=p110-p010;
  d11=p111-p011;
  p00=Trunc(d00*ox)+p000;
  p01=Trunc(d01*ox)+p001;
  p10=Trunc(d10*ox)+p010;
  p11=Trunc(d11*ox)+p011;
  d0=p10-p00;
  d1=p11-p01;
  p0=Trunc(d0*oy)+p00;
  p1=Trunc(d1*oy)+p01;
  d=p1-p0;
  return((Trunc(d*oz)+p0));
}

void MarbleTex(TDA Pt, TDA RGB)
{
  float i, d;
  float x, y, z;

  UnVec(Pt, &x, &y, &z);
  x*=0.2;
  d=x+0.0006*Noise(x, y*0.1, z*0.1);
  d*=(Trunc(d)%25);
  i=0.5+0.05*fabs(d-10.0-20.0*Trunc(d*0.05));
  if (i > 1.0)
    i = 1.0;
  Vec(i, i, i, RGB);
}

void WoodTex(TDA Pt, TDA RGB)
{
  float i, d;
  float x, y, z;
```

```
  UnVec(Pt, &x, &y, &z);
  x*=0.2;
  d=x+0.0002*Noise(x, y*0.1, z*0.1);
  d*=(Trunc(d)%25);
 i=0.7+0.05*fabs(d-10.0-20.0*Trunc(d*0.05));
  if (i > 1.0)
    i = 1.0;
  Vec(i, i, i, RGB);
}

int LC_Mtl, LC_Src;
int LC_ShadShp;
int LC_ShadObj;
float LC_ShadDist;
int LC_ObjHit;
TDA LC_LmpDir;
TDA LC_Addition;
TDA LC_Total;
float SS_Lamb;
TDA SS_Diff, SS_Spec;

void Texture(int Tex, TDA Texturing, TDA IntrPt)
{
  int x, y, z, rt;
  float lev, r;

  switch(Tex)
  {
    case Checker:
        x=Round(fabs(IntrPt[0])*Tile)%10000;
        y=Round(fabs(IntrPt[1])*Tile)%10000;
        z=Round(fabs(IntrPt[2])*Tile)%10000;
        if(((x+y+z)%2)==1)
            VecCopy(Tile1, Texturing);
        else
            VecCopy(Tile2, Texturing);
        break;
    case Grit:
        rt=random(32767);
        r=(float) rt/32768.0;
```

```
        lev=r*0.2+0.8;
        Vec(lev, lev, lev, Texturing);
        break;
    case Marble:
        MarbleTex(IntrPt, Texturing);
        break;
    case Wood:
        WoodTex(IntrPt, Texturing);
        break;
    case Sheetrock:
        rt=random(32767);
        r=(float) rt/32768.0;
        lev=r*0.1+0.9;
        Vec(lev, lev, lev, Texturing);
        break;
  }
}

void Ambient()
{
  VecElemMult(1.0, Matl[LC_Mtl].AmbRfl, AmbIntens, LC_Total);
}

void Diffuse()
{
  VecElemMult(SS_Lamb, Matl[LC_Mtl].DifRfl, Lmp[LC_Src].Intens,
                                                        SS_Diff);
}

void Specular(TDA Dir, TDA SrfNrm)
{
  TDA Temp;
  float cone, Glint;

  VecSub(LC_LmpDir, Dir, Temp);
  VecScalMult(0.5, Temp, Temp);
  VecNormalize(Temp);
  cone=VecDot(SrfNrm, Temp);
  if(cone>0.6)
  {
```

```
    Glint=exp(Matl[LC_Mtl].Gloss*Log(cone));
    VecElemMult(Glint, Matl[LC_Mtl].SpcRfl,
        Lmp[LC_Src].Intens, SS_Spec);
  }
  else
    VecNull(SS_Spec);
}

void UnShadowedSurface(TDA Dir, TDA SrfNrm)
{
  SS_Lamb=VecDot(SrfNrm, LC_LmpDir);
  if(SS_Lamb<=0.0)
  {
    VecNull(SS_Diff);
    VecNull(SS_Spec);
  }
  else
  {
    Diffuse();
    Specular(Dir, SrfNrm);
  }
  VecAdd(SS_Diff, SS_Spec, LC_Addition);
}

void ShadowFeeler(TDA IntrPt)
{
  LC_ObjHit=ShootRay(IntrPt, LC_LmpDir, &LC_ShadShp,
     &LC_ShadObj, &LC_ShadDist);
}

void GetLoclCol(int Shp, int Obj,
           TDA Dir, TDA IntrPt, TDA SrfNrm,
           float Dist, TDA LoclCol)
{
  int Tex;
  TDA Amb;
  TDA Temp;
  TDA ColorTexture;
  float IntensFactor;
  Boolean HitItself;
```

```
if(Shp==Lamp)
{
 IntensFactor=(1.0-DistEffect)+DistEffect*(-VecDot(SrfNrm,
  Dir)/sqrt(Dist));
 VecScalMult(IntensFactor, Lmp[Obj].Intens, LoclCol);
}
else
{
  switch(Shp)
  {
    case Ground:
      LC_Mtl=Gnd.MtlNum;
      Tex=Gnd.TexNum;
      break;
    case Triangle:
      LC_Mtl=Tri[Obj].MtlNum;
      Tex=Tri[Obj].TexNum;
      break;
    case Parallelogram:
      LC_Mtl=Para[Obj].MtlNum;
      Tex=Para[Obj].TexNum;
      break;
    case Circles:
      LC_Mtl=Cir[Obj].MtlNum;
      Tex=Cir[Obj].TexNum;
      break;
    case Ring:
      LC_Mtl=Rng[Obj].MtlNum;
      Tex=Rng[Obj].TexNum;
      break;
    case Sphere:
      LC_Mtl=Sphr[Obj].MtlNum;
      Tex=Sphr[Obj].TexNum;
      break;
    case Quadratic:
      LC_Mtl=Quad[Obj].MtlNum;
      Tex=Quad[Obj].TexNum;
      break;
    case Cone:
      LC_Mtl=Con[Obj].MtlNum;
```

```
          Tex=Con[Obj].TexNum;
          break;
        case Cylinder:
          LC_Mtl=Cyl[Obj].MtlNum;
          Tex=Cyl[Obj].TexNum;
          break;
      }
      Ambient();
      for(LC_Src=1; LC_Src<=ObjCnt[Lamp]; LC_Src++)
      {
        VecSub(Lmp[LC_Src].Loc, IntrPt, LC_LmpDir);
        VecNormalize(LC_LmpDir);
        ShadowFeeler(IntrPt);
        HitItself=LC_ObjHit&(LC_ShadShp==Lamp) &
          (LC_ShadObj==LC_Src);
        if((!(LC_ObjHit)) || HitItself)
        {
          UnShadowedSurface(Dir, SrfNrm);
          VecAdd(LC_Total, LC_Addition, LC_Total);
        }
      }
      if(Tex==Smooth)
        VecCopy(LC_Total, LoclCol);
      else
      {
        Texture(Tex, ColorTexture, IntrPt);
        VecElemMult(1.0, LC_Total, ColorTexture, LoclCol);
      }
    }
}

/*
 ┌───────────────────────────────────────────────────────────────┐
 │                          Calculate Sky                         │
 └───────────────────────────────────────────────────────────────┘

   Sky - blend a sky color from the horizon to the zenith

*/
```

```
void Sky(TDA Dir, TDA Col)
{
  float small=1E-03;
  float sin2, cos2;
  float x2, y2, z2;

  x2=SqrFP(Dir[0]);
  y2=SqrFP(Dir[1]);
  z2=SqrFP(Dir[2]);
  if(z2==0)
    z2=small;
  sin2=z2/(x2+y2+z2);
  cos2=1.0-sin2;
  VecLinComb(cos2, HorCol, sin2, ZenCol, Col);
}

/*
┌──────────────────────────────────────────┐
│            Recursive Ray Tracer          │
└──────────────────────────────────────────┘

   TraceRay - perform recursive ray tracing

*/

void Comb(TDA A, TDA B, TDA C, TDA D, TDA Col)
{
  TDA T1, T2;

  VecElemMult(1.0, A, B, T1);
  VecElemMult(1.0, C, D, T2);
  VecAdd(T1, T2, Col);
}
Boolean WgtMin(TDA TotWgt)
{
    if((TotWgt[0]<=MinWgt[0])&&(TotWgt[1] <=
        MinWgt[1])&&(TotWgt[2]<=MinWgt[2]))
    return(true);
  else
    return(false);
}
```

```
int TR_Shp, TR_Obj;

Boolean MaterialSpecular()
{
  int Mtl;

  switch(TR_Shp)
  {
    case Ground:
        Mtl=Gnd.MtlNum;
        break;
    case Triangle:
        Mtl=Tri[TR_Obj].MtlNum;
        break;
    case Parallelogram:
        Mtl=Para[TR_Obj].MtlNum;
        break;
    case Circles:
        Mtl=Cir[TR_Obj].MtlNum;
        break;
    case Ring:
        Mtl=Rng[TR_Obj].MtlNum;
        break;
    case Sphere:
        Mtl=Sphr[TR_Obj].MtlNum;
        break;
    case Quadratic:
        Mtl=Quad[TR_Obj].MtlNum;
        break;
    case Cone:
        Mtl=Con[TR_Obj].MtlNum;
        break;
    case Cylinder:
        Mtl=Cyl[TR_Obj].MtlNum;
        break;
  }
  if(!(TR_Shp==Lamp))
  {
    if((Matl[Mtl].SpcRfl[0] == 0)&&(Matl[Mtl].SpcRfl[1]==0) &&
        (Matl[Mtl].SpcRfl[2]==0))
```

```
      return(false);
    else
      return(true);
  }
  else
    return(true);
}

void TraceRay(TDA Start, TDA Dir, TDA TotWgt, int Depth, TDA
        Col)
{
  TDA LoclCol, ReflCol;
  TDA ReflDir, Wgt;
  TDA IntrPt, SrfNrm;
  float Dist;
  Boolean ObjHit;

  ObjHit=ShootRay(Start, Dir, &TR_Shp, &TR_Obj, &Dist);
  if(ObjHit)
  {
    GetIntrPt(Start, Dir, Dist, IntrPt);
    GetSrfNrm(TR_Shp, TR_Obj, IntrPt, SrfNrm);
    GetLoclCol(TR_Shp, TR_Obj, Dir, IntrPt, SrfNrm, Dist,
            LoclCol);
    if((Depth==MaxDepth) || (WgtMin(TotWgt)))
      VecElemMult(1.0, LoclCol, LoclWgt, Col);
    else
    {
      if(!(TR_Shp==Lamp) || (TR_Shp==Lamp)&ReflectiveLamps)
      {
        if(MaterialSpecular())
        {
        CalcDirofReflRay(Dir, SrfNrm, ReflDir);
        VecElemMult(1.0, TotWgt, ReflWgt, Wgt);
        TraceRay(IntrPt, ReflDir, Wgt, Depth+1, ReflCol);
        }
        else
        VecNull(ReflCol);
      }
      else
```

```
    VecNull(ReflCol);
      Comb(LoclCol, LoclWgt, ReflCol, ReflWgt, Col);
    }
  }
  else
    Sky(Dir, Col);
}

/*
```

Scan Pixel Display

```
   GetEye - calculate the direction of a ray from the eye
                 through a screen pixel and into the scene
   Scan   - scan the pixel display with eye-rays

*/

TDA ViewVec;
int CenterX;
int CenterY;
int ScanXRes;
int ScanYRes;
float XPitchDivFocLen;
float YPitchDivFocLen;

void PreCalculation()
{
  float Scale;

  XPitchDivFocLen=XPitch/FocalLength;
  YPitchDivFocLen=YPitch/FocalLength;
  CenterX=ScanXRes>>1;
  CenterY=ScanYRes>>1;
  Scale=CenterX;
  VecScalMult(Scale, ViewDir, ViewVec);
}

void GetInitialDir(int i, int j, TDA Dir)
{
```

```
  float x, y;
  TDA EyeToPixVec;

  x=(i-CenterX)*XPitchDivFocLen;
  y=(CenterY-j)*YPitchDivFocLen;
  VecLinComb(x, U, y, V, EyeToPixVec);
  VecAdd(ViewVec, EyeToPixVec, Dir);
  VecNormalize(Dir);
}

void Scan(Name FileName)
{
  TDA InitialDir;
  TDA Col;
  TDIA Colr;
  int Xp, Yp;

  PreCalculation();
  TextDiskFile=fopen(FileName, "w+b");
  putw(ScanXRes, TextDiskFile);
  putw(ScanYRes, TextDiskFile);
  for(Yp=0; Yp<=ScanYRes-1; Yp++)
  {
    for(Xp=0; Xp<=ScanXRes-1; Xp++)
    {
      GetInitialDir(Xp, Yp, InitialDir);
      TraceRay(ObsPos, InitialDir, MaxWgt, 1, Col);
      VecScalMultInt(63.0, Col, Colr);
      Plot(Xp, Yp, (Colr[0]+Colr[1]+Colr[2])/3);
      fprintf(TextDiskFile, "%c%c%c", Colr[0], Colr[1], Colr[2]);
    }
  }
  fclose(TextDiskFile);
}

Name FileName;

void GetFileName()
{
```

```
  Byte x, y;

  puts("");
  printf("Enter File Name -> ");
  x=wherex();
  y=wherey();
  gets(FileName);
  if(!(strcmp(FileName, "")))
  {
    strcpy(FileName, "Test");
    gotoxy(x, y);
    printf("%s", FileName);
  }
  strcat(FileName, ".RT");
  puts("");
  puts("");
}

/*
╔══════════════════════════════════════════════════════════════╗
║                         Main Program                         ║
╚══════════════════════════════════════════════════════════════╝
*/

PaletteRegister PalArray;

void main()
{
  InitNoise();
  ClearMemory();
  clrscr();
  GetFileName(FileName);
  GetData(FileName);
  ScanXRes=XRes;
  ScanYRes=YRes;
  if(XRes==1024)
    InitGraphics(56);
  else
    InitGraphics(19);
```

```
    InitPalette(PalArray);
    SetPalette(PalArray);
    Scan(OutputFile);
    ExitGraphics();
}
```

Figure 19-1. Listing of the Ray Tracing Program

The next constant is *DistEffect*, which is the fractional effect of distance upon lamp intensity. By default, it is set to 0.3; you can change it if you want the light intensity fall-off with distance to be greater or less in a particular scene. The next variable to be defined is *OutputFile,* which is the name of the disk file to which the pixel color data will be sent for storage.

This is followed by two real numbers, *XPitch* and *YPitch*. These parameters determine the coverage of the scene area. They are essentially the inverse of the focal length, in that the larger the focal length, the more restricted the area covered by the "camera lens," whereas the larger the values of the pitch parameters, the larger the area covered. However, unlike the focal length of a lens, these parameters can be separately set for the x and y directions, thereby permitting selective distortion of the scene.

The next parameters determine the weighing of color components for a particular scene. These are *LoclWgt*, the weighing of object color component; *ReflWgt*, the weighing of the reflected color component; *MinWgt*, the minimum weighing of colors in the scene; and *MaxWgt*, the maximum weighing of colors in the scene. These are all vectors, having values for the red, green, and blue components. There is also the integer variable *MaxDepth,* which is the maximum depth of the scene.

Next, the focal length and the viewer position information are defined. The geometry for ray tracing is the same as the solid modeling geometry shown in Figure 8-1. The variable *ObsPos* is the observer position (a three-dimensional vector). The variables *ObsRotate* (the observer rotate angle) and *ObsTilt* (the observer tilt angle) are *view theta* and *view phi* respectively. From these, it is possible to compute the variable *ViewDir* (the viewer direction from the origin) and U and V (the transformations from the scene coordinate system to a viewer-centered coordinate system).

Next, the sky colorings are defined. These are *HorCol* (the color of the sky at the horizon) and *ZenCol* (the color of the sky at the zenith). Next the program sets up variables for tiling with a checkerboard pattern. These are *Tile1* and *Tile2* (The two checkerboard colors) and *Tile*, the size of the side of the checkerboard square. Next the program sets up a maximum value of 20 for the number of types of material that may be defined and then defines the variables that make up a material description record. These include the name of the material type, the name of its texture type, the ambient, diffuse, and reflected color values, and the glossiness power. An array of these material records is then created.

The program then sets up a parameter for the normal ambient light intensity. Next, the maximum number of textures is set to be 6. They are *Smooth, Checker, Grit, Marble, Wood,* and *Sheetrock*. The program then establishes the number of primitive shapes as 9. They are *Ground, Lamp, Triangle, Parallelogram, Circles, Ring, Sphere, Quadratic, Cone*, and *Cylinder*.

Then the maximum value for each shape is specified. There is only one ground. There can be 15 lamps, 30 triangles, 40 parallelograms, 20 circles, 20 rings, 30 spheres, 5 quadratics, 15 cones, and 15 cylinders.

Next, the parameters associated with each primitive object are defined. These include its position, vectors that define its extent and orientation, radii (if appropriate), intensity (for lamps), surface normal, material, texture, the dot product of the normal and the location vector, and whatever other parameters are needed to define the object and compute the intersections of light rays with it. The program then sets up an array containing all of the primitive objects that may be defined. Finally, the program defines the *.RT* disk file which contains the scene definition data.

The Main Program

Now we're ready to deal with the main program, which by itself is quite simple. It begins by calling the function *InitNoise*. This function sets up the noise function that will be used to create marble textures. It then calls *ClearMemory*, which initializes all of the program parameters. We won't discuss *ClearMemory* any further, since as you can see from the listing, all it does is zero a lot of variables and null a bunch of strings.

It then calls *ClrScr*, which clears the display screen, so that it is ready to display the monochrome version of the ray-traced scene. Next, the program calls *GetFileName*. This function first displays, "Enter File Name =>". It then reads whatever file name the user types in from the keyboard. If only a return is entered, the program will use the file *Test.RT* by default. (The file name is typed in without the extension; this function then adds the extension.)

The resulting file name is stored and used throughout the program. Next, the program calls *GetData*, passing the designated file name as a parameter. This function loads all of the data from the selected scene data file into the program. The program then calls the proper *InitGraphics* function to prepare for graphics display with whatever resolution has been selected for this run of the program. It then calls *InitPalette* and *SetPalette* to set up the VGA color registers for the gray-scale display. Next, the program calls the function *Scan* which performs all of the ray tracing operations and saves the resulting scene data to the output file. Then it calls the function *ExitGraphics* to exit from the graphics mode, after which the program terminates.

Loading an .RT File

In order to observe how an *.RT* file is loaded to provide the program data base, you need to refer to the section of the program listing titled "Load an *.RT File", which describes the function *GetData*.

At the beginning of this function are a number of other functions, each of which handles the loading of a particular type of data. We'll look at a few of these now and the rest will be covered as we get into the details of the *GetData* function.

The first one that we will examine is the *LoadTDA* function. This function first reads a line from the text file into a buffer. It then creates a vector by iterating a loop three times which converts the eight characters beginning at position $14 + i*9$ (where i is the iteration index) into a real number which is stored in the indexed member of a vector. Note that this means that whatever text descriptor begins the file line is completely ignored, and that it requires the exact spacing of each of the three numbers that make up the vector. No deviation is allowed, so be careful how you space your *.RT* files.

The next function, *LoadReal*, also reads a line from the text file into a buffer. It then creates a real number by converting the eight characters beginning at position 14 into a real number. Again the text descriptor is ignored and the positioning of the numerical data in the file is critical. The next function, *LoadInteger*, also reads a line from the text file into a buffer. It then creates an integer by converting the eight characters beginning at position 14 into an integer. Again the text descriptor is ignored and the positioning of the numerical data in the file is critical. The next function, *LoadText*, also reads a line from the text file into a buffer. It then makes a text string out of the 30 characters beginning at location 14 of the file line. Again the text descriptor is ignored and the positioning of the string data in the file is critical.

For now, refer to the listing of the *GetData* function itself. It begins by opening and resetting the designated data file. It then begins a *do* loop which is iterated until the end of file is encountered. At each iteration, the first thing that the function does is to read a line from the file into a buffer. The rest of the loop is a series of *if* statements, one for each type of information that might be encountered in the buffer as a heading for a section of the file.

The first is *STATS*. If this is encountered, the function reads a line which is the output file name. It then reads two lines of integers, which are the horizontal and vertical resolution of the desired display. It then reads *XPitch* and *YPitch*, which we described earlier. If the buffer contained *ENVIRONMENT*, the function reads four vectors, *LoclWgt*, *ReflWgt*, *MinWgt*, and *MaxWgt*. It then reads the integer *MaxDepth*.

If the buffer contains *OBSERVER*, the function reads the real variable *FocalLength*, followed by the vector *ObsPos*, followed by the real number angles *ObsRotate* and *ObsTilt*. It then calls the function *GetViewDir*. This function computes the angles *Phi* and *Theta* (in radians) and then the *View* vector. It then computes the transformation vectors *U* and *V*.

Returning now to the *GetData* function, if the buffer contains *SKY* the function reads the vectors for the horizon and zenith colors. If the buffer contains *CHECK*, the function reads in the two color vectors for the checkerboard and the real number that is the length of the side of each square.

If the buffer contains *MATERIAL*, the function first increments the count of material types. It then loads the proper members of the *Matl* array at the new count location, namely the name of the material type and texture, the vectors representing the ambient, diffuse, and specular colors of the material, and the real number representing its glossiness power.

If the buffer contains *AMBIENTLIGHT*, the function loads the vector that contains the ambient light color. If the buffer contains *GROUND*, the function first loads the material name for the ground. It then calls *GetMatlNum*, which searches through the list of materials until it encounters one with the specified name, and then assigns its number to the proper member of the ground array. It then calls *GetTexNum*, which assigns a texture number corresponding to the texture specified for the designated material.

If the buffer contains *LAMP*, the function increments the number of lamps and then loads the variables needed to define a lamp into the proper members of the lamp array.

If the buffer contains *TRIANGLE*, the function increments the number of triangles and then loads the variables needed to define a triangle into the proper members of the triangle array. It then performs the vector cross product of the two vectors that define the triangle to obtain the normal to the triangle surface. It then computes and stores the dot product of the normal and the location vector of the triangle. Next, it calls *GetMatlNum* and *GetTexNum* to obtain the material and texture numbers as described above.

If the buffer contains *PARALLELOGRAM*, the function increments the number of parallelograms and then loads the variables needed to define a parallelogram into the proper members of the parallelogram array. It then performs the vector cross product of the two vectors that define the parallelogram to obtain the normal to the parallelogram surface. It then computes and stores the dot product of the normal and the location vector of the parallelogram. It then calls *GetMatlNum* and *GetTexNum* to obtain the material and texture numbers as described above.

If the buffer contains *CIRCLE*, the function increments the number of circles and then loads the variables needed to define a circle into the proper members of the circles array. It then performs the vector cross product of the two vectors that define the circle to obtain the normal to the circle surface. It then computes and stores the dot product of the normal and the location vector of the circle. It then calls *GetMatlNum* and *GetTexNum* to obtain the material and texture numbers as described above.

If the buffer contains *RING*, the function increments the number of rings and then loads the variables needed to define a ring into the proper members of the rings array. It then performs the vector cross product of the two vectors that define the ring to obtain the normal to the ring surface. It then computes and stores the dot product of the normal and the location vector of the ring. It then calls *GetMatlNum* and *GetTexNum* to obtain the material and texture numbers as described above.

If the buffer contains *SPHERE*, the function increments the number of spheres and then loads the variables needed to define a ring into the proper members of the spheres array. It then calls *GetMatlNum* and *GetTexNum* to obtain the material and texture numbers as described above.

If the buffer contains *QUADRATIC*, the function increments the number of quadratics and then loads the variables needed to define a quadratic into the proper members of the quadratic array. The function also calls *OrientQuadratic*, which performs the necessary mathematical operations to tilt the quadratic if it is not to be oriented in the upright position. It then calls *GetMatlNum* and *GetTexNum* to obtain the material and texture numbers as described above.

If the buffer contains *CONE*, the cone is actually a quadratic, but is specified in terms of the radius of its base circle and height of its apex, rather than in terms of the quadratic equation. The function thus loads these parameters and then automatically computes the necessary coefficients for the quadratic equation. It then increments the number of quadratics and stores the variables needed to define the cone quadratic into the proper members of the quadratic array. It then calls *GetMatlNum* and *GetTexNum* to obtain the material and texture numbers.

If the buffer contains *CYLINDER*, the cylinder is actually a quadratic, but is specified in terms of the radius of its circle and its height, rather than in terms of the quadratic equation. The function thus loads these parameters and then automatically computes the necessary coefficients for the quadratic equation. It then increments the number of quadratics and stores the variables needed to define the cylinder quadratic into the proper members of the quadratic array. It then calls *GetMatlNum* and *GetTexNum* to obtain the material and texture numbers.

If the buffer contains *BOX*, the function reads the location vector and the three vectors needed to define the shape and position of the box. It then calls *GetMatlNum* and *GetTexNum* to obtain the material and texture numbers as described above.

Then, the function determines the characteristics of the six parallelograms that are required to define the sides of the box and performs the same operations for each one that it ordinarily performs for a parallelogram.

If the buffer contains *PYRAMID*, the function reads the location vector, the two vectors and the height needed to define the shape and position of the pyramid. It then calls *GetMatlNum* and *GetTexNum* to obtain the material and texture numbers as described above. Then, the function determines the characteristics of the four triangles that are required to define the sides of the pyramid and performs the same operations for each one that it ordinarily performs for a triangle. When the loop has iterated until the end of file is reached, the loop terminates, the file is closed and the function returns to the calling entity.

Initializing the Noise Function

We are going to be modifying our color data by applying a noise function to it to produce interesting textures similar to wood and marble. The technique follows that described by Alan Watt in his book, *Fundamentals of Three-Dimensional Computer Graphics.*

We begin with a 28 x 28 x 28 matrix. Next, the function uses three nested *for* loops to fill every member of this array with a random number between 0 and 12000. This is all taken care of in the first statement under the innermost *for* loop. The remainder of the function is designed so that whenever one of the tree indices of the array reaches its maximum value, the array cell will be filled with the same number that is contained in the corresponding cell where the index value is zero. This assures that the end and beginning of the array are the same, and thus enables us to cycle around without any undue effects.

The array is now initialized; when we get into textures, we'll show how the array is used.

Scanning the Scene

Now let's look at the function *Scan,* which scans the pixel display. It begins by calling the function *Precalculation*. This function first modifies *YPitch* if the high-resolution display mode is to be used. This is necessary because the horizontal and vertical pixel dimensions are the same in the high-resolution mode, but not in the low-resolution mode. Because of this, if we have made the picture proportions to be correct for the low-resolution mode, we have to perform a scaling in one dimension for the picture to have the same proportions in the higher-resolution mode.

The function then computes the scaling factors *XPitchDivFocLen* and *YPitchDivFocLen*. Next, it determines the center of the screen and computes the vector *ViewVec*, which is the vector from the observer position to the center of the screen.

Getting back to the *Scan* function, the next operation is to open and prepare to rewrite the designated output file. The first thing written to the file are the *x* and *y* resolution values for the display to be generated. Next, the function starts two nested *for* loops which together iterate once for each pixel location on the display screen. For each iteration, the function first calls *GetInitialDir*. This function performs the necessary mathematical operations to compute a normalized vector *InitialDir* in the direction from the observer to the pixel on the screen that is being processed.

The *Scan* function is now going to call *TraceRay*, which will project this vector until it hits an object in the scene and then report back the resulting color for the pixel. Next, the colors, which are values in the range from 0 to 1, are scaled to be in the range of 0 to 63, which is the color information that we want to store in the output file. First, we sum the colors together and divide by 3 to get a gray scale value which is immediately plotted on the screen. Then the color information is written out to the output file.

When the loops are through, this has been done for every pixel on the screen. We have a complete gray scale image of the scene on the screen and a complete file of color data stored on the disk.

Tracing the Ray

The function *TraceRay* performs the actual chore of tracing the ray from the screen to the objects in the scene. The function begins by calling the function *ShootRay*. This function makes use of two nested *for* loops to examine every type of shape and every object of every type in the data base. For each object, it calls *Intersect* to determine the distance at which the current ray from the observer intersects the object. If this distance is greater than some minimum and the distance parameter is still at its initial value, a set of parameters is set up to indicate the shape number and object number of the object being intersected, the distance to intersection, and to indicate that an intersection has occurred. If the distance parameter is not at its initial value, the above parameters are reset only if the intersect distance for the current object is less than the distance stored in the parameter. Thus, when the loops have completed, the parameters contain information for the object for which the nearest intersection occurred.

Now let's look at *Intersect* to see how it works. We are working backward, and have already started at the observer's eye and traced a ray of light back to the screen. We have seen that we test each object to see whether that ray intersects any point on the object's surface. The *Intersect* function does this. It is essentially one big *case* statement, with a separate case to be run for each different shape that might be encountered.

Now we need to determine at some point in our computations exactly where on an object's surface the ray may be hitting the object. The math for determining the intersect point is different for each shape. We simplify as much as possible by converting the ray direction vector to the local coordinate system of the shape being tested and then using the equation of the ray in a parametric form. In particular, the equations for the coordinates of the ray are:

$$x = x_1 t + x_0 \qquad \text{(Equation 19-1)}$$

$$y = y_1 t + y_0 \qquad \text{(Equation 19-2)}$$

$$z = z_1 t + z_0 \qquad \text{(Equation 19-3)}$$

The coordinates (x_0, y_0, z_0) are the coordinates of the starting point of the ray and the coordinates (x_1, y_1, z_1) represent a unit vector in the direction in which the ray is travelling. The parameter t can be taken as time. Thus at zero time, the ray is at its origin, and as time passes, the ray travels farther and farther along its path.

We are interested in determining the time at which the ray intersects an object. We can find the shortest time for the ray to hit an object's surface and later convert this to distance. The point of intersection with a sphere is determined as follows. The equation of a sphere, centered at (0, 0, 0) and having a radius *r*, is:

$$x^2 + y^2 + z^2 - r^2 = 0 \qquad \text{(Equation 19-4)}$$

If we substitute the parametric equations of the ray into this equation (using for the ray the same coordinate system, whose origin is the center of the sphere) we obtain the following quadratic equation:

$$(x_1^2 + y_1^2 + z_1^2)t^2 + 2(x_0x_1 + y_0y_1 + z_0z_1)t$$

$$+ (x_0^2 + y_0^2 + z_0^2) - 1 = 0 \qquad \text{(Equation 19-5)}$$

Performing a straightforward solution of the quadratic equation, we obtain two roots. These roots represent intersections of the ray with the sphere; the smallest one represents the closest intersection.

Now let's consider the intersection of the ray with a quadratic curve. This is similar to the sphere intersection, since the sphere is a degenerate case of the general quadratic curve. The most common quadratic shapes are the cylinder, the elliptic paraboloid, the hyperbolic paraboloid, the elliptic cone, the hyperboloid of one sheet, the hyperboloid of two sheets. All of these shapes can be represented by the following generalized equation:

$$ax^2 + 2bxy + 2cxz + 2dxw + ey^2 + 2fyz$$

$$+ 2gyw + hz^2 + 2izw + jw^2 = 0 \qquad \text{(Equation 19-6)}$$

Although the above equation covers every possible kind of quadratic curve, it is too complex to be easily handled by this simple ray tracing program. Fortunately most of the common quadratic surfaces can be treated by a sub-set of this equation, namely:

$$Ax^2 + By^2 \; Cz^2 + Ey = D \qquad \text{(Equation 19-7)}$$

Using the same technique of substituting the parametric ray equations into the equation of the quadratic and then solving the resulting quadratic equation, we may have either of two equations, depending upon the parameters that are defined. The first is:

$$t^2(Ax_1^2 + By_1^2 + Cz_1^2) + 2t(Ax_0x_1 + By_0y_1 + Cz_0z_1)$$

$$+ (Ax_0^2 + By_0^2 + Cz_0^2 - D) = 0 \qquad \text{(Equation 19-8)}$$

the second possible equation is:

$$t^2(Ax_1^2 + Cz_1^2) + 2t(Ax_0x_1 - Ey_1 + Cz_0z_1)$$

$$+ (Ax_0^2 - Ey_0 + Cz_0^2) = 0 \qquad \text{(Equation 19-9)}$$

Next, let's consider an intersection with a ring. This is the first of three surfaces that are actually sections of a plane. First, we determine whether the ray intersects with the plane containing the ring. The equation for a plane is:

$$ax + by + cz + d = 0 \qquad \text{(Equation 19-10)}$$

The intersection of the ray with the plane is obtained, as before, by substituting the parametric equations of the ray into the equation of the plane, giving:

$$t = \frac{ax_0 + by_0 + cz_0 + d}{ax_1 + by_1 + cz_1 + d} \qquad \text{(Equation 19-11)}$$

This is a general equation, but we are going to use a coordinate system which is centered at the middle of the plane, so that the parameter d will always be zero. As you look at this equation, you need to observe that the vector *(a, b, c)* is the normal to the plane. Consequently, the denominator of the equation is the dot product of the normal to the plane and the line direction. As for the numerator, it is the dot product of the normal to the plane with the difference between the origin of the plane coordinate system and the origin of the line.

Next, we find the vector from the plane coordinate origin to the point of intersection. The length of this vector is the square root of the dot product of the vector and itself. This length, we call *rad*. If *rad* falls between the values of the inner radius of the ring and the outer radius of the ring, we have a valid intersection with the ring.

Determining the intersection point of the ray with a parallelogram starts in the same way as for the ring. We first determine whether the ray intersects the plane containing the parallelogram. If the ray intersects the plane, we have to determine if it also intersects the parallelogram which is a lot more difficult than determining whether the intersection with the plane occurs. We need to make use of the Jordan curve theorem, which simply states that if we project a line from the intersection point in an arbitrary direction, if the line has an odd number of intersections with the line segments that are the sides of the parallelogram, the intersect point is inside the parallelogram, while if there is an even number of intersections, the intersect point is outside the parallelogram.

To make things easier, we are first going to project both the parallelogram and the intersect point onto a plane defined by two axes of the coordinate system. We first decide which of the three coordinate axes should be discarded, namely the one which has the largest value for any of the vertices of the parallelogram. This is the dominant axis. We then perform the projection onto the plane formed by the other two coordinates by simply throwing away the values of the dominant coordinate for each of the vertices of the parallelogram.

We then compute the location of each vertex in the new system, with respect to the parallelogram coordinate system. The first vertex is always at (0, 0) by definition. We now take into consideration which was the dominant axis and compute the coordinates of each vertex in terms of a coordinate system centered at the intersect point. The vertices in the new coordinate system are stored in (gu[n], gv[n]), where *n* is the vertex number from 0 to 3. The new coordinate system will be considered to have the axes *u* and *v*.

The arbitrary direction in which to project the test line is, for simplicity, selected to be along the *u* axis. The function *EvenCrossings* is then used to check the test line against the line segment between each pair of adjacent vertices. We can only have an intersection of the test line and the line segment connecting adjacent vertices if *gv[i]* and *gv[j]* have opposite signs. (This puts one vertex on one side of the *u* axis and the other on the opposite side, which assures a crossing of the *u* axis. If both *gu[i]* and *gu[j]* are positive, then we know that the crossing of the *u* axis is also a crossing of the test line, and we therefore increment the number of crossings. If one of the vertex *u* coordinates is positive, and the other is negative, we next compute the value of the *u* coordinate for the intersection of the line segment with the *u* axis. If this is positive, we have an intersection with the test line and therefore increment the number of crossings; if it is negative, there is no intersection with the test line, so the number of crossings is not changed.

After completing the test for all adjacent line segment pairs, the function returns *true* if there was an even number of crossings and *false* if there was not. A return of *true* indicates no intersection; a return of *false* indicates that the intersection occurred.

Finding the intersection of the ray with a triangle works in just the same way, except that only three vertices are specified, and therefore only three line segments must be tested.

We're now getting pretty far removed from where we started, so let's try to get back as quickly as possible by noting that *Intersect* returns the distance at which the ray intercepts the designated object, and that *ShootRay* then completes its loops by identifying the object intersected and the distance from the ray origin to it. This information is returned to *TraceRay*. If there was no intersection with an object, the function *Sky* is called. This function interpolates between the horizon and zenith sky colors, as appropriate for the position in the sky that the ray is pointing toward, and returns the proper color. If the ray did intersect an object, the function *GetIntrPt* is called to establish the coordinates of the point of intersection of the ray and the object. The function *GetSrfNrm* is then called to determine the surface normal vector to the object surface at the point of intersection of the ray with the object. The mathematics for obtaining the surface normal is different for each object; what's involved can easily be seen by studying the listing for the function.

Determining the Color

The next thing that *TraceRay* does is to call the function *GetLoclCol*, which returns the local color of the object at the point of intersection. At this point you're going to find that the functions are rather convoluted so that very careful tracing through the listing is needed to understand all of the necessary interactions.

The *GetLoclCol* function begins by checking whether the object that was intersected by the ray is a lamp. If so, we don't need to go any further. The color is set to that of the lamp, with its intensity decreased by the square root of the distance from the lamp to the viewer and by the cosine of the angle between the lamp to viewer direction and the surface normal to the lamp surface.

If the object intersected by the light ray is not as lamp, the function next enters a *case* statement which determines the numbers for the type of material and texture of the intersected surface. The function *Ambient* is then called, which adds the contribution of ambient light to the total light color vector. The *GetLoclCol* function then enters a *for* loop that iterates once for each lamp (light source) that is in the scene, thereby determining the contributions of all the light sources to the lighting on the object at the point where it is intersected by the light ray. Each iteration of the loop begins by establishing a new light ray from the point of intersection on the object surface toward the lamp being processed.

Next, the function *ShadowFeeler* is called, which really only calls *ShootRay* to determine the closest object that this new ray hits. If we do intersect with an object, which is not the lamp itself, our initial intersection is shadowed from this light source, so we do not have any contribution from it to the color vector. If the new light ray doesn't intersect with anything or if it intersects the lamp itself, there is a color contribution from this light source. In this case, the function calls *UnshadowedSurface*.

This function first determines the cosine of the angle between the surface normal and the lamp direction vector. If it is negative, the light from this lamp does not contribute to the lighting of the intersection pixel. Otherwise, the function first calls *Diffuse*, which computes the diffuse light contribution and uses it to modify the total color. It then calls *Specular*, which determines the specular reflection contribution to the color.

This is obtained from the Phong shading model, which basically takes the cosine of the angle between the surface normal and a vector whose direction is the difference between the viewer and lamp directions from the point of intersection, and raises it to the power specified for glossiness. This gives the intense highlights that are particularly characteristic of reflections from spheres.

The function *UnshadowedSurface* then terminates after having included the diffuse and specular contributions to the total color vector. If the texture of the object first intersected is smooth, we have now determined the total color vector and return to *TraceRay*. If the surface has a texture, the function calls *Texture* to perturbate the color thus far determined.

Creating a Textured Surface

The function *Texture* modifies the color for each point on a surface so as to produce the appearance of one of the defined textures. The function consists of a *case* statement which permits the proper operations to be performed for whichever texture was defined. The first case is *Checker*, which produces a checkerboard pattern. For this case, the intersection point is processed to determine which colored square of the checkerboard it falls within, and the proper color is then returned to be used to modify the local color information to obtain the final pixel color.

The next case is *Grit*, which produces a slightly varied color over the surface, similar to that which might occur for a grassy surface or for dirt. All that happens for this case is that a random number between 0.8 and 1.0 is selected and used to multiply each component of the total color vector.

The next case is *Marble*. To obtain the marble texture, the function *MarbleTex* is called. This function first separates the point of intersection vector into its three components and the calls the *Noise* function to interpolate in the noise table that we created previously and obtain the proper noise value for the point in space ($0.2x, 0.1y, 0.1z$). This noise value is modified and used to create a vector (having the same value for each of its three components) which is used to multiply the local color value.

The next case is *Wood*. To obtain the wood texture, the function *WoodTex* is called. This is just the same as the function for marble except that the contribution of the noise is only one-third of that for marble.

The last case is *Sheetrock*. This is the same as for grit except that the random scalar is set to between 0.9 and 1.0 instead of 0.8 to 1.0.

Completing the Ray Trace

We are now back in the *TraceRay* function with a color for the pixel. If we have reached the maximum depth of recursion (to be explained below) or the weighing of the color on this pass is insignificant, we accept the current pixel color and terminate the function.

Otherwise, if the object material has a specular reflection capability, the function calls *CalcDirOfSpecReflRay*, which determines the direction of a ray reflected from the intersection point of the original ray and the object. The weight of the reflected ray's contribution to color is then computed and *TraceRay* is called recursively (with the depth increased by one) to perform the whole process over again and determine the color contribution for the reflected ray.

The reason for having a depth parameter is that we don't want to keep on forever with our recursive process. Thus, when the depth reaches the maximum depth that we have defined (usually 5) we cease further recursion. Next, *Comb* is called to combine all of the color contributions into a single final color vector. This completes *TraceRay* and we return one level higher in the recursion, or at the top we return to *Scan*.

CHAPTER 20

Displaying a Ray-Traced File

Using the ray tracing program produces a *.CPR* disk file which contains color information that defines a lot more than the 256 colors that are available with the present crop of VGA cards and monitors. New cards are coming, however, that will allow many more than 256 colors, so don't despair; your ray-traced files will be ready for use with the new displays. Because of the large amount of information in the ray-traced file, however, the file takes up a lot of space; in fact it is probably not possible to fit a high resolution file onto a standard 360k floppy disk.

This chapter is going to look at how we can convert from the file generated by the ray tracer to the best possible VGA display. You can then capture the screen with any of a number of commercial or shareware programs and save it in a modest sized file for re-display. One such commercial program is Pizazz Plus, which not only can capture any of the display screens which you will generate in this chapter and save them on disk for re-display, but can also print the pictures out with reasonably good quality to any of a number of color or black and white printers.

Creating a VGA Color Display

The file generated by the ray tracer begins with two integers that specify the x and y resolution of the display. After that, it consists of a triple for each pixel on the display screen. The triple is three bytes, each containing a number from 0 to 63, one byte for red, one for green, and one for blue. Each triple can represent 262,144 different shades of color.

This is adequate to represent the coloring of any scene with more precision than our human eye can distinguish. Unfortunately, the most colors that the VGA card display on the screen at one time is 256. It might seem like a rather hopeless task to attempt to create a realistic scene from our original data file with such a limited number of colors , but things are not quite as bad as they seem. Most scenes do not even come close to requiring the full range of colors. Typically, a ray-traced scene specifies from 350 to 3500 colors. Many of these colors are used in shading a surface and are thus very close to each other, and they often occur in very limited areas. Consequently, using the 256 most frequently occurring colors produces a quite realistic scene. The program to perform this operation is listed in Figure 20-1.

The program begins by clearing the memory, namely *ColorHistogram*, *Frequency*, *Hues*, and the palette. It then clears the screen, ready to paint a picture. It next displays a heading and then calls *GetFileName*. This function asks the user to "Enter File Name =>" and then reads the file name in from the keyboard. Only the main part of the file name should be entered; the program automatically adds the extension *.CPR*. If you only enter a carriage return, the program will supply the default file name of *Test*. If you don't have this file on your disk, you're out of luck.

Next the main program calls the function *CollectColorData*. This function begins by opening and resetting the selected file. It then reads the x and y resolution values and displays them on the screen. It then displays the line, "Collecting Color Data". The function then enters two nested *for* loops which read every triple from the screen, strip off the least significant bit, combine the triple into a single color number, and increment the value of the histogram array at the index defined by the color number. After all triples have been read, the file is closed.

The function then begins a *for* loop which looks at every value in the color histogram. All colors that do not occur are ignored; the others have their color number stored in the *Hues* array and their frequency of occurrence stored in the *Frequency* array. The main program then calls *SortColorData*, which first sorts the colors so that the most frequently occurring one is first and the least frequently occurring one last. The 256 VGA color registers are set to the 256 colors that occur most often in the picture.

This is all very well, but what do we do about all of the colors that were not in the first 256 in frequency of occurrence? It is instructive to look at the number of occurrences for these remaining colors. If you want to do this for several typical files, you can modify the program of Figure 20-1 so that after it completes the sort it prints out the values in the array instead of generating the color picture. You will find that many of the colors below the first 256 only occur once, so that if we get them wrong only a single pixel in the picture is affected. Even the ones that occur most frequently often have only 20 or 30 occurrences, which is not a very big section of a picture. Nevertheless, we want to do the best we can. So what we do is compare each of these colors with the 256 selected for display and assign the color to whichever of the 256 is the closest least squares fit to the actual color.

Next, the main program initiates the graphics mode of operation, selecting mode 56 (1024 x 768 pixels by 256 colors) if the x resolution was 1024 and selecting mode 19 (the standard VGA 320 x 200 pixel by 256 color mode) otherwise. The high-resolution display is only guaranteed to work with the STD Powergraph VGA card; other extended VGA cards may have different mode setting or different methods of operation that will require you to change the code.

The program then calls *MakePalette* which takes the color assignments in the *Hues* array and uses them to set the 256 VGA color registers. The program then calls *GetColorHistogramFromFrequency.* This function replaces the frequency of occurrence values in the *ColorHistogram* array with the appropriate VGA color register assignments that are stored in the *Frequency* array. The program then calls *Display.* This function reopens and resets the selected file, reads the resolution values, and then enters a pair of nested *for* loops which read each triple, synthesize the color number, use it as an index to get the proper VGA color register value, and then plot a point to the screen at the proper location using the selected color register. When the loops are through, the display is complete. The file is then closed and the program terminates.

```
/* Display.c

            Histogram VGA Color Processor

*/

#include "stdio.h"
#include "dos.h"
```

```
#include "conio.h"
#include "alloc.h"
#include "math.h"
#include "string.h"
#include "math2.inc"
#include "graph2.inc"

Byte Frequency[8192];
Word Hues[8192];

void Sort(Word First, Word Last)
{
  Word i, j, k;
  Word Pivot, Temp2;
  Byte Temp;

  if(First<Last-1)
  {
    i=First;
    j=Last;
    k=(First+Last)>>1;
   Pivot=(Frequency[i]+Frequency[j]+Frequency[k])/3;
    while(i<j)
    {
      while(Frequency[i]>Pivot)
    ++i;
      while(Frequency[j]<Pivot)
        -j;
       if(i<j)
       {
     Temp=Frequency[i];
     Frequency[i]=Frequency[j];
     Frequency[j]=Temp;
     Temp2=Hues[i];
     Hues[i]=Hues[j];
     Hues[j]=Temp2;
     ++i;
     -j;
       }
     }
```

```
      if(j<Last)
      {
        Sort(First,j);
        Sort(j+1,Last);
      }
    }
  if(Frequency[Last]>Frequency[First])
    {
      Temp=Frequency[First];
      Frequency[First]=Frequency[Last];
      Frequency[Last]=Temp;
      Temp2=Hues[First];
      Hues[First]=Hues[Last];
      Hues[Last]=Temp2;
    }
}

typedef char Name[12];

Name FileName;

void GetFileName()
{
  Byte x, y;

  printf("\nEnter File Name => ");
  x=wherex();
  y=wherey();
  gets(FileName);
  if(strlen(FileName)==0)
  {
    strcpy(FileName,"TEST");
    gotoxy(x, y);
    puts(FileName);
  }
  strcat(FileName, ".CPR");
  puts("");
  puts("");
}
```

```
PaletteRegister PalArray;
Word i, j, x, y;
int LastColor;
Word ColorNum;
Byte  far *ColorHistogram;
Word rc, gc, bc;
FILE *TextDiskFile;

void ClearMem()
{

  ClearPalette(PalArray);
  for(i=0; i<=32767; i++)
    ColorHistogram[i]=0;
  for(i=0; i<=8191; i++)
    Frequency[i]=0;
  for(i=0; i<=8191; i++)
    Hues[i]=0;
}

void CollectColorData()
{
  TextDiskFile=fopen(FileName, "r+b");
  XRes=getw(TextDiskFile);
  YRes=getw(TextDiskFile);
  printf("Image Resolution is %d by %d pixels.\n\n\n", XRes,
    YRes);
  printf("Collecting color data....\n\n");
  for(y=0; y<YRes; y++)
  {
    for(x=0; x<XRes; x++)
    {
      rc=(getc(TextDiskFile))&62;
      gc=(getc(TextDiskFile))&62;
      bc=(getc(TextDiskFile))&62;
      ColorNum=(rc>>1)|(gc<<4)|(bc<<9);
      if(ColorHistogram[ColorNum]<255)
    ColorHistogram[ColorNum]=ColorHistogram[ColorNum]+1;
    }
  }
```

```
  fclose(TextDiskFile);
  LastColor=-1;
  for(j=0; j<=32767; j++)
  {
    if(ColorHistogram[j]>0)
    {
      ++LastColor;
      Hues[LastColor]=j;
      Frequency[LastColor]=ColorHistogram[j];
    }
  }
}

void SortColorData()
{
  Word d1, Tempd, d2;
  Byte r1, g1, b1;
  Byte r2, g2, b2;

  printf("There are %d colors.\n\n",LastColor);
  puts("Starting sort.");
  Sort(0, LastColor);
  puts("Sort completed.");
  printf("\nModifying extra colors....\n");
  for(i=0; i<=255; i++)
    Frequency[i]=i;
  for(i=256; i<=LastColor; i++)
  {
    d1=32768;
    for(j=0; j<=255; j++)
    {
      r1=(Hues[i]<<1)&62;
      g1=(Hues[i]>>4)&62;
      b1=(Hues[i]>>9)&62;
      r2=(Hues[j]<<1)&62;
      g2=(Hues[j]>>4)&62;
      b2=(Hues[j]>>9)&62;
      Tempd=Sqr(r1-r2)+Sqr(g1-g2)+Sqr(b1-b2);
      if(Tempd<d1)
      {
```

```
      d1=Tempd;
      d2=j;
        }
      }
     Frequency[i]=d2;
   }
}

void MakePalette(PaletteRegister PalArray)
{
  for(j=0; j<=255; j++)
  {
    PalArray[j].Red=(Hues[j]<<1)&62;
    PalArray[j].Grn=(Hues[j]>>4)&62;
    PalArray[j].Blu=(Hues[j]>>9)&62;
  }
}

void GetColorHistogramFromFrequency()
{
  for(j=0; j<=LastColor; j++)
    ColorHistogram[Hues[j]]=Frequency[j];
}

void Display()
{
  TextDiskFile=fopen(FileName,"r+b");
  XRes=getw(TextDiskFile);
  YRes=getw(TextDiskFile);
  for(y=0; y<YRes; y++)
  {
    for(x=0; x<XRes; x++)
    {
      rc=(getc(TextDiskFile))&62;
      gc=(getc(TextDiskFile))&62;
      bc=(getc(TextDiskFile))&62;
      ColorNum=(rc>>1)|(gc<<4)|(bc<<9);
      Plot(x, y, ColorHistogram[ColorNum]);
    }
  }
```

```
  fclose(TextDiskFile);
}

void main()
{
  ColorHistogram=farmalloc(32768);
  if(ColorHistogram==0)
   {
    printf("Not enough memory!\n");
    printf(
        "Only %u bytes left to allocate.\n Hit any key to
            exit.\n", farcoreleft());
    getch();
    exit(1);
   }
  ClearMem();
  clrscr();
  printf("\t Histogram Color Image Processor using Least
        Squares Fit\n");
  printf("\t for VGA 256 Color Modes by Christopher D.
        Watkins\n\n");
  GetFileName();
  CollectColorData();
  SortColorData();
  if(XRes==1024)
    InitGraphics(56);
  else
    InitGraphics(19);
  MakePalette(PalArray);
  SetPalette(PalArray);
  GetColorHistogramFromFrequency();
  Display();
  ExitGraphics();
  farfree(ColorHistogram);
}
```

Figure 20-1. Listing of the Program to Display a Ray-Traced File

APPENDIX A

Solid Modeling Scene Definition Files

In order to produce a scene using the solid modeling technique, two data files are necessary. One of these is a *.SCN* file, which defines the scene characteristics. These files are on the disk that is available with this book, and are listed in this appendix. The other file that is needed for each scene is the *.DAT* data file. There is a C program for each of the scenes covered by this book, which generates this data file. How to create the C files for new scenes was described in Chapter 9. Before you attempt to create the scene, compile and run the proper program to generate its data file.

```
CubePlan.Scn = Cube Sitting on a Reflective Plane
```

```
TRUE     0    0 350 500
240 18
45 45
TRUE
FALSE
FALSE

Plane.Dat
7
80.0000 80.0000 80.0000
0.0000 0.0000 0.0000
0.0000 0.0000 0.0000
FALSE
FALSE
TRUE
```

```
Cube.Dat
1
25.0000 25.0000 25.0000
0.0000 0.0000 0.0000
0.0000 0.0000 25.0000
TRUE
FALSE
FALSE
```

FourCols.Scn = Four Columns with Spheres on top reflecting in 3 walls

```
TRUE  0  -18  350  500
 242  24
  45  45
TRUE
FALSE
TRUE

Cylinder.Dat
5
   15.0   15.0   35.0
    0.0    0.0    0.0
  -50.0  -50.0   35.0
TRUE
TRUE
FALSE

Sphere.Dat
6
   15.0   15.0   15.0
    0.0    0.0    0.0
  -50.0  -50.0   85.0
TRUE
TRUE
FALSE
```

```
Cylinder.Dat
5
   15.0   15.0   35.0
    0.0    0.0    0.0
   50.0  -50.0   35.0
TRUE
TRUE
FALSE

Sphere.Dat
6
   15.0   15.0   15.0
    0.0    0.0    0.0
   50.0  -50.0   85.0
TRUE
TRUE
FALSE

Cylinder.Dat
5
   15.0   15.0   35.0
    0.0    0.0    0.0
   -50.0  50.0   35.0
TRUE
TRUE
FALSE

Sphere.Dat
6
   15.0   15.0   15.0
    0.0    0.0    0.0
  -50.0   50.0   85.0
TRUE
TRUE
FALSE
```

```
Cylinder.Dat
5
   15.0    15.0    35.0
    0.0     0.0     0.0
   50.0    50.0    35.0
TRUE
TRUE
FALSE

Sphere.Dat
6
   15.0    15.0    15.0
    0.0     0.0     0.0
   50.0    50.0    85.0
TRUE
TRUE
FALSE
```

Molecule.Scn = Molecular Model of Water (108° between H-bonds)

```
FALSE   0   0  500  500
270 0
45 45
FALSE
FALSE
FALSE

Sphere.Dat
1
20.0000 20.0000 20.0000
0.0000 0.0000 0.0000
0.0000 0.0000 0.0000
FALSE
FALSE
FALSE
```

```
Cylinder.Dat
7
3.0000 3.0000 15.0000
0.0000 0.0000 0.0000
0.0000 0.0000 35.0000
FALSE
FALSE
FALSE

Cylinder.Dat
7
3.0000 3.0000 15.0000
-108.0000 0.0000 0.0000
0.0000 33.2870 -10.8156
FALSE
FALSE
FALSE

Sphere.Dat
4
10.0000 10.0000 10.0000
0.0000 0.0000 0.0000
0.0000 0.0000 60.0000
FALSE
FALSE
FALSE

Sphere.Dat
4
10.0000 10.0000 10.0000
0.0000 0.0000 0.0000
0.0000 57.0634 -18.5410
FALSE
FALSE
FALSE
```

PlotEqn1.Scn = Display an Equation Plot

```
TRUE  0  -18  450  500
 242  22
  45  45
FALSE
FALSE
FALSE

PlotEqn1.Dat
1
   100.0  100.0  100.0
     0.0    0.0    0.0
     0.0    0.0    0.0
FALSE
FALSE
FALSE
```

PlotEqn2.Scn = Display an Equation Plot

```
TRUE  0  -18  450  500
 242  22
  45  45
FALSE
FALSE
FALSE

PlotEqn2.Dat
1
   100.0  100.0  100.0
     0.0    0.0    0.0
     0.0    0.0    0.0
FALSE
FALSE
FALSE
```

PlotEqn3.Scn = Display an Equation Plot

```
TRUE  0  -18  450  500
 242  22
  45  45
FALSE
FALSE
FALSE

PlotEqn3.Dat
1
  100.0  100.0  100.0
    0.0    0.0    0.0
    0.0    0.0    0.0
FALSE
FALSE
FALSE
```

PlotEqn4.Scn = Display an Equation Plot

```
TRUE  0  -18  450  500
 242  22
  45  45
FALSE
FALSE
FALSE

PlotEqn4.Dat
1
  100.0  100.0  100.0
    0.0    0.0    0.0
    0.0    0.0    0.0
FALSE
FALSE
FALSE
```

Shapes.Scn = Collection of Shapes

```
TRUE  0  -24  400  500
 242  24
  45  45
TRUE
FALSE
TRUE

Sphere.Dat
1
   30.0   30.0   30.0
    0.0    0.0    0.0
    0.0    0.0   30.0
TRUE
TRUE
FALSE

Toroid.Dat
4
   30.0   30.0   30.0
    0.0   90.0    0.0
  -60.0   60.0   30.0
TRUE
TRUE
FALSE

Cylinder.Dat
2
   15.0   15.0   40.0
    0.0    0.0    0.0
    70.0 -70.0   40.0
TRUE
TRUE
FALSE
```

```
Cone.Dat
6
   25.0   25.0   50.0
    0.0    0.0    0.0
    0.0  -65.0   50.0
TRUE
TRUE
FALSE

Cube.Dat
5
   15.0   15.0   15.0
    0.0    0.0    0.0
  -80.0   10.0   15.0
TRUE
TRUE
FALSE

HmSphere.Dat
3
   15.0   15.0   15.0
    0.0    0.0    0.0
  -80.0  -30.0   55.0
TRUE
TRUE
FALSE

Pyramid.Dat
7
   10.0   10.0   10.0
    0.0    0.0    0.0
    0.0   70.0   10.0
TRUE
TRUE
FALSE
```

SolOfRev.Scn = 6 Solids of Revolution on a Mirrored Grid

```
TRUE    0  -20 425 500
245 18
45 45
TRUE
FALSE
FALSE

Grid.Dat
7
100.0000 100.0000 100.0000
0.0000 0.0000 0.0000
0.0000 0.0000 0.0000
FALSE
FALSE
TRUE

LgBeads.Dat
1
40.0000 40.0000 40.0000
0.0000 0.0000 0.0000
-60.0000 -60.0000 40.0000
TRUE
TRUE
FALSE

Beads.Dat
2
40.0000 40.0000 40.0000
0.0000 0.0000 0.0000
-60.0000 0.0000 40.0000
TRUE
TRUE
FALSE
```

```
Funnels.Dat
3
40.0000 40.0000 40.0000
0.0000 0.0000 0.0000
-60.0000 60.0000 40.0000
TRUE
TRUE
FALSE

MechPart.Dat
7
40.0000 40.0000 40.0000
0.0000 0.0000 0.0000
60.0000 -60.0000 40.0000
TRUE
TRUE
FALSE

Rocket.Dat
5
40.0000 40.0000 40.0000
0.0000 0.0000 0.0000
60.0000 0.0000 40.0000
TRUE
TRUE
FALSE

ChesPawn.Dat
6
40.0000 40.0000 40.0000
0.0000 0.0000 0.0000
60.0000 60.0000 40.0000
TRUE
TRUE
FALSE
```

SphrPlan.Scn = Sphere sitting on a Reflective Plane

```
TRUE    0    0 350 500
240 18
45 45
TRUE
FALSE
FALSE

Plane.Dat
7
80.0000 80.0000 80.0000
0.0000 0.0000 0.0000
0.0000 0.0000 0.0000
FALSE
FALSE
TRUE

Sphere.Dat
1
25.0000 25.0000 25.0000
0.0000 0.0000 0.0000
0.0000 0.0000 25.0000
TRUE
FALSE
FALSE
```

Sphrwall.Scn = Sphere Reflected in 3 Walls

```
TRUE  0  -18  350  500
 242  24
  45  45
FALSE
FALSE
FALSE
```

```
Grid.Dat
7
   50.0   50.0   50.0
    0.0    0.0    0.0
   50.0   50.0    0.0
FALSE
FALSE
TRUE

Grid.Dat
7
   50.0   50.0   50.0
    0.0   90.0    0.0
    0.0   50.0   50.0
FALSE
FALSE
TRUE

Grid.Dat
7
   50.0   50.0   50.0
    0.0   90.0   90.0
   50.0    0.0   50.0
FALSE
FALSE
TRUE

Sphere.Dat
1
   25.0   25.0   25.0
    0.0    0.0    0.0
   30.0   30.0   30.0
TRUE
TRUE
FALSE
```

```
StakTors.Scn = Stacked Toroids
```

```
TRUE  0  0  350  500
 242  24
  45  45
TRUE
FALSE
FALSE

Toroid.Dat
7
   80.0   80.0   80.0
    0.0    0.0    0.0
    0.0    0.0  -20.0
TRUE
TRUE
FALSE

Toroid.Dat
1
   50.0   50.0   50.0
    0.0    0.0    0.0
    0.0    0.0   10.0
TRUE
TRUE
FALSE

Toroid.Dat
4
   30.0   30.0   30.0
    0.0    0.0    0.0
    0.0    0.0   30.0
TRUE
TRUE
FALSE
```

```
Well.Scn = Well with various shapes
```

```
TRUE  0  -22  350  500
 242  16
  45  45
TRUE
FALSE
TRUE

Cylinder.Dat
1
   50.0   50.0    3.0
    0.0    0.0    0.0
    0.0    0.0    3.0
TRUE
TRUE
FALSE

Cylinder.Dat
3
   40.0   40.0    2.0
    0.0    0.0    0.0
    0.0    0.0    5.0
TRUE
TRUE
FALSE

Cylinder.Dat
1
    3.0    3.0   30.0
    0.0    0.0    0.0
    0.0   35.0   35.0
TRUE
TRUE
FALSE

Cylinder.Dat
1
    3.0    3.0   30.0
    0.0    0.0    0.0
  -25.0   25.0   35.0
TRUE
TRUE
FALSE
```

```
Cylinder.Dat
1
    3.0    3.0   30.0
    0.0    0.0    0.0
  -35.0    0.0   35.0
TRUE
TRUE
FALSE

Cylinder.Dat
1
    3.0    3.0   30.0
    0.0    0.0    0.0
  -25.0  -25.0   35.0
TRUE
TRUE
FALSE

Cylinder.Dat
1
    3.0    3.0   30.0
    0.0    0.0    0.0
    0.0  -35.0   35.0
TRUE
TRUE
FALSE

Cylinder.Dat
1
    3.0    3.0   30.0
    0.0    0.0    0.0
   25.0  -25.0   35.0
TRUE
TRUE
FALSE

Cylinder.Dat
1
    3.0    3.0   30.0
    0.0    0.0    0.0
   35.0    0.0   35.0
```

```
TRUE
TRUE
FALSE

Cylinder.Dat
1
    3.0    3.0   30.0
    0.0    0.0    0.0
   25.0   25.0   35.0
TRUE
TRUE
FALSE

Cube.Dat
5
   15.0   15.0   15.0
    0.0    0.0    0.0
  -65.0   65.0   15.0
TRUE
TRUE
FALSE

Pyramid.Dat
7
   25.0   25.0   35.0
    0.0    0.0    0.0
   65.0  -65.0   35.0
TRUE
TRUE
FALSE

Pyramid.Dat
5
    6.0    6.0   12.0
    0.0    0.0    0.0
   65.0   65.0   12.0
TRUE
TRUE
FALSE
```

```
Toroid.Dat
4
   35.0   35.0   35.0
    0.0    0.0    0.0
  -70.0  -70.0   20.0
TRUE
TRUE
FALSE

Sphere.Dat
2
   15.0   15.0   15.0
    0.0    0.0    0.0
    0.0    0.0   35.0
TRUE
TRUE
FALSE

Cone.Dat
6
   15.0   15.0   35.0
    0.0    0.0    0.0
  -80.0    0.0   35.0
TRUE
TRUE
FALSE

HmSphere.Dat
1
   45.0   45.0   20.0
    0.0    0.0    0.0
    0.0    0.0   65.0
TRUE
TRUE
FALSE
```

APPENDIX B

Materials Used in Ray Tracing

The following file shows the materials that have been developed thus far for use in ray tracing.

```
                    Materials found in *.RT files

MATERIAL
   TYPE    = ITALIANMARBLE
   TEXTURE = MARBLE
   AMBRFL  =    0.100    0.100    0.100
   DIFRFL  =    0.700    0.700    0.700
   SPCRFL  =    0.200    0.200    0.200
   GLOSS   =   10.000


MATERIAL
   TYPE    = OAKWOOD
   TEXTURE = WOOD
   AMBRFL  =    0.200    0.200    0.200
   DIFRFL  =    0.700    0.400    0.300
   SPCRFL  =    0.100    0.100    0.100
   GLOSS   =    5.000


MATERIAL
   TYPE    = MIRROR
   TEXTURE = SMOOTH
```

```
   AMBRFL  =     0.000    0.000    0.000
   DIFRFL  =     0.700    0.700    0.700
   SPCRFL  =     0.300    0.300    0.300
   GLOSS   =    50.000

MATERIAL
   TYPE    = DULLMIRROR
   TEXTURE = SMOOTH
   AMBRFL  =     0.100    0.100    0.100
   DIFRFL  =     0.100    0.100    0.100
   SPCRFL  =     0.100    0.100    0.100
   GLOSS   =    10.000

MATERIAL
   TYPE    = BLUEMIRROR
   TEXTURE = SMOOTH
   AMBRFL  =     0.100    0.100    0.100
   DIFRFL  =     0.200    0.200    0.500
   SPCRFL  =     0.100    0.100    0.400
   GLOSS   =    30.000

MATERIAL
   TYPE    = REDMIRROR
   TEXTURE = SMOOTH
   AMBRFL  =     0.100    0.100    0.100
   DIFRFL  =     0.500    0.200    0.200
   SPCRFL  =     0.400    0.100    0.100
   GLOSS   =    30.000

MATERIAL
   TYPE    = CHROME
   TEXTURE = SMOOTH
   AMBRFL  =     0.000    0.000    0.000
   DIFRFL  =     0.250    0.250    0.250
   SPCRFL  =     0.750    0.750    0.750
   GLOSS   =    40.000
```

```
MATERIAL
   TYPE    = BRASS
   TEXTURE = SMOOTH
   AMBRFL  =    0.100    0.100    0.100
   DIFRFL  =    0.300    0.300    0.300
   SPCRFL  =    0.600    0.500    0.250
   GLOSS   =   30.000


MATERIAL
   TYPE    = PLASTICTILE
   TEXTURE = CHECKER
   AMBRFL  =    0.100    0.100    0.100
   DIFRFL  =    0.700    0.700    0.700
   SPCRFL  =    0.200    0.200    0.200
   GLOSS   =    4.000

CHECK
   TILE1   =    1.000    0.000    0.000
   TILE2   =    0.200    0.200    0.200
   TILE    =    0.07


MATERIAL
   TYPE    = MATTEWALL
   TEXTURE = SHEETROCK
   AMBRFL  =    0.500    0.500    0.500
   DIFRFL  =    0.500    0.500    0.500
   SPCRFL  =    0.000    0.000    0.000
   GLOSS   =    0.000


MATERIAL
   TYPE    = CEMENT
   TEXTURE = GRIT
   AMBRFL  =    0.200    0.200    0.200
   DIFRFL  =    0.800    0.800    0.800
   SPCRFL  =    0.000    0.000    0.000
   GLOSS   =    0.000
```

```
MATERIAL
   TYPE    = LIGHTCEMENT
   TEXTURE = SHEETROCK
   AMBRFL  =    0.100    0.100    0.100
   DIFRFL  =    0.900    0.900    0.900
   SPCRFL  =    0.000    0.000    0.000
   GLOSS   =    0.000


MATERIAL
   TYPE    = BLACKANODIZED
   TEXTURE = SMOOTH
   AMBRFL  =    1.000    1.000    1.000
   DIFRFL  =    0.000    0.000    0.000
   SPCRFL  =    0.000    0.000    0.000
   GLOSS   =    0.000


MATERIAL
   TYPE    = MILKWHITEGLASS
   TEXTURE = SMOOTH
   AMBRFL  =    0.500    0.500    0.500
   DIFRFL  =    0.400    0.400    0.400
   SPCRFL  =    0.100    0.100    0.100
   GLOSS   =    4.000


MATERIAL
   TYPE    = ICEANDROCK
   TEXTURE = GRIT
   AMBRFL  =    0.150    0.150    0.150
   DIFRFL  =    0.850    0.850    0.850
   SPCRFL  =    0.000    0.000    0.000
   GLOSS   =    0.000


MATERIAL
   TYPE    = PLANET1
   TEXTURE = SHEETROCK
   AMBRFL  =    0.200    0.200    0.200
```

```
   DIFRFL  =    0.800    0.700    0.500
   SPCRFL  =    0.000    0.000    0.000
   GLOSS   =    0.000


MATERIAL
   TYPE    = PLANET2
   TEXTURE = SHEETROCK
   AMBRFL  =    0.200    0.200    0.200
   DIFRFL  =    0.700    0.800    0.700
   SPCRFL  =    0.000    0.000    0.000
   GLOSS   =    0.000


MATERIAL
   TYPE    = PLANET3
   TEXTURE = SHEETROCK
   AMBRFL  =    0.150    0.150    0.150
   DIFRFL  =    0.500    0.600    0.700
   SPCRFL  =    0.000    0.000    0.000
   GLOSS   =    0.000


MATERIAL
   TYPE    = MOON1
   TEXTURE = SHEETROCK
   AMBRFL  =    0.200    0.200    0.200
   DIFRFL  =    0.800    0.800    0.800
   SPCRFL  =    0.000    0.000    0.000
   GLOSS   =    0.000


MATERIAL
   TYPE    = STAR
   TEXTURE = SHEETROCK
   AMBRFL  =    0.500    0.500    0.500
   DIFRFL  =    0.350    0.350    0.500
   SPCRFL  =    0.000    0.000    0.000
   GLOSS   =    0.000
```

```
MATERIAL
   TYPE    = REDGIANT
   TEXTURE = SHEETROCK
   AMBRFL  =    0.500    0.500    0.500
   DIFRFL  =    0.500    0.350    0.350
   SPCRFL  =    0.000    0.000    0.000
   GLOSS   =    0.000

MATERIAL
   TYPE    = BLUEDWARF
   TEXTURE = SHEETROCK
   AMBRFL  =    0.500    0.500    0.500
   DIFRFL  =    0.300    0.300    0.500
   SPCRFL  =    0.000    0.000    0.000
   GLOSS   =    0.000

MATERIAL
   TYPE    = GRASS
   TEXTURE = GRIT
   AMBRFL  =    0.200    0.200    0.200
   DIFRFL  =    0.600    0.800    0.250
   SPCRFL  =    0.000    0.000    0.000
   GLOSS   =    0.000

MATERIAL
   TYPE    = SAND
   TEXTURE = GRIT
   AMBRFL  =    0.100    0.100    0.100
   DIFRFL  =    1.000    0.700    0.600
   SPCRFL  =    0.000    0.000    0.000
   GLOSS   =    0.000

MATERIAL
   TYPE    = WATER
   TEXTURE = GRIT
   AMBRFL  =    0.100    0.100    0.300
```

```
   DIFRFL  =    0.100    0.300    0.300
   SPCRFL  =    0.100    0.100    0.400
   GLOSS   =    3.000


MATERIAL
   TYPE    = OCEANWATER
   TEXTURE = GRIT
   AMBRFL  =    0.100    0.100    0.100
   DIFRFL  =    0.170    0.700    0.520
   SPCRFL  =    0.200    0.200    0.200
   GLOSS   =   20.000


MATERIAL
   TYPE    = LAKEWATER
   TEXTURE = GRIT
   AMBRFL  =    0.100    0.100    0.200
   DIFRFL  =    0.100    0.200    0.200
   SPCRFL  =    0.100    0.100    0.300
   GLOSS   =    2.000
```

Bibliography

Becker, K.H., and Dorfler, M., *Computergraphische Experimente mit Pascal*, Vieweg, Braunschweig, 1986.

Bouville, C., "Bounding Ellipsoids for Ray-Fractal Intersection." *SIGGRAPH '85*, Vol. 19, No. 3, (1985) pp. 45–52.

Carpenter, L. "Computer Rendering of Fractal Curves and Surfaces." *Computer Graphics*, (1980), pp. 109 ff.

Coquillast, S. and Gangnet, "Shaded Display of Digital Maps." *IEEE Computer Graphics and Applications*, Vol. 4, No. 7, (1984).

Demko, S., Hodges, L., and Naylor, B., "Construction of Fractal Objects with Iterated Function Systems." *SIGGRAPH '85*, Vol. 19, No. 3, (1985) pp. 271–278.

Dewdney, A.K., "Computer Recreations: Exploring the Mandelbrot Set." *Computer Graphics*, Vol. 20, No. 4, (1985), pp. 16 ff.

Dewdney, A.K., "Computer Recreations: Beauty and Profundity: The Mandelbrot Set and a Flock of Its Cousins Called Julia Sets." *Scientific American*, (November 1987), pp. 140–144.

Escher, M.C., *The World of M.C. Escher*, New York: H.N. Abrams, 1971.

Feigenbaum, M.J., "Quantitative Universality for a Class of Non-Linear Transformations." *Journal of Statistical Physics*, Vol. 19, No. 1, (January 1978), pp. 25–52.

Fishman, B. and Schachter, B., "Computer Display of Height Fields." *Computers and Graphics*, No. 5, (1980), pp. 53–60.

Fogg, L., "Drawing the Mandelbrot and Julia Sets." *MicroCornucopia*, No. 39, (January–February 1988), pp. 6–9.

Glassner, Andrew S., *An Introduction to Ray Tracing*, Academic Press, Ltd., 1989.

Henon, M., "A Two-Dimensional Mapping with a Strange Attractor." *Communication Math-Physics*, No. 50, (1976), pp. 69–77.

Mandelbrot, B., *The Fractal Geometry of Nature*, New York: W.H. Freeman and Company, 1983.

Mastin, G.A., Watterberg, P.A., and Mareda, J.F., "Fourier Synthesis of Ocean Scenes." *IEEE Computer Graphics and Applications*, (March 1987), pp. 16–24.

Norton, A., "Generation and Display of Geometric Fractals in 3-D." *Computer Graphics*, Vol. 16, No. 3, (July 1982), pp. 61–67.

Norton, A., "Julia Sets in the Quaternions." IBM T.J. Watson Research Center, Yorktown Heights, New York.

Peitgen, H.O., and Richter, P.H., *The Beauty of Fractals*, Berlin: Springer-Verlag, 1986.

Peitgen, H.O. and Saupe, D., *The Science of Fractal Images*, Berlin: Springer-Verlag, 1988.

Pickover, C.A., "A Note on Rendering 3-D Strange Attractors." *Computers and Graphics*, Vol. 12, No. 2, (1988), pp. 263–267.

Pickover, C.A. "Chaotic Behavior of the Transcendental Mapping (z->cosh(z) + u)." *The Visual Computer: An International Journal of Computer Graphics*, No. 4, pp. 243–246.

Pickover, C.A., "Mathematics and Beauty VII: Visualization of Quarternion Slices." *Image and Vision Computing*, Vol. 6, No. 4, (November 1988), pp. 235–237.

Sorensen, P., "Fractals." *Byte*, (September 1984), pp. 157–171.

Watt, Alan, *Fundamentals of Three-Dimensional Computer Graphics*, Addison-Wesley Publishing Co., 1989.

Whitted, Turner, "Managing Geometric Complexity with Enhanced Procedural Models." *SIGGRAPH '86*, Vol. 20, No. 4, (1986), pp. 189–195.

Index

N

O